EDINBURGH LAW AND SOCIETY SERIES

General Editors

P. Young and B. Brown

EDINBURGH LAW AND SOCIETY SERIES
Editors: P. Young and B. Brown

The Edinburgh Law and Society Series promotes scholarship that makes a significant contribution to exploring the inter-relations between legal and social spheres. It publishes empirical and theoretical work informed by classical traditions and contemporary developments in the social sciences, philosophy and political theory.

Titles in the series

P. Amselek and N. MacCormick (Eds)
Controversies about Law's Ontology

Elizabeth Kingdom
What's Wrong with Rights
Problems for a Feminist Politics of Law

D. Meyers
The Human Body and the Law

Forthcoming
S. Frith
Music and Copyright

P. Young
Punishment, Money and Legal Order

PRINCIPLED SENTENCING

edited by

Andrew von Hirsch

Andrew Ashworth

EDINBURGH UNIVERSITY PRESS

Edinburgh University Press
22 George Square, Edinburgh

Published in the USA by Northeastern University Press

Designed by Linda Koegel
Composed in Sabon
Printed, typeset and bound in the USA

A CIP record for this book is available from the
British Library

ISBN 0 7486 0381 6 (paper)

Contents

Preface

That the imposition of sentence is a decision of critical importance can scarcely be doubted. It determines how much the offender must suffer for his or her offense, and that suffering may include deprivation of liberty. When the facts of the offense are undisputed, as is often the case, the sentence is the primary decision to be made.

Before the 1970s in most English-speaking countries, however, the choice of sentence was little regulated. The law merely prescribed an (often high) maximum for the permissible sentence, and occasionally a minimum. Within these broad bounds, little further guidance was provided, either in principle or detail. The determination of the sanction in the individual case was left to the discretion of the judge. In Britain (but not the U.S.), an appellate court could review the sentence, but its decisions attracted little attention.

The objectives of sentencing also received scant exploration. In the U.S., rehabilitation was supposed to be the paramount aim—but how treatment was to determine the sanction was usually left undetermined. In Britain, the idea of deterrence was also supposed to be important—but without much exploration of the *how*.

In the 1970s, sentencing theory and practice began to receive serious attention—and the ideas changed. Faith in rehabilitation (at least, as the guide to choice of sanction) suffered a decline. Deterrence theory enjoyed a renaissance, but only a brief one. The "just deserts" philosophy—according to which the sentence is to be proportionate to the gravity of the crime—gained considerable influence. Some U.S. jurisdictions began experimenting with standards for guiding sentencing decisions. At the end of the decade, in 1980, Hyman Gross and one of the present editors put together an anthology of readings concerning these developments.[1]

Recently, interest in sentencing has intensified. There has been a further elaboration of desert theory. New controversy has emerged over the use of prediction in sentencing decisions. Experimentation with intermediate sanctions—those lying between probation and imprisonment in their onerousness—has begun in earnest. Several other U.S. jurisdictions have enacted sentencing guidelines, and two European countries—Sweden and England—have enacted statutes enunciating principles for choosing sentence.

In the present volume, we have collected a set of readings representative of current ideas about sentencing theory and policy. Each chapter consists of an introduction by one of the editors, designed to put the issues in perspective; a selection of materials that we believe to be of particular interest; and a bibliography of suggested further readings. We have included both American and British sources. In the interest of conserving space, most of the readings have been edited, and some footnotes have been omitted.

We have made one significant but intentional omission: the death penalty. A civilized state, we feel, should not have this vile sanction at all[2]—so there should be no occasion for the courts to have to decide when and why it should be imposed.

We are greatly indebted to Lisa Maher, who assisted us with excerpting the materials and who provided valuable comments on the introductions. We also thank Christie Kable for helping us put the manuscript together, Joan Schroeder for typing portions of the manuscript, and Ramona Brockett for rereading it. Most especially, we are grateful to the authors whose work appears here.

Newark and Uppsala A.v.H.
London A.A.

November 1991

Notes

1. Hyman Gross and Andrew von Hirsch, eds., *Sentencing* (New York: Oxford University Press, 1981).

2. See, e.g., Jeffrie G. Murphy, "Cruel and Unusual Punishments," in his *Retribution, Justice, and Therapy* (Dordrecht: D. Riedel, 1979). See also Hugo Adam Bedau, *Death Is Different* (Boston: Northeastern University Press, 1987). For a survey of the use of the death penalty, see Roger Hood, *The Death Penalty* (Oxford: Oxford University Press, 1989).

The discussion of the death penalty in Extracts 2.2 and 2.3 is included only to suggest certain problems of deterrence theory.

Chapter One

REHABILITATION

Rehabilitation is the idea of "curing" an offender of his or her criminal tendencies. It consists, more precisely, of changing an offender's personality, outlook, habits, or opportunities so as to make him or her less inclined to commit crimes.[1] Often, rehabilitation is said to involve "helping" the offender, but a benefit to the offender is not necessarily presupposed: those who benefit are other persons, ourselves, who become less likely to be victimized by the offender. Traditionally, rehabilitation has consisted in offering counseling, psychological assistance, training, or support—but a variety of other techniques might be used. Some of these, such as aversive therapies, may be less than pleasant.

Success in rehabilitation is measured by recidivism rates: whether the offender has been induced to desist. It is thus linked, but not wholly correlated, with the aggregate incidence of crime—which depends also on how many *new* entrants to criminal activity there are.

Success in rehabilitation involves *changing* offenders—which is why it is not easy to achieve. The treatment is applied at time *1*, in hope that the offender will desist after the treatment has been completed, at time 2. The difficulty is that at time *2*, the offender faces renewed temptations and pressures that may eradicate any effects of the treatment.

During the first six decades or so of this century, rehabilitation was supposed to be an important aim of sentencing. Sometimes, it was said to be the *primary* aim.[2] The Model Penal Code, an influential piece of draft legislation written in the early 1960s, illustrates the significance given to treatment in sentencing. Relevant portions of the code are excerpted in Extract 1.1. The sentence, according to the code, is to be directed chiefly toward preventing further crimes by the defendant. Two themes are thus stressed: resocializing the offender, and separating him from the community if he is likely to offend again.

These two themes are apparent in § 7.01 of the code, dealing with the grounds for imprisonment. According to that section, a sanction in the community—usually probation—is preferred.[3] Prison is warranted in two circumstances, chiefly. One (§ 7.01(1)(b)) is where treatment can more effectively be administered in a prison setting. The other (§ 7.01(1)(a)) is where the offender is thought likely to reoffend, is deemed unresponsive to treatment, and requires incapacitation. (This latter theme will be addressed more fully later, in Chapter 3.)

According to the code—and this was typical of the traditional rehabilitative ideology—the gravity of the actor's criminal conduct was relatively unimportant. Someone convicted of a comparatively serious crime could be given a sentence in the community if that appeared to promote his or her reintegration into society. Conversely, someone convicted of a lesser offense could be imprisoned if he or she could better be treated in confinement. Proportionality—the notion that punishment should bear a fair proportion to the blameworthiness of the offender's criminal conduct—was deemed no ideal. One saw such "retributive" thinking as impractical and unprogressive, because it meant that some offenders would continue to be punished long after they had been successfully rehabilitated, whereas others would have to be released (having completed their "deserved" sentences) before they were cured. Some rehabilitationists took this view to its logical extreme, and held that the gravity of the offense should scarcely be considered at all.[4]

The Model Penal Code takes a somewhat more restrained position. A sentence—even for someone dangerous or specially in need of treatment—may not exceed the prescribed statutory maxima set forth in §§ 6.06 and 6.07. Where the crime is sufficiently serious, moreover, even a nondangerous, potentially responsive defendant might require some period of incarceration if any lesser disposition would "depreciate the seriousness of the . . . crime" (§ 7.01(1)(c)). However, such considerations remain relatively marginal ones under the code's scheme. Ordinarily, it is the treatment needed and the likelihood of recidivism, not the gravity of the crime, that are to determine the sentence.

What also is noteworthy is the wide discretion granted the sentencing judge in pursuing these aims. Within the (quite high) statutory maxima, the judge in the individual case is free to decide the severity of the sentence. The code's provisions in § 7.01 are meant only to be principles the judge should consider. That discretion is linked also with notions of rehabilitation. Individual offenders are assumed to have differing treatment needs. The optimum sentence thus should best be decided in the particular case, not fixed in advance.

The code, like other pre-1970s sources, is quite optimistic about treatment. It is assumed that there are known and effective therapies, both inside the institution and in the community, that can be applied to a wide variety of offenders. In the 1970s, that optimism began to fade.

How does one determine whether a treatment program works? It is no proof of success that significant numbers of treated offenders later lead law-abiding lives—because they might have done so spontaneously (e.g., by virtue merely of having become older). One needs controlled experiments, in which recidivism rates for offenders who participated in a treatment program are compared with those for similar offenders who have not participated.[5] Such experiments began to be made in earnest after World War II, and surveys of the results of numerous studies became available by the end of the 1960s.[6] The results were disappointing: few programs appeared to succeed, and those succeeded only for carefully selected subgroups of offenders.

Extract 1.2, by Stephen Brody, examines these findings. It has not been shown, he points out, that *nothing* works. Experimentation was done on a fairly limited range of treatment modalities, and more novel methods might succeed better. The findings, nevertheless, raise questions about rehabilitation as a primary sentencing aim. Programs evidently do not exist that can routinely and successfully be applied to offenders coming before sentencing courts.

Meanwhile, doubts have been raised not only about the effectiveness of treatment, but about the ethics of rehabilitationism. These doubts are powerfully put in a 1968 essay by the philosopher Herbert Morris, excerpted in Extract 1.3. Morris asks us to imagine a thoroughgoing scheme of rehabilitative sanctions, in which crime is dealt with as a symptom of pathology and *any* intervention is permitted that helps toward cure. (This scheme he contrasts with an expressly desert-oriented one, in which penalties may be imposed only for voluntary criminal acts and are commensurate in severity with the gravity of the criminal conduct.) He points to two major objections to the rehabilitative scheme. The first is that it would tend to erode limits on permissible state action. The authorities could respond proactively when a mere likelihood of criminal conduct was perceived. And the intervention could be of indefinite duration or severity, without regard to any notion of proportionality. The second, and deeper, objection to the rehabilitative scheme, Morris suggests, is that it is disrespectful of the person: it would treat criminals not as responsible agents having control over their actions but as beings to be manipulated and controlled.

The thoroughgoing rehabilitationism that Morris envisions in his article is a construct—designed to bring the problems into clear relief. Actual policies have seldom gone so far, because the substantive criminal law has ordinarily required conviction for an intentional (or at least negligent) criminal act before any penal intervention is permissible.[7] Once conviction has occurred, however, Morris's scenario comes—or came—closer to reality. Several jurisdictions enacted indeterminate sentencing laws according to which convicted offenders could be confined nearly indefinitely until considered "cured"—irrespective of the gravity of their criminal acts.[8] Such laws were repealed only about two decades ago, as faith in rehabilitationism declined.

That decline of faith, and its causes, is the subject of the next selection, Extract 1.4, by Francis Allen. This author, writing in 1981, attributes the growing skepticism about the rehabilitative penal ethic to three main sources: first, a general decline in belief in the malleability of human nature; second, growing awareness of the vulnerability of the treatment ethic to various forms of debasement; and third, disclosures of how little is actually known about the means to rehabilitation. His discussion of the second and third of these factors—the tendency of treatment rhetoric toward debasement, and the vagueness about how rehabilitation might actually be achieved—is particularly illuminating. Allen concludes that although experimentation with treatments is likely to continue, rehabilitation cannot now or in the foreseeable future maintain its earlier supposed role as a central aim of punishment or of sentencing policy.

Rehabilitationism, however, has by no means lost all its defenders. Some authors suggest that a revival of the treatment ethic would make punishments more humane and help combat law-and-order sentiment. Francis Cullen and Karen Gilbert advance such arguments in their 1982 book, *Reaffirming Rehabilitation,* a portion of which appears as Extract 1.5. The authors' essential argument is that rehabilitation carries a humanizing message better than other penal theories. While the aim of treatment admittedly is to prevent offenders from committing new crimes, the message is that such prevention can best be accomplished "if society is willing to punish its captives humanely and to compensate offenders for the social disadvantages that have constrained them to undertake a life in crime."[9] Merely affirming the rights of convicted persons is a much weaker incentive to their decent treatment, the authors argue, because most people are concerned with crime prevention and not with justice or rights for offenders *per se.* Rehabilitation conveys the idea that crime prevention can best be achieved by responding to offenders' needs and treating them properly.

The final selection, by Andrew von Hirsch and Lisa Maher, Extract 1.6, is a reply to arguments such as Cullen and Gilbert's. Whether and to what extent treatment is a suitable basis for punishment decisions, von Hirsch and Maher assert, cannot be resolved by sweeping assertions about the supposed humaneness of rehabilitation. One needs to take a look at the not so easy particulars, concerning *how* treatment considerations could decide sentences. The question of effectiveness still needs to be faced: while certain treatments may work for certain carefully selected subgroups of offenders, rehabilitative cures do not exist for the bulk of cases that appear before courts for sentence. If no known treatment exists for the run-of-the-mill auto thief, burglar, or robber, how can rehabilitation possibly serve as the main basis for sentence?

The alleged humaneness of rehabilitation also needs closer examination, the authors suggest. Just why, and under what conditions, is a treatment-based sentence less onerous? The more promising treatments for drug offenders, for example, require quite intensive and protracted interventions. A treatment perspective may (and certainly did in the past) legitimate rather sweeping state scrutiny of the lifestyles of offenders.

Finally, von Hirsch and Maher suggest, the consistency of treatment-based sentencing with the requirements of justice—particularly, of proportionality—needs to be considered. Traditional rehabilitative schemes—most notably, the indeterminate sentence—flouted proportionality blatantly, and this was one reason for those schemes' demise. How are such problems to be avoided today? A possibility is to permit rehabilitative interventions only within certain bounds fixed by the blameworthiness of the criminal conduct.[10] If so, how are these bounds to be determined, and to what extent will they interfere with effective therapies? A more drastic solution would be to discard proportionality requirements entirely. But if so, how will manifestly unjust responses be avoided? Merely extolling rehabilitation, as Cullen and Gilbert do, will not make such uncomfortable questions go away.

A.v.H.

Notes

1. Or, possibly, to commit crimes of a less serious nature than the offender would have perpetrated in the absence of treatment.

2. See, e.g., National Congress on Penitentiary and Reformatory Discipline, "Statement of Principles," 1871, reprinted in H. Gross and A. von Hirsch, eds., *Sentencing* (New York: Oxford University Press, 1981), 52–56.

3. When the person is put on probation, the court is to impose such conditions

"as it deems necessary to insure that he will lead a law-abiding life or [as are] likely to assist him to do so." MODEL PENAL CODE § 301.1(1). The section then lists a number of permissible conditions of probation, the last of which is "any other condition reasonably related to the rehabilitation of the defendant and not unduly restrictive of his liberty or incompatible with his freedom of conscience." § 301.1(2)(1). The rehabilitative flavor of these provisions is evident.

4. See, e.g., the 1972 edition of the Model Sentencing Act, reproduced in Extract 3.1 below. The Act gives little or no weight to the gravity of the offense in normal sentences and states in § 1 that "sentences should not be based upon revenge and retribution."

5. For a summary of experimental techniques, see, e.g., Roger Hood and Richard Sparks, *Key Issues in Criminology* (London: Weidenfeld and Nicolson, 1970), ch. 7.

6. The most noted of these is Douglas Lipton, Robert Martinson, and Judith Wilks, *The Effectiveness of Correctional Treatment* (New York: Praeger, 1975). For other analyses, see Suggestions for Further Reading, below.

7. See, e.g., MODEL PENAL CODE §§ 2.01 and 2.02.

8. Examples are the California Indeterminate Sentence Law, in effect before 1976, and Maryland's Defective Delinquent Law, in effect before 1977. The text of the latter statute is set forth in Gross and von Hirsch, op. cit., 68–92.

9. The quote appears in Extract 1.5, page 32.

10. For the pros and cons of such an approach, see Extracts 3.5, 4.3, and 4.4.

1.1
The Model Penal Code

Section 6.06. Sentence of Imprisonment for Felony; Ordinary Terms.

A person who has been convicted of a felony may be sentenced to imprisonment, as follows:

(1) in the case of a felony of the first degree, for a term the minimum of which shall be fixed by the Court at not less than one year nor more than ten years, and the maximum of which shall be life imprisonment;

(2) in the case of a felony of the second degree, for a term the minimum of which shall be fixed by the Court at not less than one year nor more than three years, and the maximum of which shall be ten years;

(3) in the case of a felony of the third degree, for a term the minimum of which shall be fixed by the Court at not less than one year nor more than two years, and the maximum of which shall be five years.

Section 6.07. Sentence of Imprisonment for Felony; Extended Terms.

In the cases designated in Section 7.03, a person who has been convicted of a felony may be sentenced to an extended term of imprisonment, as follows:

(1) in the case of a felony of the first degree, for a term the minimum of which shall be fixed by the Court at not less than five years nor more than ten years, and the maximum of which shall be life imprisonment;

(2) in the case of a felony of the second degree, for a term the minimum

of which shall be fixed by the Court at not less than one year nor more than five years, and the maximum of which shall be fixed by the Court at not less than ten nor more than twenty years;

(3) in the case of a felony of the third degree, for a term the minimum of which shall be fixed by the Court at not less than one year nor more than three years, and the maximum of which shall be fixed by the Court at not less than five nor more than ten years.

Comment

These sections embody the main conclusions with respect to sentences of imprisonment for felony on which the draft is based. These conclusions may be summarized as follows:

1. It is desirable that the court play a substantial role in sentencing, with authority not only to determine whether the offender should be sentenced to imprisonment but also to exercise some influence upon its length. Proposals to shift such authority to a treatment board or to vest it wholly in correctional administration, such as an Adult Authority, were considered at length by the Reporters and Advisory Committee but were not accepted. . . .

2. Viewed in the foregoing terms, it is desirable that sentences of imprisonment for felony be indeterminate in all cases, with a substantial spread between the minimum and maximum, but maxima, at least for most offenses, need not be and should not be inordinately high. When they are, they have small practical utility and offer danger of abuse.

In the ordinary situation, the maximum should be fixed by the statute, but the Court should have some control of the minimum, mainly for deterrent purposes and especially in dealing with the gravest crimes, where the deterrent factor normally looms largest at the time of sentencing.

3. A distinction should be drawn between ordinary and extended terms for the same crime, based on the character of the offender. When an extended term is employed, the Court should be empowered to raise both the minimum and maximum, within prescribed statutory limits. The lesson of experience with habitual offender laws is, however, that maxima of life imprisonment should not be lightly authorized and that, in any case, long terms should be discretionary and not mandatory. When they are mandatory, they result in inequality of application and extensive nullification. . . .

4. The ordinary maxima of 5 years, 10 years, and life, with reductions contemplated for good behavior, are based in part on *a priori* considerations

but in major part on the reflection of good practice in the operation of release procedures even when longer maxima have been employed. The fact that the draft will propose that all releases be upon parole and that the parole period be fixed at some proportion of the time spent in the institution (so that the worst risks held the longest time will have the longest supervision rather than the shortest, as is now the case) were also given weight and should be kept in mind in the appraisal of these terms. . . .

Section 7.01. Criteria for Withholding Sentence of Imprisonment and for Placing Defendant on Probation.

(1) The Court shall deal with a person who has been convicted of a crime without imposing sentence of imprisonment unless, having regard to the nature and circumstances of the crime and the history, character, and condition of the defendant, it is of the opinion that his imprisonment is necessary for protection of the public because:

(a) there is undue risk that during the period of a suspended sentence or probation the defendant will commit another crime; or
(b) the defendant is in need of correctional treatment that can be provided most effectively by his commitment to an institution; or
(c) a lesser sentence will depreciate the seriousness of the defendant's crime.

(2) The following grounds, while not controlling the discretion of the Court, shall be accorded weight in favor of withholding sentence of imprisonment:

(a) the defendant's criminal conduct neither caused nor threatened serious harm;
(b) the defendant did not contemplate that his criminal conduct would cause or threaten serious harm;
(c) the defendant acted under a strong provocation;
(d) there were substantial grounds tending to excuse or justify the defendant's criminal conduct, though failing to establish a defense;
(e) the victim of the defendant's criminal conduct induced or facilitated its commission;
(f) the defendant has compensated or will compensate the victim of his criminal conduct for the damage or injury that he sustained;
(g) the defendant has no history of prior delinquency or criminal activity

or has led a law-abiding life for a substantial period of time before the commission of the present crime;

(h) the defendant's criminal conduct was the result of circumstances unlikely to recur;

(i) the character and attitudes of the defendant indicate that he is unlikely to commit another crime;

(j) the defendant is particularly likely to respond affirmatively to probationary treatment;

(k) the imprisonment of the defendant would entail excessive hardship to himself or his dependents.

(3) When a person who has been convicted of a crime is not sentenced to imprisonment, the Court shall place him on probation if he is in need of the supervision, guidance, assistance, or direction that the probation service can provide.

Comment

1. As is explained above, the draft is based upon the view that suspension of sentence or probation may be appropriate dispositions on conviction of any offense, unless of course a mandatory sentence of death or life imprisonment is prescribed. Vesting such large discretion in the court invites the effort, however, to formulate criteria to guide its exercise. Such guides, if properly defined, should serve to promote both the thoughtfulness and the consistency of dispositions, while distributing responsibility between the legislature and the court. . . .

2. Rather than attempt to state considerations making for and against a sentence of imprisonment, the draft enumerates the types of factors that may justify the Court in withholding a prison sentence, with or without probation. . . .

The factors enumerated in paragraphs (a) to (h) relate primarily to the question whether the defendant is a source of future danger to the public, but they have some bearing also on the relative necessity of a strong sanction for deterrent purposes.

1.2
How Effective Are Penal Treatments?

Stephen Brody

Until quite recently, a belief that a solution to crime would eventually be found in better and more effective ways of improving, reforming, or treating criminals was solidly entrenched in the "liberal" tradition. But over the last few years a penological *volte-face* seems to have taken place, with rather astonishing ease and speed. To put it briefly, rehabilitation has come to be seen not only as an unrealistic and unrealizable aim, but one which is positively threatening to prisoners' rights and humanitarian principles and ultimately even harmful to offenders' chances of going straight. The ramifications of such a revised attitude, of course, extend very widely into all aspects of criminology and penology, and particularly into matters of sentencing and the disposal of convicted persons. The aim of this paper is to condense what is known from existing research into a few statements—to look at it through the wrong end of a telescope, as it were, rather than through a microscope, which is the customary viewpoint—and thus to consider what sorts of research programs are needed from now on.

Is Sentencing Policy Ineffective?

A major contribution to the research literature on sentencing is Lipton, Martinson, and Wilks's (1975) encyclopedic survey of evaluative research into the effectiveness of correctional treatment. However, they missed out most English research, which has been included subsequently in a more modest review for the Home Office (Brody 1976). Along with earlier reviews, both these publications presented similar evidence which has en-

---

From Stephen Brody, "Research into the Aims and Effectiveness of Sentencing," 17 *Howard Journal of Criminal Justice* 133 (1978). Excerpted and reprinted by permission.

couraged a widespread conviction that no one type of sentence works any better—that is, is no more effective in preventing recidivism—than any other.

It has to be emphasized that even if it is true, research results have actually provided little evidence for such a belief. This is because, with one or two exceptions, only a very limited range of sentencing alternatives have ever been studied (and consequently only a relatively small proportion of the offender population has ever been considered). Most of the major North American evaluative studies have set out to establish the superiority of institutions or programs, custodial or noncustodial, which attempt by psychological means to correct or cure offenders over traditional institutions in which repression and punishment are supposed to be the authorities' prime concern, and in which context even the divisions between custody and community care tend to become blurred. The same idea has been behind research in other countries as well, except that it has generally worked on a smaller scale. This has meant that there has been a concentration on innovative and experimental schemes and on the selected offenders—most of them young—who are involved in them. The bulk of ordinary criminals, who take up most of the courts' time, have aroused little interest.

Does Treatment Really Not Work?

One good reason for not completely abandoning a faith in rehabilitation is that a number of studies have shown that improvements *can* be effected in failure rates. What is strikingly consistent about these studies is that in all of them the treatment (whatever form it took) was effective only when it was applied to certain types of offenders (Grant and Grant 1959; Adams 1961; Jesness 1965; Shaw 1974; Palmer 1974) or simply when it was adapted to the particular requirements of individuals (Bernsten and Christiansen 1965; Ditman 1967) or when it was aimed at modifying such specific aspects of behavior as addiction or aggressiveness (Cotton et al. 1976). What is more surprising is that researchers have so rarely allowed for individual variations, or "interaction effects," in their experimental designs, but have expected one particular program to work equally for all offenders and to provide a universal remedy; Martinson and his colleagues (Lipton, Martinson, and Wilks 1975) can fairly be criticized for underplaying results which pointed to individual variations (Palmer 1975).

There is an even better reason why treatment has so often been shown to have no effect, which is simply that none has been given. It is very often the case, if they are submitted to detached observation, that contrasted institutions or programs are not very different in practice or in their impact on offenders, regardless of what facilities, staff-inmate ratio, or professional services one may claim against the other. At worst, the language of therapy is employed only in the service of good public relations or to disguise, wittingly or unwittingly, the true state of affairs that pervades correctional institutions and processes.

Even where treatment programs may reasonably be said to have been properly instigated, there is a lot of confusion about what they are likely to achieve, and how. Much of this confusion can only be explained as springing from an unrealistic understanding of human nature, contaminated no doubt by a lingering equation between crime and psychopathology, as Clarke (1977) has pointed out.

Research so far has on the whole confirmed what one would expect: that individual successes may sometimes be claimed by routine psychotherapy or counseling with intelligent, articulate neurotic offenders; by guidance in personal, social, and domestic matters among those hampered by incompetence in these spheres; by sympathy and encouragement for those unsure of their limits and capabilities; and by direct assistance and support for those weighed down by practical difficulties. But none of these approaches is appropriate for other than a minority of the offender population, whose misdemeanors reflect some real psychological maladjustment and not just their social "deviance."

Are Measures of Effectiveness Good Enough?

The generally disappointing results of research into the relative effectiveness of different sentences is sometimes blamed on the insensitivity of reconviction as a criterion for success. There is, certainly, some truth in this claim, and to try to overcome it, many researchers have looked also for qualitative differences in patterns of reoffending—that is, to see whether offenders given differential treatment differ in the number of times they are subsequently arrested, in the types of offense they commit, the types of sentences they get, in the time between release and the next conviction, and so on. By and large, none of these indices has been shown to discriminate any more tellingly than simple reconviction.

Much less frequently, rehabilitative effectiveness has been judged either by changes in behavior and attitudes during the course of a sentence or by longer-term changes in personality and personal adjustment after release or termination. Although indices of behavior during a sentence—such as absconding rates, number of disciplinary infractions, "unit-management problems," and so on—*have* generally been able to demonstrate differences between different institutions, variations may partly be accounted for by differences in standards of control and supervision. In any case, offenders' compliance with a regime tells us little more than that it is being operated efficiently. Measured changes in offenders' attitudes during their sentences can be more informative, if one accepts the validity of the measuring instruments (Jesness 1965; Persons 1966). Such changes are by no means inevitable, partly for the same reasons that reconviction rates are so often unaffected by treatment.

Studies using postsentence changes in social and vocational adjustment as criteria for evaluation have been least satisfactory, and the results are difficult to interpret (Rumney and Murphy 1952). Studies of the long-term effects of probation on noncriminal behavior, such as Lohman's in California (1967) and in the IMPACT Experiment in England (Folkard et al. 1976), have been unable to claim success.

Research into changes in attitudes, personality, and adjustment has done little more than to complicate the uncertainties already mentioned with regard to the effects of different sentences on reconviction rates. There is no obvious correlation between changes in attitudes and recidivism: in some studies improvements take place in one sense but not in the other, and if occasionally both improve, more often neither do.

On the other hand, measures of long-term adjustment have often been found to relate quite well to reductions in recidivism rates. For instance, there is a reasonable negative correlation between work adjustment and reconviction among young offenders (Scott 1964; Hood 1966), and it is offenders who are released to settled homes, sound marriages, and stable jobs who always have the best prognoses (Ericson et al. 1966; Lohman et al. 1967; Davies 1969). Unfortunately, measures of both adjustment and reconviction often bear little relation to type of sentence or type of treatment, from which it may be concluded that favorable circumstances and incentives in his ordinary life play a much more important part in determining success than what happens to an offender in the course of his sentence. But more probably, what usually happens is that adverse outside circumstances or influences rapidly counteract any small psychological gains which might have been accomplished during a sentence, and former habits soon overpower what little extra stamina might have been built up. No follow-up measure, of criminal or any other sort of behavior, has yet been able to overcome this difficulty and to indicate the relative *potential* advantages of different institutions, regimes, or sentences.

References

Adams, S. (1961) "Interaction between individual interview therapy and treatment amenability in older youth authority wards," in *Inquiries Concerning Kinds of Treatment for Kinds of Delinquents* (California Board of Corrections Monograph No. 2), Sacramento, California, reprinted in N. Johnston, et al. (1970) *The Sociology of Punishment and Correction,* Second Ed., New York, Wiley.

Bernsten, K., and Christiansen, K. O. (1965) "A resocialisation experiment with short-term offenders," in K. O. Christiansen et al. (eds.), *Scandinavian Studies in Criminology,* London, Tavistock.

Beyleveld, D. (1977) "The effectiveness of general deterrents as against crime: an annotated bibliography of evaluative research" (Unpublished research report prepared for the Home Office).

Brody, S. R. (1976) *The Effectiveness of Sentencing* (Home Office Research Study No. 35), London, H.M.S.O.

Clarke, R.V.G. (1977) "Psychology and crime," *Bulletin of the British Psychological Society, 30,* 280–83.

Cotton, M., et al. (1976) "Effectiveness of a community-based treatment program in modifying aggressive or delinquent behaviour," *Corrective and Social Psychology, 22,* 35–38.

Davies, M. (1969) *Probationers in their Social Environment* (Home Office Research Study No. 2), London, H.M.S.O.

Ditman, K. S., et al. (1967) "A controlled experiment in the use of court probation for drunk arrest," *American Journal of Psychiatry, 24,* 160–63.

Ericson, R. C., et al. (1966) *The Application of Comprehensive Psychosocial Vocational Services in the Rehabilitation of Parolees,* Minneapolis, Minneapolis Rehabilitation Center.

Folkard, S., et al. (1976) *IMPACT Vol. II* (Home Office Research Study No. 36), London, H.M.S.O.

Grant, J. D., and Grant, M. Q. (1959) "A group dynamics approach to the treatment of non-conformists in the Navy," *Annals of the American Academy of Political and Social Science, 322,* 126–35.

Greenberg, D. F. (1977) "The correctional effects of corrections: a survey of evaluations," in D. F. Greenberg (ed.), *Corrections and Punishment* (Sage Criminal Justice System Annuals Vol. 8), Beverly Hills, Sage.

Hood, R. (1966) *Homeless Borstal Boys,* London, Bell and Sons.

Jesness, C. F. (1965) *The Fricot Ranch Study* (Research Report No. 47), California, Department of the Youth Authority.

Lipton, D., Martinson, R., and Wilks, J. (1975) *Effectiveness of Correctional Treatment,* Springfield, Mass., Praeger.

Lohman, J. D., et al. (1967) *The San Francisco Project* (Research Report No. 11), Berkeley, School of Criminology, University of California.

Palmer, T. B. (1974) "The youth authority's community treatment project," *Federal Probation, 38,* 3–13.

Palmer, T. B. (1975) "Martinson revisited," *Journal of Research in Crime and Delinquency, 12,* 133–52.

Persons, R. W. (1966) "Psychological and behaviour change in delinquents following psychotherapy," *Journal of Clinical Psychology, 12,* 337–40.

Rumney, J., and Murphy, J. P. (1952) *Probation and Social Adjustment,* New Brunswick, New Jersey, Rutgers University Press.

Scott, P. (1964) "Approved school success rates," *British Journal of Criminology, 4,* 525–56.

Shaw, M. J. (1974) *Social Work in Prison* (Home Office Research Study No. 22), London, H.M.S.O.

Taylor, A.J.W. (1967) "An evaluation of group psychotherapy in a girls' hostel," *International Journal of Group Psychotherapy, 17,* 168–77.

Truax, C. B., et al. (1966) "Effects of group psychotherapy with high adequate empathy and non-possessive warmth upon female institutionalised delinquents," *Journal of Abnormal Psychology, 71,* 267–74.

Wilkins, L. T., et al. (1976) *Sentencing Guidelines: Structuring Judicial Discretion,* New York, Criminal Justice Research Center.

1.3
Rehabilitation and Dignity

Herbert Morris

I want to sketch a set of institutions proceeding on a conception of man which appears to be basically at odds with that operative within a system of punishment.

In this world we are now to imagine, when an individual harms another his conduct is to be regarded as a symptom of some pathological condition in the way a running nose is a symptom of a cold. Actions diverging from some conception of the normal are viewed as manifestations of a disease in the way in which we might today regard the arm and leg movements of an epileptic during a seizure. Actions conforming to what is normal are assimilated to the normal and healthy functioning of bodily organs. What a person does, then, is assimilated, on this conception, to what we believe today, or at least most of us believe today, a person undergoes. We draw a distinction between the operation of the kidney and raising an arm on request. This distinction between mere events or happenings and human actions is erased in our imagined system.

Let us elaborate on this assimilation of conduct of a certain kind to symptoms of a disease. First, there is something abnormal in both the case of conduct such as killing another and a symptom of a disease such as an irregular heart beat. Second, there are causes for this abnormality in actions such that once we know of them we can explain the abnormality as we now can explain the symptoms of many physical diseases. The abnormality is looked upon as a happening with a causal explanation rather than an action for which there were reasons. Third, the causes that account for the abnormality interfere with the normal functioning of the body, or, in the

---

From Herbert Morris, "Persons and Punishment," 52 *Monist* 475 (1968).

case of killing, with what is regarded as a normal functioning of an individual. Fourth, the abnormality is in some way a part of the individual, necessarily involving his body. A well going dry might satisfy our three foregoing conditions of disease symptoms, but it is hardly a disease or the symptom of one. Finally, and most obscure, the abnormality arises in some way from within the individual. If Jones is hit with a mallet by Smith, Jones may reel about and fall on James, who may be injured. But this abnormal conduct of Jones is not regarded as a symptom of disease. Smith, not Jones, is suffering from some pathological condition.

With this view of man the institutions of social control respond, not with punishment, but with either preventive detention, in the case of "carriers," or therapy, in the case of those manifesting pathological symptoms. The logic of sickness implies the logic of therapy. And therapy and punishment differ widely in their implications. In bringing out some of these differences I want again to draw attention to the important fact that while the distinctions we now draw are erased in the therapy world, they may, in fact, be reintroduced, but under different descriptions. To the extent they are, we really have a punishment system combined with a therapy system. I am concerned now, however, with what the implications would be were the world indeed one of therapy and not a disguised world of punishment and therapy, for I want to suggest tendencies of thought that arise when one is immersed in the ideology of disease and therapy.

First, punishment is the imposition upon a person who is believed to be at fault of something commonly believed to be a deprivation, where that deprivation is justified by the person's guilty behavior. It is associated with resentment, for the guilty are those who have done what they had no right to do by failing to exercise restraint when they might have and where others have. Therapy is not a response to a person who is at fault. We respond to an individual, not because of what he has done, but because of some condition from which he is suffering. If he is no longer suffering from the condition, treatment no longer has a point. Punishment, then, focuses on the past; therapy, on the present. Therapy is normally associated with compassion for what one undergoes, not resentment for what one has illegitimately done.

Second, with therapy, unlike punishment, we do not seek to deprive the person of something acknowledged as a good but seek rather to help and to benefit the individual who is suffering, by ministering to his illness in the hope that the person can be cured. The good we attempt to do is not a reward for desert. The individual suffering has not merited by his disease the good we seek to bestow upon him but has, because he is a creature that has the capacity to feel pain, a claim upon our sympathies and help.

Third, infliction of a prescribed punishment carries the implication that one has "paid one's debt" to society, for the punishment is the taking from the person of something commonly recognized as valuable. It is this conception of "a debt owed" that may permit, under certain conditions, the nonpunishment of the guilty, for operative within a system of punishment may be a concept analogous to forgiveness, namely pardoning. Who is it that we may pardon and under what conditions—contrition with its elements of self-punishment no doubt plays a role—I shall not go into though it is clearly a matter of the greatest practical and theoretical interest. What is clear is that the conceptions of "paying a debt" or "having a debt forgiven" or pardoning have no place in a system of therapy.

Fourth, with punishment there is an attempt at some equivalence between the advantage gained by the wrongdoer—partly based upon the seriousness of the interest invaded, partly on the state of mind with which the wrongful act was performed—and the punishment meted out. Thus, we can understand a prohibition on "cruel and unusual punishments" so that disproportionate pain and suffering are avoided. With therapy, attempts at proportionality make no sense. It is perfectly plausible to give a pill to someone who kills and to treat for a lifetime within an institution one who has broken a dish and manifested accident proneness. We have the concept of "painful treatment." We do not have the concept of "cruel treatment." Because treatment is regarded as a benefit, though it may involve pain, it is natural that less restraint is exercised in bestowing it than in inflicting punishment. Further, protests with respect to treatment are likely to be assimilated to the complaints of one whose leg must be amputated in order for him to live, and, thus, largely disregarded. To be sure, there is operative in the therapy world some conception of the "cure being worse than the disease," but if the disease is manifested in conduct harmful to others, and if being a normal operating human being is valued highly, there will naturally be considerable pressure to find the cure acceptable.

Fifth, the rules in a system of punishment governing conduct of individuals are rules violation of which involve either direct interference with others or the creation of a substantial risk of such interference. One could imagine adding to this system of primary rules other rules proscribing preparation to do acts violative of the primary rules and even rules proscribing thoughts. Objection to such suggestions would have many sources but a principal one would consist in its involving the infliction of punishment on too great a number of persons who would not, because of a change of mind, have violated the primary rules. Though we are interested in diminishing violations of the primary rules, we are not prepared to punish too many individuals who would never have violated the rules in order to achieve this aim. In a system motivated solely by a preventive and curative ideology there would be less reason to wait until symptoms manifest themselves in socially harmful conduct. It is understandable that we should wish at the earliest possible stage to arrest the development of the disease. In the punishment system, because we are dealing with deprivations, it is understandable that we should forbear from imposing them until we are quite sure of guilt. In the therapy system, dealing as it does with benefits, there is less reason for forbearance from treatment at an early stage.

Sixth, a variety of procedural safeguards we associate with punishment have less significance in a therapy system. To the degree objections to double jeopardy and self-incrimination are based on a wish to decrease the chances of the innocent being convicted and punished, a therapy system, unconcerned with this problem, would disregard such safeguards. When one is out to help people there is also little sense in urging that the burden of proof be on those providing the help. And there is less point to imposing the burden of proving that the conduct was pathological beyond a reasonable doubt. With the world of disease and therapy the individual's free choice ceases to be a determinative factor in how others respond to him. All those principles of our own legal system that minimize the chances of punishment of those who have not chosen to do acts violative of the rules tend to lose their point in the therapy system, for how we respond in a therapy system to a person is not conditioned upon what he has chosen but rather on what symptoms he has manifested or may manifest and what the best therapy for the disease is that is suggested by the symptoms.

Apart from those aspects of our therapy model which would relate to serious limitations on personal liberty, there are clearly objections of a more profound kind to the mode of thinking I have associated with the therapy model.

First, human beings pride themselves in having capacities that animals do not. A common way, for example, of arousing shame in a child is to compare the child's conduct to that of an animal. In a system where all actions are assimilated to happenings we are assimilated to creatures—indeed, it is more extreme than this—whom we have always thought possessed of less than we. Fundamental to our practice of praise and order of attainment is that one who can do more—one who is capable of more and one who does more—is more worthy of respect and admiration. And we have thought of ourselves as capable, where animals are not, of making, of creating, among other things, ourselves. The conception of man I have outlined would provide us with a status that today, when our conduct is assimilated to it in moral criticism, we consider properly evocative of shame.

Second, if all human conduct is viewed as something men undergo, thrown into question would be the appropriateness of that extensive range of peculiarly human satisfactions that derive from a sense of achievement. For these satisfactions we shall have to substitute those mild satisfactions attendant upon a healthy well-functioning body. Contentment is our lot if we are fortunate; intense satisfaction at achievement is entirely inappropriate.

Third, in the therapy world nothing is earned and what we receive comes to us through compassion, or through a desire to control us. Resentment is out of place. We can take credit for nothing but must always regard ourselves—if there are selves left to regard once actions disappear—as fortunate recipients of benefits or unfortunate carriers of disease who must be controlled. We know that within our own world human beings who have been so regarded and who come to accept this view of themselves come to look upon themselves as worthless. When what we do is met with resentment, we are indirectly paid something of a compliment.

Fourth, attention should be drawn to a peculiar evil that may be attendant upon regarding a man's actions as symptoms of disease. The logic of cure will push us toward forms of therapy that inevitably involve changes in the person made against his will. The evil in this would be most apparent in those cases where the agent, whose action is determined to be a manifestation of some disease, does not regard his action in this way. He believes that what he has done is, in fact, "right," but his conception of "normality" is not the therapeutically accepted one. When we treat an illness we normally treat a condition that the person is not responsible for. He is "suffering" from some disease and we treat the condition, relieving the person of something preventing his normal functioning. When we begin treating persons for actions that have been chosen, we do not lift from the person something that is interfering with his normal functioning but we change the person so that he functions in a way regarded as normal by the current therapeutic community. We have to change him and his judgments of value. In doing this we display a lack of respect for the moral status of individuals, that is, a lack of respect for the reasoning and choices of individuals. They are but animals who must be conditioned. I think we can understand and, indeed, sympathize with a man's preferring death to being forcibly turned into what he is not.

Finally, perhaps most frightening of all would be the derogation in status of all protests to treatment. If someone believes that he has done something right, and if he protests being treated and changed, the protest will itself be regarded as a sign of some pathological condition, for who would not wish to be cured of an affliction? What this leads to are questions of an important kind about the effect of this conception of man upon what we now understand by reasoning. Here what a person takes to be a reasoned defense of an act is treated, as the action was, on the model of a happening of a pathological kind. Not just a person's acts are taken from him but also his attempt at a reasoned justification for the acts. In a system of punishment a person who has committed a crime may argue that what he did was right. We make him pay the price and we respect his right to retain the judgment he has made. A conception of pathology precludes this form of respect.

1.4
The Decline of the Rehabilitative Ideal

Francis A. Allen

The modern decline of penal rehabilitationism cannot be fully explained by the persuasiveness of the logical cases arrayed against it. Yet the criticisms are important, for in them may be found the assumptions on which contemporary efforts to recast criminal justice are based. Some modern reactions present very little of intellectual interest; they comprise essentially irritated responses to the prevalence of crime and offer only an all-encompassing faith in the efficacy of coercion and repression. Such a characterization, however, is in no way descriptive of the views of many who today oppose the rehabilitative ideal. The latter are troubled by the political implications of penal rehabilitationism and are sensitive to the conflicts built into a system of criminal justice that seeks to express simultaneously the values of human responsibility and the reform of offenders. Accordingly, attention needs to be given to the modern critique of the rehabilitative ideal.

The modern case against the rehabilitative ideal has been in the making at least since the years immediately preceding World War II. It derives from a variety of sources and was largely formulated before political movements in the late 1960s appropriated it for their own purposes. Although these critics share no common fund of assumptions, the modern critique of the rehabilitative ideal appears to rest on three principal propositions. First, the rehabilitative ideal constitutes a threat to the political values of free societies. Second—a distinct but closely related point—the rehabilitative ideal has revealed itself in practice to be peculiarly vulnerable to debasement

From Francis A. Allen, *The Decline of the Rehabilitative Ideal: Penal Policy and Social Purpose* (New Haven: Yale University Press, 1981).

and the serving of unintended and unexpressed social ends. Third, either because of scientific ignorance or institutional incapacities, a rehabilitative technique is lacking; we do not know how to prevent criminal recidivism by changing the characters and behavior of offenders.

The liberal political stance and penal rehabilitationism coexist in a continuing state of tension, even though the resulting unease is more acutely sensed in some periods than in others. From the liberal perspective, any system of penal regulation, however oriented, is at best a necessary evil—the necessity stemming from the presence in the community of those who unjustifiably subvert the interests and volition of other persons. The movement from penal incapacitation of offenders to their reform, however, introduces a new order of concerns; for efforts to influence by coercive means the very thoughts, feelings, and aspirations of offenders threaten trespass by the state upon areas of dignity and choice posited as immune by the liberal creed. One reason the tension between liberalism and the rehabilitative ideal has not always been seen as critical is that the means often employed in rehabilitative efforts have been such that, if at all successful, they require a considerable voluntary cooperative effort on the part of the subject. When, however, the rehabilitative effort moves from the use of devices like those of traditional psychotherapy to what have been called the extreme therapies—psychosurgery, aversive conditioning, and certain other forms of behavioral modification—the state employs rehabilitative techniques that typically impose feelings and perceptions on the subject that in a meaningful sense are not of his own making, techniques that one observer describes as "manipulating people inside the perimeter of their conscious defenses."[1] The liberal unease with such forms of rehabilitation reflects, not a Luddite rejection of scientific "advance," but rather an awareness that they constitute incursions by the state into areas of human freedom and autonomy believed to lie outside the proper province of state action.

The principles of consent and voluntarism derived from liberal political values suggest certain limitations on the methods that may legitimately be employed in rehabilitative efforts. The widespread disregard of these limitations, both in this country and around the world, constitutes one of the serious modern complaints about penal rehabilitationism.

The political implications of the rehabilitative ideal, however, encompass far more than the kinds of rehabilitative techniques employed. Regardless of the means applied, a range of problems emerge involving control of the discretion of public agencies, and these problems have proved persistent and disturbing.[2] The issues are among the most frequently discussed in the recent legal literature on corrections.

Therapeutic theories of penal treatment have often conceived of crime as symptomatic of an affliction, but the nature of the disease and how it differs from other pathologies are generally obscure. Vagueness in the conception of the disorder is communicated, in turn, to thought about its cure. Much of the political unease engendered by this version of the rehabilitative ideal stems from its central conception. One immediate consequence of a rehabilitative regime is a drastic enlargement of state concerns. The state's interests now embrace not only the offender's conduct but, as Michel Foucault has put it, his "soul": his motives, his history, his social environment.[3] A traditional restraint on governmental authority is the notion of relevance: the state is limited in its inquiries and actions to that which is pertinent to its legitimate purposes. But when there are no clear limits on what may be relevant to the treatment process and when the goals of treatment have not been clearly defined, the idea of relevance as a regulator of public authority is destroyed or impaired.

The assumption of the benevolent purpose of the rehabilitative regime and the highly subjective and ill-defined notions of how rehabilitation is to be achieved and of what it consists, generate other problems. One of these is the tendency of those engaged in rehabilitative efforts to define as therapy anything that a therapist does. Because such disabilities as loss of liberty and other privileges are defined as therapeutic, the officer's sense of self-restraint may be weakened. One consequence, frequently remarked, is the tendency of rehabilitative regimes to inflict larger deprivations of liberty and volition on its subjects than is sometimes exacted from prisoners in more overtly punitive programs.

These, then, constitute part of the catalog of political concerns that have been engendered by the rehabilitative ideal. Whether they or any part of them counsel the total abandonment of penal rehabilitationism or whether it is prudent to persist in rehabilitative efforts if forewarned of their perils, requires further consideration. For the moment, however, it is sufficient to say that the political concerns just discussed take on even greater seriousness when a second broad tendency of the rehabilitative ideal is considered: its tendency in practical application to become debased and to serve other social ends far removed from and sometimes inconsistent with the reform of offenders.

Understanding the phenomena of debasement is advanced if attention is first directed to the ways in which language has been employed by those initiating and administering programs of penal rehabilitation. What is involved is more than the usual insistence on a technical vocabulary, but rather a marked tendency toward euphemism and obfuscation. What distinguishes the language of rehabilitation is the degree of faith reflected in the efficacy of label changes, the extraordinary gaps between the epithets employed and the commonsense realities that the words are intended to describe, the amorphousness of concepts central to the system of thought. In one place or another solitary confinement has been called "constructive meditation" and a cell for such confinement "the quiet room." Incarceration without treatment of any kind is seen as "milieu therapy" and a detention facility is labeled "Cloud Nine." The catalog is almost endless. Some of the euphemisms are conscious distortions of reality and are employed sardonically or with deliberate purpose to deceive. The more serious distortions, however, are those that reflect the self-deception of correctional functionaries. The burgeoning of euphemisms and the insecure grasp on reality that their use often reveals, signal a system of thought and action under extreme pressure. They are symptomatic of factors contributing to the debasement of rehabilitative objectives in practical application.

Central among the causes of debasement is the conceptual weakness of the rehabilitative ideal. Vagueness and ambiguity shroud its most basic suppositions. The ambitious scope and complexity of its agenda make these characteristics comprehensible and perhaps inevitable. Ambiguities afflict the very notion of what rehabilitation consists. A consensus on the ends of rehabilitation sufficient to spark movements of penal reform may, however, camouflage wide diversities of orientation that become critical when institutional programs are attempted.

Equally serious is the vagueness that surrounds the means to effect rehabilitation. Much that is most bizarre in the history of penal rehabilitationism stems from scientific ignorance about how changes in the behavior of offenders are to be achieved. In general, scientific ignorance has not inspired caution in the devotees of the rehabilitative ideal. On the contrary, the very absence of knowledge has encouraged confident assertions and dogmatic claims. One consequence is the creation of expectations that are inevitably disappointed. As programs fail, euphemisms and pretext burgeon. Among the groups most seriously disenchanted by this cycle are the inmates themselves. A profound obstacle to penal rehabilitation in the contemporary world is the cynicism of the prisoners engendered, at least in part, by such institutional charades.

The weaknesses of concept and technique take on greater significance when it is recognized that even under the most favorable circumstances rehabilitation can never constitute the sole objective of a correctional system, that many other purposes compete with it for realization. Correctional institutions and programs must serve punitive, deterrent, and incapacitative ends. Penal policy must be reconciled with the reality of scarce resources and must not offend too obviously the aspirations and values of the larger society. The rehabilitative ideal has proved itself poorly armed to maintain itself against competing objectives of policy and practice. In consequence, rehabilitative efforts are frustrated, change character, and may ultimately be rejected and abandoned.

Among the various interests with which the rehabilitative ideal competes are those of the staff and the institution administering the correctional program. System maintenance is frequently confused with inmate reform. Staff positions must be justified, public relations maintained, the media and hostile reform groups kept at arm's length, the demands of political patronage contained. Because rehabilitative programs require an institutional base and because the ends and means of rehabilitation are vague, it is easy to confuse the interests of inmates with those of the institution. These pressures are insidious, in part, because they may contribute to the debasement of the rehabilitative ideal without bad faith in the correctional staff and certainly in the absence of conscious conspiracy to achieve sub-rosa objectives of social control.

Perhaps even more rigorous is the competition between rehabilitation and the punitive and deterrent purposes of penal justice. The rehabilitative ideal is ordinarily outmatched in the struggle. The amorphousness of rehabilitative theory and practice contributes to their undoing. It may on occasion be true that the detention or penal incarceration of a young offender, for example, can be defended rationally as serving a rehabilitative end. But given the intensity of the punitive pressures, on the one hand, and the vagueness of rehabilitative criteria, on the other, the temptations to self-deception of correctional personnel in such cases must often prove irresistible. In many instances the latent function of rehabilitative theory is to camouflage punitive measures that might otherwise produce protest in the community. While ordinarily described in the language of therapy, the use of aversive techniques on prisoners, such as administering the drug apomorphine to cause vomiting, can hardly be distinguished either in purpose or effect from the cruder forms of corporal punishment once defended as essential to inmate reform.

Speculation about the causes of rehabilitative debasement requires that attention be given to the effects of fiscal stringency on both the theory and practice of penal rehabilitation. The effects have been of many sorts. Occasionally in the history of the rehabilitative ideal, penal reformers have displayed a splendid disregard for the fact of scarce resources and an unawareness of insistent competing claims for public support. More devastating, however, has been the practice of rehabilitationists to seek public support of their agenda by promising savings to taxpayers. Most destructive of all is the tendency to employ the vocabulary of rehabilitation to provide elaborate rationalizations for programs and measures motivated in largest part by fiscal considerations. The point, of course, is not that a penal system can or ought to ignore inevitable fiscal limitations. It is rather that from the beginning of its modern history the rehabilitative ideal has regularly proved itself incapable of defending its nature and integrity from the erosions of fiscal policy.

Even a brief consideration of the relevant history confirms the persistent tendency toward the debasement of the rehabilitative ideal in practical application. Indeed the evidence may justify the assertion sometimes made that rehabilitative theories of penal treatment have never been accorded a fair trial. That such is true today may appear supported by estimates that no more than five cents of every dollar currently spent on penal corrections are allocated to purposes that can be considered even remotely rehabilitative.[4] Yet there are countervailing arguments. Can it reasonably be assumed that in the great variety of social and political circumstances of the past two centuries in which rehabilitation has been attempted, none provided an environment favorable to fair testing? And if so, what reason is there for supposing that the nature of Western society will alter so as to provide more favorable circumstances in the next two hundred years—at least if techniques of rehabilitation threatening to basic political values are avoided?

A consideration of the phenomena of debasement leads naturally to the third and final proposition in the critique of the rehabilitative ideal. The proposition is that there is no evidence that an effective rehabilitative technique exists, that we do not know how to prevent criminal recidivism through rehabilitative effort. The statement of the proposition that has received widest attention was that of Robert Martinson. "With few isolated exceptions," he wrote in 1974, "the rehabilitative efforts that have been reported so far have had no appreciable effect on recidivism."[5] One of the most important aspects of the Martinson study may well be that its immediate and widespread impact constitutes a demonstration of public attitudes in the 1970s receptive to the conclusions stated.

In a remarkably short time a new orthodoxy has been established asserting that rehabilitative objectives are largely unattainable and that rehabilitative programs and research are dubious or misdirected. The new attitudes resemble in their dominance and pervasiveness those of the old orthodoxy, prevailing only a few years ago, that mandated rehabilitative efforts and exuded optimism about rehabilitative capabilities. Those who resist the hegemony of the new orthodoxy have challenged the criteria of success imposed by the critics on rehabilitative programs and research and have argued that the critics' own studies provide basis for at least moderate optimism about future prospects of rehabilitative attempts.[6] Some have suggested that the methods employed in the modern attack on the rehabilitative ideal are often more polemic and ideological in their nature than scientific.[7] Even though these controversies continue, it is not too soon for certain general observations to be made. Proponents of rehabilitative research have argued with considerable force that to the extent the modern critique of the rehabilitative ideal rests on scientific ignorance of many matters vital to rehabilitative programs, the indicated response is not the abandonment of those efforts but, rather, the production of new knowledge.[8] Yet the proponents share with the critics a profound dissatisfaction with most past examples of rehabilitative research and practice. They express an awareness of the complexities inherent in such endeavors that was typically lacking in the enthusiasm for penal rehabilitation even in the recent past. A new spirit of caution pervades claims about the rehabilitative potential of correctional programs; and the era when penal rehabilitationism can be accepted as the dominant mode of crime control seems more remote today than at many times in the past.

What role is likely to be accorded the rehabilitative ideal in the emerging modern synthesis? One point seems clear: whatever functions are assigned to penal rehabilitationism in the remaining years of the twentieth century, they are likely to be peripheral rather than central to the administration of criminal justice. This is true not only because of the new awareness of the limited efficacy of rehabilitative programs and the other factors making up the modern critique of the rehabilitative ideal, but also because even an effective program of inmate reform contributes only tangentially to the strategy of public order. In that strategy the deterrence of the great majority of the population from serious criminal activity is always the consideration of first importance, not the rehabilitation or incapacitation of the much smaller number of persons convicted of criminal offenses.

Notes

1. Neville, *Ethical and Philosophical Issues of Behavior Control* (Am. Assn. for the Advancement of Science, December 27, 1972) 4.

2. Problems of discretion surfaced very early in the American experience with the rehabilitative ideal. In the 1830s Beaumont and Tocqueville noted a controversy in Pennsylvania concerning the right granted the "houses of refuge" to receive children who had neither committed a crime nor were convicted of an offense. G. de Beaumont and A. de Tocqueville, *On the Penitentiary System in the United*

States and Its Application in France (Carbondale, Ill.: Southern Illinois University Press, 1964) 139–40.

3. M. Foucault, *Discipline and Punish* (New York: Pantheon Books, 1977), at 19.

4. G. Hawkins, *The Prison: Policies and Practice* (Chicago: University of Chicago Press, 1976), at 49–50.

5. "What Works? Questions and Answers about Prison Reform," *Pub. Interest* 24, 25 (Spring 1974). The article derived from a larger work. D. Lipton, R. Martinson, and J. Wilks, *The Effectiveness of Correctional Treatment* (New York: Praeger, 1975). In his later work Professor Martinson has substantially modified the conclusions stated above. See Martinson, "New Findings, New Views: A Note of Caution Regarding Sentencing Reform," 7 *Hofstra L. Rev.* 243 (1979).

6. See, e.g., Palmer, "Martinson Revisited," 12 *J. Research in Crime and Delin.* 133 (1975). Cf. Martinson, "California Research at the Crossroads," 22 *Crime and Delin.* 180 (1976).

7. Gottfredson, "Treatment Destruction Techniques," 16 *J. Research in Crime and Delin.* 39 (January 1979).

8. McCollum, "What Works!" 41 *Fed. Prob.* 32 (June 1977); Palmer, *supra* note 6, at 143; H. Sacks and C. Logan, *Does Parole Make a Difference?* (West Hartford: University of Connecticut Press, 1979) 67.

1.5
Reaffirming Rehabilitation

Francis T. Cullen
Karen E. Gilbert

There can be little dispute that the rehabilitative ideal has been conveniently employed as a mask for inequities in the administration of criminal penalties and for brutality behind the walls of our penal institutions. However, the existence of inhumanity and injustice in the arena of crime control does not depend on the vitality of rehabilitation. Indeed, a punitive "just deserts" philosophy would serve the purposes of repressive forces equally well, if not with greater facility. It would thus seem prudent to exercise caution before concluding that the failure of the criminal justice system to sanction effectively and benevolently is intimately linked to the rehabilitative ideal and that the ills of the system will vanish as the influence of rehabilitation diminishes.

This line of reasoning is liberating in the sense that it prompts us to consider that the state's machinery of justice might well have been *more* and not less repressive had history not encouraged the evolution of the rehabilitative ideal. This suggests in turn that preoccupation with the misuses and limitations of treatment programs has perhaps blinded many current-day liberals to the important benefits that have been or can be derived from popular belief in the notion that offenders should be saved and not simply punished. In this respect, the persistence of a strong rehabilitative ideology can be seen to function as a valuable resource for those seeking to move toward the liberal goal of introducing greater benevolence

---

into the criminal justice system. Alternatively, we can begin to question whether the reform movement sponsored by the left will not be undermined should liberal faith in rehabilitation reach a complete demise. In this context, four major reasons are offered below for why we believe that liberals should reaffirm and not reject the correctional ideology of rehabilitation.

1. *Rehabilitation is the only justification of criminal sanctioning that obligates the state to care for an offender's needs or welfare.* Admittedly, rehabilitation promises a payoff to society in the form of offenders transformed into law-abiding, productive citizens who no longer desire to victimize the public. Yet treatment ideology also conveys the strong message that this utilitarian outcome can only be achieved if society is willing to punish its captives humanely and to compensate offenders for the social disadvantages that have constrained them to undertake a life in crime. In contrast, the three competing justifications of criminal sanctioning—deterrence, incapacitation, and retribution (or just deserts)—contain not even the pretense that the state has an obligation to do good for its charges. The only responsibility of the state is to inflict the pains that accompany the deprivation of liberty or of material resources (e.g., fines); whatever utility such practices engender flows only to society and not to its captives. It is difficult to imagine that reform efforts will be more humanizing if liberals willingly accept the premise that the state has no responsibility to do good, only to inflict pain. Notably, Gaylin and Rothman, proponents of the justice model, recognized the dangers of such a choice when they remarked that "in giving up the rehabilitative model, we abandon not just our innocence but perhaps more. The concept of deserts is intellectual and moralistic; in its devotion to principle, it turns back on such compromising considerations as generosity and charity, compassion and love."[1]

Now it might be objected by liberal critics of rehabilitation that favoring desert as the rationale for criminal sanctioning does not mean adopting an uncaring orientation toward the welfare of offenders. The reform agenda of the justice model not only suggests that punishment be fitted to the crime and not the criminal, but also that those sent to prison be accorded an array of rights that will humanize their existence. The rehabilitative ideal, it is countered, justifies the benevolent treatment of the incarcerated but only as a means to achieving another end—the transformation of the criminal into the conforming. In contrast, the justice perspective argues for humanity as an end in and of itself, something that should not in any way be made to seem conditional on accomplishing the difficult task of changing the deep-seated criminogenic inclinations of offenders. As such, liberals should not rely on state-enforced rehabilitation to somehow lessen the rigors of imprisonment, but instead should campaign to win legal rights for convicts that directly bind the state to provide its captives with decent living conditions.

However, we must stand firm against efforts to promote the position that the justice model with its emphasis on rights should replace the rehabilitative ideal with its emphasis on caring as the major avenue of liberal reform. Support for the principles of just deserts and determinacy has only exacerbated the plight of offenders both before and after their incarceration. But there are additional dangers to undertaking a reform program that abandons rehabilitation and seeks *exclusively* to broaden prisoner rights. Most importantly, the realities of the day furnish little optimism that such a campaign would enjoy success. The promise of the rights perspective is based on the shaky assumption that more benevolence will occur if the relationship of the state to its deviants is fully adversarial and purged of its paternalistic dimensions. Instead of the government being entrusted to reform its charges through care, now offenders will have the comfort of being equipped with a new weapon—"rights"—that will serve them well in their battle against the state for a humane and justly administered correctional system.

The rights perspective is a two-edged sword. While rights ideally bind the state to abide by standards insuring a certain level of due process protection and acceptable penal living conditions, rights also establish the limits of the good that the state can be expected or obligated to provide. A rehabilitative ideology, in contrast, constantly pricks the conscience of the state with its assertion that the useful and moral goal of offender reformation can only be effected in a truly humane environment. Should treatment ideology be stripped away by liberal activists and the ascendancy of the rights model secured, it would thus create a situation in which criminal justice officials would remain largely immune from criticism as long as they "gave inmates their rights"—however few they may be at the time.

Even more perversely, the very extension of new rights can also be utilized to legitimate the profound neglect of the welfare of those under state control. The tragic handling of mental patients in recent years is instructive in this regard. As it became apparent that many in our asylums were being either unlawfully abused or deprived of their liberty, the "mentally ill" won the right to be released to or remain in the community if it could be proven that they were of no danger to themselves or others. Yet, what has been the actual result of this "right" to avoid state enforced therapy? It brought forth not a new era in the humane treatment of the troubled but a new era of state neglect. Instead of brutalizing people within institutional structures, the state now permits the personally disturbed to be brutalized on the streets of our cities. Homeless, many of the mentally ill end up in one of the many decrepit boarding houses—"large psychiatric ghettos"—that have sprung up to exploit their vulnerability. In this context, we would do well to keep in mind Charles Marske and Steven Vargo's broader observation regarding the effects of the due process or rights movement in various sectors of our society in recent years: "Unfortunately, the darker side of legalization is its implication in depersonalization. . . . A curious irony emerges: the very groups that called for expanded legalism to establish and protect their individual rights now suffer its consequences."[2]

2. *The ideology of rehabilitation provides an important rationale for opposing the conservatives' assumption that increased repression will reduce crime.* Those embracing the conservatives' call for "law and order" place immense faith in the premise that tough rather than humane justice is the answer to society's crime problem. In the political right's view, unlawful acts occur only when individuals have calculated that they are advantageous, and thus the public's victimization will only subside if criminal choices are made more costly. This can be best accomplished by sending more offenders away to prison for more extended and uncomfortable stays.

Liberals have traditionally attacked this logic on the grounds that repressive tactics do not touch upon the real social roots of crime and hence rarely succeed in even marginally reducing criminal involvement. Campaigns to heighten the harshness of existing criminal penalties—already notable for their severity—will only serve to fuel the problem of burgeoning prison populations and result in a further deterioration of penal living standards. The strategy of "getting tough" thus promises to have substantial costs, both in terms of the money wasted on the excessive use of incarceration and in terms of the inhumanity it shamefully introduces.

It is clear that proponents of the justice model share these intense liberal concerns over the appealing but illusory claims of those preaching law and order. However, their opposition to repressive crime control policies encounters difficulties because core assumptions of the justice model converge closely with those found in the paradigm for crime control espoused by conservatives. Both perspectives, for instance, argue that (1) offenders are responsible beings who freely choose to engage in crime; (2) regardless of the social injustices that may have prompted an individual to breach the law, the nature of the crime and not the nature of the circumstances surrounding a crime should regulate the severity of the sanction meted out; and (3) the punishment of offenders is deserved—that is, the state's infliction of pain for pain's sake is a positive good to be encouraged and not a likely evil to be discouraged. Admittedly, those wishing to "do justice" would contend that current sanctions are too harsh and that prison conditions should be made less rigorous. But having already agreed with conservatives that punishing criminals is the fully legitimate purpose of the criminal justice system, they are left with little basis on which to challenge the logic or moral justification of proposals to get tough.

In contrast, the ideology of rehabilitation disputes every facet of the conclusion that the constant escalation of punishment will mitigate the specter of crime. To say that offenders are in need of rehabilitation is to reject the conservatives' notion that individuals, regardless of their position in the social order—whether black or white, rich or poor—exercise equal freedom in deciding whether to commit a crime. Instead, it is to reason that social and personal circumstances often constrain, if not compel, people to violate the law: and unless efforts are made to enable offenders to escape these criminogenic constraints, little relief in the crime rate can be anticipated. Policies that insist on ignoring these realities by assuming a vengeful posture toward offenders promise to succeed only in fostering hardships that will, if anything, deepen the resentment that many inmates find difficult to suppress upon their release back into society.

It is apparent, then, that the ideology of rehabilitation is fully oppositional to the conservatives' agenda for the repression of crime. Importantly, it thus furnishes liberals seeking to effect criminal justice reform with a coherent framework with which to argue that benevolence and not brutality should inform society's attempts to control crime. Sharing no assumptions with the right's paradigm of law and order, it does not, as in the case of the justice model, easily give legitimacy to either repressive punishment policies or the neglect of offender well-being. Instead, it remains a distinctly liberal ideology that can be utilized as a resource in the left's quest to illustrate the futility of policies that increase pain but accomplish little else.

3. *Rehabilitation still receives considerable support as a major goal of the correctional system.* While the average citizen clearly wants criminals to be severely sanctioned—in particular, sent to prison for longer stays—survey research consistently reveals that the American public also believes that offenders should be rehabilitated.[3] In a national survey which reported that the majority of Americans in July of 1981 judged prisons to be too soft, the respondents were also asked: "What do you think should be the primary purpose of putting criminals in prison?" Notably, 37 percent answered "to rehabilitate them," compared with 31 percent who favored

the alternative "to punish them" and 25 percent that favored "to remove them from society" (7 percent were "not sure").

Existing survey data suggest that rehabilitation persists as a prevailing ideology within the arena of criminal justice. This does not mean that treatment programs in our prisons are flourishing and remain unthreatened by the pragmatics and punitiveness of our day. But it is to assert that the rehabilitative ideal and the benevolent potential it holds are deeply anchored within our correctional and broader cultural heritage. That is, rehabilitation constitutes an ongoing rationale that is accepted by or "makes sense to" the electorate as well as to criminal justice interest groups and policymakers. Consequently, it provides reformers with a valuable vocabulary with which to justify changes in policy and practice aimed at mitigating the harshness of criminal sanctions—such as the diversion of offenders into the community for "treatment" or the humanization of the prison to develop a more effective "therapeutic environment." Unlike direct appeals for inmate rights to humane and just living conditions that can be quickly dismissed as the mere coddling of the dangerous, liberal reforms undertaken in the name of rehabilitation have the advantage of resonating with accepted ideology and hence of retaining an air of legitimacy. And should the confidence of citizens about specific proposals waver, it is always possible to impress upon the public that, despite overflowing penitentiaries, the average prisoner is back on the streets within two years and that fewer than 9 percent of the inmate population is serving a life sentence.[4] If the public is not willing to pay now to facilitate the betterment of those held in captivity, it can be made clear to them that they will be forced to pay in more bothersome, if not tragic, ways at a later date.

Our message here is simple but, in light of the advent of the justice model, telling in its implications: for liberals to argue vehemently against the ideology of rehabilitation—to say that treatment cannot work because the rehabilitative ideal is inherently flawed—is to undermine the potency of one of the few resources that can be mobilized in the left's pursuit of less repression in the administration of criminal punishments.

4. *Rehabilitation has historically been an important motive underlying reform efforts that have increased the humanity of the correctional system.* Liberal critics have supplied ample evidence to confirm their suspicions that state-enforced therapy has too frequently encouraged the unconscionable exploitation of society's captives.

However, while the damages permitted by the corruption of the rehabilitative ideal should neither be denied nor casually swept aside, it would be misleading to idealize the "curious" but brutal punishments of "bygone days" and to ignore that reforms undertaken in the name of rehabilitation have been a crucial humanizing influence in the darker regions of the sanctioning process. Gaylin and Rothman have thus noted that "while rehabilitation may have been used as an excuse for heaping punishment upon punishment, it was also a limiting factor, and was a rationalization and justification for what few comforts were introduced into the lives of the prisoners."[5]

Those who have traditionally sought to treat offenders have thus also sought to lessen the discomforts convicts are made to suffer. In part, this occurs, as Allen has remarked, because "the objectives both of fundamental decency in the prisons and the rehabilitation of prisoners . . . appears to require the same measures."[6] Yet the studies of Torsten Eriksson suggest that it is the case as well that those endeavoring to pioneer "the more effective treatment of criminals" have commonly been united in their "indomitable will to help their erring brother."[7] In this context, we can again question the wisdom of liberal attempts to unmask the rehabilitative ideal as at best a "noble lie" and at worst an inevitably coercive fraud. For in discrediting rehabilitation, liberal critics may succeed in deterring a generation of potential reformers from attempting to do good in the correctional system by teaching that it is a futile enterprise to show care for offenders by offering to help these people lead less destructive lives. And should rehabilitation be forfeited as the prevailing liberal ideology, what will remain as the medium through which benevolent sentiments will be expressed and instituted into meaningful policy? Will the medium be a justice model that is rooted in despair and not optimism, that embraces punishment and not betterment, that disdains inmate needs and disadvantages in favor of a concern for sterile and limited legal rights, and whose guiding principle of reform is to have the state do less for its captives rather than more? Or will, as we fear, this vacuum remain unfilled and the liberal camp be left without an ideology that possesses the vitality—as has rehabilitation over the past 150 years—to serve as a rallying cry for or motive force behind reforms that will engender lasting humanizing changes?

The thrust of our analysis has been that the inequities and inhumanities of the criminal justice system that liberals find so intolerable will be exacerbated and not diminished should the left embrace the justice model as its dominant avenue of reform. Fostering the principles of desert and determinacy runs the grave risk of adding legitimacy to the conservatives' efforts to effect a new wave of repressive legislation and incarcerative practices, and of condoning the neglect of inmate needs. We have argued as well that rehabilitation is an ideology of benevolence that not only has precipitated reform movements that have tempered the harshness of punishments but also, as a persisting rationale for criminal sanctioning, retains the potential to be mobilized to justify future ameliorations of the correctional system.

Yet in illustrating the dangers of attacking and rejecting rehabilitation, we are not insensitive to the abuse inherent in a system that links liberty to self-improvement but furnishes few means to secure this end. Under the practice of enforced therapy, the state ideally institutes comprehensive treatment programs and in return demands that offenders take advantage of these opportunities and show signs of their willingness to conform. While control officials are willing to base release decisions on an offender's "progress," they provide only minimal services that inmates can use to better equip themselves to negotiate the constraints of the wider society.

Liberal advocates of the justice model have thus argued that this link between being cured and being set free is coercive and must be broken. In place of enforced therapy which compels offenders to seek reform on the threat of longer stays behind bars, they assert that rehabilitation must become "voluntary"—that is, that both entry into and subsequent performance in a treatment program will have no impact whatsoever on when an inmate will be released from jail. With the coerciveness surrounding treatment fully dissipated, only those inmates who really desire to improve themselves will take advantage of the limited services currently available.

The logic that we should "help only those who want to be helped" is attractive but it avoids some rather sticky considerations. For one thing, if the state has been lax in its provision of rehabilitative resources when it has struck a public bargain to do so, how diligent will its commitment to this task be when rehabilitation becomes voluntary and the state's obligation to treat its captives is no longer strictly mandated? More importantly, if we conclude that rehabilitation should be left voluntary and hence that an inmate's prospect for cure is not to be a standard regulating length of incarceration (or if incarceration is appropriate at all), then what criterion will be substituted? Of course, the answer to this question is retribution or, as liberals prefer, just deserts. This brings us back to the original controversy of whether reforms that abandon notions of rehabilitation and promote the principles of the justice model will mitigate or aggravate the proclivity of the correctional machinery to victimize its charges. And as we have suggested throughout, there is good reason to surmise that a criminal justice system that seeks exclusively to inflict punishment in the name of justice will be substantially worse than one that punishes but endeavors as well to rehabilitate society's wayward members.

Yet in again rejecting the justice model as violating the "principle of least harm," we do not mean to imply that liberals should simply become resigned to accept state-enforced therapy as it is currently practiced—

however despairing this alternative might seem—because it is the lesser of two evils. While we have argued for the advantages of trumpeting treatment ideology, we believe that it is equally important that liberal reform seeks to reaffirm rehabilitation in ways that negate its more abusive features. In this regard, a crucial flaw of state-enforced therapy is that it is imbalanced: the inmate has the obligation to be reformed in order to win release, but in the absence of sufficient pressure, the state has no real obligation to rehabilitate. It is thus incumbent upon liberals to attack this imbalance by exerting pressure on the state to fulfill more adequately its half of the bargain. This would involve undertaking a persistent campaign to expose the state's failure to meet its responsibilities and to institute policies that obligate correctional officials to supply inmates with the educational, occupational, and psychological services as well as the community programs it has so long promised to deliver.

In short, we are proposing that liberals discard state-enforced therapy and embrace *state-obligated therapy* as an avenue of criminal justice reform. Since it has been tragically and repeatedly demonstrated that the state cannot be trusted through appeals to its good will to create uniformly meaningful treatment programs, reforms aimed at obligating the state to rehabilitate must be sensitive to the need to restructure the prevailing interests in the correctional system that have long undermined the provision of treatment services to offenders.

Notes

1. Willard Gaylin and David J. Rothman, "Introduction," in Andrew von Hirsch, *Doing Justice: The Choice of Punishments* (New York: Hill and Wang, 1976), xxxix.

2. Charles E. Marske and Steven Vargo, "Law and dispute processing in the academic community," *Judicature* 64 (October 1980), 175.

3. See, for instance, David Duffee and R. Richard Ritti, "Correctional policy and public values," *Criminology* 14 (February 1977), 449–59; John T. Gandy, *Community Attitudes Toward Creative Restitution and Punishment* (unpublished Ph.D. dissertation, University of Denver, 1975); Market Opinion Research Co., *Crime in Michigan: A Report from Residents and Employers,* sixth edition (Detroit: Market Opinion Research Co., 1978); Pamela Johnson Riley and Vicki McNickle Rose, "Public and elite opinion on correctional reform: implications for social policy," *Journal of Criminal Justice* 8 (No. 6, 1980), 345–56.

4. S. David Hicks, *The Corrections Yearbook* (New York: Criminal Justice Institute, Inc., 1981), 30–31.

5. Gaylin and Rothman, "Introduction," xxxix. Similarly, E. R. East, "Is reformation possible in prison today?" *Journal of Criminal Law and Criminology*

38 (1947), 130–31, has commented that "The idea of reformation, although overstressed as a function to be fulfilled by a prison, must not be abandoned. It is this principle which has effected so many progressive and commendable changes in prison life and administration tending toward the improvement of the general welfare and happiness of the men confined."

6. Francis A. Allen, *The Decline of the Rehabilitative Ideal: Penal Policy and Social Purpose* (New Haven: Yale University Press, 1981), 81.

7. Torsten Eriksson, *The Reformers: An Historical Survey of Pioneer Experiments in the Treatment of Criminals* (New York: Elsevier, 1976), 252.

1.6
Should Penal Rehabilitationism Be Revived?

Andrew von Hirsch
Lisa Maher

Penal rehabilitationism has been in eclipse since the early 1970s.[1] Treatment efforts seemed to offer only limited hope for success.[2] Relying on treatment seemed also to lead to unjust results—for example, to excessive intrusion into offenders' lives in the name of cure.[3]

Recently, however, there have been hints of an attempted revival. Some researchers claim striking new successes in treatment techniques. These successes, Ted Palmer concludes in a recent survey of treatment methods, suggest that rehabilitative intervention has gained "increased moral and philosophical legitimacy," and that it is no longer the case that rehabilitation "should be secondary to punishment . . . whether for short- or long-term goals."[4] Some penologists—for example, Francis Cullen and Karen Gilbert—argue that a revival of the penal treatment ethic could help lead to a gentler and more caring penal system.[5] Interestingly, such arguments sometimes come from the ideological and political left[6]—which had once been so critical of treatment-based punishments.[7] There is by no means unanimity, however, even from these sources. Some researchers—for example, John Whitehead and Steven Lab in their recent survey of juvenile treatments[8]—continue to be quite pessimistic about those treatments' effects. Some penologists of the left—for example, Thomas Mathiesen[9]—strongly resist treatment as the basis for sanctioning. Nevertheless, there is enough ferment to prompt the question in our title, "Should penal rehabilitationism be revived?"

Reinstatement of a treatment ethic would raise a number of questions.

This essay appears also in 11 *Criminal Justice Ethics* No. 1 (1992). Reprinted by permission.

How much more is known about the treatment of offenders now than was a few years ago? How often can treatment give us answers about how severely to sentence convicted offenders? Is treatment really as humane as it is made out to be? How fair is it to base the sentence on an offender's supposed rehabilitative needs? Rehabilitationism went into eclipse some years ago partly because it could not answer these questions satisfactorily. Are better answers available today?

We approach these issues from heterogeneous viewpoints. One of us (von Hirsch) is a philosophical liberal and has long been an advocate of the desert model.[10] The other (Maher) has a more left and feminist orientation[11] and is skeptical of a retributive penal ethic. In our present discussion of the new rehabilitationism, we will not be assuming another articulated sentencing philosophy. What we agree on are the questions, not the answers.

Questions of Effectiveness

During the late 1960s and the 1970s, critics of penal treatment were sometimes tempted to assert that "nothing works." The phrase now haunts them and confuses analysis. It assumes that the main problem of treatment is that of establishing its effectiveness, and that treatment can be declared a "success" once *some* programs are shown to work. Both assumptions are erroneous. Even when treatments succeed, their use to decide sentencing questions raises important normative questions (discussed below). And occasional successes are not enough.

The last large-scale survey and analysis of treatments, undertaken by a panel of the National Academy of Sciences,[12] is over a decade old. It was distinctly pessimistic in its conclusions: when subjected to close scrutiny, few programs seemed to succeed in reducing offender recidivism. Since then, there has been continued experimentation, and successes have been reported.[13] Some treatment advocates, such as Paul Gendreau and Robert Ross, have suggested that such findings show that rehabilitation has been "revivified."[14]

Perhaps, however, caution is in order. The extent of recent treatment successes remains very much in dispute—as witness a recent debate among researchers who have surveyed juvenile treatment programs.[15] A source of continuing difficulty is that the "whys" of treatment (that is, the processes by which successes are achieved) are seldom understood.[16] Without knowing the processes by which experimental programs produce given outcomes, it is difficult to tell which features "work," and will continue to work, when programs are extended beyond experimental groups and implemented more widely.

Programs appear to have better prospects for success when they focus on selected subgroups of offenders, carefully screened for amenability.[17] Such a screening approach, however, necessarily limits treatments' scope. Perhaps this or that type of program can be shown to succeed with this or that subgroup of offenders. Treatments do not (and are not likely to) exist, however, that can be relied upon to decide sentences routinely—that can inform the judge, when confronted with the run-of-the-mill robbery, burglary, or drug offense, what the appropriate sanction should be, and provide even a modicum of assurance that the sanction will contribute to the offender's desistance from crime. Even Palmer concedes that recent treatment surveys do not "indicate that generic *types* of programs have been found that consistently produce *major* recidivism reductions," and that programs that have positive effects for selected offender subgroups "may have limited relevance to the remaining [offender] subtypes—those which might comprise much of the sample."[18] If treatment lacks such routine, predictable applicability, how can it serve as a principal sentencing rationale?

Success depends, also, on the resources available for implementation. The programs that succeed tend to be well funded, well staffed, and vigorously implemented.[19] These features are easiest to achieve when the program is tried in an experimental setting. When the same programs are carried out more widely, program quality tends to deteriorate. Gendreau and Ross admit that "[we are] still . . . absolutely amateurish at implementing . . . experimentally demonstrated programs within . . . systems provided *routinely* by government."[20]

Questions of Humaneness

Some new advocates of penal rehabilitationism, such as Cullen and Gilbert, stress its humaneness. Reemphasizing treatment, they assert, is humane because it is more caring: it looks to the needs of the offender, rather than seeking merely to punish or prevent.[21] Is it true that rehabilitation is concerned chiefly with the offender's own needs? That depends on whether one is speaking of social service or of measures aimed at recidivism prevention.

Social service is benevolent in intent, if not necessarily in actual application: the aim is to help the offender lead a less deprived life. It can sometimes be achieved by fairly modest interventions: the unskilled offender, for example, might be taught certain skills that make him better able to cope. Providing these services is, we agree, desirable,[22] although it is far from clear to what extent they reduce recidivism. The offender who is taught to read will not necessarily desist from crime as a result.

Treatment programs, however, seldom aim merely at social service. The objective, instead, is recidivism prevention: protecting *us* against future depredations on the offender's part. To accomplish that crime-preventive aim, the intervention may well have to be more drastic. It will take more to get the drug-abusing robber to stop committing further robberies than to teach him or her a skill. (A recent review of current research suggests that the best indicator of successful drug treatment outcomes is length of time in treatment.)[23] To describe such strategies as intrinsically humane or caring is misleading: it confuses humanitarian concerns with treatment-as-crime-prevention.

Cullen and Gilbert admit this last point—that rehabilitation is aimed at recidivism prevention. They argue, however, that few people care much about being humane or benevolent to convicted criminals as an end in itself. Rehabilitationism, they argue, offers a more attractive reason—a crime-preventive one—for decent penal policies.[24] There is something circular about this argument. It assumes that rehabilitative punishments *are* capable of reducing crime significantly, or at least that people will believe they are. And it assumes that treatment-oriented punishments are inherently gentle.

Are rehabilitative responses intrinsically less onerous? Not necessarily. Consider offenders convicted of crimes of intermediate or lesser gravity. A proportionate sanction for such offenses should be of no more than moderate severity.[25] What of a rehabilitative response? That would depend on how much intervention, and how long, is required to alter the offender's criminal propensities—and to succeed, the intervention may have to be quite substantial (as in the just-noted case of drug treatments).[26]

A rehabilitative ethic also tends to shift attention from the offender's actual criminal conduct to his or her lifestyle or social/moral character. For example, the cultural presumption that women are less "rational" often results in their lawbreaking being perceived as symptomatic of social (or biological) pathology. Women found guilty of relatively minor offenses thus may more readily be subjected to substantial treatment interventions.[27] Concerns about offenders' attitudes may elicit intrusive responses aimed at "correcting" individual ways of thinking and feeling.[28]

Cullen and Gilbert, and some other new rehabilitationists, argue for a return to a treatment model, on grounds that other models (e.g., desert) have led to harsh results.[29] How supportable are such claims? The severity or leniency with which a given sentencing philosophy is implemented will vary with the manner of its implementation and the criminal justice politics of the jurisdiction involved. That legislatively mandated "deserved" penalties were harsh in California seems attributable mostly to the character of criminal justice politics in that state, and to the legislature's having the task of setting the specific penalties.[30] A similar philosophy led to different (and less harsh) results in Minnesota and Oregon, where both the form of guidance and the criminal justice politics were different.[31] Similar considerations apply also to rehabilitationism. Were California to return to a rehabilitative ethos, it is far from certain—given California's politics—how "humane" or benevolent the results would be.

Some new rehabilitationists' rejection of other models, such as desert, is based on a socially critical perspective: how the rationale is likely to be implemented in a society characterized by race, class, and gender inequalities.[32] Such a critique, however, cuts both ways: one would need also to consider how rehabilitationism might be implemented in such an unpropitious social setting. It is fallacious to reject desert, for example, because of how "they" might carry it out, and then urge a treatment ethic on the basis of how "we" might implement it—that is, on the assumption of a much more supportive social system and legal culture than exists today. If rehabilitation is kinder, gentler, or better because that is how good people would implement it, then please tell us when and how, in a society such as our own, the good people take over.

While the new rehabilitationists are taking such a critical stance, they might also apply it to the rehabilitative ethic itself. Historically, the treatment ethos supported (as Michel Foucault has pointed out)[33] expansion of official and expert power/knowledge. If penal rehabilitationism is revived, what checks are there against a further proliferation of these powers?

Questions of Fairness

Criminal punishment, by its nature, condemns. The sanction not only visits deprivation but also conveys that the conduct is wrong and the offender to blame for having committed it. This holds whatever purpose is adopted for deciding sentences. Whether the sentence is based on the seriousness of the offender's crime or on his or her need for treatment, it will still imply something about the impropriety of the behavior.

The theoretical basis for the principle of proportionality of sentence is that it comports with the criminal sanction's censuring implications. Conduct that is more blameworthy—in the sense of involving greater harm and culpability—is to be punished (and thereby condemned) more severely;

conduct that is less reprehensible is to be punished (and hence censured) more mildly.[34]

Treatment, however, seldom can rely on criteria relating to the blameworthiness of the conduct; whether the offender is amenable to a particular treatment depends, instead, on his or her social and personal characteristics. This creates the potential problem of fairness: one is using criminal punishment, a blame-conveying response, and yet deciding the intervention on the basis of those personal and social variables that have little to do with how reprehensible the behavior is.[35]

How serious is this problem? The answer depends, of course, on how much emphasis proportionality receives. A thoroughgoing desert conception would require the severity of the penal response to depend heavily on the degree of reprehensibleness of the conduct—thus leaving limited scope for rehabilitative considerations (except for deciding among responses of comparable severity).[36] Not everyone supports a desert model, and some new rehabilitationists say they reject it.[37] But then, it needs to be explained what role, if any, the degree of blameworthiness of the conduct should have.

One possibility would be to give proportionality a limiting role: the seriousness of the criminal conduct would set upper and lower bounds on the quantum of punishment—within which rehabilitation could be invoked to fix the sentence.[38] That kind of solution requires one to specify how much weight its desert elements should have—that is, how narrow or broad the offense-based limits on the sentence should be.[39] Here, one faces the familiar dilemma: the narrower that one sets those limits, the less room there would be for treatment considerations; whereas the wider one sets the limits, the more one needs to worry about seemingly disparate or disproportionate responses.

Another possibility would be to try to dispense with notions of proportionality altogether.[40] Such a strategy, however, would pose its own difficulties. It would, first, have to be explained how it is justifiable to employ punishment—a blaming institution—without regard to the blameworthiness of the conduct.[41] Or, if one proposes to eliminate the censuring element in punishment, it needs to be explained how this possibly may be accomplished. (The juvenile justice system, for example, long purported to convey no blame, but who was fooled?) Second, the absence of significant proportionality constraints could open the way for abuses of the kind that discredited the old rehabilitation—for example, long-term, open-ended intervention against those deemed to be in special need of treatment. (One thinks of the young car thief who was confined for sixteen years at Patuxent Institution, because he refused to talk to the therapists.) One might hope that we are more sophisticated now about the therapeutic value of such interventions—but are such hopes enough without some *principled* restraint upon rehabilitative responses?

Finally, one could be more ambitious and think of replacing the criminal sanction with a wholly different set of measures. Nils Christie has urged that state punishment be supplanted by communitarian responses aimed at resolution of conflicts.[42] Some feminist writers have been exploring alternative conceptions of justice.[43] These theorists are, however, aware of the scope of this undertaking: it would involve, not a change in sentencing philosophy, but a completely new set of institutions for responding to what is now termed criminal behavior. One would have to consider whether, and how, these new institutions could afford protection against excessive, or seemingly unfair, intrusions. Whatever one thinks of such suggestions (and one of us has been skeptical of Christie's),[44] they constitute a different level of argument: one that concerns basic social and institutional change. These writers are not speaking, as the new rehabilitationists are, about retaining the criminal sanction and merely giving sentencing more of a treatment emphasis.

Concluding Thoughts

In offering the foregoing criticisms of the new rehabilitationists, we are not denying that treatment might have a legitimate role in a fair system of sanctions. How large that role should be depends not only on how much is known about treatment but also on what normative assumptions one makes—including those regarding proportionality.[45] Rehabilitation, however, cannot be the primary basis for deciding the sentence, nor can it be the rationale for supporting less harsh sanctions than we have today. If we want sanctions scaled down, as they surely should be, the main and explicitly stated reason for so doing should concern equity and the diminution of suffering.

The most dangerous temptation is to treat the treatment ethic as a kind of edifying fiction:[46] if we only act as though we cared—and minister treatment to offenders as a sign of our caring—a more humane penal system will emerge. No serious inquiry is needed, on this view, about the criteria for deciding what constitutes a humane penal system or about how a renewed treatment emphasis could achieve its intended effects or lead to reasonably just outcomes.

Such thinking is a recipe for failure. It is likely to cause the new treatment ethos to be rejected, once its specifics (or lack of them) are subject to critical scrutiny. And it could do no more good than the old, largely hortatory treatment ethic: create a facade of treatment behind which decision makers act as they choose. Those who wish to revive penal rehabilitationism have yet to address the hard questions, including the ones we have tried to raise here.

Notes

1. See F. Allen, *The Decline of the Rehabilitative Ideal* (1981), ch. 3.
2. See, e.g., note 15, *infra.*
3. American Friends Service Committee, *Struggle for Justice* (1971); A. von Hirsch, *Doing Justice* (1976); N. Morris, *The Future of Imprisonment* (1974).
4. Palmer, "The Effectiveness of Intervention: Recent Trends and Current Issues," 37 *Crime & Delinq.* 330, 342 (1991).
5. F. Cullen and K. Gilbert, *Reaffirming Rehabilitation* (1982).
6. B. Hudson, *Justice Through Punishment* (1987); P. Carlen, "Crime, Inequality, and Sentencing," in *Paying for Crime* (P. Carlen and D. Cook eds. 1989); see also J. Braithwaite and P. Pettit, *Not Just Deserts* (1990), at 124–25.
7. See, e.g., American Friends Service Committee, *Struggle for Justice* (1971).
8. See note 15, *infra.*
9. T. Mathiesen, *Prison on Trial* (1989).
10. A. von Hirsch, *supra* note 3; A. von Hirsch, *Past or Future Crimes* (1985).
11. Maher, "Criminalizing Pregnancy," 17 *Social Justice* 111 (1990); Maher, "Punishment and Welfare: Crack Cocaine and the Regulation of Mothering," 3 *Women & Criminal Justice* (1991).
12. Panel on Research on Rehabilitative Effects, "Report," in *The Rehabilitation of Criminal Offenders* (L. Sechrest, S. White, and E. Brown eds. 1979).
13. See, e.g., Fagan, "Social and Legal Policy Dimensions of Violent Juvenile Crime," 17 *Crim. Justice & Behavior* 93 (1990).
14. Gendreau and Ross, "The Revivification of Rehabilitation: Evidence from the 1980s," 4 *Justice Quar.* 349 (1988).
15. Compare Lab and Whitehead, "An Analysis of Juvenile Treatment," 34 *Crime & Delinq.* 60 (1988), and Lab and Whitehead, "From 'Nothing Works' to 'The Appropriate Works,'" 28 *Criminology* 405 (1990), with Andrews, Zinger, et al., "Does Correctional Treatment Work?" 28 *Criminology* 369 (1990), and Andrews, Zinger, et al., "A Human Science Approach or More Pessimism," 28 *Criminology* 419 (1990).
16. See Fagan, *supra* note 13.
17. Palmer, "Treatment and the Role of Classification," 30 *Crime & Delinq.* 245 (1984); Sechrest, "Classification for Treatment," in *Prediction and Classification* (D. Gottfredson and M. Tonry eds. 1987); see also, Palmer, *supra* note 4.
18. Palmer, *supra* note 4, at 339.
19. See Fagan, *supra* note 13.
20. Gendreau and Ross, *supra* note 14, at 345.

21. See, e.g., F. Cullen and K. Gilbert, *supra* note 5, ch. 7.

22. For discussion of social services for offenders, see A. von Hirsch and K. Hanrahan, *The Question of Parole* (1979), ch. 8.

23. Anglin and Hser, "The Treatment of Drug Offenders," in *Drugs and Crime* (J. Wilson and M. Tonry eds. 1990).

24. F. Cullen and K. Gilbert, *supra* note 5, ch. 7.

25. von Hirsch, Wasik, and Greene, "Punishments in the Community and the Principles of Desert," 20 *Rutgers L. J.* 595, 615–16 (1989).

26. See *supra* note 23 and accompanying text.

27. See, e.g., Pearson, "Women Defendants in Magistrates' Courts," 3 *British J. L. & Society* 265 (1976); Phillips and De Fleur, "Gender Ascription and the Stereotyping of Deviants," 20 *Criminology* 431 (1982); see also C. Smart, *Women, Crime, and Criminology* (1976); *Gender, Crime, and Justice* (P. Carlen and A. Worrall eds. 1987).

28. For an exploration of the problem of humiliating and intrusive penalties, see von Hirsch, "The Ethics of Community-Based Sanctions," 36 *Crime & Delinq.* 162, 165–73 (1990).

29. See, e.g., F. Cullen and K. Gilbert, *supra* note 5; B. Hudson, *supra* note 6.

30. von Hirsch, "The Politics of 'Just Deserts,'" 32 *Canadian J. Criminology* 397, 400–402 (1990).

31. *Id.;* A. von Hirsch, K. Knapp, and M. Tonry, *The Sentencing Commission and Its Guidelines* (1987), chs. 2, 5, 8.

32. See, e.g., B. Hudson, *supra* note 6, ch. 4.

33. M. Foucault, *Discipline and Punish* (1977).

34. A. von Hirsch, *Past or Future Crimes* (1985), chs. 3–5.

35. Some personal or social variables—for example, facts relating to diminished capacity—do have a bearing on blameworthiness. However, treatment programs rely on other variables that concern the offender's amenability to the program and that seldom have such a bearing.

36. See von Hirsch, Wasik, and Greene, *supra* note 25, at 604.

37. See *supra* notes 4 and 5.

38. For a sketch of such a model, see N. Morris, *Madness and the Criminal Law* (1982), ch. 5. For a critique, see A. von Hirsch, *supra* note 34, chs. 4, 12.

39. A. von Hirsch, *supra* note 34, ch. 12.

40. An attempt to develop an alternative penal theory that dispenses with desert principles is set forth in J. Braithwaite and P. Pettit, *supra* note 6. That theory, however, relies primarily on deterrence and incapacitation rather than treatment. In our view, the theory has manifold difficulties, discussed in von Hirsch and Ashworth, "Not Not Just Deserts: A Critique of Braithwaite and Pettit," 12 *Oxford J. Legal Studies* 83 (1992).

41. Braithwaite and Pettit, *supra* note 6, try to detach censure from proportionality requirements, but their arguments are unconvincing in our judgment, for reasons set forth in von Hirsch and Ashworth, *supra* note 40.

42. N. Christie, *Limits to Pain* (1981).

43. See, e.g., Olson, "Statutory Rape," 63 *Tex. L. Rev.* 387 (1984); Lahey, "Until Women Have Told All They Have to Tell," 23 *Osgoode Hall L. Rev.* 519

(1985); Heidensohn, "Models of Justice: Portia or Persephone?" 14 *Int'l J. Sociology of L.* 287 (1986); Howe, "Social Injury Revisited: Towards a Feminist Theory of Social Justice," 15 *Int'l J. Sociology of L.* 423 (1987); West, "Jurisprudence and Gender," 55 *U. Chicago L. Rev.* 1 (1988); C. Smart, *Feminism and the Power of Law* (1989); Daly, "Criminal Justice Ideologies and Practices in Different Voices: Some Feminist Questions About Justice," 17 *Int'l J. Sociology of L.* 1 (1989); Smart, "Law's Truth/Women's Experience," in *Dissenting Opinions: Feminist Explorations in Law and Society* (R. Graycar ed. 1990).

44. von Hirsch, "Review of N. Christie," 28 *Crime & Delinq.* 315 (1982). For arguments in favor of a censuring penal response, see von Hirsch, "Proportionality in the Philosophy of Punishment," 1 *Crim. L. Forum* 259, 270–79 (1990).

45. For a limited suggested role of treatment considerations under a desert model, see von Hirsch, Wasik, and Greene, *supra* note 25, 615–16. For a somewhat expanded role under a "mixed" model, see N. Morris and M. Tonry, *Between Prison and Probation* (1990), ch. 7. For a comparison of these models, see von Hirsch, "Scaling Intermediate Punishments," in *Smart Sentencing: Expanding Options for Intermediate Sanctions* (J. Byrne, A. Lurigio, and J. Petersilia eds. 1991).

46. See Rothman, "Decarcerating Prisoners and Patients," 1 *Civil Liberties Rev.* 8 (1973).

Suggestions for Further Reading

1. *The Ideological Background of the Rehabilitative Sentence*
Wootton, B., *Crime and the Criminal Law* (2d ed., 1978); Grupp, S. E. (ed.), *The Positive School of Criminology: Three Lectures by Enrico Ferri* (1968); Menninger, K., *The Crime of Punishment* (1968); Rothman, D. J., *The Discovery of the Asylum: Social Order and Disorder in the New Republic* (1971); Rothman, D. J., *Conscience and Convenience: The Asylum and Its Alternatives in Progressive America* (1980); Garland, D., *Punishment and Welfare* (1985).

2. *Critiques of the Broad Discretion Involved in Rehabilitation-based Sentencing*
American Friends Service Committee, *Struggle for Justice* (1971); Frankel, M. E., *Criminal Sentences: Law Without Order* (1972); Gaylin, W., *Partial Justice* (1974); von Hirsch, *Doing Justice: The Choice of Punishments* (1976), ch. 2.

3. *Discussions of the Effectiveness of Rehabilitative Programs*
Bailey, W. G., "An Evaluation of 100 Studies of Correctional Outcomes," 57 *Journal of Criminal Law, Criminology and Police Science* 153 (1966); Hood, R., *Research on the Effectiveness of Punishment and Treatment* (1967); Hood, R., and Sparks, R., *Key Issues in Criminology* (1970); esp. chs. 6–8; Lerman, P., *Community Treatment and Social Control* (1971); Robison, J., and Smith, G., "The Effectiveness of Correctional Programs," 17 *Crime and Delinquency* 67 (1971); Martinson, R., "What Works?—Questions and Answers About Prison Reform," [Spring 1974] *Public Interest* 22; Lipton, D., Martinson, R., and Wilks, J., *The Effectiveness of Correctional Treatment: A Survey of Treatment Evaluation Studies* (1975); Palmer, T., "Martinson Revisited," 12 *Journal of Research in Crime and Delinquency* 133 (1975); Brody, S. R., *The Effectiveness of Sentencing* (1975); Greenberg, D. F., "The Correctional Effects of Corrections," in Greenberg, D. F. (ed.), *Corrections and Punishment* (1977); Martinson, R. "New Findings, New Views: A Note of Caution on Sentencing Reform," 7 *Hofstra Law Review* 243 (1979); Panel on Research on Rehabilitative Techniques, "Report," in Sechrest, L., et al. (eds.), *The Rehabilitation of Criminal Offenders: Problems and Proposals* (1979); Walker, N., Farrington, D., and Tucker, G., "Reconviction Rates of Adult Males after Different Sentences," 21 *British Journal of Criminology* 357 (1981); Palmer, T., "Treatment and the Role of Classification: A Review of the Basics," 30 *Crime and Delinquency* 245 (1984); Greenwood, P., and Zimring, F., *One More Chance: The Pursuit of Promising Intervention Strategies for Chronic Juvenile Offenders* (1985); Gendreau, P., and Ross, R., "Revivification of Rehabilitation: Evidence from the 1980s," 4 *Justice Quarterly* 349 (1988); Lab, S., and Whitehead, J., "An Analysis of Juvenile Correctional Treatment," 34 *Crime and Delinquency* 60 (1988); Whitehead, S., and Lab, S., "A Meta-Analysis of Juvenile Correctional Punishment," 26 *Journal of Research in Crime and Delinquency* 276 (1989);

Andrews, D. A., et al., "Does Correctional Treatment Work?" 28 *Criminology* 369 (1990); Lab, S., and Whitehead, J., "From 'Nothing Works' to 'The Appropriate Works,'" 28 *Criminology* 405 (1990); Fagan, J., "Social and Legal Policy Dimensions of Violent Juvenile Crime," 17 *Criminal Justice and Behavior* 93 (1990); Anglin, M. D., and Hser, Y., "Treatment of Drug Abuse," in Wilson, J. Q., and Tonry, M. (eds.), *Drugs and Crime* (1990); Palmer, T., "The Effectiveness of Intervention: Recent Trends and Current Issues," 37 *Crime and Delinquency* 330 (1991).

4. Discussions of the Ethics of Treatment-based Sentencing

Lewis, C. S., "The Humanitarian Theory of Punishment," 6 *Res Judicatae* 224 (1953); Morris, N., and Buckle, D., "The Humanitarian Theory of Punishment: A Reply to C. S. Lewis," 6 *Res Judicatae* 231 (1953); Lewis, C. S., "On Punishment: A Reply," 6 *Res Judicatae* 519 (1954); Smart, J.J.C., "Comment: The Humanitarian Theory of Punishment," 6 *Res Judicatae* 368 (1954); Kaufman, A. S., "The Reform Theory of Punishment," 71 *Ethics* 49 (1960); von Hirsch, *Doing Justice, supra,* ch. 15; Murphy, J. G., *Retribution, Justice, and Therapy* (1979), part 3; Bottoms, A. E., and McWilliams, W., "A Non-Treatment Paradigm for Probation Practice," 9 *British Journal of Social Work* 159 (1979).

5. Discussions of the Politics of Penal Rehabilitationism

Allen, F. A., *The Borderland of Criminal Justice* (1964); Rothman, D. J., "Decarcerating Prisoners and Patients," 1 *Civil Liberties Review* 8 (1973); Orland, L., "From Vengeance to Vengeance: Sentencing Reform and the Demise of Rehabilitation," 7 *Hofstra Law Review* 29 (1978); Scull, A., *Decarceration* (2d ed., 1984); Cohen, S., *Visions of Social Control* (1985); Garland, D., *Punishment and Welfare, supra;* Hudson, B., *Justice Through Punishment: A Critique of the "Justice Model" of Corrections* (1987), 170–76.

Chapter Two

DETERRENCE

Deterrence, as an aim of sentencing, is one of a cluster of forward-looking aims which may be termed preventive or consequentialist. Also within this cluster are rehabilitation and incapacitation. What they share is the idea that punishment is warranted by reference to its consequences. These aims are usually advanced within a utilitarian framework, the justification for punishment and the measure of punishment being found in a calculation of its utility compared with the attendant disutilities. Utilitarian theory has a range of complex and sophisticated principles, which are best exemplified still in Jeremy Bentham's ingenious and detailed writings on punishment, excerpts from which appear in Extract 2.1 below. On a broader consequentialist canvas, deterrence and the other forward-looking aims may be subsumed beneath the overall aim of the reduction or prevention of crime. This is, in turn, part of a set of social and political principles for government. Crime reduction or prevention is best regarded as an aim of the criminal justice system as a whole, including sentencing and extending to other aspects such as pretrial detention, policing, community projects to foster noncriminal behavior among teenagers, and so on. If we confine ourselves to sentencing, we find that the prevention of crime, as an aim, may be pursued by a number of different methods—rehabilitation, which seeks to alter offenders' attitudes so that they desist from crime (see Chapter 1 above); incapacitation, which seeks to restrain the offender from reoffending for a given period (see Chapter 3 below); and possibly "vindication," which aims for punishments sufficient to ensure that citizens aggrieved by offenses accept the state's response and do not seek to "take the law into their own hands."[1]

That leaves individual deterrence and general deterrence, which are the subject of the readings in this chapter. Individual deterrence seeks to further the aim of crime prevention by setting the sentence so that it is sufficient to deter the particular convicted offender from reoffending. General deterrence seeks to further the aim of crime prevention by setting it so as to induce other citizens who might be tempted to commit crime to desist out of fear of the penalty. Deterrent theories reached the height of their influence in the first half of the nineteenth century, inspired by Bentham's many writings on penal policy. Doubts about those theories' practicality and, in particular, misgivings about the resulting severity of punishments grew in the second half of the century, although in England there were some who continued to advocate a strong policy of individual deterrence toward persistent offenders. The growing interest in rehabilitation became evident toward the end of the nineteenth century and in the early twentieth century with the beginnings of probation, the American reformatory schools, and the English borstal.[2] However, deterrent assumptions continued to exert an influence on sentencing, and in the 1960s the Norwegian penologist Johannes Andenaes rekindled the theoretical debate on general deterrence.[3] Despite several reports skeptical of efforts to identify and assess the magnitude of deterrent effects of sentences,[4] deterrence philosophies retain some influence on both sides of the Atlantic in penal practice (e.g., the death penalty in some American states, and sentencing ranges for some crimes in England) and in penal theory (e.g., the writings of James Q. Wilson[5] and of Nigel Walker[6]).

A sentencing system based on individual deterrence would need to ensure that courts had detailed information on the character, circumstances, and prior record of the particular offender, and would then require courts to calculate what sentence would be necessary to deter the particular offender. Punishments would probably be increased substantially for persistent offenders,[7] even despite adherence to the limiting principle of frugality or parsimony (that the court should always impose the least punitive measure available, since punishment is an evil in itself). And such a system would give no appearance of consistency, since each sentence would be specially calculated so as to influence the individual offender involved.

In the utilitarian philosophy of Bentham, the individual deterrent approach is placed second in order of priority to general deterrence, and relatively little is heard of individual deterrence as a specific aim of sentencing in the modern debate. As appears from Extract 2.1(a), Bentham regards punishment as an evil because it involves the infliction of "pain." It can therefore be justified only if there are beneficial consequences to outweigh it, and these are to be found in the deterrence of persons from committing offenses. It is assumed that citizens are rational persons and that a well-constructed sentencing system will in general present them with a sufficient disincentive to crime. A modern version of this, forming part of the economic theory of law, will be found in Extract 2.2 from the writings of Richard Posner. Readers should consider whether Posner carries deterrence theory to unacceptable extremes, for example, in his discussion about why seldom-applied and drastic penalties might be preferable to more moderate ones.

General deterrent punishments may exert their influence over differing time periods: long-term deterrence may come about through the perpetuation of fear of punishment for certain types of conduct, although this may be difficult to disentangle from the effects of moral education and social reinforcement through the law, as emphasized in certain strands of Scandinavian legal philosophy;[8] medium-term deterrence may be associated with legislative attempts to influence social behavior by increasing certain maximum penalties or introducing some mandatory minimum penalties; and then there are "exemplary sentences" occasionally imposed in discretionary sentencing systems, visiting one or more offenders with a disproportionately high sentence in order to deter potential imitators.

What are the objections to general deterrence as a basis for penal policy? Its chief defect of principle is that since its distinctive aim and method is to create fear of the penalty in other persons, it may sometimes require the punishment of an innocent person or the excessive punishment of an offender in order to achieve this greater social effect. The calculation may be either (1) "punish someone now in order to prevent a number of probable future crimes," the sacrifice of an innocent person being regarded as justified by reference to the number of probable future victims who are thereby spared; or (2) "punish this offender with exceptional severity in order to prevent a number of probable future crimes," the excessive punishment being likewise regarded as justified by reference to the number of probable future victims who may be spared. In both instances the avoidance of a greater future harm (to victims of probable future offenses) is taken to justify the infliction of present harm which the "punishment" represents.

Deterrence theorists may attempt to avoid the reproach that they accept the punishment of the innocent, as by arguing that such practices would not be permitted because they are not "punishment." This, however, is unconvincing, because utilitarian theories do not include a principle for the distribution of punishment which restricts it to those properly convicted of an offense (see the argument of Alan Goldman in Extract 2.5 below). The objection is often expressed by recalling Kant's injunction that a person should be treated as an end in himself, and never only as a means, and it is important to notice the two elements of this formulation. One is that to regard citizens merely as numbers to be aggregated in an overall social calculation is to show no respect for the moral worth and the autonomy of each individual. This, then, is the liberal objection based on respect for individual autonomy and the separateness of persons.[9] The other element is that citizens should not be used *merely* as a means to an end—the limitation "merely" draws attention to the fact that punishment is, to some extent, a means to a social end. It is justified insofar as modern societies seem incapable of responding adequately to harmful behavior without resort to punishment. The point here is that the punishment of any given individual cannot be justified solely by reference to wider social benefits. A theory of punishment should include both a link with the general social justification for the institution of punishment[10] and principles of distribution which restrict its imposition to properly convicted offenders and which place limits on the amount of punishment.[11]

What of the justification for "exemplary sentences," imposing an unusually high sentence on an individual offender for a given type of offense, in the hope of deterring potential imitators? Bentham would consider the justification for such a sentence by reference to its wider social effects—for example, on public respect for the law—but it is by no means certain that he would rule out such sentences, especially in a situation where there is apparent public concern about a particular kind of criminal behavior. The objection to exemplary sentences is that the quantum of a convicted offender's punishment is being determined entirely by the expected future behavior of other persons, not by his own past behavior. This objection reaches into the very foundations of deterrence theory, for it raises the question whether punishments should be in some way proportional to offenses. It will be seen from Bentham's rules 2 and 3, in Extract 2.1(b) below, that the gravity of the type of offense is indeed relevant to the amount of punishment which may be justified to restrain it. This, however, does not sustain the claim that utilitarians can treat proportionality as a limiting principle on the amount of punishment. For one thing, Bentham is referring to proportionality between the punishment and probable future offenses rather than the particular crime for which this offender is now being sentenced. And, for another thing, each of Bentham's "rules" is merely one of several factors relevant to the overall utilitarian calculation: the effect of the proportionality principle may be smothered by the influence of one or more of the other rules, and not restored by the principle of frugality. Thus, if the general deterrence theorist has reason to anticipate an upsurge in a particular type of offense, this would justify the imposition of an unusually high sentence on a particular offender, as an "example" to potential offenders and in order to deter them.

Leaving aside the problems raised by "punishing" the innocent and by "exemplary" sentences, how effective might we expect a general deterrent strategy to be in achieving its goals? The logic of deterrence has an intuitive appeal, but close study of the requirements of general deterrence and of the available empirical evidence suggests that the simple logic cannot be translated easily into social situations. Three interconnected propositions may be used as a basis for discussion here. First, criminologists have found it difficult to gauge, even approximately, the extent of any general deterrent effects of penalties. Second, the effectiveness of general deterrent strategies may vary situationally. Third, it is wrong to assume that the probable penalty for an offense is always or often the most powerful influence on people's behavior. Let us examine these propositions.

There are various explanations for the difficulties which criminologists have experienced in conducting and interpreting general deterrence research. One is that it is hard to discover how often the threat of legal punishment (rather than any other motivation) turns people away from offending, since its successful operation means that those concerned are not readily discoverable in most instances. Another is that it is hard to find out about *marginal deterrence,* that is, how much extra deterrence is gained or lost by varying the severity of sanctions. This is an issue of crucial importance if sentence levels are to be set on deterrence grounds. Moreover, in respect of both these points, a statistical association which appears to establish cause and effect, such as the decrease of an offense rate following an increase in the penalty, may have an entirely different explanation: the practical example quoted by the British Royal Commission on Capital Punishment (see Extract 2.3 below) illustrates this point. Another difficulty is that criminological research has not always been designed to separate deterrent effects from the results of other influences such as situational factors. As Deryck Beyleveld argues in Extract 2.4, the first step is to formulate a proper definition of general deterrence. Surveys of the available research[12] have shown that there are relatively few studies which have genuinely identified the existence and extent of general deterrent effects flowing from the legal penalty, and that it would be unsafe to generalize from these specific studies to broad policy prescriptions. Yet this does not mean that general deterrent effects never occur; the difficulty has been in establishing in what situations and to what extent they do occur. Beyleveld makes the point that only the most drastic sanctions are likely to have deterrent effects which are easily recognizable. In less extreme situations the main contribution of criminological research has been to point out the pitfalls of simple-looking explanations and expectations of human behavior.

The second proposition is that general deterrence may only be effective in certain situations. This is not simply a repetition of the point that few studies have located a general deterrent effect. Rather, it is an assertion that the conditions must be favorable if general deterrence is to operate.

This refers, moreover, less to the actual or objective conditions in the world than to the conditions as potential offenders believe them to be: deterrence must work through the mind, and so the reasoning should always be in terms of what potential offenders believe. Thus, the risk of detection for the crime must not be thought so low as to make the threat of the penalty seem too remote and thus readily discounted. The penalty which is meant to constitute the deterrent must be publicized adequately, so that it catches the attention of potential offenders. That penalty must also be perceived as a deterrent—which may rarely be a problem, but there are some forms of sentence (such as the suspended sentence) which may be intended as a deterrent but regarded by some as a "soft option." Another point is that those who may commit the particular type of offense must be likely to consider the risks rationally: one study of English burglars found that they rarely thought they would be caught for the present offense, that they were not worried about the consequences of being caught (either because the expected sentence was accepted as an "occupational hazard" or because they refused to think about the consequences at all), and that the rewards of the burglary were rarely known in advance.[13] These findings do not exclude the possibility that others were deterred, although they do shed some light on the thought processes of those for whom deterrence appears not to have worked and therefore suggest limits to its efficacy.

One might expect that for impulsive crimes the likelihood of rational calculation is even lower, while for some organized fraud or drugs offenses the likelihood might be high. One study of weapon choice for armed robbery claims to have identified the operation of marginal deterrence, in that higher penalties turn many robbers away from the carrying of firearms.[14] Thus, general deterrence might be expected to work selectively, and only where the conditions (as perceived by potential offenders) favor it. Some of the striking apparent failures of general deterrence, such as the continued rise in "muggings" for several weeks after the widespread reporting of a twenty-year custodial sentence on a "mugger" in Birmingham, England, in 1973,[15] can only be explained by the absence of one or more of the necessary conditions.

The third proposition amounts to another attack upon, or qualification of, reasoning from "common experience" or "common sense." One of the most frequent fallacies in popular discussions of deterrence is to assume that the nature and magnitude of the probable penalty are the only or necessarily the most powerful influence on a person's behavior. There is evidence that other indirect consequences of conviction, particularly what the offender's family would think and the probability of losing one's job, exert a more powerful effect.[16] This shows the fragility of assuming that the criminal justice system and its penalty scale will be the most powerful motivating force in people's behavior (cf. Posner in Extract 2.2).

As a practical sentencing strategy, general deterrence requires the imposition (or at least the threatened or reputed imposition) of as much punishment as is necessary to reduce the frequency of offenses of a given type, preferring less painful means of crime reduction where they are available, and in any event calling for no greater punishment than the offense is "worth" in terms of its degree of harmfulness. One problem of adopting this approach in practice is that Bentham's intricate "rules of proportion" for punishment would often conflict in their application to types of crime: how should one decide on sentence levels for a relatively minor type of offense which is difficult to deter and for a relatively serious type of offense for which the prospects of deterrence seem good? Bentham's rules 2 and 5—see Extract 2.1(b)—appear to restrict the appropriate punishment for minor offenses, and yet in explaining rule 1 Bentham warns that if the punishment is insufficient to outweigh the motivation to commit the offense, "the whole lot of punishment will be thrown away." Is proportionality or maximum deterrence to be the dominant consideration in such cases of conflict?

A second problem is that we lack sufficient empirical information on which to base the calculations of penalties. General deterrence theory refers to the beliefs of potential offenders. We know too little about these, and what we do know casts some doubt on "common sense" assumptions about the effect of criminal sentences on human behavior. Moreover, Bentham's version of the theory urges restraint in the use and amount of punishment at all times, as well as maintaining that to inflict too small a punishment is to cause misery in waste: to satisfy both these injunctions would be a formidable task even if one did have perfect information.

On one point, however, there is strong empirical evidence of general deterrence. This is that the absence of a punishment structure (police, courts, and sentences) substantially reduces observance of the law. The police strikes in Melbourne, Australia, in 1918, and in Liverpool, England, in 1919, show that overall offense rates increase significantly in the absence of such a structure in practice; the imprisonment of the Danish police force in 1944 had similar consequences. Thus, one fundamental justification for the institution of state punishment is that it exerts this overall restraining effect: it deters many offenses which would be committed if there were no such institution. Thus, an advocate of proportionate sanctions—who seeks fairer principles for the distribution of punishments and for the calculation of punishments than general deterrence can offer—may still accept general deterrence as an integral part of the justification for why the institution of legal punishment should exist.[17]

A.A.

Notes

1. On the little-discussed concept of "vindicative satisfaction," see Jeremy Bentham, *Introduction to the Principles of Morals and Legislation* (1789), chapter 13, para. 1, and Sir Rupert Cross, *The English Sentencing System,* 3d ed. (London: Butterworth, 1981), 128–30 and 139–40. See also the discussion of "Montero's aim" by Nigel Walker, *Punishment, Danger, and Stigma* (Oxford: Blackwell, 1980), chapter 1.

2. For detailed analysis of trends in penal practice and theory in nineteenth-century England, see Sir Leon Radzinowicz and Roger Hood, *History of English Criminal Law: volume 5, The Emergence of Penal Policy* (London: Stevens, 1985).

3. See, e.g., "The General Preventive Effects of Punishment," 114 *U. Pa. L. R.* 649 (1966), and "The Morality of Deterrence," 37 *U. Chi. L. R.* 649 (1970).

4. See this chapter's Suggestions for Further Reading, section 2.

5. E.g., *Thinking about Crime* (1st ed., 1975; 2d ed., 1983).

6. E.g., *Punishment, Danger, and Stigma* (1980), chapter 4, and *Sentencing: Theory, Law, and Practice* (London: Butterworth, 1985), chapter 7.

7. For a nineteenth-century English approach of this kind, see the discussion of Barwick Baker's ideas by Radzinowicz and Hood, op. cit., ch. 23.

8. E.g., Karl Olivecrona, *Law as Fact* (1939).

9. See H. Morris, "Persons and Punishment," 52 *The Monist* 475 (1968).

10. For elaboration of this point, see the final paragraph of this introduction and also the introduction to Chapter 4.

11. See H.L.A. Hart, *Punishment and Responsibility* (Oxford: Oxford University Press, 1968), chapter 1.

12. See this chapter's Suggestions for Further Reading, section 2.

13. T. Bennett and R. Wright, *Burglars on Burglary* (1984), chapters 5 and 6.

14. Richard Harding, "Rational-Choice Gun Use in Armed Robbery: The Likely Deterrent Effect on Gun Use of Mandatory Additional Imprisonment," 1 *Criminal Law Forum* 427 (1990).

15. R. Baxter and C. Nuttall, "Severe Sentences: No Deterrent to Crime?" *New Society* 11–13 (1975).

16. For England, see H. D. Willcock and J. Stokes, *Deterrents and Incentives to Crime among Boys and Young Men Aged 15–21 Years* (London: H.M.S.O., 1968); for the U.S.A., cf. H. G. Grasmick and D. Green, "Legal Punishment, Social

Disapproval and Internalisation as Inhibitors of Illegal Behaviour," 71 *J. Crim. L. and Criminol.* 325 (1980).

17. See further Andrew von Hirsch, "Proportionality in the Philosophy of Punishment," 1 *Criminal Law Forum* 259 (1990), especially 276–78 and the introduction to Chapter 4 below.

2.1
Punishment and Deterrence

Jeremy Bentham

2.1(a) The Aims of Punishment

When any act has been committed which is followed, or threatens to be followed, by such effects as a provident legislator would be anxious to prevent, two wishes naturally and immediately suggest themselves to his mind: first, to obviate the danger of the like mischief in future: secondly, to compensate the mischief that has already been done.

The mischief likely to ensue from acts of the like kind may arise from either of two sources,—either the conduct of the party himself who has been the author of the mischief already done, or the conduct of such other persons as may have adequate motives and sufficient opportunities to do the like.

Hence the prevention of offenses divides itself into two branches: *Particular prevention,* which applies to the delinquent himself; and *general prevention,* which is applicable to all the members of the community without exception.

Pain and pleasure are the great springs of human action. When a man perceives or supposes pain to be the consequence of an act, he is acted upon in such a manner as tends, with a certain force, to withdraw him, as it were, from the commission of that act. If the apparent magnitude of that pain be greater than the apparent magnitude of the pleasure or good he expects to be the consequence of the act, he will be absolutely prevented from performing it. The mischief which would have ensued from the act, if performed, will also by that means be prevented.

From "The Principles of Penal Law," in *The Works of Jeremy Bentham* (J. Bowring ed. 1838–43), 396.

With respect to a given individual, the recurrence of an offense may be provided against in three ways:—

1. By taking from him the physical power of offending.
2. By taking away the desire of offending.
3. By making him afraid of offending.

In the first case, the individual can no more commit the offense; in the second, he no longer desires to commit it; in the third, he may still wish to commit it, but he no longer dares to do it. In the first case, there is a physical incapacity; in the second, a moral reformation; in the third, there is intimidation or terror of the law.

General prevention is effected by the denunciation of punishment, and by its application, which, according to the common expression, *serves for an example.* The punishment suffered by the offender presents to every one an example of what he himself will have to suffer, if he is guilty of the same offense.

General prevention ought to be the chief end of punishment, as it is its real justification. If we could consider an offense which has been committed as an isolated fact, the like of which would never recur, punishment would be useless. It would be only adding one evil to another. But when we consider that an unpunished crime leaves the path of crime open, not only to the same delinquent, but also to all those who may have the same motives and opportunities for entering upon it, we perceive that the punishment inflicted on the individual becomes a source of security to all. That punishment which, considered in itself, appeared base and repugnant to all generous sentiments, is elevated to the first rank of benefits, when it is regarded not as an act of wrath or of vengeance against a guilty or unfortunate individual who has given way to mischievous inclinations, but as an indispensable sacrifice to the common safety.

2.1(b) The Quantum of Punishment

Rule 1. The first object, it has been seen, is to prevent, in as far as it is worth while, all sorts of offenses; therefore,

From *An Introduction to the Principles of Morals and Legislation* (1789), ch. 14.

The value of the punishment must not be less in any case than what is sufficient to outweigh that of the profit of the offense.

If it be, the offense (unless some other considerations, independent of the punishment, should intervene and operate efficaciously in the character of tutelary motives) will be sure to be committed notwithstanding: the whole lot of punishment will be thrown away: it will be altogether *inefficacious.*

The above rule has been often objected to, on account of its seeming harshness: but this can only have happened for want of its being properly understood. The strength of the temptation, *cæteris paribus,* is as the profit of the offense: the quantum of the punishment must rise with the profit of the offense: *cæteris paribus,* it must therefore rise with the strength of the temptation. This there is no disputing. True it is, that the stronger the temptation, the less conclusive is the indication which the act of delinquency affords of the depravity of the offender's disposition. So far then as the absence of any aggravation, arising from extraordinary depravity of disposition, may operate, or at the utmost, so far as the presence of a ground of extenuation, resulting from the innocence or beneficence of the offender's disposition, can operate, the strength of the temptation may operate in abatement of the demand for punishment. But it can never operate so far as to indicate the propriety of making the punishment ineffectual, which it is sure to be when brought below the level of the apparent profit of the offense.

The partial benevolence which should prevail for the reduction of it below this level, would counteract as well those purposes which such a motive would actually have in view, as those more extensive purposes which benevolence ought to have in view: it would be cruelty not only to the public, but to the very persons in whose behalf it pleads: in its effects, I mean, however opposite in its intention. Cruelty to the public, that is cruelty to the innocent, by suffering them, for want of an adequate protection, to lie exposed to the mischief of the offense: cruelty even to the offender himself, by punishing him to no purpose, and without the chance of compassing that beneficial end, by which alone the introduction of the evil of punishment is to be justified.

Rule 2. But whether a given offense shall be prevented in a given degree by a given quantity of punishment, is never any thing better than a chance; for the purchasing of which, whatever punishment is employed, is so much expended in advance. However, for the sake of giving it the better chance of outweighing the profit of the offense,

The greater the mischief of the offense, the greater is the expense, which it may be worth while to be at, in the way of punishment.

Rule 3. The next object is, to induce a man to choose always the least mischievous of two offenses; therefore

Where two offenses come in competition, the punishment for the greater offense must be sufficient to induce a man to prefer the less.

Rule 4. When a man has resolved upon a particular offense, the next object is, to induce him to do no more mischief than what is necessary for his purpose: therefore

The punishment should be adjusted in such manner to each particular offense, that for every part of the mischief there may be a motive to restrain the offender from giving birth to it.

Rule 5. The last object is, whatever mischief is guarded against, to guard against it at as cheap a rate as possible: therefore

The punishment ought in no case to be more than what is necessary to bring it into conformity with the rules here given.

Rule 6. It is further to be observed, that owing to the different manners and degrees in which persons under different circumstances are affected by the same exciting cause, a punishment which is the same in name will not always either really produce, or even so much as appear to others to produce, in two different persons the same degree of pain: therefore

That the quantity actually inflicted on each individual offender may correspond to the quantity intended for similar offenders in general, the several circumstances influencing sensibility ought always to be taken into account.

Of the above rules of proportion, the four first, we may perceive, serve to mark out the limits on the side of diminution; the limits *below* which a punishment ought not to be *diminished:* the fifth, the limits on the side of increase; the limits *above* which it ought not to be *increased.* The five first are calculated to serve as guides to the legislator: the sixth is calculated, in some measure, indeed, for the same purpose; but principally for guiding the judge in his endeavors to conform, on both sides, to the intentions of the legislator.

2.1(c) Cases Where Punishment is Unjustified

All punishment is mischief: all punishment in itself is evil. Upon the principle of utility, if it ought at all to be admitted, it ought only to be admitted in as far as it promises to exclude some greater evil.

It is plain, therefore, that in the following cases punishment ought not to be inflicted.

1. Where it is *groundless:* where there is no mischief for it to prevent: the act not being mischievous upon the whole.

2. Where it must be *inefficacious:* where it cannot act so as to prevent the mischief.

3. Where it is *unprofitable,* or too *expensive:* where the mischief it would produce would be greater than what it prevented.

4. Where it is *needless:* where the mischief may be prevented, or cease of itself, without it: that is, at a cheaper rate.

From *An Introduction to the Principles of Morals and Legislation* (1789), ch. 13.

2.2
Optimal Sanctions: Any Upper Limits?

Richard Posner

[*Posner's theory is based on the assumption that criminals in general behave as "rational calculators" or, to be more precise, that a sentencing strategy which is based on this assumption will have the greatest preventive power. On this view, which is developed further in the sentencing context and more generally in Posner's* Economic Analysis of Law *(2d ed., 1977, ch. 7, and passim), crimes are committed because the expected benefits outweigh the expected costs; or, at least, significantly fewer crimes would be committed if the expected costs were known to exceed the expected benefits. In these calculations, benefits include any economic gain from the offense and other noneconomic satisfactions (e.g., in crimes of passion or revenge); and costs include not only the expected punishment but also the opportunity costs of the criminal's time, expenses necessary to commit the crime, etc. These last points are important in Posner's theory because they suggest other possibilities of controlling crime apart from increasing punishments on convicted offenders (e.g., increasing the cost or scarcity of guns, or redistributing wealth). The extract below, however, concentrates on the potential of the criminal sanction for controlling crime.*]

We have seen that the main thing the criminal law punishes is the pure coercive transfer, or, as it might better be described in a case of tax evasion or price-fixing, the pure involuntary transfer, of wealth or utility. In discussing what criminal penalties are optimal to deter such transfers, I shall

---

From Richard Posner, "An Economic Theory of Criminal Law," 85 *Columbia Law Review* 1193 (1985).

assume that most potential criminals are sufficiently rational to be deterrable—an assumption that has the support of an extensive literature.

We saw earlier that the sanction for a pure coercive transfer should be designed so that the criminal is made worse off by his act, but now a series of qualifications must be introduced. First, some criminal acts actually are wealth-maximizing. Suppose I lose my way in the woods and, as an alternative to starving, enter an unoccupied cabin and "steal" some food. Should the punishment be death, on the theory that the crime saved my life, and therefore no lesser penalty would deter? Of course not. The problem is that while the law of theft generally punishes takings in settings of low transaction costs, in this example the costs of transacting with the absent owner of the cabin are prohibitive. One approach is to define theft so as to exclude such examples; the criminal law has a defense of necessity that probably would succeed in this example. But defenses make the law more complicated, and an alternative that sometimes will be superior is to employ a somewhat overinclusive definition of the crime but set the expected punishment cost at a level that will not deter the occasional crime that is value-maximizing.

There is a related but more important reason for putting a ceiling on criminal punishments such that not all crimes are deterred. If there is a risk either of accidental violation of the criminal law or of legal error, an expected penalty will induce innocent people to forgo socially desirable activities at the borderline of criminal activity. The effect is magnified if people are risk averse and penalties are severe. If for example, the penalty for carelessly injuring someone in an automobile accident were death, people would drive too slowly, or not at all, to avoid an accidental violation or an erroneous conviction.

1. *"Afflictive" Punishment.* The foregoing analysis shows that there is a place in the criminal justice system, and a big one, for imprisonment; and perhaps for other nonmonetary criminal sanctions as well. Since the cost of murder to the victim approaches infinity, even very heavy fines will not provide sufficient deterrence of murder, and even life imprisonment may not impose costs on the murderer equal to those of the victim. It might seem, however, that the important thing is not that the punishment for murder equal the cost to the victim but that it be high enough to make the murder not pay—and surely imprisoning the murderer for the rest of his life or, if he is wealthy, confiscating his wealth would cost him more than the murder could possibly have gained him. But this analysis implicitly treats the probability of apprehension and conviction as one. If it is less than one, as of course it is, then the murderer will not be comparing the

gain from the crime with the loss if he is caught and sentenced; he will be comparing it with the disutility of the sentence discounted by the probability that it will actually be imposed. Suppose, for example, that the loss to the murder victim is one hundred million dollars, the probability of punishing the murderer is .5, and the murderer's total wealth is one million dollars and will be confiscated upon conviction. Then his expected punishment cost when he is deciding whether to commit the crime is only $500,000—much less than his total wealth.

This analysis suggests incidentally that the much heavier punishment of crimes of violence than seemingly more serious white-collar crimes is not, as so often thought, an example of class bias. Once it is recognized that most people would demand astronomical sums to assume a substantial risk of death, it becomes apparent that even very large financial crimes are less serious than most crimes of violence. The same people who would accept quite modest sums to run very small risks of death would demand extremely large sums to run the substantial risks that many crimes of violence create, even when death does not ensue. This point holds even if the white-collar crime (say, violating a pollution regulation) creates a safety hazard, provided that the probability that the hazard will result in the death of any given person is low. Even if it were a virtual certainty that some people would die as a result of the crime, the aggregate disutility of many small risks of death may be much smaller than a single large risk of death to a particular person. This is the nonlinear relationship between utility and risk of death that I have stressed.[1]

By the same token the argument sketched above for capital punishment is not conclusive. Because the penalty is so severe, and irreversible, the cost of mistaken imposition is very high; therefore greater resources are invested in the litigation of a capital case. Indeed, if I am right in suggesting that the cost of death inflicted with a high probability (a reasonable description of capital punishment) is not just a linear extrapolation from less severe injuries, it is not surprising that the resources invested in the litigation of a capital case may, as one observes, greatly exceed those invested in litigation in cases where the maximum punishment is life imprisonment, even if there is no possibility of parole. The additional resources expended on the litigation of capital cases may not be justified if the added deterrent effect of capital punishment over long prison terms is small. But there is scientific evidence to support the layman's intuition that it is great.[2]

Capital punishment is also supported by considerations of marginal deterrence, which require as big a spread as possible between the punishments for the least and most serious crimes. If the maximum punishment for murder is life imprisonment, we may not want to make armed robbery also punishable by life imprisonment, for then armed robbers would have no additional incentive not to murder their victims. But arguments based on marginal deterrence for a differentiated penalty structure are inconclusive, particularly when the greater offense is a complement of the lesser one, as is often the case with murder. Moreover, the argument does not lead inexorably to the conclusion that capital punishment should be the punishment for simple murder. For if it is, then we have the problem of marginally deterring the multiple murderer. Maybe capital punishment should be reserved for him, so that murderers have a disincentive to kill witnesses to the murder, though again the number of such complementary murders may be less if the initial murder is punished severely.

An important application of this principle is to prison murders. A prisoner who is serving a life sentence for murder and is not likely to be paroled has no disincentive not to kill in prison, unless prison murder is punishable by death. Considerations of complementarity might argue for making out-of-prison murders capital also, since reducing the number of murders and the fraction of murderers in prison would reduce the occasions for prison murder. What makes little sense is to have capital punishment for neither out-of-prison nor prison murders, so that the latter becomes close to a free good. This is the present situation in federal law. Notice that varying the probability of apprehension and conviction cannot preserve marginal deterrence in this situation. The probability of apprehension and conviction in the prison murder case is close to one; the problem is that for the murderer already fated to spend the rest of his life in prison, there is no incremental punishment from being convicted of murder again.

Of course there is no realistic method of preserving marginal deterrence for every crime, although medieval law tried. It is a reasonable conjecture (if no more than that) that because more medieval than modern people believed in an afterlife, because life was more brutal and painful, and because life expectancy was short, capital punishment was not so serious a punishment in those days as it is today. Furthermore, because society was poor, severe punishments were badly needed and law enforcement was inefficient, so that devoting much greater resources to catching criminals would not have been feasible or productive. In an effort to make capital punishment a more costly punishment to the criminal, especially gruesome methods of execution (for example, drawing and quartering)[3] were prescribed for especially heinous crimes, such as treason. Boiling in oil, considered more horrible than hanging or beheading, was used to punish murder by poisoning; since poisoners were especially difficult to apprehend in those times, a heavier punishment than that prescribed for ordinary murderers was (economically) indicated.

The hanging of horse thieves in the nineteenth-century American West is another example of a penalty whose great severity reflects the low probability of punishment more than the high social cost of the crime. But the most famous example is the punishment of all serious (and some not so serious) crimes by death in pre-nineteenth-century England,[4] when there was no organized police force and the probability of punishment was therefore very low for most crimes.[5]

Death is not the only modern form of "afflictive" punishment. Flogging is still used by many parents and, in attenuated form, in some schools. The economic objection to punishing by inflicting physical pain is not that it is disgusting or that people have different thresholds of pain that make it difficult to calibrate the severity of the punishment—imprisonment and death are subject to the same problem. The objection is that it may be a poor method of inflicting severe but not lethal punishment. Just to inflict a momentary excruciating pain with no aftereffects might be a trivial deterrent, especially for people who had never experienced such pain; while to inflict a level of pain that would be the equivalent of five years in prison would require measures so drastic that they might endanger the life, or destroy the physical or mental health, of the offender. For slight punishments, fines will do. Incidentally, I do not mean, by omission, to disparage noneconomic objections to "afflictive punishment." But this is an article about economics.

The infliction of physical pain is not the only way in which the severity of punishment can be varied other than by varying the length of imprisonment. Size of prison cell, temperature, and quality of food could also be used as "amenity variables." It may seem very attractive from a cost-effectiveness standpoint to reduce the length of imprisonment but compensate by reducing the quality of the food served the prisoners; the costs of imprisonment to the state, but not to the prisoners, would be reduced. The problem is that this would make information about sanctions very costly, because there would be so many dimensions to evaluate. Time has the attractive characteristic of being one-dimensional, and differs from pain in that it has more variability. But as a matter of fact, society does vary the amenities of prison life for different criminals. Minimum security prisons are more comfortable than intermediate security prisons, and the latter are more comfortable than maximum security prisons. Assignments to these different tiers are related to the gravity of the crime, and in the direction one would predict.

2. *Imprisonment.* If society must continue to rely heavily on imprisonment as a criminal sanction, there is an argument—subject to caveats that should be familiar to the reader by now, based on risk aversion, overinclu-

sion, avoidance and error costs, and (less clearly) marginal deterrence—for combining heavy prison terms for convicted criminals with low probabilities of apprehension and conviction. Consider the choice between combining a .1 probability of apprehension and conviction with a ten-year prison term and a .2 probability of apprehension and conviction with a five-year term. Under the second approach twice as many individuals are imprisoned but for only half as long, so the total costs of imprisonment to the government will be the same under the two approaches. But the costs of police, court officials, and the like will probably be lower under the first approach. The probability of apprehension and conviction, and hence the number of prosecutions, is only half as great. Although more resources will be devoted to a trial where the possible punishment is greater, these resources will be incurred in fewer trials because fewer people will be punished, and even if the total litigation resources are no lower, police and prosecution costs will clearly be much lower. And notice that this variant of our earlier model of high fines and trivial probabilities of apprehension and conviction corrects the most serious problem with that model—that is, solvency.

But isn't a system under which probabilities of punishment are low "unfair," because it creates ex post inequality among offenders? Many go scot-free; others serve longer prison sentences than they would if more offenders were caught. However, to object to this result is like saying that all lotteries are unfair because, ex post, they create wealth differences among the players. In an equally significant sense both the criminal justice system that creates low probabilities of apprehension and conviction and the lottery are fair so long as the ex ante costs and benefits are equalized among the participants. Nor is it correct that while real lotteries are voluntary the criminal justice "lottery" is not. The criminal justice system is voluntary: you keep out of it by not committing crimes. Maybe, though, such a system of punishment is not sustainable in practice, because judges and jurors underestimate the benefits of what would seem, viewed in isolation, savagely cruel sentences. The prisoner who is to receive the sentence will be there in the dock, in person; the victims of the crimes for which he has not been prosecuted (because the fraction of crimes prosecuted is very low) will not be present—they will be statistics. I hesitate, though, to call this an economic argument; it could be stated in economic terms by reference to costs of information, but more analysis would be needed before this could be regarded as anything better than relabeling.

There is, however, another and more clearly economic problem with combining very long prison sentences with very low probabilities of apprehension and conviction. A prison term is lengthened, of course, by adding time on to the end of it. If the criminal has a significant discount rate, the added years may not create a substantial added disutility. At a discount rate of ten percent, a ten-year prison term imposes a disutility only 6.1 times the disutility of a one-year sentence, and a twenty-year sentence increases this figure to only 8.5 times; the corresponding figures for a five percent discount rate are 7.7 and 12.5 times.

Discount rates may seem out of place in a discussion of nonmonetary utilities and disutilities, though imprisonment has a monetary dimension, because a prisoner will have a lower income in prison than on the outside. But the reason that interest (discount) rates are positive even when there is no risk of default and the expected rate of inflation is zero is that people prefer present to future consumption and so must be paid to defer consumption. A criminal, too, will value his future consumption, which imprisonment will reduce, less than his present consumption.

The discounting problem could be ameliorated by preventive detention, whereby the defendant in effect begins to serve his sentence before he is convicted, or sometimes before his appeal rights are exhausted. The pros and cons of preventive detention involve issues of criminal procedure that would carry us beyond the scope of this article, and here I merely note that the argument for preventive detention is stronger the graver the defendant's crime (and hence the longer the optimal length of imprisonment), regardless of whether the defendant is likely to commit a crime if he is released on bail pending trial.

The major lesson to be drawn from this is that criminal sanctions are costly. A tort sanction is close to a costless transfer payment. A criminal sanction, even when it takes the form of a fine, and patently when it takes the form of imprisonment or death, is not. And yet it appears to be the optimal method of deterring most pure coercive transfers—which are therefore the central concern of the criminal law.

Notes

1. This point is overlooked in "radical" critiques of criminal law. See, e.g., S. Box, *Power, Crime, and Mystification* 9 (1983).

2. See, e.g., D. Pyle, *The Economics of Crime and Law Enforcement* (London, 1983); Ehrlich, "The Deterrent Effect of Capital Punishment: A Question of Life and Death," 65 *Am. Econ. Rev.* 397 (1975); Ehrlich and Gibbons, "On the Measurement of the Deterrent Effect of Capital Punishment and the Theory of Deterrence," 6 *J. Legal Stud.* 35 (1977); Layson, "Homicide and Deterrence: A Reexamination of the U.S. Time-Series Evidence" (August 1984) (unpublished manu-

script on file at the offices of the *Columbia Law Review*). The evidence has not gone unchallenged, of course. See D. Pyle, *supra* ch. 4, for discussion and references.

3. This punishment was still "on the books" in eighteenth-century England. For the grisly details, see W. Blackstone, *Commentaries* 92.

4. See, e.g., Langbein, "Shaping the Eighteenth-Century Criminal Trial: A View from the Ryder Sources," 50 *U. Chi. L. Rev.* 1, 36–49 (1983).

5. Many capital sentences, however, were commuted to banishment to the colonies.

2.3 How "Evidence" of Deterrence Can Mislead

Royal Commission on Capital Punishment

Professor Paul Cornil quoted a case by way of illustration of the danger of the use of statistics as an argument in relation to the deterrent value of capital punishment. It took place in Belgium in 1918 and Professor Cornil described it as follows:

A series of robberies with murder were committed by gangs of criminals in the open country. The bandits penetrated at night to isolated farms and forced the farmers to tell where their money was hidden by beating them and by burning their feet (hence the name of "chauffeurs" given to the criminals).

When the farmers resisted, they were killed on the spot. One of these gangs was arrested, tried, and the five leaders were sentenced to death by the Court of Assizes of Brussels, on 29th December, 1919. Contrary to the customary rule, the Attorney-General refused in the case of the 26-year-old Pierre N. to recommend the commutation of the sentence. In his report to the Minister of Justice, the Attorney-General declared many similar crimes were being committed in the country and few of the criminals were arrested: in the district of the Court of Appeal of Liège, six such crimes had been committed and the authors of only three of these were known; in the district of Ghent, 17 crimes committed, only four of whose authors had been arrested; in the district of Brussels out of 15 cases only six had been arrested. Therefore, the Attorney-General insisted that an example should be made by the execution of Pierre N. "whose presence in the community could only be, at whatever moment, a cause of danger and scandal."

At that time the Minister of Justice was the socialist Emile Vandervelde. He refused to have the man executed and wrote on the record: "I am a decided opponent of capital punishment. As long as I am Minister, no execution shall

---

From Royal Commission on Capital Punishment, *Report* (London: H.M.S.O., 1953), Appendix 6.

take place." The sentence *was* commuted. And then, a strange thing occurred. Almost suddenly, that series of robberies died away without any apparent cause: was it the result of the return to more normal conditions of living in the country or did the members of those gangs find it more advisable to devote themselves to more lawful activities, or did the farmers take the elementary precaution to put their money in the bank instead of keeping it in their homes as they had done during the war? Whatever may be the explanation, the fact is that the crimes suddenly ceased.

Whenever I relate this incident, I cannot refrain from pointing out how narrowly we escaped a grave danger. Suppose for a moment that this man, following the Attorney-General's proposal, had been put to death, and then that special kind of crime had disappeared almost immediately. What a victory for the advocates of capital punishment! They certainly would not have hesitated to conclude that this improvement was due to the deterrent effect of capital punishment and it is quite probable that the death penalty for the common law criminal would have been reinstated and retained for a long time.

It is indeed obvious that a statistical change cannot safely be ascribed to a particular explanation without making sure that no other explanations exist which, either alone or in conjunction with each other or the suggested explanation, could account for the change. And it is impossible to be sure that variations in homicide statistics before and after the abolition of capital punishment are in fact due to abolition, or that, if the figures remain constant, abolition did not have some effect which was canceled out by some other cause.

2.4
Deterrence Research and Deterrence Policies

Deryck Beyleveld

For two or three decades ideals of rehabilitation and "treatment" of offenders have characterized the dominant control policy within the criminal justice systems of Britain and the United States. It is doubtful that this ideology ever held widespread favor among all groups of administrators and practitioners, social workers being a notable exception. Being the brainchild of "liberal" academics wedded to the positivist tradition in criminology, it has held sway largely by being imposed from above as an official or neo-official policy. At the present time, however, there is widespread disillusionment with the promise of rehabilitation, a disenchantment which affects even the ranks of those who originally fostered it. And there has been an increasingly vocal political constituency for a hard line with offenders. In Britain at least, urban terrorism, football violence, and the increasing use of guns in criminal offenses are seen by many to threaten the fabric of society. "Treatment" is no way to deal with the evil forces within our midst and its practice should be abandoned. Political pressure to placate voters is considerable and increases the urgency of finding a new official strategy.

A general deterrence policy[1] has obvious attractions as an alternative. It is compatible with models of human action which assign actors a capacity for choice. Deterrence, if successful, does not depend upon any interference with the character structure of the individual. Unlike rehabilitation, it holds out a promise of being able to prevent persons entering the criminal justice system rather than merely dealing with them after they have done so. Because it threatens punishment it has some potential for placating the

From Deryck Beyleveld, "Deterrence Research as a Basis for Deterrence Policies," 18 *Howard Journal of Criminal Justice* 135 (1979). Excerpted and reprinted by permission.

angels of vengeance. Of course, this image of being all things to all men may be an illusion once we spell out what we actually have to do in order to deter effectively. Successful deterrence may require punishment of the innocent; it may require curtailing some of the requirements of due process; or it may involve too much interference in our private lives. On all counts it may be incompatible with human rights.

In this article, I review empirical evidence on the general deterrent effectiveness of legal sanctions.[2] I argue that there exists no scientific basis for expecting that a general deterrence policy, which does not involve an unacceptable interference with human rights, will do anything to control the crime rate. The sort of information needed to base a morally acceptable general policy is lacking. There is some convincing evidence in some limited areas that some legal sanctions have exerted deterrent effects. These findings are not, however, generalizable beyond the conditions which were investigated. Given the present state of knowledge, implementing an official deterrence policy can be no more than a shot in the dark, or a political decision to pacify "public sentiment."

Do Legal Sanctions Deter?

A deterrent effect of a sanction may be defined as a modification or prevention of a threatened behavior brought about because the threatened audience considers that the sanction's presence creates too great a risk for the threatened behavior to be performed as would otherwise have been intended.[3] Because the type and degree of modification or prevention, the threatened audience, the sanction, and the threatened behavior may all vary, different types of deterrence are possible.[4] What they all share is a possible mechanism for producing compliance; modification of the intended behavior (the offense) must have been produced by a calculation that the utility of modification outweighed the utility of offending as intended. To establish a deterrent effect of a sanction it is necessary to show that the sanction produced a modification or prevention of an intended offense, *and* that this effect was due to the sanction's influence upon the threatened audience's calculation of personal utility. A sanction can only exert such an influence if certain conditions are satisfied. For example, the potential offender must be capable of acting on the basis of personal utility, and must not be prevented from offending by other considerations, must be aware of the sanction and must have specific attitudes toward the sanction and beliefs about it (notably attitudes and beliefs relating to the subjective severity and probability of incurring the sanction). These conditions, varying from one type of deterrence to the next, may be adduced *a priori* from the definition of deterrence. The adequacy of a research design which attempts to evaluate the deterrent effectiveness of sanctions can be measured by its ability to establish that the necessary criteria describe the situation being investigated: that a modification of offense behavior can be explained by the application to the situation of deterrence criteria.

Ecological Comparisons

The majority of research reports attempting to evaluate deterrent effects use, in one way or another, what might be described as "Ecological Comparisons": that is, the offense rates of different jurisdictions over the same period, or the same jurisdiction at different times, are compared in cases where the jurisdictions vary according to the manner in which they deploy sanctions. Thus, jurisdictions without a sanction may be compared with those which have one, or jurisdictions which have relatively severe sanctions may be compared with those which have less severe sanctions, and so on. The general reasoning is that if a particular sanction deters a particular offense then jurisdictions with the sanctions will have lower offense rates than those without sanctions; those with relatively more severe sanctions (as measured, for example, by the length of imprisonment) will have lower offense rates than those with less severe sanctions; and those with relatively more probable sanctions (as measured, for example, by official arrest or conviction rates) will have lower offense rates than those with less probable sanctions.

The results of these studies are impressively uniform. Almost without exception, regardless of variations in design, correlation technique, control or modeling procedure, the expected relations have been found between probability of sanctions and the offense rates, but have not been found between severity of sanctions and the offense rates. In the latter case, the only consistent exception is found with homicide, where severity is measured by the length of imprisonment for homicide.[5]

There are, however, at least three sets of problems which must be solved before these results can be interpreted as evidence for *preventive* effects of sanctions. First, it has to be shown that the data are reliable, comparable, and in no way responsible themselves or in the way in which they are constructed for any artifactual relationships. Second, it has to be shown that the relationships are due to causal relations between the investigated variables and not due to their independent causal relations with some third variable. Finally, it has to be shown that even if there is a causal relationship between the investigated variables, it is changes in sanctions which produce changes in offense rates and not *vice versa*.

Econometric analyses have addressed the third problem by using simultaneous-equations techniques. Their results, which are generally in line with ecological studies as a whole, cannot, however, be assumed to be superior. The first two problems are logically prior, and econometric analyses have done nothing to solve them. There are a few path analyses which attempt to deal with both the second and third problems, but they too are crucially subject to the first problem.

The most recalcitrant difficulties, however, arise when an attempt is made to move from an assertion of a preventive effect to a deterrent effect. With the exception of investigations using the quasi-experimental time-series design, *all* of these studies treat propositions such as "The severity/probability of sanctions varies inversely with offense rates" as criteria of deterrence. The validity of such a procedure is highly questionable. It has often been pointed out that there are a number of possible ways in which sanctions may prevent offenses, ways which may be consistent with the criteria at issue, which are not types of deterrence. Sanctions may, for example, exert moral-educative or incapacitative effects. If these propositions are to be treated as criteria of deterrence then it must be assumed *inter alia* that potential offenders are sufficiently aware of sanctions for their estimates of the severity and probability of sanctions to change in step with changes in the official estimates of these variables; that potential offenders define severity in the same way as the investigator; that they regard their estimates of probability of sanctions as the probability that they themselves will incur these sanctions; and that they always act on the basis of a personal utility calculus in which subjective severity and probability of sanctions are salient variables. Econometricians are generally quite explicit about making such assumptions in the construction of the models they use in their statistical analyses. They would no doubt contend that if the empirical estimation of these models is in line with what is predicted by the assumptions, then this is evidence for the assumptions. This claim would have some force were it not the case that the assumptions generate ambiguous predictions in their models and that direct empirical evidence is against the assumptions. Subjective perceptions of sanctions simply do not move in step with "objective" changes in sanctions, and those with the best knowledge of sanctions are also, statistically, not the least likely to offend.

The investigation by Ross et al. (1970) of the effect of the introduction of the Breathalyzer in October 1967 (which was preceded by extensive publicity) on drunken driving avoids most of the above-mentioned difficulties. These researchers plotted road accident casualties monthly from January 1961 to December 1970 making corrections for the length of month, risk of accident (measured by vehicle miles), and seasonal variations in the casualty rate. This revealed a drop in all types of casualties immediately after the introduction of the Road Safety Act of 1967 which could not be accounted for as a trend, regression to a mean, a mere random fluctuation, by more cautious driving being the effect of the Act, or by a number of other hypotheses (tested by independent data). The drop in casualties was much more significant for those times of the week when drivers could be expected to have been drinking than for other times. Ross (1973) argues that the evidence for a deterrent effect, due to an increased subjective probability of sanctions, is strong. If, instead of merely ruling out other explanations (since a possible alternative hypothesis may have been overlooked), independent evidence had been available that the subjective probability of sanctions did increase, then the inference would be more secure.

What is interesting about this study is that it attempts to do precisely what a study of deterrent effectiveness must do: establish a modifying or preventive effect, and then on the basis of properly constituted deterrence criteria show that the effect was due to the application of these criteria and not to other possible causes.

Questionnaires and Interviews

Many researchers have realized that deterrence is a function of subjective attitudes and perceptions of potential offenders. Instead of correlating official data on severity and probability of sanctions with official offense rates, they have concentrated on self-reported offense rates and measures of subjective severity and probability of sanctions. The general reasoning here has been that if a sanction deters, then those with relatively higher estimates of severity/probability of sanctions will report lower offense rates than those with lower estimates. Another strategy has simply been to ask potential offenders what considerations inhibit persons when they consider offending, and to rank these considerations (fear of legal sanctions, fear of informal sanctions, moral inhibition, etc.) in order of importance.

The first strategy has shown that the subjective probability of sanctions (arrest, conviction, etc.) generally varies inversely with self-reported offense rates (also with official offense rates, the declared intention to continue offending, and respondents' predictions of whether a hypothetical person will offend in hypothetical situations). This result holds whether subjective probability is measured by subjective estimates of what the objective probability is for "those who offend," "persons like oneself," or in just a few studies, for example Teevan (1976), "oneself." On the other hand, the subjective severity of penalties (measured by subjective perceptions of what maximum and minimum penalties are) *does not* vary inversely with offense rates, whereas the relationship *is* inverse when subjective severity is measured by how nasty the perceived penalties are considered to be.

The second strategy reveals that various population groups consider legal sanctions to be important controls of law violation (although none of the studies makes it clear whether this is a judgment about what controls others' behavior or what controls the respondent's own behavior). Other controls, however, such as moral inhibitions, are generally reported to be more important. Significantly, those who display greater involvement in offending attach more importance to legal sanctions as controls than those with a lesser involvement.

A general significant finding is that knowledge of penalties is generally inaccurate, and probabilities of arrest, etc., are generally *over*estimated. In general, groups with specific offense involvements tend to have more accurate knowledge of associated penalties and probabilities of arrest (though still overestimated), etc., and this means *lower estimates of probabilities*, etc., than the general population. Findings of this nature counsel extreme caution about interpreting the results of these studies as evidence of deterrence. As with the ecological studies, there is a problem of causal direction. An inverse relationship between subjective probability of sanction and offense rates may be due to those with greater offense involvement having lower estimates of probabilities *because* of their involvement, and not to those with lower estimates being more willing to offend *because* of their lower estimates. There is also the possibility that the relationship between subjective probability and offense rates may be spurious. Those individuals who offend less frequently may also be those with greater moral inhibitions against offending. This group may also be prone to greater overestimation of probabilities of being sanctioned *because* of their moral inhibitions. It is possible that the estimates of those morally committed to the law are prone to a wish fulfillment that those not morally committed won't get away with it.

In general, we should question any results as relevant deterrence evidence which do not attend to subjective estimates by a respondent of severity/probability for himself. Few people regard themselves as "the average man." Whatever the statistical chances, objective or subjective, each person is likely to regard himself as an exception. He may think himself more or less gifted or lucky than average when it comes to his chances of "getting away with it." Estimates of general chances are simply not relevant. Once we are dealing with personal estimates, however, we need to consider that those who commit more offenses may be inveterate optimists. Although the pessimists may be deterred, the optimists may always think they can "get away with it," no matter what the general objective chances against this are. The crucial thing to realize about these studies is that, *even if* they do show that some persons are being deterred *by their beliefs* about sanctions, this does not show that they are being deterred by actual legal sanctions, nor that changing sanctions will affect the beliefs of those who are most likely to offend. By failing to show how actual legal sanctions may or may not be productive of beliefs about them, these studies fail to say anything about the deterrent effectiveness of actual legal sanctions.

Field Experiments

Field experiments are potentially an excellent means for evaluating deterrent effects. Unfortunately, their scope is limited by their cost and the need to secure cooperation from officials. A study by Schwartz and Orleans (1967) of tax evasion and the study by Buikhuisen (1974) of a campaign to deter driving with worn tires are particularly fine examples of this kind of research. Although other studies report evidence for preventive effects of their sanctions, these are the only two which are immune from the usual caveats about the use of official statistics, adopt reasonably adequate control procedures, and provide plausible evidence that the prevention of their target behavior is by deterrence.

Buikhuisen's study is worth describing in some detail: he investigated the potential deterrent effect of penalties for driving with worn tires in The Netherlands (imprisonment for up to two months or a fine of up to three hundred Dutch guilders; driving licenses could also be revoked for a period of up to two years). Groningen was chosen as the experimental city, and Leeuwarden as the control. The cities are similar in size, and a pilot investigation showed that in both cities 80 percent of car owners parked their cars outside at night. This enabled the tires of samples of cars to be checked in both cities on two occasions, three months apart, before a police campaign against driving with worn tires. Cars were investigated during the early hours of the morning and the car number and the position of worn tires were noted. During the three months there was a "spontaneous" renewal rate of worn tires of 46.3 percent in Groningen and 43.5 percent in Leeuwarden.

In Groningen, special patrol cars and newspapers conducted a two-week campaign warning drivers about the need to have legal tires. In Leeuwarden, there was no publicity and no special patrols during the experimental weeks or for four months preceding the experiment. Immediately before the campaign samples of cars in both cities were inspected using the method of the pilot study. Immediately after the campaign these same cars were relocated to see if they had replaced worn tires. Checks were made to ensure that none of the sample had been located by the police during the campaign.

During the two weeks of the experiment 54 percent of the cars with worn tires before the campaign had them replaced in Groningen; but the figure was only 27 percent in Leeuwarden. Furthermore, during the campaign the Groningen police inspected 13,474 cars and found that only 189 had worn tires: a much lower percentage than in The Netherlands generally. Eighty persons who had renewed their tires during the campaign, and ninety-one who had not, were interviewed after the campaign. The majority of both groups knew about the campaign, but far more of the renewers than nonrenewers did. More nonrenewers than renewers claimed that they would risk driving with worn tires if there was another campaign. Nonrenewers tended to be younger, had less education, older cars, less need of a car for professional reasons, and paid less attention to their cars.

The particular merits of this study lie in the attempts to establish the "real" offense rate, to establish the spontaneous renewal rate, and to ascertain why the police succeeded or failed in terms of the characteristics and perceptions of the threatened audience. However, the renewal rate in Leeuwarden during the campaign was four times the spontaneous rate[6] (vs. six times in Groningen), and this is not explained. The interview questions were also not detailed enough to rule out the hypothesis that the renewals were prompted by the campaign raising safety consciousness rather than by drawing attention to legal penalties. Nevertheless, such faults are remediable within the general design.

Conclusion

Taking deterrence research as a whole, it must be concluded that, although there is some persuasive evidence for deterrent effect in some situations, most notably that reported by Ross et al. (1970) and Buikhuisen (1974), most studies are inconclusive, the main reasons being methodologically defective designs or procedures and inadequate deterrence criteria.

Can We Predict Deterrent Effects of Legal Sanctions?

Many studies which primarily attempt to identify deterrent effects, also attempt to draw policy conclusions from their results.

The inference most commonly drawn in ecological studies is that increasing the probability of arrest or conviction is likely to deter potential offenders, whereas increasing the severity of penalties is unlikely to have an effect. More specific statements are also made on occasion; for example, that the severity of sanctions can be decreased without affecting deterrence, sometimes even that severity should be decreased because high severity may militate against securing a high probability of conviction (as may happen if juries show reluctance to convict when very severe penalties are threatened); that certain types of offenses are less deterrable than others (for example, violent crimes less than property crimes); that increasing, for example, police manpower (taken to index probability of arrest), by some exact amount, will deter an exactly specified number of offenses.

Such inferences are of highly dubious validity. Even if we could assume, as we cannot, that the correlations upon which they are based are evidence about deterrence, a number of totally unwarranted assumptions must be made. These inferences are merely extrapolations from the magnitude and direction of empirically estimated correlation coefficients. Suppose, for example, that a particular set of studies does show that increasing severity of sanctions fails to deter. To draw a policy inference they must then *explain* why increasing the severity of sanctions does not deter. They can hardly claim that severity is not a deterrence criterion, so the likely explanation would be that severity levels are already above their upper thresholds (which is plausible when serious crimes are the topic of investigation). But if severity is decreased then it is possible that the upper threshold will be crossed. Below this threshold decreasing severity will then lead to decreasing deterrence.

It must also be assumed that the deterrence potential of the threatened audience (the ratio of those who need to be, and can be, deterred to those who need not or cannot be deterred) is not exhausted in the present situation by the existing values of probability/severity; that is, that all those who can *and* need to be deterred are not already deterred as much as possible.

In any case, this sort of discussion, as well as the policy proposals, are fanciful. In order to be discussing deterrence it must be assumed that changes in the objective probability/severity values will produce corresponding changes in the subjective values. The inferences, however, simply ignore the fact that deterrence involves people acting in a social setting. We really do not know how people come to have their attitudes toward, and perceptions of, laws and offenses. People may simply not tolerate the sorts of things which may have to be done in order to increase the subjective probabilities of arrest and conviction. It may, for example, be necessary to alter police search and questioning procedures, to interfere with due process and to introduce identity cards and compulsory fingerprinting of the entire population. In any case, even if such "drastic" measures are not required, by not telling us what is required, the proposals are really empty as practical and practicable policy suggestions.

In general, these policy inferences rest upon a methodological error. They treat their correlations, not only as causal relationships, but as causal laws. Instead, they should be regarded as empirical relationships which are produced by hidden social processes and actions. It is from knowledge of these processes, not from the empirical generalizations which they explain, that scientific predictions can be drawn.

Questionnaires and interviews fare no better as a basis for policy proposals. They are sometimes used to generate policy predictions which correspond in all respects to those inferred in ecological investigations; the only difference being that subjective and self-report data are correlated rather than objective and official data. These inferences are subject to exactly corresponding objections relating to the possible operation of thresholds, the unknown deterrence potential, and the inutility of prescribing what it is not known how to accomplish.

The irony of the general run of policy inferences is that they provide information of little different order from what can quite legitimately be inferred *a priori* from an analysis of what it means to be deterred. "*If* someone views offending in terms of its utility; *if* the subjective probability/severity of sanctions is high enough, etc., then he will be deterred" is inferable from deterrence criteria. In order to implement a policy we need to know how to write out the hypotheticals. It is this very knowledge which is missing and which these studies circumvent by making unwarranted and often implausible assumptions.

One partial exception to these criticisms is Ross's (1973) discussion of the effect of the British Road Safety Act of 1967. Ross suggested that a reduction in the severity of penalties for drunken driving, the use of a more reliable Breathalyzer (which does not require blood- and urine-test backups), the introduction of random testing, and a lowering of the legal limit, would not only be adequate to deter drunken driving but would help ensure that any deterrent effect achieved by a publicity campaign would not quickly wear off. Ross's analysis shows that the initial deterrent effect of the 1967 campaign started to wear off as early as January 1968. He argues that the publicity for the campaign initially led to an increased subjective probability of incurring what were perceived to be rather severe penalties for drunken driving. However, examination of the ways in which alcohol tests were actually given, charges brought, and convictions secured, reveals that there was little objective basis for the supposed public belief that the sanctions were not easily avoided. The need to back up the Breathalyzer with blood and urine tests led to lowered charge and conviction rates because the delay allowed some "illegal" blood levels to become legal in the interim. The police were also reluctant to enforce the Act because they feared worsening police-public relations. Ross postulates that the gap between the objective and subjective probabilities of sanctions led to an erosion of the initially high subjective probability. If this were so then the declining effect of the legislation would be explained. Ross's policy proposals are made on the basis of this explanation of the consequences of the 1967 Act in terms of the operation of social processes; and it should further be noted that he suggests that random testing may not be implementable because of public antagonism, despite the fact that, if implemented, it is likely to be an effective measure.

Ross's reasoning is by no means flawless; it rests on a number of plausible rather than tested assumptions, and he is rather cavalier and vague when he suggests that the severity of penalties can be decreased without lessening deterrence. In essence, however, the general design appears to be sound and his procedure is worth outlining in a schematic form.

1. Evaluate the deterrent effectiveness of a measure by assessing the likelihood that a preventive effect can be explained by the application of deterrence criteria. If no preventive effect is found (or if one declines) then assess how likely it is that this can be explained by the failure of application of a deterrence criterion.
2. Analyze the social situation attending the introduction of the measure and attempt to explain what social processes were responsible for the application or failure of application of the deterrence criteria (necessary attitudes, perceptions, etc., of potential offenders).
3. Evaluate the feasibility of actions which, if performed, would ensure that deterrence criteria will apply.

Such a procedure can be applied to field experiments as well as to the quasi-experimental design used by Ross. This has not, however, been the case when policy suggestions have been inferred from field experiments. For example, Kelling et al. (1975) conducted an experiment to determine the deterrent effectiveness of random patrol exercises in Kansas City. They failed to find such an effect and concluded that random patrols would be no more effective at deterring crime than a policy of only answering calls for service. This is unwarranted. Findings generated in particular experimental circumstances cannot form a basis for general policy predictions. The proper basis is an explanation of why the particular policy failed. This might identify some absent deterrence requirement in the original experimental situation which may be present in another situation.

It cannot be emphasized too strongly that the chief defect of deterrence research for policy purposes, ignoring the fact that most investigations have not been adequate even as evaluative studies, is not that research has concentrated on a limited range of offenses and penalties as Brody (1978) suggests. Brody reasons that studies have failed to find convincing deterrence evidence because they have dealt mainly with crimes of passion which, on *a priori* grounds, may be thought to be less deterrable anyway, but that "For other categories it is less easy to resist the simple and old-fashioned idea that firm penalties resolutely applied must do something to frighten off would-be malefactors" (Brody 1978, 145). If, however, offenses such as shoplifting and penalties such as fines had received as much attention as serious crimes and imprisonment the situation would not necessarily be improved. First, it is not true that there are no studies of other offenses. The problem is that they are as inadequate as the serious crime investigations. Second, it is not the case that serious crime investigations have shown that no deterrence occurred: all one can say is that they have not shown that deterrence did occur. Third, the point is not whether penalties can deter, but how to set up the conditions in which they will deter, and this applies to potential offenders regardless of the type of offense or penalty, provided only that the potential offender needs to be deterred and can be deterred in principle. No penalty is a deterrent or not a deterrent *in itself*, and *any* penalty *may* be a deterrent in suitable circumstances.

Far more serious than a concentration upon limited offenses and penalties has been the concentration upon a limited range of types of deterrence. Investigators have only been interested in types of deterrence in which the offense rate is lowered. However, a measure can exert a deterrent effect without preventing the action which it is designed to deter. When a potential offender takes steps to avoid detection as his response to a policy, then this is a type of deterrence if he previously regarded these steps to be unnecessary. What explains the failure of prevention may not be the sanctions but the social circumstances which attend them: they allow him to find ways of avoiding the sanctions. This neglect of what may be termed "qualitative deterrence" is both a function and a cause of the neglect of attention to deterrence as a social process. If the emphasis in deterrence research had been upon the explanation of behavior and not upon blind statistical manipulation of data, then this would have been obvious.

Ross's procedure has its merits when it is possible to investigate a particular policy in detail. It can only base particular deterrence programs relating to specific penalties, offenses, and social circumstances. A different program is required if it is desired to have a general basis for predicting the effects of policies in novel situations. A general theory for predicting deterrence is required. It may be thought that this can be generated by applying Ross's procedure to a wide range of penalties, offenses, and social circumstances; but this is mistaken. How people react or act in specific situations is a function of the situations themselves, the principles which govern their behavior, and their perceptions of the situations. The principles in question are not empirical generalizations of their behavior in a wide variety of situations: it is doubtful that there can be such uniformities. When situations vary, behavior will vary. Instead, the principles have to be abstracted from different situations, and must in no way be dependent upon them. In an adequate theory for predicting deterrence, principles will be stated which, in conjunction with statements about the social position of individuals or groups, will generate predictions about the attitudes and perceptions of these subjects. A theory for predicting deterrence is impossible without a theory of the generation of attitudes toward laws and offenses and a theory of the communication of threats. Such theories are not available and so no scientific basis exists for a general policy of deterrence.

Can a General Policy of Deterrence Be Justified?

The concluding sentence of the last paragraph needs to be qualified. We do not know what difference doubling police manpower or increasing a fine from £10 to £100 would have on a potential offender's perceptions or calculation of the utility of an offense. But this does not mean that we don't know, with a fair degree of certainty, what would be the effect of a mandatory death penalty without trial administered in good science fiction style by robot parking meters on parking offenders. There are extreme policies which we can virtually guarantee will deterrently affect the perceptions and responses of all but those who are perfectly willing to suffer the penalty, cannot appreciate it, or do not act voluntarily. We could fingerprint the entire population, force everyone to carry identity cards, keep universal computer records, give the police unlimited powers of arrest, search, and questioning, dispense with due process, litter our cities and even the "privacy" of homes with spy cameras, and to cap it all we could institute extremely severe penalties for every offense. No doubt there are some who would be prepared to go to such lengths to eliminate any behavior which offends them. It is to be hoped that they are and will remain the tiny minority. Such a policy would represent a gross violation of human rights, and fortunately, while this group remains a minority, such a policy will not be implementable.

It may also be stated as a general principle that the adequacy of our knowledge of deterrence for policy purposes varies inversely with the political morality and feasibility of the proposed deterrence policy. In general, we have good reason to believe that immoral, unimplementable policies would "work"; rarely reason to believe that more sane and realistic policies will achieve anything. This is quite simply because human behavior is much more predictable in situations in which freedom of choice is severely limited.

If the choice is a clear one between compliance and, for example, certain death, then it is a good bet that a deterrable individual will comply. But to make choices clear and restricted the social milieu must either be extremely repressive or else we require far more knowledge of human behavior and institutions than we presently possess.

I do not want to give the impression that I am suggesting that the powers that be are intending a crusade of repression. I am sure that they are not. But barring some extreme policy, specific campaigns can be no more than tentative and hopeful experiments. On the other hand, to speak of a general policy is more sinister. The airing of a general policy is typical electioneering rhetoric. There are almost no specific policies which are scientifically grounded, and the idea as a general policy of control is appealing only while it is vague and unspecified. The rhetoric has attractions as a ploy to satisfy "public opinion"; "'Getting tough' with offenders or potential offenders by deterrence" is a slogan which may well attract votes. But would it continue to do so if it were generally realized that the slogan is empty, or else that implementation would involve social actions which would interfere with everybody's lives and not just with those whom the political constituency for deterrence views as the social enemy? The constituency will only be placated, except for short-term electioneering purposes, by results. When these results cannot be guaranteed, barring much unavailable knowledge, without alienating the constituency itself, then we do not have to look far for the motives behind the promises.

I do not want to suggest, however, that I am against any general policy of deterrence as a matter of principle. There would be a case for such a policy if it were scientifically grounded, and involved no violation of human rights in excess of the violations it could be expected to prevent by successful deterrence. I realize that there are some who may object to any deterrence policy on the grounds that it is "conservative." If this means that it is a policy which is directed at preserving whatever happens to be the present social and legal order, then it *is* conservative; but then the morality of conservatism depends upon the morality of that order. Then there are those who may suggest that a wholly moral order will not require deterrence: in Utopia all will obey the law by free choice; indeed, there may be no need for law. At most, however, this suggests that deterrence should not be the primary ideology of control. Our primary efforts should be directed at constructing Utopia, but until we succeed, deterrence may be necessary. In general, we must avoid a tendency to assume that alternative offense control and response policies are mutually exclusive options selected by different scientific theories and political ideologies. We should avoid thinking that if treatment doesn't work for all offenders then it should be replaced by deterrence *or* social change, etc., in a wholesale manner. People offend for different reasons and different responses are accordingly appropriate. Ideologies, furthermore, do not dictate treatment *or* deterrence, etc.: instead they dictate different hierarchical orderings of different sorts of responses; they dictate what should be the primary policy and what should be secondary policies according to a general theory of social goals and the desirable social order. Someone who approves of the existing social order may resist any radical social change; but room can be found for both treatment and deterrence within such an attitude. On the other hand, someone who disapproves of the existing order will primarily want to see it changed; but unless he disapproves of all existing laws and regards no one as needing treatment, both deterrence and treatment can play subordinate roles.

"Deterrence" has for too long been associated with the sorts of policies which I regard as extreme. This has made the notion a politically loaded one. This is unfortunate, for deterrence is, in fact, a pervasive fact of human existence. When someone looks before crossing a road, that is probably because of deterrence; when he takes an umbrella to avoid getting wet, that too may manifest deterrence. We tend to associate deterrence with a legal context, but we need not do so, and doing so does not alter the phenomenon, only the context. For this reason it is important to understand its limits and operation, not only for purposes of control, but also for purposes of understanding social behavior generally. If deterrence is not studied seriously or if deterrence policies are suggested and implemented without adequate grounding, we will achieve neither of these purposes, but merely add fuel to the flames of political passion.

Notes

1. This article concentrates on general deterrence: the deterrent effect of threats on potential offenders who have not as yet suffered the implementation of the threats. It is not concerned with the effects of implementing penalties on individuals.
2. This review draws upon Beyleveld (1978). It should be assumed that unreferenced remarks may be traced to this source.
3. For reasons for adopting such a narrow definition rather than equating deterrence with prevention, or allowing it to cover a number of mechanisms, see Beyleveld (1978), Introduction.
4. For a typology, see Beyleveld (1978), Introduction.

5. This should not be confused with the issue of the effectiveness of capital punishment.

6. That is to say, 27% in two weeks vs. 44% in three months.

References

Beyleveld, D. (1978) *The Effectiveness of General Deterrents Against Crime: An Annotated Bibliography of Evaluative Research*, Cambridge, University of Cambridge, Institute of Criminology (Microfiche).

Brody, S. (1978) "Research into the aims and effectiveness of sentencing," *The Howard Journal of Penology and Crime Prevention, 17,* 133–48.

Buikhuisen, W. (1974) "General deterrence: research and theory," *Abstracts on Criminology and Penology, 14,* 285–98.

Kelling, G. L., Pate, T., Dieckman, D., and Brown, C. E. (1975) *The Kansas City Preventive Patrol Experiment: A Technical Report*, Washington, D.C., Police Foundation.

Ross, H. L. (1973) "Law, science, and accidents: the British Road Safety Act of 1967," *The Journal of Legal Studies, 2,* 1–78.

Ross, H. L., Campbell, D. T., and Glass, G. V. (1970) "Determining the social effects of a legal reform: the British 'Breathalyser' crackdown of 1967," *American Behavioral Scientist, 13,* 493–509.

Schwartz, R. D., and Orleans, S. (1967) "On legal sanctions," *The University of Chicago Law Review, 34,* 274–300.

Taylor, I., Walton, P., and Young, J. (1973) *The New Criminology*, London, Routledge and Kegan Paul.

Teevan, Jr., J. J. (1976) "Subjective perception of deterrence (continued)," *Journal of Research in Crime and Delinquency, 13,* 155–64.

2.5
Deterrence Theory: Its Moral Problems

Alan H. Goldman

[*This essay was written as a reply to an article by Ernest van den Haag, "Punishment as a Device for Controlling the Crime Rate," 33* Rutgers Law Review *706 (1981). For present purposes the statement of van den Haag's views in the Goldman essay is sufficient.*]

Ernest van den Haag's initial defense of deterrence theory against an old objection to it, that deterrence justifies only the appearance of punishment, or the threat of punishment, and not its actual imposition, is sound. Van den Haag correctly points out that for threats to be plausible and effective, they must be carried out when their antecedent conditions are met. The deterrence theorist need only state his argument in two steps in order to avoid this objection: first, that threats of punishment are justified to reduce crime, and second, that the threats must be made good to achieve their purpose.

Van den Haag concludes from these premises that "every effort must be made to let no actually guilty persons escape punishment." Here this author begins to part company with him. The many procedural rights and safeguards of our legal system are founded on the premise that it is worse to punish an innocent person than to let a guilty one go free. This asymmetry is based on the certainty of harm in the former case, as opposed to its mere probability in the latter. The difference between imposing unjustified harm and simply not preventing it is recognized throughout our moral system: the bystander who fails to thwart the preventable crime is not as culpable as the criminal.

From Alan H. Goldman, "Beyond the Deterrence Theory," 33 *Rutgers Law Review* 721 (1981). Excerpted and reprinted by permission.

Van den Haag's emphasis on the duty to punish the guilty allows an internal criticism as well. The deterrence theory he advocates might not allow punishment of all those who deserve it. He points to the match between deterrence and other theories in requiring fault before punishment may be imposed. We cannot deter actions for which the agents are not responsible. Unfortunately there may be undeterrable crimes involving fault as well. Crimes without premeditation, so-called "crimes of passion," may fall into that class. If such crimes could be separated from others whose perpetrators attempt to make them appear unpremeditated, then the goal of deterrence would not justify punishing truly unpremeditated crimes. Yet surely the fact that a crime is unplanned, that the criminal does not contemplate the consequences to him of his action, should not entirely exempt it from punishment.

More serious than the failure of deterrence theory to justify deserved punishments are its excesses in the other direction, its seeming capacity to warrant punishments beyond those deserved. The well-known problem of justifying not punishing innocents when this would successfully deter a greater number of potential criminals is but one instance of this broader affliction of the theory. Van den Haag argues that the goal of deterrence does not necessarily require punishing innocent persons, even when officials can reduce crime and protect others by doing so. He asserts that only the utilitarian versions of deterrence theory authorize such punishment if it serves to minimize the sum of harm or misery. Deterrent threats are justified ultimately to prevent violations of certain fundamental moral rules. But these rules need not be utilitarian. They might themselves prohibit deceptive policies and practices. Van den Haag argues that because punishment of the innocent is deceptive, and because it is also a crime, nonutilitarian deterrence theories need not hold this practice justified, even when it might succeed in its aim.

The problem with this argument as a way of avoiding the standard objection is that it fails to capture what is seriously wrong in punishing the innocent. It is not the deception of third parties that is so wrong; and certainly the victim himself is not deceived, although it is he who is primarily and most seriously wronged. The injustice lies in the violation of the victim's right not to be harmed. Few moral theories would prohibit deception of parties not directly involved in particular cases if great gains in welfare could be achieved by it. Most would prohibit the more serious harm imposed by punishment of a person who does not deserve to be punished. But deterrence theory, utilitarian or not, in seeking to justify punishment, looks only to the future good to be gained by it. Looking instead to the past and to individual deserts arising from past conduct is the orientation of the rival retributive theory. It is this alternative view that appears necessary, not only to protect the innocent, but also to protect the guilty against excessive punishment. Both needs arise from the broader requirement to treat people as they deserve in relation to their past conduct. Neither seems capable of capture by future-looking deterrence theory.

Van den Haag sees retributive theory as telling us only that we punish because we feel we ought to. Of course it tells us much more. As he points out, Kantian retributive theory involves the notion of consent by the criminal to his own punishment. The idea is not that criminals actually consent, but that we must treat them as rational subjects who responsibly choose certain courses of conduct. According to Kant, rational subjects, in recognizing the moral equality of others, universalize their principles of action. They act only in ways they would will or approve for all other agents. In punishing criminals, we universalize the consequences of their actions in relation to them; we treat them as they treat their victims. Since they cannot find morally relevant differences between themselves and their victims, as rational subjects they would have to consent to equal treatment. Thus punishment within retributive limits treats them as rational moral beings and restores their moral status in the community.

While Kant's theory does provide a deeper moral justification for the retributive demand that the punishment equal the crime, the premise that the recognition of others as moral equals constitutes a requirement of rationality itself remains questionable. Hence the notion of hypothetical consent no longer figures prominently in modern retributive theory. Van den Haag himself suggests that the rational criminal at least consents to the rules under which he is punished, but this is equally doubtful and in any case not necessary to the justification of his punishment. What remains accepted of Kant's theory is his model of society as a community of equal subjects (the "kingdom of ends"). Such citizens have equal rights, which they retain only as long as they continue to respect the same rights of others. When instead they violate certain rights of others, they forfeit those same or equivalent rights themselves. They may then be treated in a way equivalent to losing those rights, with the harm that results.

Hence the modern retributive theory, modeled not upon Kant's idea of rational consent, but upon his idea of a community of equal subjects all ends in themselves rather than means to communal welfare, continues to provide support for the equation of punishment with crime in determining degrees of harm imposed. This limit to justified punishment in relation to desert guarantees not only that innocents not be punished at all, but also that criminals not suffer more harm than they deserve. Certainly a criminal, in violating some rights of his victim, does not thereby forfeit all his own rights. We cannot slowly torture all criminals to death. If we ask which rights they do forfeit, the plausible answer appears to be the very ones they fail to respect. Forfeiture of rights is consequent upon and depends only upon the nature of the offending action, not upon how many more potential perpetrators remain to be deterred. This equation sets limits to justified punishments, limits necessary in the case of the guilty no less than in the case of the innocent. Only some form of retributive theory oriented toward past actions seems able to generate them.

Van den Haag is sensitive to this broader criticism of deterrence theory. He points out that the goal of deterrence itself tends to proportion penalties to the gravity of crimes. As Bentham argued, in order to discourage the escalation of minor crimes into major ones, in order to encourage the criminal to choose the lesser evil, deterrent threats must be more severe in relation to more serious potential crimes. If the penalty for rape or kidnapping is the same as for murder, for example, the rapist or kidnapper is encouraged to kill his victim and reduce his chances of apprehension. On utilitarian grounds, greater punishments for more serious crimes are further justified, first, to offset the greater gain to the potential criminal and so continue to deter him, and second, to protect the potential victim from greater harm.

Proportionality in deterrence is not equivalent, however, to the absolute limit on punishment entailed by retributive theories, nor is it sufficient to express our full moral sensibility. It is easy to provide examples in which all punishments are too severe. The state might, for example, impose penalties ranging from ten to thirty years in prison for crimes from shoplifting to armed robbery. It would be possible to create such a range of penalties, excessive in the author's view, and still have punishments outside this range for greater and lesser crimes. Thus proportionality is insufficient. The charge can be leveled that even fully proportionate penalties use criminals unjustly as means to better protect the community against other potential criminals. If it is not permissible to use those innocent of crimes for such purposes, then it does not seem right to so use those convicted either, that is, to inflict on them a level of punishment beyond that called for by their actions.

Van den Haag denies that deterrence theories use criminals merely as means, in violation of the Kantian injunctions. He asserts that punishments are not imposed simply to deter others; rather, it is the threat of punishment that is intended to be sufficient to deter criminal activity. Once threats have been made, failure to carry them through against criminals would amount to reneging on a promise made to others. These others would then have been deceived into forgoing gains on the understanding that they would have been punished for seeking them.

This argument resembles the retributivist claim that, in the absence of punishment, criminals achieve an unfair advantage over noncriminals. The difference is that van den Haag uses it only to justify the imposition of punishment once threatened. The threats themselves are strictly for deterrence purposes, and they must be adequate for those purposes. Perhaps his most important point here, however, is that criminals can avoid the punishment altogether because they are adequately forewarned. Therefore, when they assume the risks involved in criminal activity, despite the warnings, they must be seen as having done so voluntarily. Even given the risks, they must consider themselves as well off in relation to the rules as noncriminals, since they too could forgo the risks if they so chose. Thus van den Haag asserts that lesser threats would again give them an unfair advantage over others. Although they do not consent to their punishments, there is a sense in which they consent to taking the risk that they know may result in their being punished. In this sense van den Haag sees deterrence theory as meeting the Kantian requirement. Since criminals can avoid the harm imposed upon them while their victims cannot, the state is justified, according to this theory, in threatening criminals with whatever is necessary to protect their victims.

These points may be countered one at a time. First, representing the imposition of punishment as keeping a promise made to noncriminals does not show that criminals are not being unjustly used. Rather than used directly to deter others, they are used to maintain the plausibility of the threats and to honor the supposed promises. Promises, however, lack moral force when what is promised is itself morally impermissible. If *A* promises *B* that he will unjustly harm *B*'s rival, his promise ought not to be kept. Similarly, if the promise to punish criminals beyond retributive limits lacks independent moral warrant, it cannot justify the imposition of the punishment. It is of course also questionable whether noncriminals understand threats of punishment as promises made to them. The normally moral person presumably forgoes commission of serious crimes on independent moral grounds, not solely because of legal threats. The noncriminal might regret that a criminal who goes free did not receive his just deserts, but he would hardly regret his own missed chance at getting away with murder.

Similar reasoning applies to the relevance of having warned criminals of the risks of punishment assumed in their activities. Warning that a certain reaction will follow a certain course of conduct does not suffice to justify the reaction if it lacks independent warrant. *A*'s warning that he will assault *B* if *B* criticizes his argument does not warrant his doing so. Warning thieves that their hands will be cut off does not justify the punishment, even if, having been forewarned, they can avoid the penalty by refraining from further stealing. Advance announcements of penalties attached to various crimes may be a necessary condition for their just imposition; it is never sufficient. That punishment be within the limits set by retributive considerations of desert seems to be another necessary condition. Van den Haag does not succeed in showing that these considerations can be captured by deterrence theories alone.

Suggestions for Further Reading

1. The Concept of Deterrence

Zimring, F. E., *Perspectives on Deterrence* (1971); Zimring, F. E., and Hawkins, G., *Deterrence: The Legal Threat in Crime Control* (1973); Andenaes, J., *Punishment and Deterrence* (1974); Gibbs, J. P., *Crime, Punishment, and Deterrence* (1975); Posner, R., *Economic Analysis of Law* (2d ed., 1977); Beyleveld, D., "Identifying, Explaining, and Predicting Deterrence," 19 *British Journal of Criminology* 205 (1979); Pyle, D., *The Economics of Crime and Law Enforcement* (1983); Quinn, W., "The Right to Threaten and the Right to Punish," 4 *Philosophy and Public Affairs* 327 (1985).

2. Empirical Evidence of Deterrent Effects

The two most systematic analyses, both including extensive bibliographies, are Panel on Research on Deterrent and Incapacitative Effects, "Report," in Blumstein, A., Cohen, J., and Nagin, D. (eds.), *Deterrence and Incapacitation: Estimating the Effects of Criminal Sanctions on Crime Rates* (1978), and Beyleveld, D., *The Effectiveness of General Deterrents against Crime: An Annotated Bibliography of Evaluative Research* (1980). For other empirical evidence, see Willcock, H. D., and Stokes, J., *Deterrents and Incentives to Crime among Boys and Young Men Aged 15–21 Years* (1968); Buikhuisen, W., "General Deterrence: Research and Theory," 14 *Abstracts on Criminology and Penology* 285 (1974); Brody, S. R., *The Effectiveness of Sentencing* (1976); Grasmick, H. G., and Green, D., "Legal Punishment, Social Disapproval and Internalisation as Inhibitors of Illegal Behaviour," 71 *Journal of Criminal Law and Criminology* 325 (1980); Cook, Phillip J., "Research in Criminal Deterrence: Laying the Groundwork for the Second Decade," in Morris, N., and Tonry, M. (eds.), *Crime and Justice: An Annual Review,* vol. 2 (1980); Ross, H., *Deterring the Drinking Driver* (1982); Thornton, R., et al., *Tougher Regimes in Detention Centres* (1984), chs. 5 and 6; Bennett, T., and Wright, R., *Burglars on Burglary* (1984); Riley, D., "Drinking Drivers: The Limits to Deterrence?" 24 *Howard J.C.J.* 241 (1985); Cousineau, F. D., *Legal Sanctions and Deterrence* (1986); Williams, K. R., "Perceptual Research on General Deterrence: A Critical Review," 20 *Law and Society Review* 545 (1986); Harding, R., "Rational-Choice Gun Use in Armed Robbery: The Likely Effect on Gun Use of Additional Imprisonment," 1 *Criminal Law Forum* 427 (1991); Riley, D., *Drunk-Driving: The Effects of Enforcement* (1991); Nagin, D., and Paternoster, R., "The Preventive Effects of Perceived Risk of Arrest," 29 *Criminology* 561 (1991).

3. On the Pros and Cons of Deterrent Sentencing

De Tarde, G., *Penal Philosophy* (1912), esp. sec. 90; Becker, G. S., "Crime and Punishment: An Economic Approach," 76 *Journal of Political Economy* 169 (1968); Tullock, G., "Does Punishment Deter Crime?" [Summer 1974] *Public*

Interest 103; Becker, G. S., and Landes, W. M., *Essays in the Economics of Crime and Punishment* (1974); von Hirsch, A., *Doing Justice: The Choice of Punishments* (1976), ch. 7; Walker, N. D., "The Efficacy and Morality of Deterrents," *Criminal Law Review* 129 (1979); van den Haag, E., "Punishment as a Device for Controlling the Crime Rate," 33 *Rutgers Law Journal* 706 (1981); Goldman, H., "The Paradox of Punishment," 9 *Philosophy and Public Affairs* 42 (1981).

Chapter Three

INCAPACITATION

Incapacitation is the idea of simple restraint: rendering the convicted offender incapable, for a period of time, of offending again. Whereas rehabilitation involves changing the person's habits or attitudes so he or she becomes less criminally inclined, incapacitation presupposes no such change. Instead, obstacles are interposed to impede the person's carrying out whatever criminal inclinations he or she may have. Usually, the obstacle is the walls of a prison, but other incapacitative techniques are possible—such as exile or house arrest.

Incapacitation has, usually, been sought through predicting the offender's likelihood of reoffending. Those deemed more likely to reoffend are to be restrained, for example, by imposition of a term of imprisonment—or of a prison term of longer duration than they otherwise would receive. This predictive approach is evident in the Model Penal Code, set forth in part in Excerpt 1.1, above. The offender, according to § 7.01(1)(a) of the code, is to be imprisoned if "there is undue risk that [he or she] will commit another crime."

Who, then, is likely to reoffend? Prediction research in criminology has had a more than sixty-year history, beginning with S. B. Warner's statistical studies of recidivism among Massachusetts parolees in the 1920s and the Gluecks' prediction studies among juvenile delinquents in the 1930s. The basic research technique has been straightforward enough. Various facts about convicted criminals are recorded: previous arrests and convictions, social and employment history, prior drug use, and so forth; and those factors that are, statistically, most strongly associated with recidivism are identified. The prediction instrument, based on these factors, is then constructed and tested. The studies suggest that a limited capacity to predict does exist. Certain facts about offenders—principally, their previous criminal records, drug habits, and histories of unemployment—are (albeit only to a modest extent) indicative of increased likelihood of recidivism.[1]

Incapacitation was an important (although often less visible) element in the traditional rehabilitative penal ethic. Sentencing judges and correctional officials were supposed to gauge not only offenders' treatment needs but their likelihood of recidivism. "Curable" offenders were to be treated (in the community, if possible), but those judged bad risks were to be restrained. The traditional view had its appeal precisely because it thus offered both therapy and restraint. One did not have to assume that all criminals really were treatable, but merely that some might be. Therapy could be tried on the potentially responsive, but always with a fail-safe: the offender who seemed unsuitable for treatment could be separated from the community.

Illustrative of this dual approach—treatment in the community for seemingly treatable offenders, restraint for the bad risks—is the National Council on Crime and Delinquency's proposed Model Sentencing Act,[2] reproduced in part as Extract 3.1. The Act makes much of treatment: offenders, § 1 asserts, "shall be dealt with in accordance with their potential for rehabilitation, considering their individual characteristics, circumstances, and needs." In their commentary to that section, the drafters also emphasize their preference for community sanctions and for reduced reliance on imprisonment. Nevertheless, the scope for predictive confinement is great. Section 1 states that whereas nondangerous offenders are to be dealt with by noncustodial sentences, "dangerous offenders shall be identified [and] segregated . . . for long terms as needed." (During that custody, they are also to be "correctively treated.") Terms of up to five years are authorized for such individuals.[3] What constitutes a sufficient degree of dangerousness to warrant confinement is not defined by the Act.

A further provision, § 5, authorizes extraordinary terms—of up to *thirty* years—for offenders deemed especially dangerous. Here, the Act supplies something of a definition: such offenders include those who have inflicted or attempted to inflict serious bodily harm, provided the court finds the person "is suffering from a severe mental or emotional disorder indicating a propensity toward continuing dangerous criminal activity." That disorder, however, need not be so severe as to amount to legal insanity. (Indeed, the legally insane defendant would ordinarily be acquittable.)

The Act prompts a number of questions. Under § 1 and its associated provisions, the seriousness of the defendant's crime of conviction does not matter at all: a defendant convicted of *any* crime can be confined for up to five years if deemed dangerous. (It is only for extended terms up to thirty years, under § 5, that the Act requires the current crime to be one involving violence.) Does this almost complete disregard of the gravity of the current crime pose questions of fairness—particularly, of proportionality? The drafters of the Act, in their comments, say not—because concern over the gravity of the current offense would fail to take the actor's personality, and hence his possible dangerousness, into account. Is this a sufficient reply? Another question is the degree of discretion the Act allows. For sentences up to five years, the judge has unfettered leeway to decide whether and how long to imprison any defendant. Even for the longer terms under § 5, wide discretion remains: the judge merely "may" impose such extended terms. Is such broad leeway consistent with the idea of government by law? (This issue will be considered at length in Chapter 5.) Finally, how reliable are the predictions? For terms under five years, under the Act, the judge need consult only his or her own sense of how likely the defendant is to recidivate; for the longer terms, the judge is required to obtain a diagnostic report. But how trustworthy is a judge's (or even a diagnostician's) assessment of dangerousness?

The Model Sentencing Act is unusual in the very wide sweep of predictive power it allows. Actual sentencing statutes in most jurisdictions did not go quite so far. Usually, they imposed a maximum permitted sentence—and occasionally, a minimum sentence as well.[4] This meant that persons convicted of minor crimes could not receive sentences beyond the permitted maximum, on predictive grounds. For most felonies, however, the statutory maxima were high—giving wide scope to judges wishing to resort to incapacitative sentences.

In the early 1970s, some penologists began raising doubts about predictive restraint in sentencing. One such discussion by Andrew von Hirsch—which appeared, incidentally, in the same year as the Model Sentencing Act[5]—is excerpted in Extract 3.2.

Von Hirsch begins by noting that prediction in sentencing does not have to be left to a judge's personal judgment. Before a defendant is incarcerated on incapacitative grounds, the degree of harmfulness of the predicted conduct, and its required degree of likelihood, could be specified in advance. The predictions could also rely, not on someone's intuitive sense of who is a bad risk, but on statistically tested forecasting methods. The question asked is whether—once these threshold requirements are met—it is fair to rely on forecasts of dangerousness in deciding the sentence.

In this connection, von Hirsch points to the tendency of forecasts of criminality to overpredict. Although statistical forecasting methods can identify groups of offenders having higher than average probabilities of recidivism, these methods show a disturbing incidence of "false positives." Many of those classified as potential recidivists will, in fact, not be found to offend again. The rate of false positives is particularly high when forecasting serious criminality—for example, violence. The majority of those designated as dangerous turn out—when the predictions are followed up—to be persons who are not found to commit the predicted acts of violence when allowed to remain at large.

This tendency to overpredict, von Hirsch suggests, is not easily remediable because it results from the comparative rarity of the conduct to be forecasted. Serious crimes, such as acts of violence, are, statistically speaking, rather infrequent events. The rarer the event, the greater will be the incidence of false positives. When the conduct to be predicted occurs infrequently in the sample—and when the prediction method relies (as it must) on rough correlations between criminals' observed characteristics and their subsequent unlawful behavior—the forecaster will be able to spot the actual violators only if he or she includes a large number of false positives. It is like trying to shoot at a small, distant target with a blunderbuss: one can hit the target only if much of the discharge hits outside it.

False positives put the justice of predictive sentencing into question. Ostensibly, the offender classified as dangerous is confined to prevent him or her from infringing the rights of others. But to the extent the classification is mistaken, the offender would not have committed the infringement. The person's liberty is lost merely because people *like* him or her will offend again, and we cannot specify which of them will actually do so.

It should be noted, however, that the false positives argument is only a conditional challenge to predictive sentence: it questions not the propriety *per se* of confining an offender to prevent injury to others in future, but only the propriety of doing so erroneously. Concern about false positives might thus conceivably diminish were it possible to make predictions more accurate.[6]

The question of dangerousness became the focus of debate in Great Britain, after the publication of the so-called Floud Report in 1981.[7] Extract 3.3 is drawn from an article summarizing the report, by the report's principal author, Jean Floud. Floud concedes the recalcitrance of the false positive problem: in predictions of dangerousness, she admits, at least half of those classified as risks will mistakenly be so classified. With such a high incidence of error, how then can sentencing on the basis of dangerousness be justified? It can only be, she suggests, by the idea of shifting the burden of risk. An unconvicted dangerous person is entitled to remain at large, and any risk to potential victims must be borne by them. Once the person acts on the dangerous inclinations and is convicted for seriously harming others, however, we become entitled to shift the risk of victimization (in this case, of mistaken confinement) to the offender. Error is unavoidable, and the question is, who should bear its costs? However, Floud wishes to limit the scope of predictive sentencing. The protective sentence—which she defines as any duration of imprisonment exceeding the deserved term for the past crime—should be limited to cases where the predicted harm from the offender is quite severe.

The Floud report drew a number of replies, including that by David Wood, appearing as Extract 3.4. Wood notes that even if restraining the dangerous were justifiable on grounds such as Floud's "shifting of risk," one still has not explained why an offender's *punishment* should be extended on that ground. Punishment, Wood's argument assumes, involves not only deprivation but blame—so that increasing a punishment implies the offender to be more blameworthy. (For more discussion of this issue, see Excerpt 4.2.) There is nothing about a convicted offender's dangerousness—that is, the mere likelihood of offending again as contrasted with the degree of culpability for crimes already committed—which renders him or her more to blame. Thus if confining offenders beyond their deserved term of punishment were justifiable at all, that confinement should be civil, not criminal.

A defense of predictive sentencing—within certain limits—is provided by Norval Morris, in Extract 3.5. Morris begins by questioning whether false positives really are a problem. A prediction of dangerousness, Morris asserts, is a statement of present condition: it is saying that a person is now able and inclined to injure someone. That statement of present capability and inclination is not falsified by the fact that the person turns out not to commit the harm. Morris draws the analogy to the unexploded bombs found after World War II in various London sites. There were few injuries—hence the rate of false positives was high. Yet who would deny that the bombs were dangerous? One wonders, however, about such analogies. Bombs are not thought of as individuals with rights, so that the destruction of a bombshell that might have exploded is not something that should trouble us. Offenders, by contrast, are persons with rights—ones which they lose by being confined. If that loss is justified by reference to the injury such persons would have visited on others, is it not a matter of legitimate concern how often such predictions turn out correct?

False positives, however, may not be the central issue. What is fundamental, instead, is the extent to which predictive sentencing is consistent with notions of proportionality. Extending a person's *punishment* beyond his or her deserved term is problematic (as Wood notes),[8] and it would remain so even if the predictions were quite accurate. If notions of desert are less precise, however—if they offer merely a range of permitted punishment—then relying on predictions within that permitted range could be morally permissible even if prediction errors inevitably do occur.

Morris adopts this latter view of desert as offering only certain bounds on permitted punishment. He defends it in a subsequent selection (Extract 4.3), and his point here is simply that prediction is justified within such bounds. If a fair reflection of the blameworthiness of a given offense consists of a term of imprisonment somewhere between *x* and *y* months, then a nondangerous offender may legitimately receive a sentence closer to the lower bound, *x*, and the high-risk offender may legitimately receive one closer to the upper bound, *y*. Of course, this view is only as strong as its major premise, that desert offers only broad limits; and would require a theory about how those limits are to be identified. The justification of this premise—and the question of whether Morris can specify such limits adequately—is debated later (see, particularly, Extracts 3.8 and 4.4).

If one accepts Morris's premise, the further question arises about whether—within his purported desert limits—there should be *any* requirement regarding the accuracy of the prediction. Could one offender get near the lower limit, *x*, and another near the upper limit, *y*, merely on the basis of a decision maker's hunch that the latter person is more dangerous? Here, Morris adopts a fairly stringent criterion of predictive acuity: the prediction needs to be *statistically* supported, and those statistics must show the person has a significantly higher likelihood of offending than other offenders of comparable crimes and criminal record. He does not, however, explain why this criterion should be imposed. Could any reasons be offered?

In the early 1980s, a number of studies, based mainly on interviews with incarcerated offenders, suggested that offense patterns are highly skewed, even among those individuals who recidivate after being convicted. While some recidivists reoffended only occasionally, others appeared to revert to serious criminality frequently. If incapacitative techniques could be targeted to the latter group—to the frequent, serious violators—might these techniques not offer hope, after all, for reducing crime?

It was during this period that Peter Greenwood, a Rand Corporation researcher, published a report on a prediction technique which he termed "selective incapacitation." The technique, derived from interviews with confined offenders, made use of a few simple indicia of dangerousness, concerned mainly with the offender's criminal, unemployment, and drug-use histories. It was designed to identify "high-rate" predators—those who would commit violent offenses (such as robbery) frequently. Because so many robberies were being committed by a small group of active predators, he argued, identifying and isolating these persons could considerably reduce the incidence of such crimes. Greenwood devised a method of projecting the resulting crime reduction effect. He estimated that imposing longer prison terms for the high-rate offenders could reduce the robbery rate by as much as 15 to 20 percent, without even any significant increase in prison populations.

Greenwood's suggestions generated considerable interest among criminologists and policymakers. Selective incapacitation is described with approval by James Q. Wilson, in a 1983 book from which Extract 3.6 is taken. It provides a useful summary of the technique and of the studies from which it is drawn.

Wilson, at the end of the extract, turns to the possible moral objections to selective incapacitation, and dismisses them. Selective incapacitation is not unfair or undeserved, he asserts, because desert sets merely the broadest outer limits on permissible punishments. Reliance on status factors such as employment is no serious problem, because such factors are used by the criminal justice system in other contexts. The possible inaccuracies of the prediction technique should be no bar to use, because the technique is superior to the informal predictive judgments that judges and prosecutors make today. How convincing are these arguments?

The optimism that Wilson shows about selective incapacitation was soon challenged, however. Objections were raised both about the empirical soundness of the technique and about its ethics. These objections are summarized in Extract 3.7, by Andrew von Hirsch.

The empirical objections need not be rehearsed at length here, as Extract 3.7 describes them. It is uncertain whether Greenwood's factors can identify high-rate offenders, once official data that courts must rely upon are utilized, instead of offenders' self-reports of their own criminal activities. The projections of large crime-reduction effects are also suspect. Those projections rely on questionable extrapolations, from the criminal activity of *incarcerated* offenders to the activity of offenders generally. The projections also appear to make unrealistic estimates of such important factors as the anticipated length of offenders' criminal careers. In 1986, a research panel of the National Academy of Sciences examined these issues, and concluded that selective incapacitation, at least today, has a much more modest crime-reduction potential than Greenwood and Wilson claim.[9]

The ethical objection to selective incapacitation, also addressed in Extract 3.7, consists chiefly in the strategy's conflict with the requirements of proportionality. Selective incapacitation relies upon factors (e.g., early criminal history, drug use, and so forth) that have little bearing on the blameworthiness of the criminal conduct for which the offender stands convicted. The strategy can have significant crime prevention effects by its own proponents' reckoning, moreover, only if disparities among those convicted of comparable offenses are very large: the prison sentences visited on "high-risk" felons must be *much* longer than those visited on lower-risk felons convicted of the same offense. To sustain such large disparities, proportionality must either be disregarded entirely or be treated as only marginal constraint.[10]

A final selection by Michael Tonry, Extract 3.8, takes a closer look at the debate over the ethics of predictive sentencing. He suggests how the force of ethical objections to such strategies depends on the role and weight given to the idea of proportionality. This essay is particularly helpful, because it addresses specifically the views of several authors whose writings appear in previous excerpts.[11]

A.v.H.

Notes

1. For a fuller description of such prediction techniques and their methodology and results, see Don M. Gottfredson, "Assessment and Prediction Methods in Crime and Delinquency," in President's National Commission for Law Enforcement and Administration of Justice, *Task Force Report: Juvenile Delinquency and Youth Crime* (Washington, D.C.: U.S. Government Printing Office, 1967).
2. The Act was prepared by an advisory council of judges, sponsored by the National Council on Crime and Delinquency. The Act is model legislation only. This is the second edition, published in 1972. The first edition appeared in 1963.
3. This five-year limit is set forth in another provision of the Act, § 9.
4. See MODEL PENAL CODE §§ 6.06 and 6.07, set forth in Extract 1.1, above.
5. The year was 1972.
6. For a fuller discussion, see Andrew von Hirsch, *Past or Future Crimes* (New Brunswick, N.J.: 1985), App. 1.
7. The report is Jean Floud and Warren Young, *Dangerousness and Criminal Justice* (London: Heinemann, 1981).
8. See Extract 3.4.
9. The report is set forth in National Academy of Sciences, Panel on Research on Criminal Careers, *Report,* in A. Blumstein, J. Cohen, J. Roth, and Christy Visher, eds., *Criminal Careers and "Career Criminals"* (Washington, D.C.: National Academy Press, 1986). For analysis of this report, see Andrew von Hirsch, "Selective Incapacitation Reexamined," 7 *Criminal Justice Ethics* 19 (1988).
10. For fuller discussion, see A. von Hirsch, *Past or Future Crimes,* op. cit., chs. 11 and 14. Note the emphasis is on the issue of proportionality—no longer on false positives as in Extract 3.2. For reasons why this shift of emphasis, see *id.,* App.1.
11. These include Floud (Extract 3.3), Morris (Extract 3.5), and von Hirsch (Extracts 3.2 and 3.7).

3.1
Sentencing on the Basis of Risk: The Model Sentencing Act

§ 1. Purpose and Policy

The purpose of penal codes and sentencing is public protection. Sentences should not be based upon revenge and retribution. The policy of this Act is that dangerous offenders shall be identified, segregated, and correctively treated in custody for long terms as needed and that other offenders may be committed for a limited period. Nondangerous offenders shall be dealt with by probation, suspended sentence, or fine wherever it appears that such disposition does not pose a danger of serious harm to public safety.

Persons convicted of crime shall be dealt with in accordance with their potential for rehabilitation, considering their individual characteristics, circumstances, and needs.

Although in general the nature of penal treatment is determined primarily by the quality of the custodial, supervisory, and administrative personnel, the philosophy and legal structure of sentencing are highly influential.

The legal structure controls the use of community treatment, suspended sentence, probation, and fines; specifies the length and place of confinement; and limits or facilitates a parole board's operation.

A model sentencing system must point the way to adequate protection of the public, as far as that can be obtained by the sentence. Sentencing on

From Council of Judges, National Council on Crime and Delinquency, "Model Sentencing Act, 2d Edition," 18 *Crime and Delinquency* 335 (1972).

the basis of the offense does not satisfactorily provide public protection, because it does not sufficiently take into account the offender's personality.

A sentence that allows a defendant to remain in the community is preferred if it does not substantially compromise public safety—preferred because it entails lower cost to the taxpayer and less disruption to the life of the defendant and his family. The philosophy stated in this section supports noninstitutional sentences wherever commitment is not clearly needed for public protection. Hence the statement at the outset that the purpose of penal codes and sentences is public protection.

In cases where the harm was slight or where the mere apprehension and prosecution are deemed sufficient for the purposes of deterrence, a suspended sentence may be the best alternative. Where greater control is required, probation or commitment is indicated, but not because the judge thinks it will do the defendant some good. Vengeance or punishment is not a proper motive for a sentence; so neither is treatment. The dominant purpose of the sentence—not only commitment but also suspended sentence, probation, and fine—is public protection.

§ 5. Dangerous Offenders

Except for the crime of murder in the first degree, the court may sentence a defendant to a term of commitment of years stated but not more than thirty years if either of the following grounds is found to exist:

1. The defendant is being sentenced for a felony in which he (a) inflicted or attempted to inflict serious bodily harm or (b) seriously endangered the life or safety of another and he was previously convicted of one or more felonies not related to the instant crime as a single criminal episode, and (c) the court finds that he is suffering from a severe mental or emotional disorder indicating a propensity toward continuing dangerous criminal activity.

Whenever the court, upon entering the conviction or receiving the investigation report, has reason to believe the defendant falls within the category of subdivision 1(a) or 1(b), it shall refer him to [a diagnostic facility] for study and report as to whether he is suffering from a severe mental or emotional disorder indicating a propensity toward continuing dangerous criminal activity.

The Model Act establishes a legally and socially precise delineation of dangerous persons and a legally and clinically careful procedure for identifying them. It proposes that an offender be sentenced as dangerous if he fits into these categories: (1) he inflicted or attempted to inflict serious bodily harm, and he has a propensity to commit crime; (2) he committed a crime (such as arson) which, intended or not, seriously endangered the life or safety of another, he has a previous criminal conviction, and he has a propensity to commit crime.

The Assaultive Offender

The requirement of diagnosis of severe mental or emotional disorder indicating a propensity toward continuing dangerous criminal activity is admittedly difficult to accept, and we do not dismiss its uncertainties in theory and practice. The behavioral sciences do not now have sufficient expertise to carry out this assignment adequately. How, then, can the procedure be made operable?

First, contrary to the impression that some people receive or give, the effect of the diagnosis provision will be in general to shorten terms, not to lengthen them. In almost all jurisdictions today, in the absence of usable criteria and wholly at the discretion of the sentencing judge, sentences of thirty years and more are not rare.

In contrast, a term of such length may, under the Model Act, not be imposed without meeting certain criteria.

A diagnostic clinic has no difficulty determining whether a man is suffering from a severe mental or emotional disorder. Relating that kind of diagnosis to a likelihood that he will commit further crimes does present a problem. But even here the Model Act says that the defendant's likelihood of committing further crimes must be supported by his record.

In the light of today's limited knowledge of prediction of criminal behavior (or any behavior), we make it clear that the judge, representing society, makes a commonsense decision based on as much relevant information as possible. Sentencing of *any* offender is a judicial task, not a decision for doctors or behavioral scientists.

But the expertise of psychologists and psychiatrists can be helpful to the judge.

Only a small percentage of offenders in penal institutions today meet the criteria of dangerousness. In any state no more than one hundred persons would have to be confined in a single maximum-security institution, which, because of its small size, could be staffed for genuine treatment; other offenders would be either on probation or in institutions of less than maximum security. The reduction in costs would be considerable, protection of the public would not suffer, and the treatment of offenders, both dangerous and nondangerous, would probably be more effective.

We also make clear that a mentally disordered offender who commits an offense other than those cited in the section (for example, a writer of bad checks) may not be committed as a dangerous offender.

In subdivision 1(c) the language used is "severe mental or emotional disorder," contrasting with "severe personality disorder" in the first edition. The change was adopted because a number of psychiatrists had pointed out that the term "personality disorder" might be mistakenly construed as the classification of a specific type of disorder. Our intent, now clarified, was to refer to defendants who, in the terms of laymen, were suffering from some mental or emotional disorder and not to limit the disorder to any one specific diagnosis.

Terms of Commitment of Dangerous Offenders

Section 5 authorizes commitment of dangerous offenders for a period long enough—up to thirty years—to protect the public against them and to afford ample opportunity for therapeutic efforts to be made. The statutory maximum is not mandatory; the judge may fix the maximum at any period less than thirty years. This discretion is provided for in the case of long-term commitments to give scope to individualized consideration of the defendant.

Consideration was given to the suggestion that a defendant sentenced to a term of more than five years should be given a right to have his continuing confinement reexamined by a court upon an institutional report at regular intervals. Such a proposal was not incorporated in the Act. Periodic review by the institution and parole authorities should occur—and it does—without requirement by statute. A statutory requirement might have a limiting effect on administrative review. A statute that would make review mandatory every year would be disapproved by administration as too rigid; on the other hand, expressly authorizing review at some significantly greater interval, such as five years, might induce laxity and would encourage an acceptance of long-term incarceration.

3.2
Prediction and False Positives

Andrew von Hirsch

We might start our analysis by examining the following theoretical model:

The Preventive Confinement Model. In an imaginary jurisdiction, a person convicted of a criminal offense would be subject to preventive confinement for an indeterminate term, if specified predictive criteria indicated a high probability of his committing a serious offense in the future. Following completion of his term in prison for the offense of which he was convicted, he would be transferred to and confined in a special facility designed solely for preventive purposes, in which living conditions would be made as "pleasant," that is, as little punitive, as possible, consistent with the fact of incarceration itself. The individual would not be subjected to mandatory rehabilitative treatment during confinement in this special facility. The duration of confinement could substantially exceed the maximum statutory term of punishment prescribed for the offense of which he had been convicted. He would be released only at such time as he is found no longer to meet the predictive criteria for dangerousness.

In actual practice, preventive confinement frequently is mixed with other elements. By giving the parole board plenary discretion to determine an adult offender's release date, the California indeterminate sentence law allows preventive considerations to be mixed with judgments concerning punishment, treatment, and institutional convenience.[1] In these contexts, it is difficult to isolate and analyze the preventive component of decisions to confine.

In our theoretical model, however, the preventive component is separately identified. The offender serves an indeterminate term in a special

---

From Andrew von Hirsch, "Prediction of Criminal Conduct and Preventive Confinement of Convicted Persons," 21 *Buffalo Law Review* 717 (1972). Excerpted and reprinted by permission.

facility in which confinement is *for preventive purposes only*. The duration of confinement in that facility would be set *solely on the basis of a prediction of his individual future dangerousness, without regard to the nature of his past offense.*

Thus the model gives us the opportunity to evaluate preventive confinement in its more or less "pure state."

To have any possible merit, the model should satisfy three important threshold requirements: (1) there must be reasonably precise legal standards of dangerousness; (2) the prediction methods used must be subjected to careful and continuous validation; and (3) the procedure for commitment must provide the defendant with certain minimal procedural safeguards. These requirements, however, are seldom met by current practices of preventive confinement.

Explicit Legal Standards of Dangerousness

As Dershowitz[2] and Goldstein and Katz[3] have pointed out in connection with the law of commitment of the insane, a supposedly "dangerous" person should never be preventively confined, unless the "danger" he poses is of sufficient gravity—and sufficient likelihood—to warrant deprivation of his freedom. That determination—of the seriousness and likelihood of the predicted misconduct required to justify confinement—is a value judgment the *law* should make; it is not a factual judgment within the professional competence of psychiatrists or other expert witnesses. Failure to provide explicit legal standards of "dangerousness" creates the unacceptable situation where, for example, one psychiatrist can decide that only those mental patients who are likely to perpetrate violent crimes ought to be confined, while another psychiatrist, depending upon his personal philosophy, can employ the concept of "dangerousness" to confine potential minor offenders as well.

These considerations apply with equal force to the preventive incarceration of convicted persons. Yet existing preventive confinement schemes seldom, if ever, provide legal standards of dangerousness which have any definiteness.

Validating the Predictive Method

In commitment proceedings for the mentally ill, there is rarely any effort made to check the accuracy of psychiatric predictions of dangerousness by following up and tabulating their results.[4] The same absence of validation pervades the existing preventive confinement practice for some offenders.

Not surprisingly under these circumstances, unverified predictions of dangerousness prove fallible, indeed, when their accuracy is subsequently examined by scholars.

Predictions by supposedly "expert" correctional personnel show this proneness to error, as a study by Hakeem suggests.[5] He requested ten trained parole officers and ten laymen with no correctional experience to make a series of predictions of parole survival on the basis of case summaries of two hundred parolees, half of whom had been recommitted for parole violations and half of whom had not. He found that the laymen were substantially *more* accurate predictors than the parole officers. Moreover, both groups combined made fewer correct identifications of the nonviolators than would have been made by random selection.

Thus a second threshold requirement for acceptability of the model would be that its predictive method carefully be validated *in advance* of being applied in actual decisions to confine; and be subject to continual follow-up and review.

Even if these threshold requirements are satisfied, however, the preventive model will encounter a formidable theoretical impediment to prediction: the false positive problem.

The Significance of False Positives

Starting in the early 1920s with S. B. Warner's statistical study of recidivism among prisoners paroled from the Massachusetts State Reformatory and with the Gluecks' widely publicized prediction studies, an extensive literature has developed concerning the statistical prediction of parole recidivism and of delinquency.[6]

As Wilkins points out in his perceptive *Evaluation of Penal Measures*,[7] there has been a tendency in this predictive literature to adopt a rather one-sided criterion for success. A prediction table for delinquency or recidivism is thought effective if it can correctly forecast a relatively high proportion of those individuals who actually become delinquent or recidivist. The other side of the coin is less often considered: the so-called *false positives*—those mistakenly predicted to engage in such deviant conduct. There has been an inclination to overlook how many nondelinquents or nonrecidivists a prediction table incorrectly classifies as potentially deviant.

In certain types of prediction, the criteria for success need not be too seriously concerned with false positives. If, for example, we develop a prediction table for recruitment into the army,[8] the table may well be useful if it successfully identifies a high percentage of individuals actually unsuitable for the service, who can then be screened out. If the manpower pool is ample, it does not really matter that the predictive index also yields a substantial number of false positives—individuals actually suitable for the service who are rejected as a result of a mistaken prediction of unsuitability. For the army does not need to recruit all suitable persons, and the impact upon affected individuals of a mistaken prediction of unsuitability generally is not damaging.

In predicting criminal conduct, however, the consequences of ignoring the false positives are much more serious. As Wilkins points out:

> Taking a sample of offenders and showing that a large proportion would have scored in the delinquent category does not validate the prediction. Yet claims of this kind are frequently found. If decisions are made upon the basis of prediction statements, it is to be expected that the consequences of errors in each class will be different. It may be more damaging to regard (predict) a person as delinquent or recidivist when this is incorrect, than to incorrectly regard a person as nondelinquent or nonrecidivist. Some recent writers have claimed that the first kind of error can lead to a self-fulfilling prophecy—the labeling process of classification as "likely delinquent" may change the perception of the person by others, and through this, his own self-image.[9]

In the context of our model system of preventive incarceration, we can afford little tolerance, indeed, of prediction methods that show a high yield of false positives. Here, mistakenly predicting nondangerous individuals to be dangerous is gravely damaging—for it can lead to their prolonged incarceration.

The Rare Event and False Positives: The Rosen Suicide Model

It might be hoped that with increased attention to the false positive problem and sufficient expenditure of time, money, and effort, superior predictive indices could be developed which would be relatively free of false positives. That hope, however, may be misplaced—for there exist theoretical impediments to prediction of criminal conduct notwithstanding such efforts at improvement.

Generally speaking, criminal conduct tends to have two characteristics which make it resistant to accurate prediction:

1. It is comparatively rare. The more dangerous the conduct is, the rarer it is. Violent crime—perhaps the most dangerous of all—is the rarest of all.
2. It has no known, clearly identifiable symptoms. Prediction therefore becomes a matter of developing statistical correlations between observed characteristics of offenders and subsequent criminal conduct.

Where those two conditions obtain, false positives show a high degree of persistence, even in a theoretical predictive model.

In a valuable 1954 article,[10] Albert Rosen of the University of Minnesota developed a theoretical model for predicting suicide among mental patients that illustrates this problem. Rosen constructed a hypothetical suicide detection index for an assumed population of 12,000 mental patients. On the basis of existing suicide statistics, he assumed that the rate of suicides was very low—one-third of one percent of the total patient population. With this low rate, only 40 patients out of the initial population of 12,000 would actually commit suicide. Thus, without any test, *all* patients in this population could be predicted to be nonsuicidal, and the prediction would be right in 99⅔ percent of all cases. A hypothetical suicide detection index would have to perform better than this in identifying the potential suicides.

Rosen assumes such a hypothetical index is developed as follows: (1) the patient population is divided into two groups—patients who actually committed suicide during confinement (suicide population) and patients who did not (nonsuicide population); (2) a random sample is selected and analyzed from each population; (3) a predictive index is developed, based upon the test data which significantly differentiate the two criterion samples; (4) a cutting line is established—that is, a differentiating score on the index, so that patients testing above that score would be classified as suicidal and patients testing below that score would be classified as nonsuidal; and (5) the cutting line is cross-validated—that is, it is validated with new suicide and nonsuicide samples, every psychiatric patient over a period of years being scored on the index.

Such an index, Rosen finds, can identify a significant number of true positives only by misidentifying a very much larger number of false positives. If an effort is made to reduce the false positives to a manageable number, only a tiny fraction of the true positives can be spotted—and even then, there are many more false positives than true positives.

Suppose the cutting line is established at a point where, after cross-validation, the index will correctly identify 75 percent of the patients in both the suicide and the nonsuicide populations. Using this cutting line, the index *will correctly identify 30 of the 40 actual suicides.* However, Rosen indicates, *it will also incorrectly identify 2,990 nonsuicidal patients as potentially suicidal.* The false positive rate here is so high as to make the prediction, in his words, "[of] no appreciable value, for it would be impractical to treat as suicidal the prodigious number of misclassified cases."[11]

Suppose, then, a much higher cutting line is established—one which, when cross-validated, will correctly identify 90 percent of the nonsuicide cases. It is assumed that the new cutting line reduces to 60 percent (regarded by Rosen as a liberal estimate) the proportion of correctly classified suicidal patients. Using this new cutting line, the index *will correctly identify 24 out of 40 actual suicides,* but still *will misidentify as suicidal 1,196 false positives.* This is still "an impractical instrument because of the large number of false positives."[12]

With every elevation of the cutting line, Rosen shows, there would be some reduction in the number of false positives. However, there would be a corresponding shrinkage in the number of true positives. And the false positives will continue to greatly outnumber the true.

To achieve a better result, the experimenter might try to seek to develop a predictive index for a special diagnostic subgroup that has a substantially higher suicide rate than the general mental patient population. But, as Rosen points out, there are inherent limitations in this approach. Any such diagnostic subgroup would be unlikely to have a suicide rate much higher than 2 percent, and that still would yield an excessive number of false positives. Moreover, a considerable proportion of the actual suicidal patients in the entire sample population would then be *excluded* from the diagnostic subgroup.

Violent Crimes and False Positives

Like suicide, crimes of violence are infrequent events. They are rare not only among the general population, but also (as will be discussed below) among previous offenders who have been released. The Rosen model thus has applicability to violent crimes, as well as to suicide. Predictions of violence tend to yield large numbers of false positives.

What makes violence so particularly difficult to predict is not merely its rarity, but its situational quality. Deterministic models to the contrary notwithstanding, violence generally is not a quality which inheres in certain "dangerous" individuals: it is an occurrence which may erupt—or may not—in certain crisis situations. Whether it does erupt, whether it is reported, whether the perpetrator is apprehended and punished, depend upon a wide variety of fortuitous circumstances, largely beyond the actor's control. Not only the actor's proclivities, but the decisions of other individuals—the victim, the bystanders, the police, the magistrate—may determine whether an act of violence occurs and whether it comes to be included in the criminal statistics.

The difficulty of predicting violent criminal behavior is strikingly illustrated by a recent study by Wenk and Robison of violent recidivism among California Youth Authority wards.[13] Wenk and Robison examined the records of all juvenile offenders who were processed during 1964–66 through the Deuel Reception-Guidance Center, a diagnostic unit that examines older juvenile offenders at the time they are committed to the Youth Authority. A follow-up study was made of their behavior on parole for a period of fifteen months after release from confinement—with a view to determining how many were recommitted for a violent offense. As nearly one-quarter of the sample had originally been committed for a violent offense or had a history of known violent behavior, the violence potential of the group might have been expected to be relatively high. Nevertheless, the investigators found that of this entire group, the incidence of violent recidivism during the fifteen-month follow-up period was only 2.4 percent. As Rosen's analysis of his suicide model indicates, constructing a hypothetical predictive index upon a base rate as low as that—only 2.4 percent—would yield an unmanageable number of false positives.

Wenk and Robison's own tentative analysis supports this conclusion. They requested a psychologist and a statistician to project hypothetical predictive indices for violent recidivism, based upon the data in their sample. The *less* pessimistic projection—that of the psychologist—was that a multivariable multiple regression equation could be developed from the data, which could identify about one-half of the true positives, *but in which the false positives would outnumber the true positives by a discouraging eight to one.*

Selection of High-Risk Subgroups

One strategy mentioned by Rosen for avoiding the false positive problem was to develop a predictive index only for narrowly defined subgroups of the original sample population, which manifest a considerably higher rate of the behavior to be tested.[14] Applying this strategy to predictions of violent crime, we might try to construct a predictive instrument only for special subgroups of the convicted offender population, which manifest a substantially higher rate of violence.

The Wenk and Robison study suggests, however, that there may be serious obstacles to such a strategy. Their investigation identified five subgroups which manifested higher rates of violent recidivism than the general sample population.[15] The subgroups were: (1) offenders with known histories of violence; (2) offenders originally committed on a violent offense charge; (3) offenders committed to the Youth Authority for the fourth time or more (i.e., multiple recidivists); (4) offenders with histories of "moderate to serious" opiate involvement; and (5) offenders referred to a psychiatrist for violence potential upon commitment to the Youth Authority. The investigators' results indicated that *none* of these subgroups manifested a high enough incidence of violent recidivism to avoid the false positive problem. The highest rate (for category 5) was 6.2 percent; the other categories showed rates of about 5 percent or less. These rates are well below the frequency needed for constructing an instrument relatively free of false positives—which should be closer to 50 percent.

Moreover, Wenk and Robison found that all these subgroups, except the first, account for a rather small fraction of the total incidence of violent recidivism in the sample population. For example, offenders in category 5, which manifests the highest rate of violence, account for only 15 percent of the total incidence of violence on parole in the entire group. This creates another difficulty. If to construct an accurate predictive index we are forced to limit its application to defined, high-risk subgroups that account for only a small fraction of the total occurrence of violence, then the public obtains little additional protection from preventive confinement so limited in scope.

Inclusion of Lesser Offenses

Another avoidance strategy might be to include nonviolent offenses—since they are much more frequent. In the Wenk and Robison study, for example, if all parole violations are considered—which include not only violent crimes but also property crimes and other lesser offenses—then the recidivism rate climbs to a more statistically manageable 39.9 percent. Another serious objection is encountered here, however. To obtain the needed higher offense rates, we would find ourselves fast descending the scale of seriousness toward the minor offenses. Then, it becomes increasingly difficult to demonstrate a need for societal protection of the degree of urgency that could conceivably warrant the kind of deprivation of liberty contemplated in the model.

Concealing Overprediction

Even were we to extricate ourselves from this last difficulty we face another formidable theoretical problem: any system of preventive incarceration *conceals erroneous confinements, while revealing erroneous releases.*[16] The individual who is wrongly identified as dangerous is confined, and thus has little or no opportunity to demonstrate that he would not have committed the crime had he been released. The individual who is wrongly identified as nondangerous remains at large, so it comes to public attention if he later commits a crime. Thus, once a preventive system is established, it creates the illusion of generating only one kind of evidence: *evidence of erroneous release, that prompts decision makers to expand the categories of persons who are preventively confined.* In short, a system of preventive confinement creates a self-fulfilling prophecy for the need of *more* preventive incarceration.[17]

Moreover, the problem of distortion of evidence would greatly be compounded by political-bureaucratic pressures. Under a system of preventive confinement, the public undoubtedly would hold officials responsible if they fail to incarcerate (or if they release) persons who subsequently do commit violent criminal acts. This would create overwhelming pressures upon officials to overpredict—since it would entail much less risk to the institution and to their own careers for them to confine (or fail to release) persons who actually are or have become harmless, than to release persons who are actually dangerous and do subsequently perpetrate crimes.

We are now ready to evaluate our model of preventive confinement. Let us begin by assuming that the technique of prediction used in the model manifests a relatively high incidence of false positives. More specifically, let us suppose that the prediction method *generates false positives at a rate which substantially exceeds the rate of erroneous convictions under the existing system of criminal justice for those categories of offenses.* (Since there is little available evidence concerning the rate of mistaken convictions, it is difficult to confirm that any given rate of false positives would, or would not, substantially exceed it. But if the rate of false positives is of the high order of magnitude discussed in the preceding analysis—say, the eight false positives to every one true positive suggested by the Wenk and Robison study—it is fairly safe to conjecture that, in Dershowitz's words, "any system of predicting future crimes would result in a vastly larger number of erroneous confinements"[18] than could be expected to occur under the present criminal justice system.)

To sustain the model where false positives are present, a cost-benefit rationale must be assumed. Proponents of preventive confinement must argue in terms of "balancing" the individual's interest in not being mistakenly confined against society's need for protection from the actually dangerous person. It has to be contended that the "benefit" of preventing the really dangerous individual from committing future crimes exceeds, in the aggregate, the "cost" of mistakenly identifying and confining the nondangerous one.

Even if this kind of cost-benefit thinking were appropriate, it is highly questionable whether the preventive confinement model could be justified in its terms—once the magnitude of the "cost" of confining large numbers of false positives is fully taken into account. That is especially true because—for reasons just noted—strategies designed to minimize the number of false positives also sharply reduce the number of true positives that can be identified—and hence, minimize the social benefits of the system as a crime prevention device.

The more basic point, however, is that *cost-benefit thinking is wholly inappropriate here.* If a system of preventive incarceration is known systematically to generate mistaken confinements, then it is unacceptable in absolute terms because it violates the obligation of society to do *individual* justice. Such a system cannot be justified by arguing that its aggregate social benefits exceed the aggregate amount of injustice done to mistakenly confined individuals.

Notes

1. See, e.g., Mitford, "Kind and Usual Punishment in California," *The Atlantic,* March 1971, at 46. [This indeterminate sentence law was repealed subsequently in 1976—Eds.]
2. Dershowitz, "The Law of Dangerousness: Some Fictions about Predictions," 23 *J. Legal Ed.* 24 (1970).
3. Goldstein and Katz, "Dangerousness and Mental Illness: Some Observations on the Decision to Release Persons Acquitted by Reason of Insanity," 70 *Yale L.J.* 225 (1960).
4. Dershowitz, "The Law of Dangerousness," *supra* note 2.
5. Hakeem, "Prediction of Parole Outcome from Summaries of Case Histories," 52 *J. Crim. L.C. & P.S.* 145 (1961).
6. The Warner, Glueck, and other studies are summarized in H. Mannheim and L. Wilkins, *Prediction Methods in Relation to Borstal Training* (1955), ch. 1.
7. L. Wilkins, *Evaluation of Penal Measures* (1969), ch. 5.
8. For an example of such a prediction study designed for army recruitment purposes, see Danielson and Clark, "A Personality Inventory for Induction Screening," 10 *J. Clin. Psychol.* 137 (1954). The design of that study, however, was criticized in Meehl and Rosen, "Antecedent Probability and the Efficiency of Psychometric Signs, Patterns, and Cutting Scores," 52 *Psychol. Bull.* 194 (1955).
9. L. Wilkins, *supra* note 7, at 69–70.
10. Rosen, "Detection of Suicidal Patients: An Example of Some Limitations in the Prediction of Infrequent Events," 18 *J. Consulting Psych.* 397 (1954).
11. *Id.* at 399.
12. *Id.* at 400.
13. E. Wenk and J. Robison, "Assaultive Experience and Assaultive Potential," May 1971 (unpublished paper, National Council on Crime and Delinquency Research Center, Davis, Cal.).
14. See previous discussion.

15. Wenk and Robison, *supra* note 13, at 27–38.

16. Dershowitz, "On Preventive Detention," in *Crime, Law, and Society* 307–19 (A. S. Goldstein and J. Goldstein eds. 1971).

17. To avoid this distortion of the evidence, it has been suggested that a random sample of the population of those preventively confined be released from time to time, and the accuracy of the prediction be tested upon that sample. That may get us involved, however, in the problem of infrequent events. If we are trying to predict violent crimes, where the offense rate is very low, a substantial number of persons would have to be released at random in order to be able to measure the effectiveness of the criteria. This would pose serious problems of fairness for those who remain subject to confinement. Also, any large-scale random release could reduce the effectiveness of the system as a measure of public protection—and rekindle much of the public anxiety that the preventive system is designed to alleviate.

18. Dershowitz, *supra* note 16, at 313.

3.3 Extending Sentences for Dangerous Offenders

Jean Floud

Few serious offenders repeat their serious offenses, so that there is no reason, in most cases, to keep them out of circulation on that account for very long periods of time. The question of penalties for serious offenses—even for the worst cases of such offenses—must not be confused with the question of protecting the public from the few serious offenders who *do* present a continuing risk and who *are* likely to cause further serious harm. So long as retribution is thought to require very long sentences for serious offenders, the problem of the risky minority is obscured and can be neglected; but if, as is now widely accepted, the demands of retribution can be met with much shorter sentences, even for serious offenders, the problem of the exceptional minority is exposed and cannot be neglected. It seems irrational to tolerate longer sentences for serious offenses than nowadays would meet the demands of retribution, in order to avoid the notorious difficulties and dilemmas of dealing justly with the exceptional few; but this seems to be the price of refusing to entertain the idea of bringing protective sentencing into the open and placing it under statutory control.

I need hardly remind this audience that our high maximum sentences are irrelevant and inappropriate for a modern penal policy. They are irrelevant because the normal range of sentences imposed is appreciably lower than the permitted maxima. Over the years, the sentences actually passed appear to have settled around an established average; but wide deviations in particular cases raise a risk of unequal treatment and are a source of

From Jean Floud, "Dangerousness and Criminal Justice," 22 *British Journal of Criminology* 213 (1982). Excerpted and reprinted by permission of Oxford University Press. This article summarizes the views developed in Jean Floud and Warren Young, *Dangerousness and Criminal Justice* (London: Heinemann, 1981).

unrest in prisons. They are inappropriate because a modern penal policy should clearly distinguish the main purposes of imprisonment and see that these are reflected in the sentencing structure: viz., protection, denunciation, and dealing with defaulters from the obligations imposed by other penalties. Long sentences of imprisonment are required only in the few cases which call for the separation of the offender for the protection of others; the requirements of denunciation or retribution can nowadays be met by short sentences even for serious offenses (e.g., flagrant breaches of trust or offenses of violence) so long as the offenders do not present a continuing risk to other persons; and more or less nominal sentences will serve to deal with defaulters from the obligations imposed by other penalties (e.g., fines).

The practical difficulties and ethical dilemmas of protective sentencing are mutually reinforcing. We paid a great deal of attention to the practical difficulty of identifying, with any degree of confidence, serious offenders against whom protection is needed because they present a continuing risk of serious harm. As will be evident from our report, we sifted a considerable quantity of theoretical argument and empirical evidence bearing directly or indirectly on the state of the art of assessing "dangerousness." We reached a conclusion which is not surprising, insofar as it amounts to saying that, since it is impossible to be sure how people will behave in the future, if only because of the working of chance, any attempt to apply precautions selectively against some persons for the sake of others is bound to be more or less wide of the mark. What *is* surprising—and very alarming—is to discover just how wide of the mark it turns out to be, whenever it is possible to put predictive judgments to the test by following the postrelease careers of "dangerous" offenders. Statisticians have calculated the probabilities: so many judgments of *dangerous* falsified by the offender's subsequent behavior (that is to say, by his failure to cause further grave harm) and so many judgments of *safe* falsified by the further serious offenses he commits. Not surprisingly, it tends to be the critics of protective sentencing who worry about the former and members of the general public who worry about the latter. But the former figure, the proportion of falsified judgments of *dangerous,* even at its lowest, is so uncomfortably high that no one engaged in making predictive judgments in the administration of justice can fail to be impressed—or, more likely, depressed. As matters now stand, parole boards and similar bodies, to say nothing of courts, are, on average, at best as likely to be wrong as right in thinking that the offenders they decide to detain as dangerous will actually do further serious harm if left at large. Whatever be the prospects of improvement—and it must be admitted that, though they exist, they are not rosy and are forever constrained by a large factor of chance, it is likely that at least two persons are detained for every one person who is prevented from doing serious harm. This is to say that each offender in protective custody probably suffers, in addition to the usual hardships of imprisonment, at least a 50 percent risk of being unnecessarily detained. On what grounds are we justified in doing him this grave harm?—for grave harm it undoubtedly is, on any reckoning.

The justification can only be that we are thereby relieving someone else of a substantial risk of grave harm—that we are justly redistributing a burden of risk that we cannot immediately reduce. This formulation of the answer, in terms of redistributing risk, seems to us to be more appropriate to the jurisprudence of protective sentencing than the one that is frequently given in terms of social utility. The objections to that approach, which involves the abstract and unacceptable concept of social defense, are by now familiar and I will not rehearse them, even briefly, here. Our own formulation has its difficulties and I prefer to say something about these—or at least about those of which we are aware. I will mention two fundamental problems.

We speak of redistributing risk between potential victims and potential aggressors. But we are all potential aggressors—differently placed and variously motivated to harm our fellows. Why shift the burden of risk, if any is to be shifted, only onto the shoulders of convicted offenders? Why confine tests of dangerousness to them? Why not, some critics ask, apply tests of dangerousness to us all and, in the interests of social defense, introduce what has been called "civil preventive confinement"?

Another problem arises from the fact that we are talking about redistributing risk between two parties only one of whom—the convicted offender—is, generally speaking, actually and immediately identifiable and certain to bear the cost of the redistribution in person. We have to make a moral choice between competing claims: the claim of a known individual offender, not to be unnecessarily deprived of his liberty; and the claim of an innocent (unconvicted), unknown person (or persons), not to be deprived of the right to go about their business without risk of grave harm at the hands of an aggressor. Where does justice lie? The debate has recently concentrated heavily on the rights of offenders.

The general objective of our proposals is to bring protective sentencing under statutory control, while leaving ample scope for the necessary exercise of judicial discretion in the sentencing of a very heterogeneous group of exceptional offenders. To this end, we have formulated categories of grave harm, against which the public, in certain circumstances, may claim the protection of a special sentence outside the permitted maximum for a relevant serious offense; and we have defined a severely restricted class of offenders who might be eligible for such a sentence, and mandatory evidential and procedural requirements within which judicial and executive discretion would be exercised in the administration of the proposed sentence.

We took it as axiomatic that the public is entitled to the protection of a special sentence only against *grave* harm, and that no offender should be eligible for a protective sentence unless grave harm is manifested in his criminal conduct. The problem of distinguishing between "serious" and other harm cannot be wholly objectified; harms to the person are *sui generis* and enjoy special moral status, whatever their degree, but a protective sentence, which carries the risk to the offender that he will be unnecessarily deprived of his liberty, should be used only where the victims of the anticipated harm are themselves exposed to the risk of unusual hardship (pain and suffering, shock and fear, injury to health, or beggary). We therefore propose that grave harm for the purposes of protective sentencing should be interpreted as comprising the following categories: death, serious bodily injury, serious sexual assault, severe or prolonged pain or mental stress, loss of or damage to property which causes severe personal hardship, damage to the environment which has a severely adverse effect on public health or safety, serious damage to the security of the state.

This is perhaps the point at which I should say something about our view of the role of discretionary powers in protective sentencing. The argument that these powers are indispensable but that they should be no greater than necessary and should be subject to reasonable guidelines applies, we think, with particular force to protective sentencing. Such sentences, I need not reiterate, represent a more serious infringement of the offender's rights than an ordinary retributive sentence and they should not be freely available to the courts. The protective sentence we propose may be of any determinate length and, like an ordinary sentence, will obey the proportionality rule. The court will have regard to the gravity of the anticipated harm and the risk of its occurring. The sentence will represent the length of time beyond which the offender could not justly be detained, even if he were still thought to present a risk; it will represent, so to say, the outside limit of the grant of additional protection to the public. The responsibility then rests with the executive to release the offender as soon as it becomes clear that control without custody is practicable.

I come now to the difficult question of determining an offender's dangerousness—that is, making a predictive judgment about him. We had envisaged formulating restrictive criteria of dangerousness for the courts to apply, or, at any rate, guidelines for the making of predictive judgments. We had in mind, for example, indications of a pattern of behavior or a mental condition which would justify a conclusion of continuing risk, and a requirement that the court should be satisfied in fairly specific terms as to the level of the risk which would justify a protective sentence (for example, that the offender is all but certain to cause further serious harm; or, at least, is more likely than not to do so; or merely, perhaps, more likely to do so than others of similar age and circumstances).

The road to our conclusion was long and hard; but in the end we agreed that statutory tests of dangerousness were not feasible. The nature of predictive judgments, the limited scope for precision and confidence in such judgments, the widely varying characteristics of the relatively few offenders likely to meet the qualifying conditions we propose for a protective sentence, call for the exercise of a broad discretion rather than the application of statutory tests.

3.4
Extending Sentences for Dangerous Offenders: Some Objections

David Wood

This article is concerned with the justifiability of protective sentencing. Three broad approaches need to be distinguished. The first holds that such sentences are in principle supportable. Where offenders genuinely constitute a threat to the physical well-being of members of the public, their continued detention is warranted despite their having served their normal sentence. According to the second approach, protective sentences are on the contrary unjustifiable. The dangerous offender should be treated no differently from other offenders and released once his ordinary sentence has been served. To detain him further is to punish him not for offenses he has committed, but for those he might commit in the future. The third approach seeks a *via media* between the other two. This approach appeals to a distinction between imprisonment on the one hand and forms of detention such as quarantine which do not constitute punishment on the other. It claims that although the continued imprisonment of dangerous offenders is quite unjustified, detaining such offenders further in some form of civil institution may be warranted.

1. Walker's Defense of Protective Sentencing

Rather than treating incapacitation as in some way an inferior reason for imprisoning someone, Walker asks why, on the contrary, it should not "be regarded as a justification which is quite as sound as retribution, deterrence,

From David Wood, "Dangerous Offenders and the Morality of Protective Sentencing," *Criminal Law Review* 424 (1988). Excerpted and reprinted by permission.

or the need for treatment." The major objection to protective sentencing is that "incapacitation as a reason for penal interventions means that a person is punished, not for what he has done but for what it is believed he may do in the future." After stating that this objection assumes that "the only justifiable aim of a sentence must be retributive punishment," Walker goes on to claim that, insofar as incapacitation is concerned, the "sterility" of a purely retributive approach to sentencing can be "la[id] bare" by considering what a proponent of such an approach would approve in two hypothetical situations.[1] These situations warrant close attention, for they turn out to be very different from the simple knockdown arguments Walker takes them to be.

To start with the first hypothetical situation:

> In Situation A the offender to be sentenced is certain to commit a crime of serious violence unless detained for longer than the "just deserts tariff" would allow. Must he be released and reincarcerated only when he has committed the crime he was certain to commit? Or would certainty justify incarcerating him before he commits it? To be consistent the pure retributivist must insist on the former answer. He might protest that the case as posed is unreal and artificial; but the answer to that is that an uncompromising philosophical position must be defensible in any conceivable situation.[2]

Certainly the pure retributivists must hold (as must any retributivist) that the offender cannot be punished for a crime he has not committed, even if *ex hypothesi* there is no doubt about his committing a further crime. But this does not mean that the retributivist, of any sort, is committed to the offender's being released once he has served his tariff sentence. The retributivist, *qua* retributivist, offers only a theory of punishment, not a comprehensive account of the circumstances and conditions under which individuals can be forcibly detained. It is absurd to suppose that he is committed to the view that every social measure, or even every preventive measure, must be justified on retributive grounds. If this were the case, he would be required to hold that the epileptic could only be denied a driver's license if this was something he rightfully deserved, or homes could only be compulsorily purchased in order to build a new motorway if this were somehow to give their occupants their due. In a whole range of cases, questions of desert are simply irrelevant. However, Walker seems to see the retributivist precisely as offering an account according to which desert is always relevant, and therefore he sees him as being unable to justify, for example, the compulsory commitment of psychotics, or the quarantining of those carrying life-threatening diseases. Why, otherwise, does Walker suppose in the above example that detention or incarceration of any form can be justified only as a form of punishment? To portray the retributivist as Walker does is merely to caricature him.

It might be claimed, however, that Walker's point is not that the retributivist cannot accept the principle that social protection is a justifiable ground for intervention. Rather his point is that it is inconsistent for the retributivist not to extend this principle to the sphere of punishment, given that he is forced to accept it quite generally outside this sphere. (Consider the examples in the previous paragraph.) Walker says, after all, that "[t]he traditional retributivist, who asserts that the law enforcement system ought not to take account of the harm which people might do, must either explain why it should be subject to a restrictive principle which we do not apply outside the system, or else argue that we should apply the same principle outside it."[3] But the retributivist's reply here is obvious. He can acknowledge quite openly that considerations of social protection are just as relevant in the law enforcement system as they are outside it, and go on to say that they are not relevant so as to justify further imprisonment as opposed to merely detention. Beyond that which is required on normal tariff grounds, punishment is just as much out of place in the case of the dangerous offender as it is in the case of the typhoid carrier. It is equally unjust to continue to imprison the dangerous offender once he has served his tariff sentence as it is to imprison, as opposed to merely quarantine, the typhoid carrier in the first place. (The term "imprisonment" is used here in its everyday sense, rather than in the broader legal sense in which any deprivation of liberty constitutes imprisonment.) In both cases, isolation alone is required, and no harsher treatment is defensible.

This criticism of Walker can be reinforced by comparing the case of two persons who are equally dangerous but only one of whom has committed violent offenses in sufficient number of sufficient gravity to be classified as a dangerous offender. Social protection requires that they be treated similarly and both incapacitated. But if dangerousness is a reason for punishing the dangerous offender beyond whatever is justified on normal tariff principles, why is not dangerousness similarly a reason for punishing the equally dangerous person who is yet so to qualify? (Let's call him "the dangerous nonoffender.") It seems that Walker is forced to hold either that dangerousness constitutes a sufficient reason for punishment in the case of the dangerous offender and dangerous nonoffender alike, or in neither of these cases. Of course, Walker does not see the matter this way. He categorically rejects the idea that subjecting a prisoner to further restraint once he has served his tariff sentence is like punishing the innocent. He claims that in no sense does a person "regain his innocence" once he has served his tariff sentence: "One is innocent of a crime until one commits it, after which one is guilty of it forever. One may be pardoned, or have one's conviction quashed, or eventually become 'rehabilitated' . . . but one does not become innocent in any literal sense." According to Walker, to suppose that the dangerous offender cannot be subjected to a protective sentence is again to beg the question of "whether a sentence should ever be anything but retributive punishment."[4] The point remains, however, that the connection between guilt and dangerousness is yet to be explained. How does the dangerous offender's record of violence make him liable to social protection measures in a way in which the nonoffender is not so liable? The frequently raised criticism that the dangerous offender is being regarded as a second-class citizen, that he has lost his equal status in virtue of being categorized as a dangerous offender, appears highly plausible. Walker accuses the retributivist of begging the question of why punishment should be limited to retributivist grounds—or at least, in the case of the limiting retributivist, the question of why "just deserts" should be regarded as placing a ceiling on penalties. But Walker could equally be accused of begging the question of why being convicted of crimes of a certain degree of violence should be regarded as merely setting a threshold for various forms of intervention. He seems to think that because the fact of conviction can never be changed (once the appeal channels have all been exhausted), there are only uncertain limits to the social protection measures that can be taken against the guilty person. It seems far more reasonable, however, to endorse some principle of commensurability between the seriousness of the offenses in question and the severity of the punishment administered in relation to them.

The proposition that the continued imprisonment, as opposed to civil detention, of dangerous offenders cannot be justified prompts a further criticism of Walker. Even if the required connection between guilt and dangerousness could be established, this would be of no assistance in the case of the dangerous nonoffender. We are still left with the question of what action, if any, can be taken against him. The absurdity Walker supposes in simply releasing the offender in situation A has nothing to do with his being dangerous.[5]

Walker draws a parallel between the quarantining of carriers of life-threatening diseases and the protective sentencing of dangerous offenders. The appropriate analogy, however, is rather with the civil detention of dangerous persons generally, whether dangerous offenders or not. That a dangerous person is also classifiable as a dangerous offender is only epistemically or evidentially significant, and not morally relevant. Walker can only draw his parallel with quarantine on the assumption either that quarantine is a form of punishment, and not merely detention, or that a protective sentence is merely detention, and not punishment. Walker can hardly adopt the first alternative, as then he would be no better placed to handle the dangerous nonoffender than would be the retributivist, according to his own criticism of that position rejected above. That is, Walker could only civilly detain a dangerous offender if it is presumed that such treatment was somehow deserved. The latter alternative is hardly plausible either. If a protective sentence is merely detention, why should it be served in a normal prison as opposed to (what we shall call) a civil detention center?[6] If incapacitation is all that is required, the more stringent measure of imprisonment cannot be justified.

Turning to the second of Walker's hypothetical situations, in situation B

> the violent offender declares his intention of committing further violence when he is released, and there is no reason to disbelieve him or to doubt his capacity for doing what he says he will do. Would the retributivist allow him to be kept inside any longer than the just deserts tariff permits, in order to stop him doing what he promises to do? Must his answer in this situation also be "No"? If so, he is in effect saying that his principles do not allow him to take any steps to save a person from becoming a victim of violence if those steps involve the extension of incarceration. If he is completely consistent he would also be unwilling to allow any non-custodial precautionary measure that would involve even inconvenience for the offender.[7]

In situation A we know only that it is certain that the offender will commit a further violent crime, not how we are certain of this. One way of taking the offender's declaration of intention in situation B is as just filling out situation A, as informing us of the way in which we know that the offender will undoubtedly commit the crime. On this interpretation, rather than presenting a different story, situation B presents a more detailed version of the same story. If this is how situation B is to be viewed, it clearly does not warrant separate treatment.

It may seem more reasonable, then, to take the declaration of intention in situation B as possessing moral and not just epistemic status, as making it plain that the offender is responsible for his future crime. Interpreted this way, however, situation B provides no additional difficulties for the retributivist. If anything, it makes his position easier, for he is provided with separate grounds for intervention: he has not just a prediction of future conduct to rely upon, but a statement of present intention. A substantive criminal law based more soundly on retributivist principles could well regard this statement itself as an offense. (Of course, this would require the legal concept of assault to be extended to threats of future harm, but there seems to be no reason why the retributivist should not agree to this.) It would still have to be considered, however, whether such an offense would be sufficient to justify detaining the maker of such a statement for so long as he is dangerous. It seems that it would be quite fortuitous if this were to be the case.[8]

2. Floud and Young's Defense of Protective Sentencing

Floud and Young argue for positions diametrically opposed to the two propositions defended here. Contrary to our first proposition (and also to Walker), they claim that the civil detention of dangerous nonoffenders is never warranted. The risk presented by such persons must be borne by the community at large. Concerning our second proposition, they dismiss the option of civil detention, arguing (or at least implying) that the more stringent step of subjecting dangerous offenders to protective sentences is defensible.

Floud and Young defend their first claim, that the civil detention of dangerous nonoffenders is never warranted, by appealing to what they call "the right to be presumed harmless." The "crucial objection" to taking protective measures against dangerous nonoffenders is that

> such measures would entail abrogating [this] right . . . which, like the right to be presumed innocent, is fundamental to a free society. In such a society people do not simply expect or hope to be treated as harmless; they have a right to be so treated, even if it is more probable than not that they do intend harm: just as they have a right to be treated as innocent even if it is more probable than not that they are guilty.[9]

Floud and Young's "right to be presumed harmless" raises two important questions, which will be considered in turn. The first question is why it should be supposed that this right is sufficiently powerful to exclude the civil detention of dangerous nonoffenders. It needs to be asked why they should regard this right as excluding civil detention when they do not take it as ruling out quarantining those with life-threatening diseases. Floud and Young hold that the risks presented by disease carriers can fairly be redistributed, so that the disease carriers suffer the burden of quarantine rather than the public at large running the risk of infection. It must be asked, then, why the risks presented by dangerous nonoffenders should not likewise be redistributed.

The conclusion that civil detention is morally indistinguishable from quarantining can be arrived at another way. Floud and Young argue that subjecting dangerous offenders to protective sentences is morally unobjectionable because, first, such persons have forfeited the right to be presumed harmless, and second, what could be termed "the principle of just redistribution of risks" justifies the redistribution of risks that is entailed by protective sentences. They hold, at least implicitly, that the presence of the right to be presumed harmless provides immunity from the application of this principle. This is why they believe that the risks posed by dangerous nonoffenders cannot be redistributed (at least not on the grounds of this principle), but must be borne by the community at large. However, it is not clear why the right to be presumed harmless should be regarded as being more significant than the principle of redistribution of risks and given preference to it.

Outside the area of punishment, or at least where preventive measures can be justified according to the principle of just redistribution of risks, rather than retributively, it seems that individuals who are required to carry the burden of such redistribution cannot object that the Kantian constraint on using them merely as means to an end has been violated. Certainly, this constraint is not being violated so as to subvert their moral status in the same way it would be were they to be wrongly punished. (The moral distinction here between forms of incarceration which do and do not constitute punishment is vital.) It seems, then, that the right to be presumed harmless is not sufficient to exclude the civil detention of dangerous non-offenders, as opposed to their imprisonment, where the term "imprisonment" is understood, as in this article, in the ordinary sense as a form of punishment rather than in the technical legal sense of any deprivation of liberty.

Whereas the first question raised by the right to be presumed harmless asks whether this right is strong enough for Floud and Young's purposes, the second queries whether it is not too powerful. It may well be that in appealing to this right Floud and Young have bought far more than they bargained for. Why should it be supposed that, once they have been convicted of violent crimes of sufficient number and seriousness to satisfy the dangerous offender threshold, individuals are capable of losing this right, and therefore of being made liable to a protective sentence? Once again, the analogy with the right to be presumed innocent is misplaced, for this right is never lost, irrespective of the defendant's past criminal record. Indeed, in the English legal system at least, it is considered of great importance that the jury is kept ignorant of any such record. To talk of a class of persons who might be treated as having lost this right, or at least the benefit of this right insofar as it provides immunity from liability to protective sentences, raises once again the specter of a second-class citizenry.

The other main proposition of Floud and Young that we are concerned with here, that it is not merely the civil detention of dangerous offenders that is justified, but their continued imprisonment under protective sentences, can be dealt with more briefly. If it is only the incapacitation of dangerous offenders that is required, civil detention suffices. Floud and Young do not consider this issue explicitly. But they appear to believe that if merely the civil detention of dangerous offenders were to be accepted, there would be a serious risk of the practice spreading to nonoffenders. However, this fear appears to be quite misplaced. There is no reason to suppose that the practice of detaining dangerous offenders would spread to dangerous persons generally. Floud and Young provide no grounds for thinking that the practice cannot be kept so confined. Even if there were a distinct possibility of the practice spreading in this way, this is not a sufficient reason to subject dangerous offenders to the more stringent measure. If dangerous offenders were to be imprisoned rather than merely detained for this reason, they could clearly object that they were merely being used as a means to a social end. They could rightfully complain that they were being imprisoned for the dubious reason that, were they only to be civilly detained, the idea that dangerous nonoffenders likewise should be subjected to this measure might become fashionable. The central point remains of why dangerous offenders should be subjected to further periods of imprisonment when civil detention centers could serve the end of incapacitation equally well.

This article has so far been mainly concerned with defending the third option set out at the beginning, namely civil detention, against the first option of protective sentencing. It might be objected, however, that we have not sought to defend civil detention against the second option, that of intervening no further in the case of dangerous offenders once their ordinary tariff sentences have been served. We have done no more in this regard than appeal to the analogy with quarantining. Furthermore we have done so, according to this objection, simply assuming that quarantining is morally quite blameless.

It is not to be supposed, however, that quarantining is completely free of moral difficulties. Certainly the question must be faced as to why it is justified as a forcible measure, given that most carriers of serious diseases would willingly cooperate and remain in a quarantine center voluntarily. It is the risk of the small minority who cannot be relied upon that seems to justify forcible quarantining. However, the main point to note here is that there is a vital moral difference between quarantining and imprisonment, namely that the latter is a form of punishment, whereas the former is not. Two further points regarding the second option are also in order. First, as already pointed out, Floud and Young are quite happy to let the community at large bear the risk presented by dangerous nonoffenders. It could well be asked whether it would not be more consistent for them to endorse the same strategy in respect of dangerous offenders, and drop their argument for protective sentences completely. This seems particularly plausible given that, owing to the general absence of "career paths" among dangerous offenders, the risk presented by this class of persons is scarcely considerable in comparison with that presented by dangerous nonoffenders. Second, and following on from this point, it needs to be reiterated that, given the epistemic difficulties involved in correctly identifying those likely to commit violent crimes, the option of simply releasing dangerous offenders once they have served their ordinary sentence in practice could well be the most reasonable.

Notes

1. Nigel Walker, "Unscientific, Unwise, Unprofitable, or Unjust?" 22 *British Journal of Criminology* 276, 280 (1982).
2. *Id.*, 281.
3. Nigel Walker, *Sentencing: Theory, Law, and Practice* (Butterworths, London, 1985), 95.
4. *Supra,* n. 1, 280.
5. As we shall see shortly, Floud and Young seem to deny such absurdity. They hold that the risk presented by dangerous nonoffenders must be borne by the community at large, and cannot justifiably be restricted by detaining such persons.
6. *Cf.* Ferdinand D. Schoeman, "On Incapacitating the Dangerous," in H. Gross and A. von Hirsch (eds.) *Sentencing* (Oxford University Press, New York, 1981), 175.
7. *Supra,* n. 1, 281.
8. A connected issue here is the form protective sentences should take, whether they are to be determinate or not.
9. Jean Floud and Warren Young, *Dangerousness and Criminal Justice* (Heinemann, London, 1981), 44.

3.5
Incapacitation within Limits

Norval Morris

In the criminal law, if not in international relations, the preemptive strike has great attraction; to capture the criminal before the crime is surely an alluring idea. In a variety of ways, implicit and expressed, that idea has been pursued for centuries and is being more vigorously pursued today—and, of course, it is also at the foundation of the civil commitment of those mentally ill or retarded persons who are thought likely to be a danger to themselves or others.

My purpose here, as I have tried to define it, is not at all to attack the idea of the preemptive strike. I think one could easily attack it—it is far from invulnerable—but my effort is different, and is clearly more difficult. I will try to enunciate those principles under which such preemptive strikes would be jurisprudentially acceptable.

I have reduced my argument to the following seven submissions, which I shall try to defend in this lecture. Here they are:

1. Clinical predictions of dangerousness unsupported by actuarial studies should not be relied on for other than short-term intervention.
2. The autonomy of the individual should sometimes be restricted because of his predicted dangerousness. The relevant considerations are:
   —the extent of the harm that may occur,
   —the likelihood of its occurrence,
   —the extent of individual autonomy to be limited to avoid the harm.

From Norval Morris, "On 'Dangerousness' in the Judicial Process," 39 *Record of the Association of the Bar of the City of New York* 102 (1982). This lecture was the Thirty-eighth Annual Cardozo Lecture of the Association of the Bar of the City of New York. Excerpted and reprinted by permission.

3. A prediction of dangerousness is a statement of a present condition, not the prediction of a particular result.
4. It is a mistake to confuse the sufficiency of proof of dangerousness with the decision on whether to require proof beyond a reasonable doubt, or by clear and convincing evidence, or on a balance of probability.
5. Punishment should not be imposed, nor the term of punishment extended, by virtue of a prediction of dangerousness, beyond that which would be justified as a deserved punishment independently of that prediction.
6. Provided the previous limitation is respected, predictions of dangerousness may properly influence sentencing decisions (and other decisions under the criminal law).
7. The base expectancy rate of criminal violence for the criminal predicted as dangerous must be shown by reliable evidence to be substantially higher than the base expectancy rate for another criminal, with a closely similar criminal record and convicted of a closely similar crime, but not predicted as unusually dangerous, before the greater dangerousness of the former may be relied on to intensify or extend his punishment.

I am confining analysis in this lecture to the prediction of behavior that is dangerous to the person or threatens the person, in effect, to assaultive criminality. I do not mean to deprecate the significance of the threats of predatory theft, or of many other crimes, to social welfare; I have narrowed my focus primarily to assist analysis and in the belief that if I can struggle toward principle here the task will be easier in relation to other criminal conduct.

The problem then is: Suppose we knew with some precision how well we could predict future violent behavior; how and to what extent should we in justice apply that knowledge?

I must make one self-protective comment at this point.

To discuss the definition and application of concepts of dangerousness in the criminal law, and in the law relating to mental health, may give the impression that I favor the widespread application of this concept. I certainly do not. My submission is different. It is that a jurisprudence that pretends to exclude such concepts is self-deceptive; they will frequently figure prominently in decision making, whether or not they are spelled out in jurisprudence. One can pretend to ignore such predictions, but it will be a pretense. My view is that it is better to recognize the reality of such predictions and try to put them into their proper jurisprudential place, difficult though that may be.

But that is not the only reason for pursuing this topic of reliance on predictions of dangerousness. If such predictions are in fact made and relied on and cannot be banished from the criminal law, that circumstance may be one reason for studying them, for trying to improve their validity and stability over time, and even for making speeches about them (though you may already begin to doubt that). But there is a larger justification. Suppose our present weak predictive capacity proves to be the best we can do for decades, which I think quite likely. Suppose for a high risk of a crime of violence the best we can do at present is to predict one in three, in the sense that to be sure of preventing one crime we would have to lock up three people. My submission is, and it is a difficult one, that it is still ethically appropriate and socially desirable to take such predictions into account in many police, prosecutorial, judicial, correctional, and legislative decisions.

That is an unfashionable position. It may well be a wrong position. So let me approach its defense with caution, starting with the obvious question of how well we can predict violent behavior. I shall skim over the literature—you will either take it as truth from me or you will pursue it somewhere else. Current research supports the working hypothesis that we can predict about one in three crimes of violence in a high risk group.

Prediction and Risk Shifting

Classifications are often arbitrary, and the classification that follows is not necessarily compelling, but for me there are only three paths to the prediction of a person's future behavior.

First: This is how he behaved in the past when circumstances were similar. It is likely that he will behave in the same way now. Let me call this an *anamnestic* prediction.

Second: This is how people like him, situated as he is, behaved in the past. It is likely that he will behave as they did. This, of course, is an *actuarial* prediction. It is the basis of all insurance, of a great deal of our efforts to share and shift risk in the community.

And the third type of prediction, which is harder to state, is this: From my experience of the world, from my professional training, from what I know about mental illness and mental health, from my observations of this patient and efforts to diagnose him, I think he will behave in the following fashion in the future. This is a *clinical* prediction; it has elements of the first two in it but it includes professional judgmental elements that the psychiatric literature treats as distinct from the others.

Anamnestic predictions are often very reliable. Indeed, they reach the highest levels of validity. He has taken out the old raincoat and exposed his rampant self to the young girls in the park every Friday for the past year. Here he is, this Friday, wearing his raincoat though the weather be fine and he is heading again for the park. Who says a prediction of only one in three is all you can make?—of course you can make a higher prediction in that situation. But that does not controvert what I said earlier; it is a short-term prediction and it does not concern a crime of violence.

Actuarial predictions also are often very reliable—the insurance industry lives by them. Clinical predictions are of a different order. They are intuitive rather than verifiable, except in the result. At first blush it would seem that the best predictions of human behavior would be based on a combination of all three of these types of prediction, that is to say, would take in the pattern of behavior of the person under consideration, would be advised by how others like him behaved in the past, and would also be guided by a total clinical consideration of his case, which would improve on the prediction from the first two categories by taking into account what was distinctive in him—that is to say, would individualize the prediction to his particular circumstances. And that is correct for the prediction of certain types of human behavior—how someone will hit a tennis ball, whether he will be late to work one day next week, and so on. But it is not true for the prediction of violent behavior at the present level of our knowledge. It has not been demonstrated, and psychiatrists have not claimed, that clinical predictions can improve upon actuarial and anamnestic predictions—certainly not on actuarial predictions. That leads me to my first formal submission to you: Clinical predictions of dangerousness unsupported by actuarial studies should not be relied on for other than short-term intervention.

As lawyers, we should insist on testing psychiatric predictions by probing the actuarial and anamnestic bases for such prediction. And the organized profession of psychiatry is pressing us to do just that.

The next proposition that I want to make—my third submission [listed at the outset]—may be thought to be only linguistic, but I think it is necessary in order to develop several major points. A statement of a prediction of dangerousness is a statement of a present condition, not the prediction of a particular result. The belief that it is the prediction of a result is an error that is constantly made and leads many astray. An analogy to a dangerous object rather than to a dangerous person may help clarify my point.

I remember the drab postwar days in London. The bombing had stopped but the scars of war were pervasive. And on occasion the risks of war returned in their earlier force. An unexploded bomb would be found and would have to be moved and rendered safe. Death and severe injuries were very rare; the base expectancy rate was very low; there were large numbers of "false positives" for every "true positive"—bombs that didn't go off, as distinguished from those that did. The area would be cleared; the bomb disposal crew would begin their delicate work and in all but a few instances manage it successfully. When the talk resumed that night in the neighboring pub, would anyone say the bomb was not dangerous because it did not go off? Would anyone say that because it proved to be a "false positive" it was not dangerous? Of course not; that is not how words are used when the focus is on dangerous things as distinct from dangerous people. Yet the similarities of risk and analysis are great. Why the difference of usage? In part, I think, because we tend to think of dangerous people as those who intend harm—yet that view conceals the psychological reality.

In sum, that the person predicted as dangerous does no future injury does not mean that the classification was erroneous.

Let me take you along another definitional path to the same result. I think the journey is worthwhile, giving a different perspective on the contours of the country that has to be crossed.

Assume that in every instance the question is: who shall bear the risk of harm, the individual or the community? This assumption presupposes, of course, that the risk can be quantified as a base expectancy rate and the harm defined with some precision and, further, that it can substantially be shifted from the community, the cost of the shift being paid by the individual by his being controlled in one or another fashion, usually by detaining him in custody.

Consider the case of a sixteen-year-old black youth who has just dropped out of school and who has no employment, whose mother was herself a child on welfare when he was born, who does not know his father, who runs with a street gang, and who lives in a destroyed inner-city neighborhood. How should we assess the risk of his being involved in the next six months in a crime of personal violence? Since we own the numbers, let us give him a base expectancy rate of, say, to be conservative, one in twenty. That risk now rests on the community in which he lives. May we, without further justification, at this one-in-twenty level, shift that risk from the community and make him bear the cost of the shift in the coinage of institutional detention until we can do something to reduce the risk, by retraining him or by allowing time to pass while the threat he presents diminishes? Clearly no. But let him be involved in a nonviolent crime, say, shoplifting, and even if that conviction makes no difference to his base expectancy rate of a crime of violence, there is no doubt that in practice we would then take into account the risk of a crime of violence in deciding what to do about him and for how long. Within our sentencing discretions we would take into account the risk of violence he presents. How should it be taken into account?

The Burden of Proof of Dangerousness

The discussion of sentencing that young criminal was in large part only a restatement of the position earlier advanced, but it allows me to bring out one point that I think important. What elements of the "dangerousness" sentencing of that hypothetical young man are capable of proof and at what level of persuasiveness? His personal circumstances, the historical facts of his mother and his absent father, his truancy, his school and employment records, his gang membership are all capable of what I might call absolute proof. It makes very little difference whether the burden of their proof is on a balance of probabilities, or has to be by clear and convincing evidence, or has to be beyond reasonable doubt. And is that not also true of his base expectancy rate of violence? The scientific work to define a group and to assess its base expectancy rate of criminal violence within a given period has been done or it has not been done. Its stability over time and in different regions has either been tested or has not been tested. If the facts of the future criminal behavior of the group to which he is said to belong have been found actuarially, then the question of his risk to the community is not properly related to the different burdens of proof of those actuarial facts. The difficulty of proof of the base expectancy rate is not in any inherent sense more difficult than proof of the historical facts on which the rate was calculated. Hence my fourth formal submission to you: It is a mistake to confuse the sufficiency of proof of dangerousness with the decision to require proof beyond a reasonable doubt, or by clear and convincing evidence, or on a balance of probability.

False Positives and the Conviction of the Innocent

Under this heading I want to defend three submissions that complete the argument in this lecture. The three submissions are:

5. Punishment should not be imposed, nor the term of punishment extended, by virtue of a prediction of dangerousness, beyond that which would be justified as a deserved punishment independently of that prediction.
6. Provided the previous limitation is respected, predictions of dangerousness may properly influence sentencing decisions (and other decisions under the criminal law).

7. The base expectancy rate for the criminal predicted as dangerous must be shown by reliable evidence to be substantially higher than the base expectancy rate for another criminal, with a closely similar criminal record and convicted of a closely similar crime, but not so predicted as unusually dangerous, before any distinction based on his higher dangerousness may be relied on to intensify or extend his punishment.

These three submissions form an effort to state a jurisprudence of predictions of dangerousness for punishment purposes that would achieve both individual justice and better community protection. It would seem futile to deny the relevance and propriety of such predictions to a wide range of discretions exercised under the aegis of the criminal law, and in particular to decisions whether to imprison and for how long. Yet, if moral issues are to be taken seriously, the fact of approved use is not compelling and the morality of applying predictions based on group behavior to predict the likely behavior of the individual requires justification.

Thought has been led astray here, by equating the assumption of power (or of extra power) over the individual on a basis of a prediction of dangerousness to reluctance to risk convicting the innocent. The model of the criminal trial has confused analysis.

If it is true that it is better that nine guilty men be acquitted rather than one innocent man be convicted, why does not a similar though more compelling equation apply to the prediction of dangerousness—so that it is better that two men who would not in fact injure or threaten others (two false positives) should be released rather than one who would (one true positive) be detained? If one to nine is unacceptable in one case, how can two to one be acceptable in the other?

This line of reasoning, though it has persuaded many commentators and some judges, seems to me deeply flawed. The equation with the proof of guilt misses the point. Let us assume a properly convicted criminal, criminal X, with a one-in-three base expectancy rate of violence (as we have defined it), and another criminal, criminal Y, also properly convicted of the identical offense, but who has a very much lower base expectancy rate—same record, same offense. Unlike X, Y was not a school dropout; he has a job to which he may return and a supportive family who will take him back if he is not imprisoned, or after his release from prison. May criminal X be sent to prison while criminal Y is not? Or may criminal X be sent to prison for a longer term than criminal Y, despite the same record and the same gravity of offense, the longer sentence being justified by the utilitarian advantages of selective incapacitation? My answer to both questions is in the affirmative; he may. But since this appears to be the advocacy of locking up two "innocent" men to prevent crime by a third, I must offer a brief defense of my view.

The central idea that moves me in defending submissions 5, 6, and 7 and the conclusion about criminal X is recognition of the imprecision of our moral calipers. In no exact sense can one say of punishment: "That was a just punishment." St. Peter is reputed to be informed on those matters and I am prepared to yield that he can make a statement like that; but I cannot, and I have never met anyone who can. All I have ever been able to say about the justice of a particular sentence on a convicted criminal, and all I have ever thought people sensibly said was: "As we know our community and its values, that does not seem to be an unjust punishment." Retributive sentiments properly limit but do not define a just punishment.

The injustice of a punishment, assuming proper proof of guilt, is thus defined in part deontologically, in limited retributivist terms and not solely in utilitarian terms. The upper and lower limits of "deserved" punishment set the range in which utilitarian values, including values of mercy and human understanding, may properly fix the punishment to be imposed. There is always a range of a "not unjust" punishment, measured in relation to the gravity of an offense and the offender's criminal record.

The philosophy of punishment I am offering is that of a limiting retributivist, and I suggest that punishments, and a just scale of punishment, should always allow for discretion to be exercised, under proper legislative guidance, by the judicial officer of the state. I have developed that argument at excessive length elsewhere and I am not going to inflict it again on you now. The key to the argument that I am advancing is submission 7; let me illustrate its operation by an example or two.

Submission 7—that the base expectancy rate for the criminal predicted as dangerous must be shown by reliable evidence to be substantially higher than the base expectancy rate for another criminal, with a closely similar criminal record and convicted of a closely similar crime, but not so predicted as unusually dangerous, before any distinction based on his higher dangerousness may be relied on to intensify or extend his punishment—may seem a pallid and toothless proposition, but if accepted it would have a dramatically restrictive effect on the acceptability of predictions of dangerousness in the criminal law. Rightly or wrongly, prior record and severity of the last offense are seen in all legal systems as defining the retributive range of punishment. Once criminal record and severity of the last offense are included, the definition of groups with higher base expectancy rates than those with similar crimes and similar criminal records becomes very much more difficult of proof.

Let me test my submission in relation to my criminals X and Y and show you one real defect in what I am offering.

Criminals X and Y had identical criminal records and had committed identical crimes, but Y was not a school dropout, Y had a job to which he could return if not sent to prison, and Y had a supportive family who would take him back if allowed to do so, while the unfortunate X was a school dropout, was unemployed, and lacked a supportive family. And let us suppose that past studies reveal that criminals with X's criminal record and with his environmental circumstances have a base expectancy rate of 1 in 10 of being involved in a crime of personal violence. While no such calculations have been made for criminals like Y, it is quite clear that they have a much lower base expectancy rate of future violent criminality. I suggest that X should be held longer than Y based on these predictions.

In fairness I must note that I have lured myself onto some very unpleasant terrain, for the reality in this country at this time will be that my apparently aseptic principles will grossly favor the wealthy to the detriment of the poor, and will be used to justify even more imprisonment of blacks and other underclass minorities than at present obtains—as will the whole "selective incapacitation" process. Put curtly, without knowing more about our hypothetical criminals, we already confidently guess the pigmentation of X and Y. As a matter of statistical likelihood, Y is white and X is black.

I do not take lightly this line of criticism of the thesis I have offered tonight. I do not enjoy advancing principles which if accepted would have those effects. So let me offer one or two comments by way of explanation—not really apology—for my thesis. The sad fact is that in our society predictors of violence are not racially neutral. How could they be racially neutral, when at this moment one of every twenty black males in their twenties is either in prison or in jail. And that really underestimates the difference between blacks and whites in prisons and jails, since when black youths move into the middle class their crime rates are just the same as those of white youths. It is the black underclass, left behind, which has these enormously high rates of imprisonment and jailing and very much higher rates of violence. Predicting violence in the inner-city slum is grossly easier than predicting it in the dormitory suburb. And what else is characteristic of the inner-city ghetto? Much else that distinguishes our criminal X from our criminal Y—school absenteeism, unemployment, functional illiteracy, generations on welfare, no supportive families. Blackness and a higher base expectancy rate of violence overlap. And that is the problem of all these preemptive sentencing processes.

What, then, is the conclusion properly to be drawn from these sad realities? Some would say: "Don't base decisions in the criminal justice system at all on predictions of dangerousness; they are racially skewed, and we already lock up too many members of our minorities." I sympathize with the reason, but reject the conclusion. The criminal justice system cannot rectify racial inequalities and social injustices; it will do well if it does not exacerbate them. It is proper that predictions of violence should figure in many decisions in applying the criminal law, and if they are applied within principles that I am seeking to tease out, that is all that can be expected. My submissions may be in error, but if they are, then anyone seeking to apply predictions should offer alternative predictions. We cannot properly close our eyes to the different threats that criminal X and criminal Y pose to the community. But it is of first importance that we base our decisions about their respective dangerousness on validated knowledge and not on prejudice, particularly racial prejudice, and hence that we insist on the most careful validation of such stereotypes of dangerousness; my submissions are an effort to define what is required to achieve such validation. We must insist, if predictions are to be used, that they be reliable.

To conclude. As is so often the case with issues of justice, procedural and evidentiary issues become of central importance. Let me put the point curtly and again. Clinical predictions of dangerousness unsupported by actuarial studies should never be relied on. Clinical judgments firmly grounded on well-established base expectancy rates are a precondition, rarely fulfilled, to the just invocation of prediction of dangerousness as a ground for intensifying punishment. My conclusions then are my seven submissions—I know that they are unrealistic, but I affirm they provide a rational process by which one can think of the just use of predictions. Unless they or something like them are fulfilled the present movement to the overuse of predictions of dangerousness is a threat to justice.

I must admit that, if my submissions are accepted, I doubt the availability of sufficient knowledge to meet the necessary preconditions of just sentencing based on express predictions of violence. Further, that gap in our knowledge should make us skeptical about our present widespread reliance on implicit and intuitive predictions of dangerousness in exercising discretion—in situations where we do not declare that usage as we do in the situations I have been discussing.

3.6 Selective Incapacitation

James Q. Wilson

When criminals are deprived of their liberty, as by imprisonment (or banishment, or very tight control in the community), their ability to commit offenses against citizens is ended. We say these persons have been "incapacitated," and we try to estimate the amount by which crime is reduced by this incapacitation.

Incapacitation cannot be the sole purpose of the criminal justice system; if it were, we would put everybody who has committed one or two offenses in prison until they were too old to commit another. And if we thought prison too costly, we would simply cut off their hands or their heads. Justice, humanity, and proportionality, among other goals, must also be served by the courts.

But there is one great advantage to incapacitation as a crime control strategy—namely, it does not require us to make any assumptions about human nature. By contrast, deterrence works only if people take into account the costs and benefits of alternative courses of action and choose that which confers the largest net benefit (or the smallest net cost). Though people almost surely do take such matters into account, it is difficult to be certain by how much such considerations affect their behavior and what change, if any, in crime rates will result from a given, feasible change in either the costs of crime or the benefits of not committing a crime. Rehabilitation works only if the values, preferences, or time-horizon of criminals can be altered by plan. There is not much evidence that we can make these

---

From James Q. Wilson, "Dealing with the High-Rate Offender," 72 *The Public Interest* 52 (1983). Reprinted by permission of the author and publisher.

alterations for large numbers of persons, though there is some evidence that it can be done for a few under certain circumstances.

Incapacitation, on the other hand, works by definition: its effects result from the physical restraint placed upon the offender and not from his subjective state. More accurately, it works provided at least three conditions are met: some offenders must be repeaters, offenders taken off the streets must not be immediately and completely replaced by new recruits, and prison must not increase the postrelease criminal activity of those who have been incarcerated sufficiently to offset the crimes prevented by their stay in prison.

The first condition is surely true. Every study of prison inmates shows that a large fraction (recently, about two-thirds) of them had prior criminal records before their current incarceration; every study of ex-convicts shows that a significant fraction (estimates vary from a quarter to a half) are rearrested for new offenses within a relatively brief period.[1] In short, the great majority of persons in prison are repeat offenders, and thus prison, whatever else it may do, protects society from the offenses these persons would commit if they were free.

The second condition—that incarcerating one robber does not lead automatically to the recruitment of a new robber to replace him—seems plausible. Although some persons, such as Ernest van den Haag, have argued that new offenders will step forward to take the place vacated by the imprisoned offenders, they have presented no evidence that this is the case, except, perhaps, for certain crimes (such as narcotics trafficking or prostitution) which are organized along business lines.[2] For the kinds of predatory street crimes with which we are concerned—robbery, burglary, auto theft, larceny—there are no barriers to entry and no scarcity of criminal opportunities. No one need wait for a "vacancy" to appear before he can find an opportunity to become a criminal. The supply of robbers is not affected by the number of robbers practicing, because existing robbers have no way of excluding new robbers and because the opportunity for robbing (if you wish, the "demand" for robbery) is much larger than the existing number of robberies. In general, the earnings of street criminals are not affected by how many "competitors" they have.

The third condition that must be met if incapacitation is to work is that prisons must not be such successful "schools for crime" that the crimes prevented by incarceration are outnumbered by the increased crimes committed after release attributable to what was learned in prison. It is doubtless the case that for some offenders prison is a school; it is also doubtless that for other offenders prison is a deterrent. The former group will commit more, or more skillful, crimes after release; the latter will commit fewer crimes after release. The question, therefore, is whether the net effect of these two offsetting tendencies is positive or negative. In general, there is no evidence that the prison experience makes offenders as a whole more criminal, and there is some evidence that certain kinds of offenders (especially certain younger ones) may be deterred by a prison experience. Moreover, interviews with prisoners reveal no relationship between the number of crimes committed and whether the offenders had served a prior prison term.[3] Though there are many qualifications that should be made to this bald summary, there is no evidence that the net effect of prison is to increase the crime rates of ex-convicts sufficiently to cancel out the gains to society resulting from incapacitation.

To determine the amount of crime that is prevented by incarcerating a given number of offenders for a given length of time, the key estimate we must make is the number of offenses a criminal commits per year free on the street.[4] If a community experiences one thousand robberies a year, it obviously makes a great deal of difference whether these robberies are the work of ten robbers, each of whom commits one hundred robberies per year, or the work of one thousand robbers, each of whom commits only one robbery per year. In the first case, locking up only five robbers will cut the number of robberies in half; in the second case, locking up one hundred robbers will only reduce the number of robberies by 10 percent.

Shlomo and Reuel Shinnar have produced an elegant mathematical formula for estimating the crime-reduction potential of incapacitation under various assumptions. Their key assumption was that the average rate of offending—that is, the number of crimes committed by the average criminal per year free—was ten. On the basis of this assumption and others, they estimated that the street robbery rate in New York State would be only one-fifth what it was in 1970 if every person convicted of such a crime spent five years in prison.[5] About the time the Shinnars published this argument, other scholars were appearing in print with estimates of the individual offense rate that were much lower than ten.

At this point, the matter was taken up by a panel of experts appointed by the National Research Council (a part of the National Academy of Sciences). Jacqueline Cohen of Carnegie-Mellon University prepared, at the invitation of the panel, a careful analysis of the competing claims of various scholars.

Cohen and the panel concluded in 1978 that the most important research task confronting persons interested in incapacitation was to obtain better estimates of individual offense rates.[6] A major step in that direction was taken the following year with the publication of a new estimate, the most sophisticated to date, of those rates. Working with individual adult criminal records of all those persons arrested in Washington, D.C., during 1973 for any one of six major crimes (over five thousand persons in all), Alfred Blumstein and Jacqueline Cohen suggested that the individual offense rate varied significantly for different kinds of offenders. For example, it was highest for larceny and lowest for aggravated assault. But they also found, as had other scholars before them, that there was not a great deal of specialization among criminals—a person arrested today for robbery might be arrested next time for burglary. The major contribution of their study was the ingenious method they developed for converting the number of times persons were arrested into an estimate of the number of crimes they actually committed, a method that took into account the fact that many crimes are not reported to the police, that most crimes known to the police do not result in an arrest, and that some crimes are likely to be committed by groups of persons rather than by single offenders. Combining all the individual crime rates, the offenders in this study (a group of adults who had been arrested at least twice in Washington, D.C.) committed between nine and seventeen serious offenses per year free.[7]

This number was strikingly similar to the original estimates used by the Shinnars that had provoked so much criticism. And confidence in the Blumstein-Cohen estimates was increased when the results of a major study at the Rand Corporation became known. Researchers there had been interviewing prisoners (first in California, then in other states) to find out directly from known offenders how much crime they were committing while free. No one can be certain, of course, that the reports of the convicts constitute an accurate record of their crimes, undetected as well as detected, but the Rand researchers cross-checked the information against arrest records and looked for evidence of internal consistency in the self-reports. Moreover, the inmates volunteered information about crimes they had committed but for which they had not been arrested. Still, it is quite possible that the self-reports were somewhat inaccurate. However, it is reasonable to assume that inmates would be more likely to conceal crimes they did commit rather than admit to crimes they did not commit. Thus, any errors in these self-reports probably lead to an underestimate of the true rate of criminality of these persons.

The Rand group found that the average California prisoner had committed about fourteen serious crimes per year during each of the three years he was free.[8] This number falls squarely within the range estimated, using very different methods, by Blumstein and Cohen and, again, is comparable to the original estimate of the Shinnars. To state the California findings in slightly different terms, if no one was confined in state prison, the number of armed robberies in California would be about 22 percent higher than it now is.[9]

After their initial survey of 624 incarcerated male felons in California, the Rand group enlarged their study to include about 2,200 inmates in the states of California, Michigan, and Texas. Again, they gathered self-reports on crimes committed while free. This larger survey produced even higher estimates of individual offense rates. A person serving time in California for robbery, for example, would on the average admit to committing fifty-three robberies per year free; in Michigan, the number was seventy-seven. Those who were active burglars reported committing ninety burglaries per year in California. Interestingly, the offense rates of Texas inmates were much lower—on the average, robbers committed nine robberies a year and burglars committed twenty-four burglaries.[10]

But the Rand group learned something else which would turn out to be even more important. The "average" individual offense rate was virtually a meaningless term because the inmates they interviewed differed so sharply in how many crimes they committed. A large number of offenders committed a small number of offenses while free and a small number of offenders committed a very large number of offenses. In statistical language, the distribution of offenses was highly skewed. For example, the median number of burglaries committed by the inmates in the three states was about 5 a year, but the 10 percent of the inmates who were the highest-rate offenders committed an average of 232 burglaries a year. The median number of robberies was also about 5 a year, but the top 10 percent of offenders committed an average of 87 a year. As Peter W. Greenwood, one of the members of the Rand group, put it, incarcerating one robber who was among the top 10 percent in offense rates would prevent more robberies than incarcerating eighteen offenders who were at or below the median.[11]

All the evidence we have implies that, for crime-reduction purposes, the most rational way to use the incapacitative powers of our prisons would be to do so selectively. Instead of longer sentences for everyone, or for persons who have prior records, or for persons whose present crime is especially grave, longer sentences would be given primarily to those who, when free, commit the most crimes.

But how do we know who these high-rate, repeat criminals are? Knowing the nature of the present offense is not a good clue. The reason for this is quite simple—most street criminals do not specialize. Today's robber can be tomorrow's burglar and the next day's car thief.[12] When the police happen to arrest him, the crime for which he is arrested is determined by a kind of lottery—he happened to be caught red-handed, or as the result of a tip, committing a particular crime that may or may not be the same as either his previous crime or his next one. If judges give sentences based entirely on the gravity of the present offense, then a high-rate offender may get off lightly because on this occasion he happened to be caught snatching a purse. The low-rate offender may get a long sentence because he was unlucky enough to be caught robbing a liquor store with a gun.

Prosecutors have an understandable tendency to throw the book at persons caught committing a serious crime, especially if they have been caught before. To a certain extent, we want to encourage that tendency. After all, we not only want to reduce crime, we want to see criminals get their just deserts. Society would not, and should not, tolerate a system in which a prosecutor throws the book at purse snatchers and lets armed robbers off with a suspended sentence. But while society's legitimate desire for retribution must set the outer bounds of any sentencing policy, there is still room for flexibility within those bounds. We can, for example, act so that all robbers are punished with prison terms, but give, within certain relatively narrow ranges, longer sentences to those robbers who commit the most crimes.

If knowing the nature of the present offense and even knowing the prior record of the offender are not accurate guides to identifying high-rate offenders, what is? Obviously, we cannot ask the offenders. They may cooperate with researchers once in jail, but they have little incentive to cooperate with prosecutors before they go to jail, especially if the price of cooperation is to get a tougher sentence. But we can see what legally admissible, objective attributes of the offenders best predict who is and who is not a high-rate offender. In the Rand study, Greenwood and his colleagues discovered, by trial and error, that the following seven factors, taken together, were highly predictive of a convicted person being a high-rate offender: he (1) was convicted of a crime while a juvenile (that is, before age sixteen), (2) used illegal drugs as a juvenile, (3) used illegal drugs during the previous two years, (4) was employed less than 50 percent of the time during the previous two years, (5) served time in a juvenile facility, (6) was incarcerated in prison more than 50 percent of the previous two years, and (7) was previously convicted for the present offense.

Using this scale, Greenwood found that 82 percent of those predicted to be low-rate offenders in fact were, and 82 percent of those predicted to be medium- or high-rate offenders also were. To understand how big these differences are, the median California prison inmate who is predicted to be a low-rate offender will in fact commit slightly more than one burglary and slightly less than one robbery per year free. By contrast, the median California inmate who is predicted to be a high-rate offender will commit ninety-three burglaries and thirteen robberies per year free. In other states, this prediction scale may be more or less accurate.

Opinions differ as to the effect on the crime rate and prison population of making sentences for high-rate offenders longer than those for low-rate ones. Greenwood applied his scale to California and found that if all low-rate robbers received two-year prison terms (most now receive longer ones) and all high-rate robbers received seven-year terms (most now receive shorter ones), the number of robberies committed in the state would drop by an estimated 20 percent with no increase in the prison population.[13]

Obviously, a policy of reducing crime by selective incapacitation (that is, by adjusting prison terms to reflect predicted individual offense rates) raises a number of issues. Though these issues are important, one must bear in mind that they cannot be resolved by comparing selective incapacitation to some ideal system of criminal justice in which everyone receives exactly his just deserts. No such system exists or ever will. One must compare instead the proposed policy with what exists now, with all its imperfections, and ask whether the gains in crime reduction are worth the risks entailed when we try to make predictions about human behavior.

The first issue is whether it is permissible to allow crime-control to be an objective of sentencing policy. Some persons, such as Andrew von Hirsch, claim that only retribution—what he calls "just deserts"—can be a legitimate basis for sentencing.[14] To some extent, he is undoubtedly correct. Even if we were absolutely certain that a convicted murderer would never murder again, we would still feel obliged to impose a relatively severe sentence in order to vindicate the principle that life is dear and may not be unlawfully taken without paying a price. Moreover, the sentences given low-rate offenders must reflect society's judgment as to the moral blame such behavior deserves, and the sentences given high-rate offenders ought not exceed what society feels is the highest sentence appropriate to the crime for which the offenders were convicted. And low-rate offenders should get a sufficiently severe sentence to help persuade them, and others like them, not to become high-rate offenders. Still, after allowing for all of these considerations, there will inevitably remain a range of possible sentences within which the goal of incapacitation can be served. The range will exist in part because there is no objective way to convert a desire for retribution into a precise sentence for a given offense and in part because legislatures will almost invariably act so as to preserve some judicial discretion so that the circumstances of a case which cannot be anticipated in advance may affect the sentence. Among those circumstances is a concern for protecting society from the threat that a given offender represents.

The second issue is whether our prediction methods are good enough to allow them to influence sentence length. The answer to that question depends on what one will accept as "good enough." Absolute certainty will never be attainable. Moreover, criminal justice *now,* at almost every stage, operates by trying to predict future behavior. When a prosecutor decides how much plea bargaining he will allow, he is trying to predict how a judge or jury will react to his evidence, and he is often trying to guess how dangerous an offender he has in his grasp. When a judge sets bail, he is always making a prediction about the likelihood of a person out on bail showing up for his trial and is frequently trying to predict whether the person, if out on bail, will commit another crime while free. When a defense attorney argues in favor of his client being released on his own recognizance, without bail, he is trying to persuade the judge to accept his prediction that the accused will not skip town. When the judge passes a sentence, he is trying, at least in part, to predict whether the convicted person represents a future threat to society. When a parole board considers a convict's application for early release, it tries to predict—often on the basis of a quantitative system, called a "base expectancy table"—whether the person will become a recidivist if released. Virtually every member of the criminal justice system is routinely engaged in predicting behavior, often on the basis of very scant knowledge and quite dubious rules of thumb. The question, therefore, is this: are the kinds of predictions that scholars such as Greenwood make about future criminality better (more accurate) and thus fairer than the predictions prosecutors and judges now make?

A third issue is tougher. Is it fair for a low-rate offender who is caught committing a serious crime to serve a shorter sentence (because he is not much of a threat to society) than a high-rate offender who gets caught committing a relatively minor offense? Probably not. Sentences would have to have legal boundaries set so that the use of selective incapacitation could not lead to perverse sentences—armed robbers getting one year, purse-snatchers getting five.

Finally, there is bound to be a debate about the legal and even ethical propriety of using certain facts as the basis for making predictions. Everyone would agree that race should not be a factor; everyone would probably agree that prior record should be a factor. I certainly believe that it is proper to take into account an offender's juvenile as well as his adult record, but I am aware that some people disagree. But can one take into account alcohol or drug use? Suppose the person claims to be cured of his drinking or his drug problem; do we believe him? And if we do, do we wipe the slate clean of information about these matters? And should we penalize more heavily persons who are chronically unemployed, even if unemployment is a good predictor of recidivism? Some people will argue that this is tantamount to making unemployment a crime, though I think that overstates the matter. After all, advocates of pretrial release of arrested persons, lenient bail policies, and diverting offenders away from jail do not hesitate to claim that having a good employment record should be counted in the accused's favor. If employment counts in favor of some, then obviously unemployment may be counted against others. Since advocates of "bail reform" are also frequent opponents of incapacitation, selective or collective, it is incumbent on them to straighten out their own thinking on how we make use of employment records. Nonetheless, this important issue deserves thoughtful attention.

On one matter, critics of prison may take heart. If Greenwood and the others are correct, then an advantage of selective incapacitation is that it can be accomplished without great increases (or perhaps any increases) in the use of prisons. It is a way of allocating more rationally the existing stock of prison cells to produce, within the constraints of just deserts, greater crime-control benefits. Many offenders—indeed most offenders—would probably have their sentences shortened, and the space thereby freed would be allocated to the small number of high-rate offenders whom even the most determined opponents of prison would probably concede should be behind bars.

Notes

1. "Prisons and Prisoners," Bureau of Justice Statistics *Bulletin,* January, 1982.
2. Ernest van den Haag, *Punishing Criminals* (New York: Basic Books, 1975), 52–60.
3. Mark A. Peterson and Harriet B. Braiker, *Doing Crime: A Survey of California Prison Inmates* (Santa Monica, Calif.: Rand, 1980), x, 50.
4. Scholars who study incapacitation call the number of crimes committed per offender per year free "lambda," or λ. To avoid technical terminology, I will refer to it as the "individual offense rate."
5. James Q. Wilson, *Thinking About Crime* (New York: Basic Books, 1975), 201; Shlomo and Reuel Shinnar, "The Effects of the Criminal Justice System on the Control of Crime: A Quantitative Approach," 9 *Law and Society Review* 581–611 (1975); Benjamin Avi-Itzhak and Reuel Shinnar, "Quantitative Models in Crime Control," 1 *Journal of Criminal Justice* 196–97 (1973).
6. Jacqueline Cohen, "The Incapacitative Effect of Imprisonment: A Critical Review of the Literature," in *Deterrence and Incapacitation: Estimating the Effects of Criminal Sanctions on Crime Rates,* ed. Alfred Blumstein et al. (Washington, D.C.: National Academy of Sciences, 1978), 206.
7. Alfred Blumstein and Jacqueline Cohen, "Estimation of Individual Crime

Rates from Arrest Records," 70 *Journal of Criminal Law and Criminology* 585 (1979).

8. Peterson and Braiker, *Doing Crime,* vii, 32.

9. Ibid.

10. Peter W. Greenwood, *Selective Incapacitation* (Santa Monica, Calif.: Rand, 1982), 43–44.

11. Ibid.

12. Blumstein and Cohen, "Estimation of Individual Crime Rates," 581; Peterson and Braiker, *Doing Crime,* 40; Marvin Wolfgang et al., *Delinquency in a Birth Cohort* (Chicago: University of Chicago Press, 1972), 206.

13. Greenwood, *Selective Incapacitation,* Figure 5-2.

14. Andrew von Hirsch, *Doing Justice: The Choice of Punishments,* a report of the Committee for the Study of Incarceration (New York: Hill and Wang, 1976).

3.7
Selective Incapacitation: Some Doubts

Andrew von Hirsch

Prediction research in criminology has, by and large, focused on characteristics of offenders. Various facts about criminals are recorded: age, previous arrests and convictions, social history, and so forth. It is then statistically determined which of these factors are most strongly associated with subsequent offending.[1] The result is a "selective" prediction strategy: among those convicted of a given type of offense, some will be identified as bad risks and others not.

Traditional Prediction Methods

Traditional statistical prediction techniques pursued this selective approach. Generally, they found that certain facts about an offender—principally, previous criminal history, drug habits, and history of unemployment—were to a modest extent indicative of increased likelihood of recidivism.[2]

These techniques did not, however, distinguish between serious and trivial recidivism. Both the offender who subsequently committed a single minor offense and the individual who committed many serious new crimes were lumped together as recidivists. Moreover, the techniques offered no promise of reduced crime rates, as they did not attempt to estimate aggregate crime-prevention effects. Locking up the potential recidivist thus assured only that he or she would be restrained; since other criminals remained at large, it did not necessarily diminish the overall risk of

This essay is published here for the first time.

victimization. By the 1970s, these limitations reduced penologists' interest in traditional prediction techniques.[3]

"Selective Incapacitation"

Surveys of imprisoned offenders, conducted in the United States in the early 1980s, found that a small number of such persons admitted responsibility for a disproportionate number of serious offenses. If that minority of dangerous offenders could be identified and segregated, perhaps this could reduce crime rates after all. These surveys thus generated a renewed interest in prediction research.

The most notable product was a Rand Corporation study published in 1982 by Peter W. Greenwood.[4] Greenwood named his prediction strategy "selective incapacitation." His idea was to target *high-rate, serious* offenders—those likely to commit frequent acts of robbery or other violent crimes in future. For that purpose he took a group of incarcerated robbers, asked them how frequently they had committed such crimes, and then identified the characteristics of those reporting the highest robbery rates. From this, he fashioned a seven-factor predictive index, which identified the high-rate offenders on the basis of their early criminal records and histories of drug use and unemployment.[5]

Greenwood also devised a method of projecting the crime reduction impact of his technique. On the basis of offender self-reports, he estimated the annual rate of offending of those robbers who were identified as high risks by his prediction index. He then calculated the number of robberies that, supposedly, would be prevented by incarcerating such individuals for given periods. By increasing prison terms for the high-risk robbers while reducing terms for the others, he concluded, one could reduce the robbery rate by as much as 15 to 20 percent—without causing prison populations to rise.[6]

Questions of Effectiveness

While the study initially attracted much interest,[7] serious problems have become apparent. One difficulty is making the predictions hold up when official data of the kind a sentencing court has available are relied upon. The objective of selective incapacitation is to target the potential high-rate serious offenders, and distinguish them from recidivists who reoffend less frequently or gravely. To make this distinction, the Rand studies, including Greenwood's, relied upon offender self-reports. A sentencing court, however, is seldom in the position to rely upon the defendant facing sentence to supply the necessary information about his criminal past. The court would have to rely on officially recorded information about offenders' adult and juvenile records, and such records make the distinction poorly. When Greenwood's data were reanalyzed to see how well the potential high-risk serious offenders could be identified from information available in court records, the results were disappointing. The officially recorded facts—arrests, convictions, and meager information about offenders' personal histories—did not permit the potential high-rate robbers to be distinguished from (say) the potential car thieves. The factors in the self-report study that had proved useful—such as early and extensive youthful violence and multiple drug use, were not reflected in court records.[8] To make the predictions work, the courts would have to obtain and rely on information in school and social-service files—with all the problems of practicability and due process that would involve.[9]

Serious flaws were found, also, in the projections of preventive impact. Greenwood based his crime reduction estimates on the self-reported activities of *incarcerated* robbers, and then extrapolated those estimates to robbers generally. Incarcerated robbers, however, are scarcely a representative group: they may well rob more frequently than robbers generally in the community. (It is like trying to learn about the smoking habits of smokers generally by studying the self-reported smoking activity of admittees to a lung cancer ward.) When this extrapolation is eliminated, the projected crime reduction impact is reduced by about one-half.[10] Other defects in the projections exist. Greenwood assumed, for example, that his high-rate robbers have lengthy criminal careers. When shorter and more realistic criminal careers are assumed instead, the estimated preventive effect shrinks.[11]

These doubts are confirmed by the 1986 report of the National Academy of Sciences' panel on criminal careers.[12] The panel included several noted advocates of predictively based sentencing, and the report endorses the idea of predictive strategies (within certain limits) *if* these could be shown to be effective.[13] Nevertheless, the panel's conclusions on the crime-preventive effects of selective incapacitation are skeptical.[14] After recalculating Greenwood's results and scaling his initial preventive estimates down considerably, the panel notes that even those revised estimates (1) do not hold up in two of the three jurisdictions studied; (2) would shrink further were the scale drawn from a broader and potentially more heterogeneous population than persons in confinement and were it to utilize officially recorded rather than self-reported information; and (3) could nearly disappear if the estimated length of the criminal career were scaled down. While the report urges further research, it does not claim that selective incapacitation methods now exist that yield more satisfactory results.

Prospects for Improvement

Can these difficulties be overcome? Greenwood's research is only the beginning, and future selective incapacitation studies might conceivably do better. The obstacles are considerable, however. If the aim is to distinguish potential high-rate, serious offenders from lesser potential criminals, this remains difficult to achieve using the scant official records courts have at their disposal. Records of early offending might become somewhat more accessible, with a change in the law concerning the confidentiality of juvenile records—but such records, notoriously, suffer from incompleteness and inaccuracy. Social histories, such as drug use and employment, will be even more difficult to ascertain accurately.[15]

Estimation of the impact of selective incapacitation on crime rates involves difficult problems of sampling. Analyses of convicted or incarcerated offenders' criminal activities suffer from the difficulty mentioned already: it is not clear to what extent these persons' activities are representative of the activity of offenders in the community. Samples drawn from the general population are free from such bias, but usually contain too small a number of active offenders.[16]

Another obstacle concerns estimating the length of criminal careers. The serious offenders with whom selective incapacitation is concerned generally would be imprisoned in any event; the main policy issue is the length of their confinement. The strategy is to impose longer terms on the supposed high-risk offenders, but that assumes they will continue their criminal activities. Little prevention is achieved if the bad risks who are confined are those whose careers will end fairly soon. This means that selective incapacitation, to succeed, needs not merely to pick out high-risk offenders but *those who are likely to continue offending for an appreciable time*. But how much do we know about forecasting the residual career? At the moment, very little. The National Academy panel suggests that career termination may depend on new variables—not so much prior criminal history but later events, including steady employment and marriage. Those are scarcely matters concerning which a court can readily obtain information at time of sentencing.[17]

Proportionality Problems

Selective prediction strategies—whether the traditional sort or newer methods such as Greenwood's—suffer also from a serious ethical problem: their conflict with the requirements of proportionality. The conflict stems from the character of the factors relied upon to predict. Those predictive factors have little bearing on the degree of reprehensibleness of the offender's criminal choices.

Proportionality requires that penalties be based chiefly on the gravity of the crime for which the offender currently stands convicted.[18] The offender's previous criminal record, if considered at all, should have only a secondary role (see Extract 4.6),[19] and the offender's social status is largely immaterial to the penalty he or she deserves.

With selective risk prediction, the emphasis necessarily shifts *away* from the seriousness of the current offense. Since the aim is to select the higher-risk individuals from among those convicted of a specified type of crime, the character of the current crime cannot have much weight. Traditional prediction indices largely ignored the gravity of the current offense and concentrated on the offender's earlier criminal and social histories.[20] The new "selective incapacitation" techniques have a similar emphasis. Of Greenwood's seven predictive factors, three do not measure criminal activity of a significant nature at all, but the offender's personal drug consumption and lack of stable employment, instead. Of the four other factors, only two measure the offender's recent criminal record; and *none* measure the heinousness (e.g., the degree of violence) of the offender's current offense.[21]

When one tries to take aggregate preventive impact into account, matters become worse. Selective incapacitation techniques, by their own proponents' reckoning, could promise significant crime reduction effects only by infringing proportionality requirements to a *very* great degree. Greenwood's projection of a significant reduction in the robbery rate is made on the assumption that robbers who score badly on his prediction index would receive about *eight* years' imprisonment, whereas better-scoring robbers would receive only *one* year in jail.[22] This means a huge difference in severity—one of over 800 percent—in the punishment of offenders convicted of the same offense of robbery; and one that can scarcely begin to be accounted for by distinctions in the seriousness of the offender's criminal conduct. When this punishment differential is narrowed—when high-risk robbers receive only modestly longer terms than robbers deemed lower risks—the crime reduction payoff shrinks to slender proportions, even by Greenwood's estimation methods.[23]

Conclusions

Where does this leave us? A limited capacity to forecast risk has long existed: persons with criminal records, drug habits, and no jobs tend to recidivate at a higher rate than other offenders, as researchers have known for years. However, the limitations in that forecasting capacity must be recognized—for selective incapacitation as well as more traditional forecasting techniques. Identifying high-risk, serious offenders will be impeded by the quality of information available (or likely to become available) to sentencing courts. The potential impact of selective incapacitation on crime rates is far below proponents' initial estimates, and is likely to be quite modest. Considerations of proportionality limit the inequalities in sentence that may fairly be visited for the sake of restraining high-risk offenders; and limiting these permissible inequalities will, in turn, further restrict the technique's impact on crime. Selective incapacitation—far from being the near panacea some of its advocates have asserted it is—is both on empirical and ethical grounds a device of limited potential, at best.

Notes

1. For a description of prediction techniques, see D. M. Gottfredson, "Assessment and Prediction Methods in Crime and Delinquency," in President's National Commission for Law Enforcement and Criminal Justice, *Task Force Report: Juvenile Delinquency and Youth Crime* (Washington, D.C., 1967).
2. *Id.;* see also D. Gottfredson, L. Wilkins, and P. Hoffman, *Guidelines for Parole and Sentencing* (Lexington, Mass., 1978).
3. A. von Hirsch, *Past or Future Crimes: Deservedness and Dangerousness in the Sentencing of Criminals* (New Brunswick, N.J., 1986), 5–7 [hereafter referred to as *Past or Future Crimes*].
4. P. Greenwood, *Selective Incapacitation* (Santa Monica, Cal., 1982).
5. Greenwood's seven predictive factors are: (1) prior convictions of instant offense type; (2) incarceration for more than half the preceding two years; (3) conviction before age of sixteen; (4) time served in a state juvenile facility; (5) drug use during preceding two years; (6) drug use as a juvenile; (7) employment for less than 50 percent of the preceding two years. (*Id.*)
6. *Id.* His projection method was a modification of methods devised by Reuel Shinnar. See R. Shinnar and S. Shinnar, "The Effects of Criminal Justice on the Control of Crime," *Law and Society Review* 9 (1975): 581.
7. For favorable initial comment, see J. Q. Wilson, *Thinking About Crime,* rev. ed. (New York, 1983), ch. 8 [set forth in part in Extract 3.6]; M. Moore et al., *Dangerous Offenders* (Cambridge, Mass., 1985).

8. M. Chaiken and J. Chaiken, "Offender Types and Public Policy," *Crime and Delinquency* 30 (1985): 195.

9. *Past or Future Crimes,* 111–13.

10. *Id.,* ch. 10; for the method of estimation, see A. von Hirsch and D. M. Gottfredson, "Selective Incapacitation: Some Queries on Research Design and Equity," *N.Y.U. Review of Law and Social Change* 12 (1983–84): 11.

11. *Past or Future Crimes,* 121 n. 2.

12. The panel's report is set forth in A. Blumstein, J. Cohen, J. Roth, and C. Visher, eds., *Criminal Careers and "Career Criminals"* (Washington, D.C., 1986), vol. 1, 1–209 [hereafter referred to as *Criminal Careers*]. For an examination of the report, see A. von Hirsch, "Selective Incapacitation Reexamined," *Criminal Justice Ethics* 7 (1988): 19–35.

13. See *Criminal Careers,* 129–30.

14. *Criminal Careers,* 131–34.

15. *Id.,* 181; *Past or Future Crimes,* 112–13.

16. *Criminal Careers,* 101–4; von Hirsch, "Selective Incapacitation Reexamined," op. cit., 22–23.

17. *Id.,* 23; *Criminal Careers,* 206.

18. For a general analysis of proportionality and its rationale, see *Past or Future Crimes,* chs. 3–8; A. von Hirsch, "Proportionality in the Philosophy of Punishment," *Criminal Law Forum* 1 (1990): 259–90. See also Extracts 4.2 and 4.4 in this volume.

19. See also *Past or Future Crimes,* ch. 7.

20. *Id.,* ch. 11, especially 132–38.

21. *Id.*

22. Greenwood does not publish these proposed durations in his report, but they are estimated in the reanalysis of his data done for the National Academy of Sciences' panel. See *Criminal Careers,* 131–32.

23. For his estimates, see Greenwood, *Selective Incapacitation,* 78–79.

3.8
Selective Incapacitation: The Debate over Its Ethics

Michael Tonry

Much of the debate over predictions of dangerousness in sentencing turns on the debaters' differing views of the importance of equality and proportionality in the distribution of punishment. These different views, in turn, derive from different theories of the justification and properties of criminal punishment.

Retributive and Utilitarian Theories

In the interest of efficiency, the issues commonly raised concerning prediction are considered here primarily from two polar hypothetical positions—that of the ultimate utilitarian (UU) and that of the thoroughgoing retributivist (TR), which are stereotyped exemplars of two kinds of philosophical views called, respectively, teleological (or "consequentialist") theories and deontological theories. In general, teleological theories are concerned with justification for actions as means to ends, deontological theories with justification of actions in themselves.

1. Utilitarian Theories

Utilitarianism is the best-known teleological theory and is concerned ultimately with maximizing social utility and the aggregate public good. In the arcane reaches of utilitarianism, there is considerable debate about how

---

From Michael Tonry, "Prediction and Classification: Legal and Ethical Issues," in Don M. Gottfredson and Michael Tonry, eds., *Prediction and Classification: Criminal Justice Decision Making* (Chicago: University of Chicago Press, 1987).

one could best measure social utility, but for the purposes of this essay "the greatest good for the greatest number" should suffice. Applied to crime, UU would support the crime control strategy that costs least in economic and social terms when one takes fully into account the cost of crime and fear of crime; the cost of law enforcement and sanctioning; the cost to offenders, their families, and associates, and the state of the offender's being punished.

Utilitarians believe in incentives and rationality and therefore see the punishment of offenders as a device for reducing the incidence and cost of crime through deterrence, incapacitation, and rehabilitation. To UU, then, what is important in punishing individual offenders is not anything about them but rather the likely crime-preventive effects of their punishment. Strictly speaking, if no crime prevention effects would be realized from punishing an individual, no punishment would be justified. Conversely, if punishment of an individual will on balance increase social utility, then that punishment should be imposed even if, for example, a severe punishment is needed for a petty offense. Thus, for UU, equality and proportionality are relatively unimportant properties or objectives of punishment.

2. *Retributivist Theories*

The thoroughgoing retributivist, TR, finds UU's views shocking and believes that people must be viewed as ends, not means. Punishments must be deserved; the relevant moral calculus concerns the offender and his culpability and not the consequences of his punishment. People deserve punishment because they knowingly and wrongly inflict injury to the person or interests of others. Exactly why this is so varies for different theorists, just as the methods for measuring social utility vary among utilitarian theorists.

A number of criticisms of prediction-based classifications have been offered. These are summarized in the following pages with, where appropriate, the different views of UU and TR set out alongside those of major contemporary writers.

Problems with Predictions

The mainstream case made for use of predictions of dangerousness goes something like this. Judges, parole boards, and correctional administrators have *always* taken an offender's apparent dangerousness into account in making critical decisions, although, of necessity, they have done so in an intuitionist way with wide divergence in the decisions reached; it is far better explicitly to rely on general predictive rules that are based on the best available evidence and that are systematically applied than to go on as before; so long as the resulting penalties do not exceed what the offender deserved, he has no ground for complaint, and the rest of us will be better off because crime will be incrementally reduced by virtue of the incapacitation of offenders predicted to be dangerous. If the accuracy of predictions can be significantly improved, we may be able to target resources on dangerous offenders, to extend greater leniency to nondangerous offenders, to reduce prison populations, and thereby to achieve greater crime control at less financial cost. Thus the public's interests in crime control and economy will be served, sentencing (or bail release or parole release) disparities will be diminished, and offenders will suffer punishments that are not undeserved. It is not the best of all possible worlds, but it is better than what now exists.

Arguments for marginal improvements in justice and efficiency are hard to resist because we know that more ambitious efforts tend to fail. Nonetheless, powerful arguments have been offered against reliance on predictions.

1. Simple Injustice

Some simply reject prediction's incapacitative premise. If, like TR, one believes that the offender's blameworthiness or culpability determines how much punishment he should suffer, an increase of that punishment for incapacitative reasons is, by definition, unjust. The promised decrease of punishment for the nondangerous is not necessarily a good thing; the resulting differences between punishments of dangerous and nondangerous offenders who have committed the same offense exacerbate existing inequalities in punishment.

A standard rejoinder is that, for obvious metaphysical reasons, it is impossible to say precisely what punishment is deserved for any particular offense and, consequently (barring aberrantly severe punishments), it is difficult ever to say that a punishment is undeserved. Norval Morris, for example, has argued that one can meaningfully speak of punishments as being "undeservedly lenient" or "undeservedly severe" but can say of punishments within the range thereby defined only that they are "not undeserved": "Hence, a deserved punishment must mean a not undeserved punishment which bears a proportional relationship in the hierarchy of punishments to the harm for which the criminal has been convicted" (1982, 150) [see also Extract 4.3].

John Monahan has extended this argument by noting that, because neither moral theory nor empirical research on public attitudes and opinions can precisely determine crime seriousness, "it is affirmatively preferable [to consider crime control in making punishment decisions], in that, justice to the offender being equal (within our large measurement error), a scheme which promotes justice to potential victims is superior to one that does not" (Monahan 1982, 104; see also Bedau 1977, 65).

Andrew von Hirsch has offered a surrejoinder to arguments like those of Morris and Monahan. He concedes that no available moral calculus will allow one to identify the single punishment appropriate in any individual case. However, he argues that moral principles can give much more guidance than does Morris's "not undeserved" punishment. Von Hirsch distinguishes between "cardinal" and "ordinal" desert (1985, 39, 43–46). With Morris he agrees that cardinal desert—that is, some absolute metaphysically appropriate punishment—is beyond the knowledge of mortal mind. Ordinal desert, however, deals with relations between punishments, and regarding this man's moral principles can offer guidance. Robbery, most people agree, is more serious than is petit larceny and should be more severely punished, and similar comparative statements can be made about most offenses. If one concedes that, other things equal, more serious offenses should precipitate more severe sanctions, then the logic of a comprehensive listing of offenses scaled to reflect notions of their comparative seriousness carries with it an ordinal ranking of deserved punishments [see Extract 4.4].

Norval Morris responds to this by observing that the "ranges" for deserved punishments for particular offenses must be quite broad and overlap substantially because the least severe version of higher-rated offenses may be less deserving of punishment than the most severe version of lower-rated offenses: "some rapes are less serious than some aggravated batteries that are not rapes" (Morris 1982, 151).

The force of Morris's response to some extent depends on the kind of criminal law sentencing system one has in mind. In systems in which criminal offenses are defined broadly and in which judicial sentencing discretion is not structured by guidelines or a meaningful determinate sentencing law, surely Morris is correct. Some batteries are more serious than some rapes, and a generalization that all rapes must be sentenced more severely than any battery would be morally unconvincing and unduly rigid.

In a jurisdiction with tightly specified offense definitions, Morris's argument loses much of its force; various grades of rape could be distinguished, as could various grades of battery, and it would not be surprising if some battery subtypes were regarded as more serious than some rape subtypes. Even then, exceptional cases can be imagined in which offenses of a less serious type (e.g., vindictive destruction of property known to have enormous sentimental value to the owner) seem worse than offenses of a more serious type (e.g., mercy killing of an aged spouse who has clearly and repeatedly asked to be relieved of intense incessant pain and who will in any event soon die), but these will be exceptional cases, and any sensitive ethical or legal system must allow for the existence of difficult special cases.

Thus Morris's rebuttal can be avoided mechanically, if imperfectly. Inevitably, there must be marginal cases and gray areas, but in the main it should be possible to establish an offense ranking of sufficient detail to permit a coherent system of "ordinal" desert.[1]

If one sees desert or retribution as defining principles governing the amount of punishment, as von Hirsch largely does,[2] then achievement of equality and proportionality in punishment are paramount goals. Predictive sentencing conflicts with achievement of equality and proportionality in outcomes and violates the limits set by concern for ordinal desert.

However, von Hirsch in my view wins the skirmish but loses the conflict unless he can persuade Morris or others to adopt his premise that desert *should* be both a justifying aim of punishment and the primary defining principle in determining amounts of punishment. Almost by definition, proponents of predictive sentencing subscribe to a significant degree to utilitarian premises of punishment and so, rejecting von Hirsch's premises, can reject his critique of predictive sentencing.

2. *Past and Future Crimes*

A second, more general, criticism of predictive sentencing is that it punishes people for crimes they have not yet committed and might not commit if released (von Hirsch 1985, 2, 167–69). This criticism is related to, but different from, the argument that predictions of dangerousness are unacceptably unreliable: this latter claim is the empirical basis for the assertion that some of those "incapacitated" would not reoffend, but the "false positive" argument is a different argument.

On this point, TR and UU simply differ in principle. To TR, deserved punishment for the current crime can be calibrated reasonably precisely; extension of punishment beyond that amount is not deserved in respect of the current offense and can be seen as an additional increment of punishment for a crime not committed. Von Hirsch (1981) argues that some increase in punishment is permitted in respect of prior offenses (actually, that offenders should be given the benefit of the doubt and given more lenient sentences than they deserve for the first, or first few, offenses); to the extent that accumulated prior convictions predict future offending, some incapacitative effect will be coincident with increased penalties for successive convictions and is to that extent not objectionable. For von Hirsch, the values of equality and proportionality are not seriously undermined since all offenders convicted of the same offense and with the same criminal history will receive the same sentence [see Extract 4.6].

Norval Morris and Marc Miller would go further because their position of "limiting retributivism" does not require equality of suffering. It seems to them entirely proper "within the range of not unjust punishments, to take account of different levels of dangerousness of those to be punished; but the concept of the deserved, or rather the not undeserved, punishment properly limits the range within which utilitarian values may operate" (Morris and Miller 1985, 37). The imprecision of "the range of not undeserved punishments" makes it difficult to say precisely where the Morris-Miller view would limit the scope of predictive sentencing; however, if for a hypothetical offender any prison sentence from within the range of two to five years would be not undeserved, an incapacitative sentence not to exceed five years would be acceptable. There the line would be drawn, however, and an incapacitative sentence of ten years would be unjust, even if it would optimize the incapacitative effects of punishment.

The Morris-Miller view can be tested by trying to apply it in a determinate sentencing jurisdiction that has narrow ranges of approved sentences for individual cases. If, as a matter of authoritative policy-making, the applicable range has been set at thirty-two to thirty-six months, can predictive considerations be looked to only within that narrow range? If so, much of their disagreement with TR and von Hirsch disappears. The underlying issue is whether "not undeserved punishment" is a normative and cultural question or whether it is a policy-making question. If it is the former, the thirty-two- to thirty-six-month boundaries are not confining if cultural norms would regard a sixty-month sentence for the offense (to which the thirty-two- to thirty-six-month range applies) as "not undeserved." If this is the argument, it is hard to see how it can be incorporated into legal rules, because it is difficult to see what source of credible authoritative declarations of moral and cultural views of not undeserved punishment there can be other than legally constituted policymakers.[3]

Finally, UU, who cares nought for equality and proportionality, would opt for a ten-year sentence if that would most enhance social utility even if two to five years is the agreed range of not undeserved punishment in an individual case. Richard Posner, for example, has argued that the utilitarian principle of parsimony may require stark inequality (Posner 1977, 163–73). He argues that, if crime prevention goals required imposition of ten years of punishment, it would be preferable to sentence one person to a ten-year term than to sentence ten people to one-year terms. This is because subjective suffering would diminish as the years passed, and, consequently, the ten, each suffering an especially grievous first year's loss of freedom, would suffer more in the aggregate than would the one over time. To impose the greater aggregate subjective suffering on the ten is unnecessary and therefore unjust.

Thus, like the previous criticism that predictive sentencing is prima facie unjust, the argument against sentencing in respect of future crimes turns out to be another disagreement over the premises of punishment. Only for UU is there no problem—UU, however, is a mythological beast, and few people subscribe to this polar view. For "limiting retributivists" like Norval Morris, predictive sentencing is unjust only when the resulting aggregate sentence is "undeserved." Von Hirsch allows much less scope for predictive considerations than does Morris's range of "not undeserved punishments."[4] Finally, to TR, predictive sentencing is prima facie objectionable because it treats individuals as means to crime control ends.

3. *False Positives and the "Conviction-of-Innocents" Analogy*

By this point in the argument, TR has rejected predictive sentencing. To Andrew von Hirsch, predictive sentencing is acceptable only insofar as it can be achieved in ways that are consonant with the limited scope that he would permit for increased sentence on account of prior convictions. For those who remain unconvinced or skeptical, another major problem remains—predictions of violence are not very accurate. The conventional wisdom for some years has been that for every three persons predicted to commit serious violent offenses, only one will do so, and the other two will be "false positives" (see, e.g., Morris and Miller 1985; Floud and Young 1981). Perhaps this 33 percent accuracy rate has improved, but even at 50 percent accuracy, an argument can be made that this is too inaccurate to serve as the basis for denying liberty [see Extract 3.2].[5]

To some extent, people's views of this criticism are subsumed within their views on "punishment for future crimes," but not completely. For Norval Morris and Marc Miller, even within the range of not undeserved punishments, predictive sentencing is appropriate only if

> the base expectancy rate of violence for the criminal predicted as dangerous must be shown by reliable evidence to be *substantially higher* than the base expectancy rate of another criminal *with a closely similar criminal record* and *convicted of a closely similar crime* but not predicted as unusually dangerous. [Morris and Miller 1985, 37; emphasis added]

This is a very demanding test that few proposals for predictive sentencing could satisfy. Information concerning past criminality has repeatedly been shown to be the best predictor of future criminality. If, as the Morris-Miller formula prescribes, one controls for criminal history and the nature of the current crime, the offender's remaining characteristics are seldom likely to lead to predicted base expectancy rates "substantially higher" than those for other individuals with comparable criminal histories convicted of comparable crimes. Thus the Morris-Miller view concedes that the false positive problem is a serious problem and sidesteps it by setting a test for predictive sentencing that few, if any, systems could meet.

A number of arguments are commonly made about the false positive problem. The first, the "conviction-of-innocents" analogy, is to analogize *extension* of incarceration to conviction by contrasting the standards of proof that apply at a criminal trial and the levels of predictive accuracy that now characterize violence predictions. Proof beyond a reasonable doubt is seldom quantified, but surely it is equivalent at least to a 90 percent probability. Thus, one can argue, the requisite *90 percent probability* of commission of a *past crime* that must be proven before a person can be convicted and deprived of liberty should be contrasted with the best case *33 percent probability* of commission of a *future crime* that can be used to extend incarceration. If liberty is an important value, the argument goes, we should not extend deprivations of liberty on so much lower a probative standard than justifies its deprivation in the first place.

The standard response to this, as given by Floud and Young (1981) and Morris and Miller (1985), is that the analogy is misconceived. Per Floud and Young, "The question is not 'How many innocent persons are to sacrifice their liberty for the extra protection that special sentences for dangerous offenders will provide?' but 'What is the moral choice between the alternative risks: the risk of harm to potential victims or the risk of unnecessarily detaining offenders judged to be dangerous'" (1981, 49). This argument, again, is an argument about premises. To TR or Andrew von Hirsch, the deserved punishment imposed for the current offense is relatively specific, and conviction of the offense is an essential condition precedent; Floud and Young's balancing of harms is simply inappropriate. A significant increment added to the deserved punishment for those predicted to commit future crimes is imposition of an additional term of incarceration, and, so seen, a 33 percent probability standard of proof is shockingly low. Floud and Young, by contrast, simply assume that a limited utilitarian calculus is appropriate.

To limiting retributivists, the increment of punishment added for predictive reasons may be acceptable so long as the total punishment is "not undeserved" (though recall that the Morris-Miller test is so stringent that it could seldom be met). Whatever the level of predictive accuracy, an aggregate sentence exceeding the upper limit of not undeserved punishment would be unjust. For UU, Floud and Young are absolutely correct, and the trade-off between offenders' liberty and crimes prevented is simply another appropriate utilitarian calculus.

A second response to the conviction-of-innocents analogy that is sometimes offered by proponents of predictive sentencing is that the false positive problem is itself misconceived. This argument has two components. The first component is that "statistical predictions are made for groups and not for individuals" (Farrington and Tarling 1983, 20). The false positives, say Floud and Young (1981, 26), "are statistical errors and it is fallacious to think of them as misjudged individuals." All members of the group predicted to be violent (assuming reliable information) were correctly identified as having the characteristics that, in general, are possessed by those predicted to commit future violence. One could say that there was 100 percent correct identification of members of a group that has a 33 percent violence probability.

The second component of this argument is that "a statistical prediction of dangerousness, based on membership in a group for which a consistent and tested pattern of conduct has been shown, is the statement of a *condition* [membership in the group] and not the prediction of a result [future violence]" (Morris and Miller 1985, 18).

Clearly, neither component of this second argument would convince TR or Andrew von Hirsch. I doubt that they would convince an agnostic or a skeptic either, for the distinctions offered beg the critical question. That this argument does not resolve the false positive problem can be shown by imagining that a criminal code expressly authorized an incremental prison term for dangerous offenders to be served after the "deserved" sentence imposed for the current offense (as English habitual offender laws once did; see Morris 1951). The question to be decided would be "is there an X percent [possibly 33 percent, possibly 50 percent] probability that this individual will commit future acts of serious violence?" That the defendant had the attributes of membership in a group with a 33 percent base rate would be admissible in evidence to show what is equivalent to membership—that the probability of that individual committing serious violence is 33 percent. The legislative draftsmen in their wisdom could specify 33 percent or 50 percent or 90 percent as the required probability, but the policy question concerning the punishment of individuals must surely be focused on the individual's probability of future violence, and that question is the same whether one considers group or individual probabilities (see also Monahan and Wexler 1978).

A third response to the conviction-of-innocents analogy put by proponents of predictive sentencing is that the seemingly low "false positive" rates are misleading. Some seeming false positives may be true positives who were overlooked either because their violent acts did not come to the attention of the authorities or researchers or because, for some reason, police, prosecutor, judge, or jury elected to overlook violent acts. Other false positives may in fact have committed no violent acts, not from innocence, but from the lack of appropriate opportunities or circumstances.

Here too I think the proponents of prediction offer a weak case. The effective argument is that the false positive problem is less serious than it appears to be because the predictions are more accurate than they appear to be. Given the attention that violence predictions have received, it seems reasonable to place on prediction's proponents the burden of proving predictive accuracy higher than the state-of-the-art appears to allow. If substantially more accurate predictions can be made, that could significantly alter the debates over predictive sentencing, and it seems only fair that the higher accuracy levels be demonstrated empirically rather than be surmised.

4. *Inappropriate Predictors*

One major criticism of predictive sentencing (or paroling or bailing) is that many factors correlated with future violence are controversial. Although the Constitution apparently precludes use only of race, religion, ethnicity, political affiliation, and possibly sex as sentencing factors, many people object to other factors on policy grounds.

a) Factors beyond the offender's control. Many people believe it unjust to base punishment decisions on factors over which the offender has no control. For example, sex is seen by many to be an inappropriate factor, even though it is highly predictive of violence, because it has no moral relevance to punishment. Similarly, race, age, ethnicity, intelligence, and national origin are factors beyond the offender's control and are therefore not logically related to culpability. Some people would also place drug or alcohol addiction (as contrasted with nonaddicted use) in the same category.

b) Status variables. A considerable number of social and economic status variables are correlated with recidivism and violence probabilities but are nonetheless widely regarded as inappropriate factors for consideration in punishment decisions. These include various measures of educational attainment, vocational skills and experience, residential stability, and income. Incorporation of such variables in decision-making criteria systematically adversely affects people of lower income and social status. On policy grounds, the sentencing commission in Minnesota expressly prohibited reliance on such factors in sentencing precisely because of their socially skewed impact.

Patently, retributivists in principle oppose consideration of such factors, and utilitarians in principle should not object, though in practice many do.

Many people object to consideration of such factors, and, to the extent that they are purged from prediction formulas, their accuracy will be by that much reduced (and the false positive problem thereby exacerbated).

c) Nonconviction criminal history. Past involvement in crime is the best single predictor of future involvement in crime (see, e.g., Blumstein et al. 1986). Numerous research findings confirm this conclusion. Generally, however, researchers' analyses incorporate self-reports or information on arrests that did not result in convictions.

Arrests and alleged criminality not resulting in an arrest present one kind of problem. Researchers generally justify use of arrests in their analyses in three ways. First, arrests are much closer in time than are convictions to the commission of crimes, and in the aggregate they offer a fuller picture of crime. For analyses of aggregate data, the fullest picture of crime involvement is best, and it is not important to know which of those arrests proved unfounded. No harm will come to any individual because of research use of arrests (or self-reports) as indicators of crime. Second, relatively few arrests result in convictions, and reliance solely on convictions as crime indicators would impoverish the analyses. Third, there is no reason to doubt that most people who are arrested for crimes committed those crimes.

The problem results from the interaction of several of the preceding propositions. From a predictive perspective, the more indicators there are of past criminality, the more likely that a prediction of continued involvement in crime will be accurate. From the defendant's perspective, and from a civil liberties perspective, that is beside the point. If past crimes are to influence current sentencing, then they should be considered only when they have been admitted or proved beyond reasonable doubt (see, e.g., Monahan 1982). Reliance on arrests creates an unacceptable risk that the defendant will be additionally punished now for offenses he did not commit (or could not have been proven to have committed) then.

From an incapacitative perspective, reliance solely on past convictions defeats the system. Many much-arrested individuals have been seldom convicted and, without arrest information, will escape the incapacitative net.

The split resembles that on many prediction issues. While UU would have little doubt about the appropriateness of use of arrests in making predictive judgments (though were he a proceduralist, he would want to establish procedures for assessing defendants' claims that their apparent arrest records were incorrect), TR would probably say that the benefit of the doubt should operate for the individual and against the state and, therefore, that taking liberty seriously requires that punishment be imposed or extended in respect only of criminal behavior admitted or proved beyond a reasonable doubt.

5. Disparate Racial Impacts

For both constitutional and policy reasons, no one has proposed that race be used as a factor in setting sentences or implementing incapacitation programs, even though race is significantly correlated with recorded criminality. Indirectly, however, race effects may occur in prediction systems if those systems incorporate variables that are correlated with race. Insofar as class is associated with race, many of the status variables described in the preceding subsection will, if used in sentencing as prediction factors, systematically adversely affect blacks. Many criminal history factors are also correlated with race.

Although in this context there are apparently no constitutional problems in adopting policies known (but not intended) to affect minorities systematically and adversely, there may be powerful policy grounds for wanting to purge criminal justice decision making of practices that operate to the systematic detriment of minorities. This is one reason why the Minnesota Sentencing Guidelines Commission elected to prohibit reliance on status variables in sentencing.

To conclude this section, whether the ethical and policy criticisms of predictive sentencing summarized here are regarded as devastating depends largely on the premises that shape one's views of punishment. Retributivists tend strongly to disapprove of predictive sentencing; utilitarians tend to accept it. However, almost every analyst of predictive sentencing is uncomfortable with some of its features.

Notes

1. There is another complication here. Even if offense categories are precisely delineated, variations in offender characteristics may for some decision makers result in very different sentences. This problem is actually a conflict over premises. For those who believe that punishment should be based solely, or primarily, on the offender's culpability and the harm that resulted, offender characteristics by definition should play only a small role. For those who believe that culpability and harm are but some of the factors that should shape punishment decisions, then, by definition, a tight offense-based punishment scheme will be too confining.

2. "Largely" because von Hirsch would permit prior criminal history to play a modest role in setting appropriate punishments. See von Hirsch (1981, 1985).

3. At the reductionist extreme, the answer is that each decision maker must

decide which punishment is "not undeserved" in each case, but this answer effectively rejects the value of general rules and culpability-influenced punishment.

4. But it is not clear whether this is true. If, as is discussed in the text, Morris would defer to policymakers, such as a sentencing commission, to specify what is "not undeserved," there is little difference in their views, and the seemingly large difference is an artifact of their assumptions about the kind of sentencing system in which each addresses his arguments.

5. It is true that predictions of participation in *any crime* can be made at much higher rates of accuracy (see Farrington 1979; Blumstein, Farrington, Moitra 1985). Most discussions of dangerousness prediction focus on violent crime. This seems reasonable to me. Liberty—even that of property offenders—seems to me a sufficiently important value that one should rely on deterrence as a crime prevention strategy for property crimes and not extend offenders' incarceration because of property crimes they might later commit.

References

Bedau, Hugo, 1977. "Concessions to Retribution in Punishment." In *Justice and Punishment,* edited by J. B. Cedarblom and William Blizek. Cambridge, Mass.: Ballinger.

Blumstein, Alfred, Jacqueline Cohen, Jeffrey Roth, and Christy Visher, eds. 1986. *Criminal Careers and "Career Criminals."* Washington, D.C.: National Academy Press.

Blumstein, Alfred, David P. Farrington, and Soumyo Moitra. 1985. "Delinquency Careers: Innocents, Desisters, and Persisters." In *Crime and Justice: An Annual Review of Research,* vol. 6, edited by Michael Tonry and Norval Morris. Chicago: University of Chicago Press.

Farrington, David P. 1979. "Longitudinal Research on Crime and Delinquency." In *Crime and Justice: An Annual Review of Research,* vol. 1, edited by Norval Morris and Michael Tonry. Chicago: University of Chicago Press.

———. 1987. "Predicting Individual Crime Rates." In *Prediction and Classification: Criminal Justice Decision Making,* edited by Don M. Gottfredson and Michael Tonry. Chicago: University of Chicago Press.

Farrington, David, and Roger Tarling. 1983. *Criminal Prediction.* Albany: State University of New York Press.

Floud, Jean, and Warren Young. 1981. *Dangerousness and Criminal Justice.* London: Heinemann.

Monahan, John. 1982. "The Case for Prediction in the Modified Desert Model for Criminal Sentencing." *International Journal for Law and Psychology* 5:103–13.

Monahan, John, and David B. Wexler. 1978. "A Definite Maybe: Proof and Probability in Civil Commitment." *Law and Human Behavior* 2:37–42.

Morris, Norval. 1951. *The Habitual Criminal.* London: London School of Economics.

———. 1982. *Madness and the Criminal Law.* Chicago: University of Chicago Press.

Morris, Norval, and Marc Miller. 1985. "Predictions of Dangerousness." In *Crime and Justice: An Annual Review of Research,* vol. 6, edited by Michael Tonry and Norval Morris. Chicago: University of Chicago Press.

Posner, Richard A. 1977. *Economic Analysis of Law.* 2d ed. Boston: Little, Brown.

von Hirsch, Andrew. 1981. "Desert and Previous Convictions in Sentencing." *Minnesota Law Review* 65:591–634.

———. 1985. *Past or Future Crimes: Deservedness and Dangerousness in the Sentencing of Criminals.* New Brunswick, N.J.: Rutgers University Press.

Suggestions for Further Reading

1. A Brief History of Prediction Methods in Criminal Law and in Criminology

See Mannheim, H., and Wilkins, T., *Prediction Methods in Relation to Borstal Training* (1955); Dershowitz, M., "The Origins of Preventive Confinement in Anglo-American Law—Part I: The English Experience," 43 *University of Cincinnati Law Review* 1 (1974).

2. Methodology of Prediction Techniques

Gottfredson, D. M., "Assessment and Prediction Methods in Crime and Delinquency," in President's Commission on Law Enforcement and Administration of Criminal Justice, *Task Force Report: Juvenile Delinquency and Youth Crime* (1967); Floud, J., and Young, W., *Dangerousness and Criminal Justice* (1981), Appendix C; Monahan, J., *Predicting Violent Behavior: An Assessment of Clinical Techniques* (1981); Hinton, W. (ed.), *Dangerousness: Problems of Assessment and Prediction* (1983); Farrington, D. P., and Tarling, R. (eds.), *Prediction in Criminology* (1985); Gottfredson, S. D., "Prediction: An Overview of Selected Methodological Issues," in Gottfredson, D. M., and Tonry, M. (eds.), *Prediction and Classification: Criminal Justice and Decision Making* (1987).

3. General (i.e., Nonselective) Incapacitation Methods

Wilson, J. Q., *Thinking About Crime* (1975), chs. 8 and 10; Shinnar, R., and Shinnar, S., "The Effects of Criminal Justice on the Control of Crime," 9 *Law and Society Review* 581 (1975); Greenberg, D. F., "The Incapacitative Effect of Imprisonment: Some Estimates," 9 *Law and Society Review* 541 (1975); Cohen, J., "The Incapacitative Effect of Imprisonment: A Critical Review of the Literature," in A. Blumstein, J. Cohen, and D. Nagen (eds.), *Deterrence and Incapacitation: Estimating the Effects of Criminal Sanctions on Crime Rates* (1978); Panel on Research on Deterrent and Incapacitative Effects, "Report" in *id.;* Brody, S., and Tarling, R., *Taking Offenders out of Circulation* (1980); Cohen, J., "Incapacitation as a Strategy for Crime Control: Possibilities and Pitfalls," in M. Tonry and N. Morris (eds.), *Crime and Justice: An Annual Review of Research,* vol. 5 (1983); von Hirsch, *Past or Future Crimes: Deservedness and Dangerousness in the Sentencing of Criminals* (1985), ch. 13.

4. Selective Incapacitation: Methods and Effects

Greenwood, W., *Selective Incapacitation* (1982); Chaiken, M., and Chaiken, R., *Varieties of Criminal Behavior* (1982); von Hirsch, A., and Gottfredson, D. M., "Selective Incapacitation: Some Queries About Research Design and Equity," 11 *New York University Review of Law and Social Change* 12 (1983–84); Chaiken, J., and Chaiken, M., "Offender Types and Public Policy," 30 *Crime and Delinquency* 195 (1984); von Hirsch, *Past or Future Crimes, supra,* chs. 9 and 10; Panel on Research on Criminal Careers, "Report," in A. Blumstein, J. Cohen, J. Roth, and C. Visher (eds.), *Criminal Careers and "Career Criminals"* (1986); Visher, C., "The Rand Inmate Survey: A Reanalysis," in *id.;* Reiss, A. J., Jr., "Co-Offender Influences on Criminal Careers," in *id.;* von Hirsch, "Selective Incapacitation Reexamined: The National Academy of Sciences' Report on Criminal Careers and 'Career Criminals,'" 7 *Criminal Justice Ethics* 19 (1988).

5. Ethical and Policy Issues in Incapacitation

Dershowitz, A., "The Law of Dangerousness: Some Fictions About Predictions," 23 *Journal of Legal Education* 24 (1970); Morris, N., *The Future of Imprisonment* (1974), esp. 62–73; von Hirsch, *Doing Justice: The Choice of Punishments* (1976), esp. chs. 3 and 15; Radzinowicz, L., and Hood, R., "A Dangerous Direction for Sentencing Reform," *Criminal Law Review* 713 (1978); Sherman, M., and Hawkins, G., *Imprisonment in America: Choosing the Future* (1981), esp. chs. 4 and 5; Floud, J., and Young, W., *Dangerousness and Criminal Justice* (1981); Radzinowicz, L., and Hood, R., "Dangerousness and Criminal Justice: A Few Reflections," *Criminal Law Review* 756 (1981); Walker, N., "Unscientific, Unwise, Unprofitable, or Unjust?" 22 *British Journal of Criminology* 276 (1982); Honderich, T., "On Justifying Protective Punishment," 22 *British Journal of Criminology* 268 (1982); Bottoms, A. E., and Brownsword, R., "The Dangerousness Debate After the Floud Report," 22 *British Journal of Criminology* 229 (1982); Monahan, J., "The Case for Prediction in the Modified Desert Model for Criminal Sentencing," 5 *International Journal of Law and Psychology* 103 (1982); Bottoms, A. E., and Brownsword, R., "Dangerousness and Rights," in J. W. Hinton (ed.), *Dangerousness: Problems of Assessment and Prediction* (1983); Morris, N., and Miller, M., "Predictions of Dangerousness," in M. Tonry and N. Morris (eds.), *Crime and Justice: An Annual Review of Research,* vol. 6. (1985); Moore, M., et al., *Dangerous Offenders: The Elusive Target of Justice* (1985); von Hirsch, *Past or Future Crimes, supra,* chs. 11 and 12; Zimring, F. E., and Hawkins, G., "Dangerousness and Criminal Justice," 85 *Michigan Law Review* 481 (1986); Miller, M., and Morris, N., "Predictions of Dangerousness: An Argument for Limited Use," 3 *Violence and Victims* 263 (1988); von Hirsch, "Selective Incapacitation Reexamined," *supra.*

Chapter Four

DESERT

Retributivist theories of punishment have a long history which includes the writings of Kant and Hegel, but their revival in modern times can be traced to various philosophical writings in the 1960s[1] and to John Kleinig's book *Punishment and Desert* in 1973. This increased philosophical interest percolated through into penal theory later in the 1970s—most notably, in the espousal of "just deserts" in the report of the Committee for the Study of Incarceration, *Doing Justice* (1976).[2] Since then, desert theory has had a continuing (though sometimes disputed) influence in sentencing policies of several countries, illustrated by the prominence it has achieved in the sentencing guidelines of Minnesota, Washington, and Oregon (see Extracts 5.2 and 5.4 below), in the Swedish sentencing law of 1988 (see Extract 5.4), and in the English law of 1991 (see Extract 5.3).

For present purposes, a desert theorist will be regarded as someone who claims that the seriousness of crimes should, on grounds of equity, be the chief determinant of the quantum of punishment. In terms of the three main issues in the justification of punishment—why punish, whom to punish, how much to punish—desert theorists will agree in principle about the second and third.

In response to the first question, Why punish? there appear to be at least two different approaches among modern desert theorists. One approach, advanced in Extract 4.1 by Michael Moore, is essentially that those who commit crimes deserve to be punished for the same reason that those who commit civil wrongs deserve to be made to pay damages: there is a fundamental intuitive connection between crime and punishment, of the same order as the promissory theory of contract or the corrective theory of tort liability. Punishment as a practice or institution needs no further justification than this. The second approach, adopted in the writings of von Hirsch, regards this intuitive connection as only one element in the justification. Thus desert is "an integral part of everyday judgments of praise and blame," and it is institutionalized in state punishment "to express disapprobation of the conduct and its perpetrators."[3] This is the censuring function of punishment. But the other element of von Hirsch's justification is preventive: legal punishment provides a disincentive against engaging in certain conduct. Without the regular official punishment of crimes, "it seems likely that victimizing conduct would become so prevalent as to make life nasty and brutish, indeed."[4] For von Hirsch, therefore, the notion of deserved censure is necessary but not sufficient as a justification. General deterrence must also be invoked.[5] Critics of desert theory have argued that "a judgment that D has behaved wrongly does not involve or justify the further judgment that [he or she] should be punished."[6] Those who adopt von Hirsch's view would agree, since general prevention forms part of their justification. But those who follow Moore's view would disagree, as Extract 4.1 shows.

In answer to the second question, Whom to punish? desert theorists agree that only those who have been proved to have committed an offense ought to be punished. This marks an important difference from deterrence theory, as noted in the introduction to Chapter 2. The limitation to punishing convicted offenders stems from Kant and has been advanced strongly in modern debate by H.L.A. Hart in his principle of "retribution in distribution."[7] It will not be taken further here.

The third question, How much to punish? leads to the main distinguishing feature of desert theory. Desert theorists' answer to the question is the principle of proportionality: sentences should be proportionate in their severity to the seriousness of the criminal conduct. The proportionality principle's contours, and its difference from the deterrent and rehabilitative rationales, are set out in Extract 4.2 by Andrew von Hirsch. Within the general principle of proportionality there are two distinct sets of concepts, and some of the criticisms leveled at desert theory stem from a failure to keep them apart. One is ordinal proportionality: this concerns "how a crime should be punished compared to similar criminal acts, and compared to other crimes of a more or less serious nature."[8] Thus, once the penal sanction has been established as a condemnatory institution to respond to criminal acts, its sentences ought to reflect the relative reprehensibleness of those acts. Crimes must be ranked according to their relative seriousness, as determined by the harm done or risked by the offense and by the culpability of the offender. Ordinal proportionality is thus concerned with preserving a correspondence between relative seriousness of offense and relative severity of sentence.

This is to be contrasted with cardinal proportionality, which requires that the overall levels of the penalty scale be kept in some reasonable relation to the gravity of the offending behaviors. In practice, the anchoring points of a particular country's penalty scale seem to derive from tradition and from the habit of associating offenses of a certain gravity with penalties of a certain severity. In principle, there is room for criminological arguments about the effect on crime rates of different levels of penalties, so as to generate debate on the appropriate anchoring points.

Some writers have accepted only parts of desert theory's answer to the question, How much to punish? Thus Norval Morris, in Extract 4.3 below, argues that proportionality should merely set the limits of permissible punishment, allowing decisions within those limits to be taken on various other theories which may appear appropriate in particular cases. Andrew von Hirsch, in Extract 4.4, argues that this kind of "limiting retributivism" involves a confusion between cardinal and ordinal proportionality.

To establish a principled basis for desert theory is no more than the first step in fashioning a coherent theory of sentencing. Several of the elements of desert theory stand in need of further exploration, both in their own right and in relation to the theory itself. First, by what criteria can it be assessed whether or not a sentencing system achieves cardinal proportionality? The answer is somewhat at large: von Hirsch accepts that "commensurate deserts is a limiting but not a defining principle when cardinal magnitudes are concerned,"[9] and that social convention and general policy factors have much to do with it.[10] Thus, von Hirsch himself has argued strongly in favor of a reduction in the severity of penal sanctions and has always presented this as part of the desert approach. Some have contended that in practice the adoption of "just deserts" leads to increased punitiveness,[11] but—as discussed more fully in Chapter 7 below—no such claim seems generally sustainable, especially when one considers the experience of such jurisdictions as Minnesota, Oregon, Finland, and Sweden.[12] The crucial elements seem to be the social conventions and the political climate of each jurisdiction. There are ample criminological and moral-social arguments in favor of lowering the penalty levels: one might start with the absence of proof that different levels of sanction severity produce different crime rates and move to the proposition that it is morally unjustified to set a scale's anchoring points at a given level when the balance of evidence might suggest that a lower level would achieve a similar effect in terms of crime prevention. It is arguments of this kind which need to be articulated separately and vigorously, since they have been too readily overlooked by many opponents and some proponents of desert.

Second, by what criteria can it be assessed whether or not a sentencing system achieves ordinal proportionality? How can we determine whether robberies of a given kind should be regarded as more or less serious than certain forms of rape or certain forms of drug importation? Many would maintain that these are largely uncontroversial matters: not only do most members of most societies rank most offenses in a similar order of relative gravity,[13] but also those states which have recently introduced new sentencing guidelines have not found this to be a contentious part of the enterprise.[14] Critics would assail this cozy, consensus view from various angles. First, there is no agreement on some matters such as the determinants of culpability (e.g., should intoxication ever mitigate?) and the relevance of the presence or absence of resulting harm (e.g., in attempted crimes).[15] Second, the writings of desert theorists have focused on "conventional" crimes, and it is unclear whether and in what way so-called "white collar" crimes can be accommodated.[16] Third, and more generally, the quantification of harms is both a complex and a changing enterprise. Recent years have seen changes, for example, in the assessment of such conduct as domestic violence, drunk driving, and use of hard drugs. How can desert theory prescribe criteria for offense seriousness in such changing social contexts? One response to this challenge, sketched in Extract 4.5 from a study by Andrew von Hirsch and Nils Jareborg, is to seek an overarching framework for rating crimes according to their effect on "living standards." This line of inquiry is necessarily at a high level of generality. It may need to be supplemented by a more culturally specific examination of the values implicit in existing offense ratings, although even in pluralist societies there are probably some shared values which are relevant to crime seriousness.[17] It may also need to be adapted to take account of the many crimes which do not have individual victims: there is a need to develop the theory so as to comprehend not only crimes against the state (such as espionage or perjury) but also offenses which affect public welfare (such as pollution). Once it is accepted that ordinal proportionality is a requirement of fairness, the importance of pursuing this inquiry into how it is structured is beyond doubt.

Third, the effect of previous convictions on sentence remains an unsettled issue among desert theorists, as Martin Wasik demonstrates in Extract 4.6. Some argue that each offense should be treated in isolation, without prior record having any effect on sentence. On this view, any increases in sentence on account of prior record stem from social protection arguments which are inconsistent with the desert rationale. A counterargument would be that a first offender ought to receive a reduced sentence because this recognizes humans as fallible and shows respect for their capacity to respond to censure.[18] Such discount should diminish with the second and third convictions, and eventually be lost. Another disputed question is *how much* reduction in sentence is warranted for the absence of a criminal record. It has been argued by von Hirsch that desert theory requires "primary but not exclusive emphasis on the current offense," so as to retain clear differentials between minor and serious crimes.[19] Several further questions about the precise application of desert theory to prior record remain: while it is often assumed that only the number of previous convictions is relevant, Martin Wasik in Extract 4.6 raises questions about the relevance of such matters as the similarity or otherwise of the previous offenses, their relative seriousness, their frequency, and their recency or staleness.

Fourth, it is argued that desert theorists have been preoccupied by serious crimes and custodial sentences, without devoting adequate attention to the bulk of less serious offenses. It will be seen from Chapter 6 below that the deficiency is now being remedied by study of the application of desert theory to noncustodial measures (see particularly Extract 6.6). Rather less attention has been paid to the compatibility of policies of selective nonprosecution with the desert approach. Many sentencing systems now operate schemes for the formal cautioning of offenders or other forms of "diversion." As argued in Chapter 7 below, they might be incorporated into desert theory by regarding them as proportionate responses to minor forms of lawbreaking or to offenses of certain kinds by persons of low culpability. So long as the criteria are clear and their use reflects ordinal proportionality, these schemes can be regarded as a manifestation of a lowering of the overall penalty level.

Fifth, desert theory may be criticized as an uncaring approach to the problems of crime and criminals, ignoring the causes of crime and showing little interest in constructive ways of tackling crime problems. As a general line of criticism this somewhat misses the target: desert theory is an approach to sentencing and not a set of prescriptions for the criminal justice system as a whole. There is no incompatibility between desert theory and the idea of new community correction programs or innovative prison regimes, but the desert theorist would insist that sentences should not be prolonged so as to accommodate treatment programs. A more specific question is whether desert theory has been little more than equivocal about sentences whose aim is to treat the particular needs of particular offenders, such as probation orders. As will be seen in Chapter 6, a desert model for noncustodial penalties such as that proposed by von Hirsch, Wasik, and Greene (Extract 6.6) can accommodate probation as an alternative measure for certain levels of offense. This would ensure that probation orders are used in a proportionate manner, while allowing the court to select probation on the overtly rehabilitative ground that there is "particular reason to believe that this type of offender is potentially responsive." A further criticism of a similar kind is that desert theorists have too little to say about the victims of crime, in terms of restitution and compensation. This question is taken up in Chapter 7 below.

Considerable interest has been shown in hybrid sentencing schemes, which combine desert theory with aspects of other approaches to punishment. A taxonomy of different ways of constructing hybrids is supplied by Paul Robinson, in Extract 4.7. An example of a hybrid is the new Swedish sentencing law (see Extract 5.4), which declares proportionality as the leading aim but which provides for other aims such as deterrence or rehabilitation to be pursued in respect of certain types of offense (e.g., drunk driving) or certain types of offender (e.g., nonserious offenders with a need for social support). Such approaches may be politically attractive where a full implementation of desert theory is resisted by reference to a particular group of allegedly "dangerous" offenders, or to the need to deter a particular offense, etc.

The strengths of desert theory may be recognized in its basis in everyday conceptions of crime and punishment,[20] in its close links with modern liberal political theory, in its insistence that state power be subject to limitations, in its model of individuals as autonomous, choosing beings, and in its protagonists' insistence that sentencing systems should have coherent aims and predictable sentences. One important aspect of desert theory is that it explicitly rejects the relevance of race, culture, family circumstances, and employment to the severity of sentence: it sets out to be nondiscriminatory and, insofar as it results in clear sentencing guidance, it should exclude such factors from the calculation of sentence. But matters such as social deprivation might be relevant to culpability and might therefore tell in mitigation of sentence.

A.A.

Notes

1. E.g., K. G. Armstrong, "The Retributivist Hits Back," 70 *Mind* 471 (1961); H. G. McCloskey, "A Non-Utilitarian Approach to Punishment," 8 *Inquiry* 249 (1965).
2. Andrew von Hirsch, *Doing Justice* (1976).
3. Andrew von Hirsch, *Past or Future Crimes* (1985), 52.
4. Ibid., 48.
5. See the introduction to Chapter 2, at 55.
6. Nicola Lacey, *State Punishment: Political Principles and Community Values* (1988), 21.
7. H.L.A. Hart, *Punishment and Responsibility* (1968), ch. 1.
8. Von Hirsch, *Past or Future Crimes,* 40.

9. Ibid., 44.

10. Ibid., ch. 8; a well-documented example of this is the level of penality in the Netherlands, which is significantly lower than in many other European countries for various cultural and attitudinal reasons: see David Downes, *Contrasts in Tolerance* (Oxford, 1988).

11. E.g., Barbara Hudson, *Justice through Punishment* (1987), ch. 4.

12. See Chapter 7, and more fully, Andrew von Hirsch, "The Politics of Just Deserts," 23 *Canadian Journal of Criminology* 397 (1990).

13. Cf. the introduction to the 1978 edition of T. Sellin and M. Wolfgang, *The Measurement of Delinquency.*

14. For extensive discussion, see Andrew Ashworth, "Criminal Attempts and the Role of Resulting Harm under the Code and in the Common Law," 19 *Rutgers L.J.* 725 (1988).

15. For references, see Andrew Ashworth, *Sentencing and Penal Policy* (1983), 173–81.

16. See John Braithwaite, "Challenging Just Deserts: Punishing White Collar Criminals," 73 *J. Crim. L. & Criminology* 723 (1982), and reply by Andrew von Hirsch, ibid., 1164. See also J. Braithwaite and P. Pettit, *Not Just Deserts* (1990), chs. 8 and 9.

17. Paul Rock, "The Sociology of Deviancy and Conceptions of Moral Order," 14 *British Journal of Criminology* 139–51 (1974).

18. For elaboration, see Andrew von Hirsch, "Criminal Record Rides Again," 10(2) *Criminal Justice Ethics* 2 (1991).

19. Von Hirsch, *Past or Future Crimes,* 78 and 86–87.

20. For a recent and sophisticated survey of public opinion on sentencing aims in five different countries, see Nigel Walker and Mike Hough, *Public Attitudes to Sentencing* (Gower, 1988).

4.1
The Moral Worth of Retribution

Michael S. Moore

Retributivism is a very straightforward theory of punishment: we are justified in punishing because and only because offenders deserve it. Moral culpability (desert) is in such a view both a sufficient as well as a necessary condition of liability to punitive sanctions. Such justification gives society more than merely a right to punish culpable offenders. It does this, making it not unfair to punish them, but retributivism justifies more than this. For a retributivist, the moral culpability of an offender also gives society the *duty* to punish. Retributivism, in other words, is truly a theory of justice such that, if it is true, we have an obligation to set up institutions so that retribution is achieved.

Retributivism, so construed, joins corrective justice theories of torts, natural right theories of property, and promissory theories of contract as deontological alternatives to utilitarian justifications; in each case, the institutions of punishment, tort compensation, property, and contract are justified by the rightness or fairness of the institution in question, not by the good consequences such institution may generate. Further, for each of these theories, moral desert plays the crucial justificatory role: Tort sanctions are justified whenever the plaintiff does not deserve to suffer the harm uncompensated and the defendant by his or her conduct has created an unjust situation that merits corrective action; property rights are justified whenever one party, by his or her labor, first possession, or intrinsic ownership of his or her own body, has come by such actions or status morally

---

From Michael S. Moore, "The Moral Worth of Retribution," in Ferdinand Schoeman, ed., *Responsibility, Character, and the Emotions: New Essays in Moral Psychology* (Cambridge: Cambridge University Press, 1987).

to deserve such entitlements; and contractual liability is justified by the fairness of imposing it on one who deserves it (because of his or her voluntary undertaking, but subsequent and unexcused breach).

Once the deontological nature of retributivism is fully appreciated, it is often concluded that such a view cannot be justified. You either believe punishment to be inherently right, or you do not, and that is all there is to be said about it. As Hugo Bedau (1978) once put it:

> Either he [the retributivist] appeals to something else—some good end—that is accomplished by the practice of punishment, in which case he is open to the criticism that he has a nonretributivist, consequentialist justification for the practice of punishment. Or his justification does not appeal to something else, in which case it is open to the criticism that it is circular and futile.

Such a restricted view of the justifications open to a retributivist leads theorists in one of two directions: Either they hang on to retributivism, urging that it is to be justified "logically" (i.e., nonmorally) as inherent in the ideas of punishment (Quinton, 1954) or of law (Fingarette, 1977); or they give up retributivism as an inherently unjustifiable view (Benn and Peters, 1959). In either case, retributivism is unfairly treated, since the first alternative trivializes it and the second eliminates it.

Bedau's dilemma is surely overstated. Retributivism is no worse off in the modes of its possible justification than any other deontological theory. In the first place, one might become (like Bedau himself, apparently) a kind of "reluctant retributivist." A reluctant retributivist is someone who is somewhat repelled by retributivism but who nonetheless believes: (1) that there should be punishment; (2) that the only theories of punishment possible are utilitarian, rehabilitative, retributive, or some mixture of these; and (3) that there are decisive objections to utilitarian and rehabilitative theories of punishment, as well as to any mixed theory that uses either of these views in any combination. Such a person becomes, however reluctantly, a retributivist by default.

In the second place, positive arguments can be given for retributivism that do not appeal to some good consequences of punishing. It simply is not true that "appeals to authority apart, we can justify rules and institutions only by showing that they yield advantages" or that "to justify is to provide reasons in terms of something else accepted as valuable" (Benn and Peters, 1959, 175–76). Coherence theories of justification in ethics allow two nonconsequentialist possibilities here:

1. We might justify a principle such as retributivism by showing how it follows from some yet more general principle of justice that we think to be true.

2. Alternatively, we can justify a moral principle by showing that it best accounts for those of our more particular judgments that we also believe to be true.

In a perfectly coherent moral system, the retributive principle would be justified in both these ways, by being part of the best theory of our moral sentiments, considered as a whole.

The first of these deontological argument strategies is made familiar to us by arguments such as that of Herbert Morris (1976), who urges that retributivism follows from some general ideas about reciprocal advantage in social relations. Without assessing the merits of these proposals one way or another, I wish to pursue the other strategy. I examine the more particular judgments that seem to be best accounted for in terms of a principle of punishment for just deserts.

These more particular judgments are quite familiar. I suspect that almost everyone at least has a tendency—one that he may correct as soon as he detects it himself, but at least a tendency—to judge culpable wrongdoers as deserving of punishment. Consider some examples Mike Royko has used to get the blood to the eyes of readers of his newspaper column:

> The small crowd that gathered outside the prison to protest the execution of Steven Judy softly sang "We Shall Overcome." . . .
>
> But it didn't seem quite the same hearing it sung out of concern for someone who, on finding a woman with a flat tire, raped and murdered her and drowned her three small children, then said that he hadn't been "losing any sleep" over his crimes. . . .
>
> I remember the grocer's wife. She was a plump, happy woman who enjoyed the long workday she shared with her husband in their ma-and-pa store. One evening, two young men came in and showed guns, and the grocer gave them everything in the cash register.
>
> For no reason, almost as an afterthought, one of the men shot the grocer in the face. The woman stood only a few feet from her husband when he was turned into a dead, bloody mess.
>
> She was about 50 when it happened. In a few years her mind was almost gone, and she looked 80. They might as well have killed her too.
>
> Then there was the woman I got to know after her daughter was killed by a wolfpack gang during a motoring trip. The mother called me occasionally, but nothing that I said could ease her torment. It ended when she took her own life.
>
> A couple of years ago I spent a long evening with the husband, sister and parents of a fine young woman who had been forced into the trunk of a car in a hospital parking lot. The degenerate who kidnapped her kept her in the trunk, like an ant in a jar, until he got tired of the game. Then he killed her.
>
>

Most people react to such atrocities with an intuitive judgment that punishment (at least of some kind and to some degree) is warranted. Many will quickly add, however, that what accounts for their intuitive judgment is the need for deterrence, or the need to incapacitate such a dangerous person, or the need to reform the person. My own view is that these addenda are just "bad reasons for what we believe on instinct anyway," to paraphrase Bradley's general view of justification in ethics.

To see whether this is so, construct a thought experiment of the kind Kant originated. Imagine that these same crimes are being done, but that there is no utilitarian or rehabilitative reason to punish. The murderer has truly found Christ, for example, so that he or she does not need to be reformed; he or she is not dangerous for the same reason; and the crime can go undetected so that general deterrence does not demand punishment (alternatively, we can pretend to punish and pay the person the money the punishment would have cost us to keep his or her mouth shut, which will also serve the ends of general deterrence). In such a situation, should the criminal still be punished? My hypothesis is that most of us still feel some inclination, no matter how tentative, to punish. That is the particular judgment I wish to examine. (For those persons—saints or moral lepers, we shall see which—who do not have even a tentative inclination to punish, I argue that the reason for affirming such inclinations are also reasons to feel such inclinations.)

The Case against Retributive Judgments

The puzzle I put about particular retributive judgments is this: Why are these particular judgments so suspect—"primitive," "barbarous," "a throwback"—when other judgments in terms of moral desert are accorded places of honor in widely accepted moral arguments? Very generally, there seem to me to be several explanations (and supposed justifications) for this discriminatory treatment of retributive judgments about deserved punishment.

1. First and foremost there is the popularly accepted belief that punishment for its own sake does no good. "By punishing the offender you cannot undo the crime," might be the slogan for this point of view. I mention this view only to put it aside, for it is but a reiteration of the consequentialist idea that only further good consequences achieved by punishment could possibly justify the practice. Unnoticed by those who hold this position is that they abandon such consequentialism when it comes to other areas of morals. It is a sufficient justification not to scapegoat innocent individuals, that they do not deserve to be punished; the injustice of punishing those

who do not deserve it seems to stand perfectly well by itself as a justification of our practices, without need for further good consequences we might achieve. Why do we not similarly say that the injustice of the guilty going unpunished can equally stand by itself as a justification for punishment, without need of a showing of further good consequences? It simply is not the case that justification always requires the showing of further good consequences.

Those who oppose retributivism often protest at this point that punishment is a clear harm to the one punished, and the intentional causing of this harm requires some good thereby achieved to justify it; whereas *not* punishing the innocent is not a harm and thus does not stand in need of justification by good consequences. Yet this response simply begs the question against retributivism. Retributivism purports to be a theory of justice, and as such claims that punishing the guilty achieves something good—namely, justice—and that therefore reference to any other good consequences is simply beside the point. One cannot defeat the central retributivist claim—that justice is achieved by punishing the guilty—simply by assuming that it is false.

The question-begging character of this response can be seen by imagining a like response in areas of tort, property, or contract law. Forcing another to pay tort or contract damages, or to forgo use and possession of some thing, is a clear harm that corrective justice theories of tort, promissory theories of contract, or natural right theories of property are willing to impose on defendants. Suppose no one gains anything of economic significance by certain classes of such impositions—as, for example, in cases where the plaintiff has died without heirs after his cause of action accrued. "It does no good to force the defendant to pay," interposed as an objection to corrective justice theories of tort, promissory theories of contract, or natural right theories of property simply denies what these theories assert: that something good *is* achieved by imposing liability in such cases—namely, that justice is done.

This "harm requires justification" objection thus leaves untouched the question of whether the rendering of justice cannot in all such cases be the good that justifies the harm all such theories impose on defendants. I accordingly put aside this initial objection to retributivism, relying as it does either on an unjustifiable discrimination between retributivism and other deontological theories, or upon a blunderbuss assault on deontological theories as such.

2. A second and very popular suspicion about retributive judgments is that they presuppose an indefensible objectivism about morals. Sometimes this objection is put metaphysically: There is no such thing as desert or

culpability (Mackie, 1982). More often the point is put as a more cautious epistemological modesty: "Even if there is such a thing as desert, we can never know who is deserving." For religious people, this last variation usually contrasts us to God, who alone can know what people truly deserve. As Beccaria (1964, 17–18) put it centuries ago:

[W]hat insect will dare take the place of divine justice . . . ? The gravity of sin depends upon the inscrutable wickedness of the heart. No finite being can know it without revelation. How then can it furnish a standard for the punishment of crimes?

We might call this the "don't play God" objection.

One way to deal with this objection is to show that moral judgments generally (and judgments about culpability particularly) are both objectively true and knowable by persons. Showing both is a complicated business, and since I have attempted such a showing elsewhere (Moore, 1982), let me try a different tack. A striking feature of the "don't play God" objection is how inconsistently it is applied. Let us revert to our use of desert as a limiting condition on punishment: We certainly seem confident both that it is true and that we can know that it is true, that we should not punish the morally innocent because they do not deserve it. Neither metaphysical skepticism nor epistemological modesty gets in our way when we use lack of moral desert as a reason not to punish. Why should it be different when we use presence of desert as a reason to punish? If we can know when someone does *not* deserve punishment, mustn't we know when someone *does* deserve punishment? Consider the illogic in the following passages from Karl Menninger (1968):

The very word *justice* irritates scientists. No surgeon expects to be asked if an operation for cancer is just or not. No doctor will be reproached on the grounds that the dose of penicillin he has prescribed is less or more than *justice* would stipulate. (17)

It does not advance a solution to use the word *justice*. It is a subjective emotional word. . . . The concept is so vague, so distorted in its applications, so hypocritical, and usually so irrelevant that it offers no help in the solution of the crime problem which it exists to combat but results in its exact opposite—injustice, injustice to everybody. (10–11)

Apparently Dr. Karl knows injustice when he sees it, even if justice is a useless concept.

Analogously, consider our reliance on moral desert when we allocate initial property entitlements. We think that the person who works hard to produce a novel deserves the right to determine when and under what conditions the novel will be copied for others to read. The novelist's labor gives him or her the moral right. How can we know this—how can it be true—if desert can be judged only by those with godlike omniscience, or worse, does not even exist? Such skepticism about just deserts would throw out a great deal that we will not throw out. To me, this shows that no one really believes that moral desert does not exist or that we could not know it if it did. Something else makes us suspect our retributive judgments than supposed moral skepticism or epistemological modesty.

References

Beccaria, C. 1964. *On Crimes and Punishments* (J. Grigson, trans.) in A. Manzoni (ed.), *The Column of Infamy* (Oxford: Oxford University Press).

Bedau, H. 1978. "Retribution and the Theory of Punishment," 75 *Journal of Philosophy* 601.

Benn, S. I., and R. S. Peters. 1959. *Social Principles and the Democratic State* (London: Allen and Unwin).

Fingarette, H. 1977. "Punishment and Suffering," 50 *Proceedings of American Philosophical Association* 499.

Mackie, J. 1982. "Morality and the Retributive Emotions," 1 *Criminal Justice Ethics* 3.

Menninger, K. 1968. *The Crime of Punishment* (New York: Viking Press).

Moore, M. S. 1982. "Moral Reality," *Wisconsin Law Review* 1061.

Morris, H. 1976. *On Guilt and Innocence* (Berkeley and Los Angeles: University of California Press).

Quinton, A. M. 1954. "On Punishment," 14 *Analysis*.

4.2
Proportionate Punishments

Andrew von Hirsch

If one asks how severely a wrongdoer deserves to be punished, a familiar principle comes to mind: *Severity of punishment should be commensurate with the seriousness of the wrong.* Only grave wrongs merit severe penalties; minor misdeeds deserve lenient punishments. Disproportionate penalties are undeserved—severe sanctions for minor wrongs or vice versa. This principle has variously been called a principle of "proportionality" or "just deserts"; we prefer to call it *commensurate deserts,* a phrase that better suggests the concepts involved. In the most obvious cases, the principle seems a truism (who would wish to imprison shoplifters for life, or let murderers off with small fines?). Yet, whether and how it should be applied in allocating punishments has been in dispute.

In an earlier era, the principle of commensurate deserts had a firmly established place in criminal jurisprudence. Cesare Beccaria's *Of Crimes and Punishments,* written in 1764, gives it much emphasis. Punishments, he stated, should be carefully graded to correspond with the gravity of offenses. To Beccaria and his followers, the principle was grounded on commonsense notions of fairness—and on utilitarian considerations as well: if penalties were not scaled commensurately with offenses, criminals, it was feared, would as soon commit grave crimes as minor ones. Criminal codes of the era—such as the French Code of 1791 and the Bavarian Code of 1813—reflected this conception. The framers of the original New Hampshire Constitution considered the principle so central to a fair and workable system of criminal justice that they embodied it in the state's bill of rights.

From Andrew von Hirsch, *Doing Justice: The Choice of Punishments* (New York: Hill and Wang, 1976; reprint ed., Boston: Northeastern University Press, 1986), ch. 8. Excerpted by permission.

Yet, with the rise of the rehabilitative ideology in the nineteenth century, the principle of commensurate deserts went into eclipse.

One school of thought dismissed the principle entirely. Desert was seen as relevant only before conviction—when it was being decided whether the violator had acted with the requisite degree of culpability to be held criminally liable. After conviction, the seriousness of his offense was not to be considered at all; his punishment was instead to be determined by his need for treatment and his likelihood of returning to crime. The Model Sentencing Act (in both its 1963 and its 1972 versions) takes this view. [See Extract 3.1 above.] The Act does not provide scaled maximum penalties for different categories of offenses. Instead, it gives the judge discretion to impose up to a five-year sentence on an offender convicted of any felony: within this limit, irrespective of the character of the offense, the judge is supposed to fix a sentence on the basis of the risk the offender poses to society.

Others have not been quite so uncompromising, conceding a residual significance to the seriousness of the offense. Most criminal codes provide maximum penalties for different offenses, ranked according to some approximate scale of gravity. But these legislative maxima are set so much higher than the sentences ordinarily expected that they have not much influence on actual dispositions. The American Law Institute's Model Penal Code recommends also that the judge should not set the sentence so low as to "depreciate the seriousness of the offense"; the code fails, however, to clarify how much weight should be given this factor of "depreciating the seriousness" as contrasted with other possible goals of sentencing. Although H.L.A. Hart comments briefly in the "Prolegomenon" on how the principle serves as a constraint of fairness, his thoughts on this subject (unlike so much else in his influential essay) did not stimulate much further interest. The justification for the principle; the weight to be assigned it as contrasted with other possible aims of punishing; the meaning of "seriousness"; and the relevance of the principle to the knotty question of sentencing discretion—all these have remained largely unexplored until quite recently.

The principle looks retrospectively to the seriousness of the offender's past crime or crimes. "Seriousness" depends both on the harm done (or risked) by the act and on the degree of the actor's culpability. (When we speak of the seriousness of "the crime," we wish to stress that we are *not* looking exclusively to the act, but also to how much the actor can be held to blame for the act and its consequences.) If the offender had a prior criminal record at the time of conviction, the number and gravity of those prior crimes should be taken into account in assessing seriousness. (The meaning of "seriousness" and the significance of a prior criminal record will be explored more fully later. [See Extracts 4.5 and 4.6, below.])

The principle of commensurate deserts, in our opinion, is a requirement of justice;[1] thus:

The principle has its counterpart in commonsense notions of equity which people apply in their everyday lives. Sanctions disproportionate to the wrong are seen as manifestly unfair—whether it be an employee being fired for a minor rule infraction to make an example of him, or a school inflicting unequal punishments on two children for the same misdeed.

The principle ensures that offenders are not treated as more (or less) blameworthy than is warranted by the character of the offense. Punishment, as we noted earlier, imparts blame. A criminal penalty is not merely unpleasant (so are taxes and conscription): it also connotes that the offender acted wrongfully and is reprehensible for having done so.[2] The offender, in other words, is being treated *as though he deserves* the unpleasantness that is being inflicted on him. That being the case, it should be inflicted only to the degree that it is deserved.

Where standards of criminal liability are concerned, this is a familiar point—for Henry M. Hart made it nearly two decades ago in his defense of the criminal law's *mens rea* requirements.[3] Since punishment characteristically ascribes blame, he contended, accidental violations should not be punished—because they are not blameworthy.

What is often overlooked, however, is that the same holds true after conviction. By then, it has been decided that the offender deserves punishment—but the question *how much* he deserves remains. The severity of the penalty carries implications of degree of reprobation. The sterner the punishment, the greater the implicit blame: sending someone away for several years connotes that he is more to be condemned than does jailing him for a few months or putting him on probation. In the allocation of penalties, therefore, the crime should be sufficiently serious to merit the implicit reprobation. The principle of commensurate deserts ensures this. If the principle is not observed, the degree of reprobation becomes inappropriate. Where an offender convicted of a minor offense is punished severely, the blame which so drastic a penalty ordinarily carries will attach to him—and unjustly so, in view of the not so very wrongful character of the offense. (This last argument, it should be noted, does not presuppose a desert-based general justification of punishment. Whatever the ultimate aim of the criminal sanction—even if one were to defend its existence on purely utilitarian grounds—punishment still *in fact* ascribes blame to the person. Hence the severity of the penalty—connoting as it does the degree of blame ascribed—ought to comport with the gravity of the infraction.)[4]

Equity is sacrificed when the principle is disregarded, even when done for the sake of crime prevention. Suppose there are two kinds of offenses,

A and *B*, that are of approximately equal seriousness; but that offense *B* can more effectively be deterred through the use of a severe penalty. Notwithstanding the deterrent utility of punishing offense *B* more severely, the objection remains that the perpetrators of that offense are being treated as though they are more blameworthy than the perpetrators of offense *A*—and that is not so if the crimes are of equivalent gravity.

It is sometimes suggested that the principle of commensurate deserts sets only an upper limit on severity—*no more* than so much punishment. We disagree. Imposing only a slight penalty for a serious offense treats the offender as *less* blameworthy than he deserves. Understating the blame depreciates the values that are involved: disproportionately lenient punishment for murder implies that human life—the victim's life—is not worthy of much concern; excessively mild penalties for official corruption denigrate the importance of an equitable political process. The commensurateness principle, in our view, bars disproportionate leniency as well as disproportionate severity.[5]

It has been objected (by the drafters of the Model Sentencing Act, for instance) that applying the principle in sentencing decisions would aggravate disparities, given judges' divergent views of the seriousness of offenses. But that holds true only if, as in current practice, the assessment of seriousness is left to the discretion of the individual judge. The principle has to be consistently applied; and consistent application requires the articulation of standards and the placing of limits on the individual decision maker's discretion [see Chapter 5, below].

The commensurate deserts principle may sometimes conflict with other objectives: for example, if an offense is not serious but can better be deterred by a severe penalty, commensurate deserts and deterrence may suggest divergent sentences. To deal with such conflicts, it becomes necessary to decide what priority should be given the principle.

We think that the commensurate deserts principle should have priority over other objectives in decisions about how much to punish. The disposition of convicted offenders should be commensurate with the seriousness of their offenses, even if greater or less severity would promote other goals. For the principle, we have argued, is a requirement of justice, whereas deterrence, incapacitation, and rehabilitation are essentially strategies for controlling crime. The priority of the principle follows from the assumption we stated at the outset: the requirements of justice ought to constrain the pursuit of crime prevention.

In giving the principle this priority, we need not claim the priority to be absolute: perhaps there are some unusual cases where it will be necessary to vary from the deserved sentence. But the principle derives its force from the fact that it applies *unless* special reasons for departing from it are shown: the burden rests on him who would deviate from the commensurate sentence.

Giving commensurate deserts this prominence will have practical usefulness in sorting out decisions about punishment. An often-repeated theme in the literature has been that the offender's disposition should be decided by "balancing" the different aims of punishment: the diverse considerations—rehabilitation, predictive restraint, deterrence, possibly desert as well—are to be weighed against each other, to yield an optimum penalty in the offender's particular case. When the different objectives are in conflict, however, saying they should be "balanced" against each other does not offer a principled way of resolving the issue. One escapes this difficulty by giving the commensurate deserts principle prima facie controlling effect. No longer would it be necessary to weigh these conflicting objectives in each case. Rather, the disposition would be presumed to be—unless there are overriding grounds for deciding otherwise—the one which satisfies the principle of commensurate deserts. Instead of juggling competing rationales to reach a decision, one has a workable starting point.

Notes

1. There also are utilitarian arguments for the principle (e.g., Bentham's argument that penalties should be proportioned so as "to induce a man to choose always the least mischievous of two offenses"). But were utilitarian arguments the only basis for the principle, it could be disregarded in those classes of cases where there would be still greater social benefits in so doing. We want to argue that departures from the principle—even when they would serve utilitarian ends—inevitably sacrifice justice.

2. The unpleasantness of punishment and its reprobative connotations are inextricably mixed. Being severely punished—sent to prison, for example—signifies a high degree of blame; but being imprisoned is painful not only because one is being deprived of one's freedom of movement but because one is being so deprived as a symbol of obloquy.

The reprobative connotations of punishment stem, essentially, from the context in which it is imposed—from the fact that it is inflicted mainly on persons who have intentionally done forbidden acts (acts that in most instances also strongly offend the society's moral norms). As long as that is the occasion for punishment, reprobation would be present even if the authorities were to try to label the disposition "preventive" or "therapeutic."

3. Henry M. Hart, "The Aims of the Criminal Law," 23 *Law and Contemporary Problems* 401 (1958).

4. This argument would not apply, admittedly, to a ritual so different from punishment that the reprobative overtones were largely absent. An example might be a purely preventive system that isolated "dangerous" persons regardless of whether any prohibited act was found to have been committed. But such a system would be open to other kinds of objections. Many of those confined would be false positives. Worse still, an individual would have no assurance that he can remain at liberty as long as he takes care to comply with the rules; his continued freedom would depend not upon his voluntary acts, but upon his *propensities* for future conduct as they are seen by the state. . . . his liberty would depend upon predictive determinations which he would have little ability to foretell, let alone alter by his own choices.

5. If the concern is not to allow the punishment to become so lenient as to depreciate the blameworthiness of the conduct, the penalty scale could still be kept to modest dimensions. It would not be necessary, for example, to inflict as much suffering on the offender as he did on the victim ("an eye for an eye"), as the penalty would merely have to impart blame enough to express a sense of the gravity of the crime.

4.3
Desert as a Limiting Principle

Norval Morris

There is an important element in the recommendations of von Hirsch and others which cannot be as cursorily dismissed as can the argument for mandatory minimum sentences. Their recommendations lead to an issue of principle central to the relationship between equality and desert. They all favor, as do I, a system of sentences which is primarily retributive, which does not pretend to a personal curative effect on the criminal, and in which the proper sentence to be imposed is strongly influenced by what the criminal has done. Thus, concepts of just desert are of overwhelming importance. Indeed, von Hirsch and the Committee for the Study of Incarceration build their entire sentencing system on a *defining* relationship between the deserved and the imposed punishment. My view is different: It is that desert is not a *defining* principle, but is rather a *limiting* principle; that the concept of a just desert properly limits the maximum and the minimum of the sentence that may be imposed, but does not give us any more fine-tuning to the appropriate sentence than that.

Is this only a quibble, or does it push to issues of principle concerning just sentencing? I think the latter, of course, and hope to prove that conclusion to you today. Let me offer some examples where it seems to be accepted, and is in my view proper and just, not to treat like cases alike. The exemplary sentence is such a case. As Professor Nigel Walker put it, judges "will sometimes impose sentences which are markedly more severe than the norm for the express purpose of increasing their deterrent effect."[1] He gives as an example the imposition of a sentence of four years imprisonment on each of nine young white men who were involved in attacks on

From Norval Morris, *Punishment, Desert, and Rehabilitation* (Washington, D.C.: U.S. Government Printing Office, 1976).

blacks in the Nottinghill District of London in 1958. This sentence was at least double the sentence normally imposed for their offenses, and was stated by the sentencing judge to be in excess of his normal sentence for such offenses, but it was within the legislatively prescribed maximum for those offenses. It was imposed expressly as an exemplary punishment, to capture public attention and to deter such behavior by a dramatic punishment. It needs no refined analysis to demonstrate that these nine offenders were selected for *unequal* treatment before the law. Please do not misunderstand me, I am not opposing such sentences, quite the contrary. Rather, I am arguing that if the increased penalty is within the legislatively prescribed range, then any supposed principle of equality does not prevent such a sentence from being in the appropriate case a just punishment. There are many such examples, they occur in all countries and are generally accepted. Let me give you just one more example. Annually, in Chicago, there is what is called a "crackdown on drunken driving." It occurs in the latter weeks of November and the early weeks of December. It is designed expressly to reduce the carnage from drunken driving in Chicago over the Christmas period. Often, those selected for punishment during this crackdown commit their offenses in the summer or autumnal months, when the thought of the allegedly jolly penury of Christmas is far from their minds; but such are the delays in the courts that an opportunity to serve their country as recipients of exemplary punishment is vouchsafed them—in this instance, a jail term for what would at other times be punished by lesser sanctions. My excellent colleague Franklin Zimring has done a close study of this practice and has concluded, cautious fellow that he is, addicted as he is to methodological niceties, that it is not disproved that the "crackdown" may have reduced the Yuletide devastation in Chicago from the combination of the ingestion of alcohol and the activation of the internal combustion engine.

Exemplary punishment is surely discordant to the principle that like cases should be treated alike, if that principle is regarded as either a limiting or defining principle of just punishment.

At the other end of the punishment process another example is to be found of general acceptance of not treating like criminal cases alike. The pardon and amnesty power is exercised in dramatically different ways in different jurisdictions, but it exists in all, at home and abroad. Pressures outside the prisoner and his crime, factors plainly extrinsic to the deserved punishment, the birth of a prince, the inauguration of a new government, the cessation of a foreign war, and political processes far removed from whatever makes criminal cases alike, except differences of date of the commission of the crime or imposition of the sentence, will lead to clemency to one prisoner which was denied to another. The pardon and amnesty power is difficult to reconcile with the equality principle if that principle is regarded as either defining or limiting just punishment.

Let us consider another hard case for that principle, this time a law teacher's hypothetical, which, however, I shall later argue is realistic, presenting some empirical data to that end.

Let us suppose what is, no doubt, wildly unlikely, that six medical practitioners in Denver are discovered to have a preference for patients who pay them in cash and who do not require receipts. Let us suppose that on full investigation we discover that all six doctors have understated their income last year by, say, $20,000 each. For some time we have been doubtful of the precision of tax returns by medical practitioners in this city and, as advisers to the Internal Revenue Service, we discuss what should be done about the six doctors. Well, to start with, it is quite clear that all six must pay tax on the income they have failed to declare, interest at appropriately high rates on that tax, and substantial financial penalties for their criminality. All this can, of course, be arranged without the need for their prosecution before a federal district court. Most of the six and their tax advisers will be happy indeed to arrange such settlements with IRS agents or, if necessary in relation to disputed issues of fact, through the tax court. Do we need to prosecute all six in the federal district court and do we need to send all six to prison? I submit not. Our purposes are utilitarian, deterrent. We wish, as Voltaire said of the English practice of killing an occasional admiral to encourage the others to bravery, publicly to punish by sending to prison an occasional medical practitioner "to encourage the others" to integrity in their tax returns. We do not need to send all six to prison. The extra increment of deterrence would be bought at too high a cost. It would be wasteful of our own resources, wasteful of the court's time and, what is perhaps also in point, it would inflict unnecessary suffering on those doctors whose punishment did not substantially increase the deterrent impact we would gain by the imprisonment of, say, two of their number. The principle of parsimony overcomes the principle of equality.

How should we select those to be imprisoned? Perhaps we should struggle for some distinguishing characteristic of deserved severity or some opportunity of extra deterrent utility in the punishment of some among the six; but what is important to recognize is that we are involved in a conscious breach of a principle that like cases should be equally punished. It may be that we would select those doctors whose lives had achieved the larger contribution to social welfare and who, as a consequence, were the better known of the six; their punishment would thus achieve the larger deterrent impact. *That* can hardly be a reason of equality for selecting them for the larger punishment.

This principle of parsimony in the imposition of punishment is, I think, of great importance, and is too often neglected. Let me offer some figures to demonstrate the frugality with which the Internal Revenue Service in practice applies its massive punitive powers. In 1975, throughout this vast country, only 1391 defendants were indicted for federal income tax violations, of whom 1158 were convicted and sentenced, and of whom only 367 were sent to prison or jail. This is an astonishingly selective and cautious use of the sanction of imprisonment for deterrent purposes. Is it unjust? It cannot be treating like cases alike if any reasonable concepts of the quality of guilt and deserved suffering are to be applied. In my view, on the data that have been published about the implication of the prison term in federal district courts, the system is both unequal and just, and it is precisely that apparent paradox I am seeking to defend.

When I put this type of case to many people, academic and civilian (if the distinction will be accepted), they tend to reply that this discriminatory selective invocation of the prison sentence by prosecutorial agencies, by administrators, is to be approved, provided it is properly controlled by K. C. Davis–like criteria that can be announced and tested as to their validity, but that it would be grossly unjust for a judge to act in this fashion in exercising his sentencing discretion. This distinction puzzles me. You will note that it is not made about exemplary punishment, where there seems to be general acceptance of the judge as the selector of the individual for the exemplary punishment. Why should the judge not be equally capable of being the selector of the four of my six doctors not to receive the more severe punishment? It can hardly be that the sentence of two of the six to prison, if only two are taken by the prosecutor to trial and four are handled administratively, is a just sentence, but that it would not be a just sentence if the selection were made by a judge. Equality in that case would serve only to protect the judicial role, to protect the oracle, the black robe—although that too is an important value which cannot be dismissed out of hand.

As you will gather, I have difficulty with these problems and by no means pretend to their solution; but I do strenuously argue that I have demonstrated situations in which justice and the principle of equality are not coterminous.

Our entire present criminal justice system is infested with discretion in the exercise of the punishment power, and much of this discretion must continue to be exercised, guided but not determined by principles of equality in punishment. At present, the shortage of police, prosecutorial, defense, judicial, and punishment resources compels the discretionary selection of cases to be prosecuted; but the constraint that the principle of parsimony in punishment properly imposes on the principle of equality in just punishment would remain were such resources unlimited. Equality would still remain only a guiding principle; even with adequate resources in the criminal justice system, equality would neither define nor limit just punishment. By contrast, the principle of a deserved punishment is and should remain a limiting principle of just punishment. Let me try to unpack that blunt affirmation.

Let me propose that the death penalty be the mandatory sentence for anyone convicted of abortion. I am not talking only about an abortion in which the mother dies but the run-of-the-mill legally unjustified abortion in which the life of the well-grown, third-trimester fetus is terminated. Well, why do you not leap to accept such a proposition? Why does no one, so far as I know, advocate *that* punishment? Not even the most perfervid advocates of the right-to-life position seem to take themselves that seriously in relation to abortion being murder. On deterrent utilitarian grounds there would be a great deal to be said for such a penalty if you are a true believer in the right to life. It would certainly push the price of the backyard abortion up to a very high figure; it would greatly reduce the number of fetuses whose existence was terminated; it would greatly increase the number of tickets that were purchased on international airlines and I would, for my own part, immediately reinvest in TWA. Well, why not? The answer must surely be that no one would see such a punishment as an appropriately *deserved* punishment, even those who are both in favor of protecting the fetus and in favor of capital punishment for convicted murderers. The limiting principle is the principle of desert. As elsewhere, it is hard to quantify this principle, but it clearly operates in this case to hold that such a punishment would be undeserved.

Desert thus operates categorically to limit the maximum of punishment. Sometimes it operates to limit the minimum, when it is argued that a too lenient punishment would unduly depreciate the seriousness of the offense that the accused has committed. An example of this was the sentencing of Spiro Agnew which, in my view, was entirely correct, for utilitarian and governmental practical reasons, but which certainly strained at the lower level of the deserved punishment.

By contrast, I am suggesting that the principle of equality, that like cases should be treated alike, is not a limiting principle at all, but is only a guiding principle which will enjoin equality of punishment unless there are other substantial utilitarian reasons to the contrary; such as those that favor exemplary punishment or the parsimonious punishment of some of my six doctors, or in situations where there are inadequate resources for or high costs attached to the application of equal punishments. The equality principle neither restricts nor limits; it merely guides. The principle of desert is not much of a guide, but it does restrict and limit.

When we say a punishment is deserved we rarely mean that it is precisely appropriate in the sense that a deterrent punishment could in principle be. Rather we mean it is not undeserved; that it is neither too lenient nor too severe; that it neither sentimentally understates the wickedness or harmfulness of the crime nor inflicts excessive pain or deprivation on the criminal in relation to the wickedness or harmfulness of his crime. It is not part of a utilitarian calculus, in the properly restricted Rawlsian sense of utilitarianism. The concept of desert defines relationships between crimes and punishments on a continuum between the unduly lenient and the excessively punitive within which the just sentence may on other grounds be determined.

Note

1. Nigel Walker, *Sentencing in a Rational Society* (London: Penguin Press, 1969), 69.

4.4
Ordinal and Cardinal Desert

Andrew von Hirsch

[*The extract is from a review of Norval Morris's book* Madness and the Criminal Law *(1982), part of which restates the theory of "limiting retributivism" advanced by Morris in the lecture printed as Extract 4.3 above. Page references in the text of the extract below are to* Madness and the Criminal Law.]

I

The debate over sentencing theory in the last decade has focused in large part on the respective roles that should be given to utilitarian considerations and to desert in deciding quanta of punishments. The positions have varied from those giving crime-preventive concerns exclusive emphasis, to those giving preeminence to notions of proportionality and desert. The debate is by no means a purely abstract one: on it turns the choice of factors that a rule-making body such as a sentencing commission should use in fashioning its rules or guidelines on the choice of sentence. On a desert-oriented rationale, the sentence must be based upon the seriousness of the defendant's criminal conduct. The more one moves away from desert and toward utilitarian models, the greater the entitlement to use factors that are unrelated to the blameworthiness of the conduct and that concern instead the likelihood of the defendant's recidivating or the effect of the penalty in deterring others.

In this debate, Professor Morris has been the primary exponent of what he calls "limiting retributivism"—namely, a mixed model somewhere be-

From Andrew von Hirsch, "Equality, 'Anisonomy,' and Justice," 82 *Michigan Law Review* 1093 (1984). Reprinted by permission, with changes approved by the author.

tween pure utilitarianism and the more thoroughgoing desert outlook which some of my colleagues and I have been advocating. In *Madness and the Criminal Law,* he attempts to defend his view against the criticisms of those who advocate more reliance on desert.

Before exploring the differences between Morris and the desert advocates, it is important to take note of essential similarities. Morris, like the modern retributivists, insists that desert is to be taken seriously as a constraint on utilitarian pursuits. Throughout his book, there is a clearly visible thread of argument that desert is a separate, retrospectively oriented conception based on the blameworthiness of the offender's conduct; that desert and prospectively oriented utilitarian notions have to be kept distinct and are in potential conflict; and that the problem of sentencing theory is not to try to obliterate that crucial distinction but to find the just and proper balance of emphasis between retributive and utilitarian notions (179–209).[1] I could not agree with all this more strongly.

Let us turn, then, to the areas where Morris and the modern desert advocates disagree. I shall spend more space on these issues because they are the ones on which Morris concentrates his own arguments in this book.

Morris's basic position in sentencing is that desert supplies the upper and lower bounds within which a penalty may justly be levied; but that within those bounds, utilitarian concerns—for example, the amount of punishment needed to achieve a socially acceptable level of deterrence—should be decisive. He is attempting to defend this view here against those, such as myself, who have been urging that desert be given a more central role in deciding punishments. Morris insists that we are mistaken: desert, he says, should properly serve only as a *limiting* principle that sets bounds on permissible punishments. It should not be used as a *determining* (he uses the less apt word "defining") principle—one purporting to guide decisions on actual quanta of punishments. In Morris's words:

> Desert is not a defining principle; it is a limiting principle. The concept of "just desert" sets the maximum and minimum of the sentence that may be imposed for any offense and helps to define the punishment relationships between offenses; it does not give any more fine-tuning to the appropriate sentence than that. The fine-tuning is to be done on utilitarian principles. [199]

The reason desert can only be limiting, Morris goes on to argue, is that none of us has any idea of precisely how much punishment is deserved for any given category of offense; we can grasp only what would be manifestly *disproportionate* in lenience or severity. As Morris puts it:

> When we say a punishment is deserved, we rarely mean that it is precisely appropriate in the sense that a deterrent punishment could in principle be.

Rather we mean that it is not undeserved; that it is neither too lenient nor too severe; that it neither sentimentally understates the wickedness or harmfulness of the crime nor inflicts excessive pain or deprivation on the criminal in relation to the wickedness or harmfulness of his crime. It is not part of a utilitarian calculus. . . . The concept of desert defines relationships between crimes and punishments on a continuum between the unduly lenient and the excessively punitive within which the just sentence may be determined on other grounds. [198]

Since desert is only a limiting principle, Morris goes on to assert, the sentencer is not obligated to impose equal sentences on equally deserving (or rather, undeserving) criminals: cases that are like in respect to the blameworthiness of the defendant's conduct may be treated *unlike* where necessary for utilitarian ends.

When one asks whether desert is limiting or determining, however, it is essential to specify: *determining or limiting for what purpose?* One must distinguish between *ordinal* and *cardinal* magnitudes of punishment: That is, between (1) the question of how defendants should be punished relative to each other, and (2) the question of what absolute severity levels should be chosen to anchor the penalty scale. To view desert as a determinative principle in deciding how crimes should be punished relative to each other does *not* commit one to the claim that it is determinative for deciding their cardinal magnitude.

For modern desert theory, this distinction is critical. Advocates of desert-oriented sentencing such as myself do not assert that desert is determinative for all purposes. Rather, our claim is a more restricted one, to wit: desert is a determinative principle in deciding ordinal magnitudes, but only a limiting principle in deciding cardinal magnitudes. To see what this means in practice, consider the crime of burglary. The issues of ordinal magnitude deal with how a particular burglary should be penalized compared to other burglaries and to other more or less serious crimes. When desert theorists assert that desert is a determining principle here, they mean that the ordering of penalties must meet the following two requirements. The first is the requirement of *parity:* criminal conduct of equal seriousness should be punished equally, with deviations from such equality permitted only where special circumstances alter the harm or culpability—that is, the degree of blameworthiness—of the defendant's conduct. The other is that of *rank ordering*: penalties should be ranked and spaced to reflect the ranking and spacing in degree of seriousness among crimes. What desert theorists object to is deciding these questions of *comparative* punishments on grounds other than the blameworthiness of the defendant's conduct: for example, to punish a particular burglar more severely than other burglars not because his particular crime is any worse but because he is a worse risk or because giving him a higher-than-usual punishment would make him an example to others.

To espouse this view does not, however, require one to hold that desert is determinative in deciding cardinal magnitudes. Here, rather, most modern desert theorists—certainly I—would admit that desert is a limiting principle only. I do not claim to know precisely how tough or lenient a sentencing scale should be, but only that punishments beyond certain levels of harshness or leniency are *undeserved*. But to make that concession about cardinal magnitude does not in logic compel one to abandon desert as the principle for deciding relative severities.

This distinction between ordinal and cardinal magnitudes may seem elementary, but Morris sometimes ignores it in his book. He seems to hold that desert must either be limiting for all purposes or determinative for all purposes. He quotes, for example, a passage of mine,[2] where I am speaking of how a sentencing commission in writing its guidelines might draw the dividing line on a sentencing grid between crimes serious enough to warrant imprisonment and those warranting lesser sanctions. I state that cardinal proportionality requires severe punishment such as imprisonment for the most serious crimes and lesser punishments for the least serious, but that the notion of a reasonable proportion between crimes and punishments may not be precise enough to determine exactly where to draw the dividing line through intermediate-level crimes, and hence that the rule maker might properly invoke various nondesert considerations in deciding this latter issue. Morris seizes upon this statement of mine as suggesting some kind of inconsistency with a desert orientation. In his words:

> Professor von Hirsch would thus allow utilitarian considerations within desert constraints to guide a sentencing commission but would deny them to a judge. I don't see why, except to protect the elegance of his thesis or the robe of the judge. [204–5]

In fact, my point has nothing to do with theoretical or sartorial elegance. It has to do with the difference between ordinality and cardinality. A sentencing commission, within broad limits of cardinal proportionality, might anchor the penalty scale by deciding to locate the "in-out" (i.e., prison vs. nonprison) dividing line a little higher or lower on the sentencing grid, so that intermediate-level crimes such as burglary receive either a short period of imprisonment or a noncustodial sentence instead. But once the scale has been so anchored, the rule maker is required to observe parity among convicted burglars—and to rank higher or lower on the penalty scale crimes which are, respectively, more or less serious than burglaries.

The fact that I may have no precise quantum in mind as the precise deserved penalty for burglary does not mean I am precluded from insisting that the punishment for burglaries should be ranked vis-à-vis the punishment of other crimes so as to reflect the relative gravity of those acts.

If one does bear in mind the distinction between cardinal and ordinal magnitudes, what is Morris's thesis? Morris *is* saying that desert is a significant limiting principle in deciding cardinal magnitudes. A penalty system, he is saying, ought not to be so inflated or deflated that penalties cease to bear any reasonable relationship to the degree of reprehensibleness of crimes. Here, Morris's view does not seem so different from that of desert theorists. The difference comes when one deals with ordinal magnitudes. There, Morris is saying that one need not observe parity in punishment among equally serious criminal acts if there are utilitarian reasons for imposing different punishments. And he seems also to take the rank-ordering principle less seriously than desert theorists would: one may, for deterrent or incapacitative purposes, punish a few burglars more severely than most convicted robbers—so long as one is not being so very harsh as to breach the cardinal limits on the punishment of burglary.

II

Professor Morris's thesis, in my view, faces two main difficulties. One, internal to his own statement of his thesis, concerns the width of the desert limits. The other problem concerns the condemnatory implications of punishment. Let me take each of these issues in turn.

Width of the Desert Limits

If desert is to be treated as only a "limiting" principle, as Morris suggests, the question that immediately comes to mind is the breadth of those limits. Is desert to be a significant constraint on utilitarian punishments, or only some kind of wide outer limit, that merely bars outrageous disproportion in lenience or severity?

The tendency of theorists who speak of desert as being only a "limiting" principle is to adopt the latter interpretation. Sentences are to be decided ordinarily on utilitarian grounds alone, and desert comes in only as a constraint against extremes: it should be little more than a protection against, say, inflicting very long prison sentences on car thieves or burglars, or giving probation to those convicted of the most violent offenses. Suffice to say here that this view is scarcely an advance over traditional positivism of two decades ago. Morris, to his credit, firmly rejects this view of desert as inconsistent with his own basic insistence on taking desert seriously.

Desert, he argues, must be treated as a significant restraint on utilitarian punishments, not merely as a rule against unlikely extremes in punishment that defy common sense and the common morality.

So far, so good. The next question, however, is *how* significant desert's role should be: how wide or narrow should the desert-based limits be, within which utilitarian concerns are permitted to operate? Fairly wide limits—say, a few months' to five years' confinement for the serious offense of armed robbery—would mean that utilitarian considerations would still play the primary role in determining the choice of penalty. Narrower limits—say, a range of two years to three for a first offense of armed robbery—would mean that desert would carry a greater, perhaps the primary weight in the choice of penalties.[3] Which does Morris prefer, the narrower or the wider desert limits? He does not say.[4] I am not speaking here of a mathematical formula. Rather, the problem is that Morris does not even suggest any principles that would guide one in deciding the latitude of the desert limits. When he refers to the use of utilitarian considerations for "fine-tuning,"[5] this would suggest rather narrow limits. Some of his examples, however, suggest otherwise[6]—a broad scope for utilitarian concerns. Without any specification of the nature of the desert limits or of how those limits might be derived from his theory, one does not know what one is dealing with: a substantially desert-oriented system, a primarily utilitarian one, or something in between. As a result, Morris's formula for "limiting retributivism" seems less of a theory than something akin to a party platform: a broad formula attractive because it accommodates what are in fact substantially different positions.

Is the more thoroughgoing desert model I have been advocating less ambiguous than Morris's scheme? Here, we must resort again to the cardinal/ordinal distinction. Desert theorists, at least as yet, have hardly done better than Morris in specifying the precise extent of the limits which desert imposes on the cardinal magnitudes of punishment. But our model calls for considerably more specificity in dealing with ordinal magnitudes: to meet the requirements of parity and rank ordering, crimes will have to be graded according to their seriousness; normally recommended penalties will have to be assigned to those gradations; and deviations from those penalties permitted only in special circumstances related to the harm or culpability of the offender's conduct. This will not, in pure theory, provide for a unique set of solutions, since (given the open-endedness of the cardinal requirements) the penalty scale as a whole could be inflated or deflated to a considerable extent while the *relative* proportions among punishments were held constant. But in practice, such a theory will provide substantially more guidance to the rule makers. A sentencing commission does not in fact have all that much leeway in inflating or deflating overall severity levels, without encountering limits on the availability of prison resources on the one hand and political constraints on reducing severities on the other. Where the commission's power resides, and where it needs guidance, is in deciding questions of *relative* severity and in determining how much to emphasize the gravity of the criminal conduct versus other factors in deciding who is to be confined and for how long. It is precisely on this issue of distribution that the desert-oriented view, with its strong ordinal requirements, provides definitive guidance as to which defendants should be punished more severely, and which less, and as to what aspects of the crime and the criminal's history should be relied upon in the guidelines.[7] And it is on that crucial issue that Morris leaves his model so little specified, because he downgrades the ordinal desert requirements and looks only to the much less clear cardinal requirements of desert.

The Blaming Implications of Punishment

The case for the ordinal requirements—that is, for equal treatment of the equally undeserving and for ranking punishments according to the seriousness of crimes—rests on the condemnatory implications of punishment. The reason, according to desert theorists, why the ordinal proportionality requirements must be observed is that to do otherwise means blaming equally reprehensible conduct unequally, or blaming less reprehensible conduct more than worse conduct.

How does Morris deal with this issue of the reprobative overtones of punishment? He ignores it. To desert advocates who object to his model as permitting unequal punishment of the equally blameworthy, his answer is that such arguments are merely circular: "[T]hey seem to me rather to restate the conflict than to resolve it against my view" (202).

But the argument is *not* circular. It can be stated in general terms as follows:

1. Suppose X is an institution having strong praising or blaming implications, such that the quantum of *X* distributed to any recipient connotes how much he or she is to be praised or blamed for his or her conduct.
2. It follows that *X* should as a matter of fairness be distributed among recipients so as to comport with the degree of praiseworthiness or blameworthiness of the recipient's conduct in the relevant respect.
3. Therefore if one does not wish to distribute *X* according to recipients' deserts, one must make one of these two moves:
   a) Deny the premise; that is, show that institution X has no such praising or blaming implications, as customarily understood; or else

b) Reform institution X so that its praising or blaming implications are eliminated or diminished so far as possible.

Let me give a modest illustration. Each year, the School of Criminal Justice at Rutgers University awards a certain number of fellowships and assistantships to graduate students. The fellowships are explicitly designated as awards, and carry a stipend but no added work. The assistantships are not so designated, and involve working with a faculty member. Because of the different character of the two institutions, our faculty uses different criteria to distribute them. The fellowships, in virtue of their character as awards, are distributed according to desert: that is, according to the quality of the student's past academic performance. The assistantships, however, are distributed according to more utilitarian criteria: since they are viewed as jobs, the student's usefulness for and experience in a faculty member's area of research are considered, along with academic grades. Were a faculty member to propose distributing fellowships similarly, he would need to argue for changing their character to make them less an award and more a form of employment.

Applying the point to punishment, the logic runs similarly. Desert theorists' crucial claim is that punishment is, and ought to be, a blaming institution—and hence that penalties should be distributed according to the degree of blameworthiness of criminal conduct. In order to do that, one must observe the ordinal requirements of desert: to punish equally blameworthy criminal conduct equally, and to grade severities of penalties so as to comport with the rank ordering of seriousness of crimes. To resist these conclusions, one needs to deny the premise; that is, to assert that punishment either (1) is not or (2) should not be essentially a blaming institution.

Assertion (1), denying that punishment connotes blame, seems to me pretty implausible. The only perceptible difference between a tax and a fine, for example, resides in the condemnatory character of the fine, not in the material deprivation, which in both cases is a taking of money.[8] I doubt Professor Morris would wish to deny the blaming character of punishment.

Assertion (2) is not quite so implausible: one conceivably *could* say that the blaming element of punishment is an historical relic, and that one should seek to reform the criminal sanction so as to make it only a material disincentive against undesirable conduct, with little or no moralizing overtones. One could argue, further, that disregarding ordinal proportionality requirements would be a step toward thus reforming the sanction, to be taken along with other symbolic changes (such as, if one wished to go far enough, even eliminating morally laden terms such as "innocence" or "guilt"). This is not merely hypothetical: juvenile justice reformers in the United States tried for years to recast the juvenile system so as to eliminate all traces of moral stigma.

But I wonder if this route would have much attraction for Professor Morris. It might, in the first place, carry utilitarian costs he would not like: were the criminal sanction to involve only material deprivation and not much moral obloquy, much higher levels of material deprivation might conceivably have to be resorted to in order to achieve even a minimal level of crime prevention. Second and more seriously, eliminating or downgrading the blame element in punishment might eliminate desert requirements *too* well. Not only might it dispense with the need for parity and rank ordering in punishments, but it might also dispense with the desert requirement Morris *does* wish to keep: to wit, the cardinal proportionality principle barring absolute disproportion in punishment. After all, the civil commitment law has had no similar principle, precisely because no moral stigma has been seen as involved in its sanctions, as Morris himself has noted. No, I doubt that he is any more willing than I to excise the blaming element in punishment. But if that element is retained, I find it hard to understand how ordinal desert requirements can justly be disregarded.

III

In support of his sentencing conception, Morris offers some pragmatic arguments concerning existing sentencing practice and the notion of "parsimony." He also mentions the idea of mercy. Let me consider these issues briefly.

Existing Sentencing Practice: Exemplary Punishments

Judges sometimes impose extra punishment on selected offenders for deterrent effect. Morris cites the instance of the exemplary sentence imposed on nine white hoodlums convicted of racial assaults on blacks in the Notting Hill district of London in 1958. Such a practice, he points out, does not comport with the parity requirements of desert. The difficulty with this argument should be apparent: citing the *existence* of a sentencing practice does not demonstrate the *justice* of that practice. Yes, judges, when left to their discretion, sometimes impose exemplary deterrent sentences; they also often impose extra punishments on the basis of predictions of debatable accuracy. They may also engage in a variety of other practices that are not necessarily defensible. Such facts, however, no more establish that exemplary sentences are appropriate than they show that predictive sentencing is desirable. Some jurisdictions, moreover, have reformed their sentencing systems so as to sharply restrict judges' powers to impose exemplary or predictive sentences. The Minnesota and Washington sentencing guidelines are examples of this.

The Parsimony Argument

Elaborating on his earlier writings, Morris asserts that it is "parsimonious" to impose unequal punishments—that is, to ignore or downgrade the requirements of desert parity. Suppose, he says, that a sentencing commission is deciding what is to be the normally applicable penalty for second-time purse snatchers. If parity is not required, one can give most such purse snatchers probation and achieve such deterrence as is necessary by giving a few six months in jail. He thus would recommend that the commission adopt a probation-to-six-months range as the standard penalty. If equally culpable purse snatchers must be punished equally, however, then the commission may, as a realistic matter, have to require that *all* of them be sent to jail for a short period—a less parsimonious result in Morris's view.

The most natural and straightforward response of the desert theorist would be to hold his ground. If blame is and should be so central to the idea of punishment, then it simply is unjust to impose unequal punishments on those found guilty of equally reprehensible crimes; and that inequality remains unjust even when urged in the name of parsimony. But Morris's argument strikes me as questionable even within his framework of "limiting retributivism." Is it really so obvious that abandoning desert parity will produce more "parsimonious" results?

Morris has made his conclusion sound plausible through his choice of example. People tend to be only moderately exercised about how purse snatchers are punished. If we change the example to a substantially more fear-instilling crime, things may work differently.

Consider the crime of armed robbery. In devising the penalty for armed robbery and other crimes, the Minnesota Sentencing Commission did adopt a strong parity requirement. This meant that when limited prison resources were taken into account, terms for armed robbery had to be in the two-to-three-year range (depending on the offender's criminal record), with longer terms reserved for the minority of defendants having quite long criminal records. Suppose the commission had instead rejected parity. This could have meant that some armed robbers (say, those deemed favorable risks) would get shorter terms than Minnesota's two-to-three years. But it would also have meant that other robbers would get longer terms, and a few could be visited with *extremely* long terms. To prevent excessive severity, Morris might apply his retributive ceiling by, for example, limiting the prison terms of robbers (other than those with the worst records) to no more than, say, five years. But if we are speaking of a commission's realistic choices, as Morris claims he is, how easy would it be to defend such a limit? Once a commission abandons parity in the treatment of robbery, how effectively can it defend a maximum of five years when it is practically feasible to imprison some robbers for ten, fifteen, or twenty years, and when that may appear to be the more effective incapacitant? The more one downgrades parity and permits selectivity among those convicted of a crime of a given degree of gravity, the harder it will be in practice to prevent the extraordinarily severe treatment of a selected few. As the crime becomes more serious and demands for a tough response increase, this problem will become all the worse.

The problem of harsher punishment for the unlucky few raises the question of *parsimony for whom?* Suppose the penalty for crime *A* has been set at *x* years' confinement and that there are one hundred defendants per year convicted of the crime. Suppose that, by abandoning the parity requirement, one will reduce the penalty for fifty defendants by one-half, keep the penalty the same for another twenty-five, and *double* the penalty for the remaining twenty-five. Has one produced a more parsimonious result? That depends on how one defines parsimony. If one counts only the number of defendants, a larger number get lower punishment than before. Were one to use the more sophisticated utilitarian criterion of aggregate cost—by factoring in the amount of penalty change per person as well as the number of persons involved—there would be no change in net severity. Were one to adopt the nonutilitarian criterion of considering the position of potentially the worst-off persons[9]—a criterion that Morris has not hesitated to use in other contexts[10]—then the change does not seem parsimonious at all: instead of facing a punishment of *x* years, the potentially disadvantaged defendant faces *double* that amount. And his extra suffering—as a separate person with only his own life to lead—is scarcely made good by the benefit accruing to other defendants.

The Mercy Argument

Throughout his book, Morris keeps asserting that his scheme is more "merciful" than a more thoroughgoing desert approach. The claim is not easily responded to, because penologists (including myself) have hardly touched upon the concept of mercy.

In the philosophical literature, however, there has been some discussion. One useful analysis is entitled "On Mercy," written a decade ago by Claudia Card.[11] Mercy, Dr. Card suggests, is not a utilitarian concept at all. If a judge reduces an offender's penalty below the norm for that offense because he or she finds the offender is not dangerous or would better respond to correctional treatment in the community, or because the offender is a noted scientist who needs to be at liberty in order to discover a new cancer cure, these are prudential reasons for being more lenient but not for acts of mercy in the commonly understood sense. Mercy, Card contends, is a conception that is tied to the idea of desert. It involves reducing the penalty on grounds that go beyond the normal reasons of diminished culpability but nevertheless are concerned with the suitability and commensurability of punishment for someone who has been visited by much collateral suffering.[12]

If Card is right—and I think she is at least on the right track—then desert advocates should think more seriously than they have about the issue of mercy. Perhaps there exist a variety of circumstances where one should be permitted to go below the normally applicable penalty on grounds related to mercy. A beginning would be to consider the appropriateness of reducing the punishment in cases where the act has visited the offender himself with sufficiently injurious consequences.

I find it difficult to understand, however, how the idea of mercy fits into Morris's scheme. If it is an act of prudence rather than mercy to fix penalties for utilitarian ends, then how has Morris made his system more merciful by limiting the scope of desert considerations and expanding the scope of utilitarian ones in deciding the appropriate sentence? Morris has not explained what he means by mercy or how mercy is to be distinguished from other concepts that he uses (such as parsimony). Without such an explanation, his talk of mercy strikes me as more rhetorical than illuminating.

Notes

1. Morris thus implicitly rejects the views of those, such as Ernest van den Haag, who assert that the idea of proportionate punishments can be explained purely in terms of a deterrence calculus or other crime-prevention notions. See van den Haag, "Punishment as a Device for Controlling the Crime Rate," 33 *Rutgers L. Rev.* 706 (1981).

2. See von Hirsch, "Utilitarian Sentencing Resuscitated: The American Bar Association's Second Report on Criminal Sentencing," 33 *Rutgers L. Rev.* 772, 788 (1981).

3. The nature of these limits might conceivably be affected by how broadly or narrowly the prohibited conduct is defined: the desert limits on punishing armed robbery, for example, might have to be wider the more comprehensively robbery is defined to embrace forcible takings of various types and shadings of gravity. But supposing one were operating with offense definitions of a given degree of breadth or specificity, it still needs to be explained how wide or narrow the desert limits should be for such offenses under Morris's theory.

4. He admits he does not specify the width of the limits. In his words: "I am well aware that I have not defined the proper range fixed for all crimes and for criminals by the upper and lower limits of undeserved severity and excessive leniency which exaggerate or depreciate the gravity of the crime. My view is merely that

such ranges exist, that they should be defined as punishment categories in some form such as that set forth by the Minnesota Sentencing Commission. . . ." I doubt, however, that endorsement of the Minnesota commission's guideline format would really be consistent with Morris's view. The commission's guidelines come close to adopting the desert parity that Morris wishes to reject: there is a recommended presumptive prison sentence for each cell in the commission's sentencing grid for which imprisonment is prescribed, surrounded by a quite narrow range of permissible variation.

5. It is also unclear precisely how that utilitarian "fine-tuning" might be accomplished, given the imprecision of our efforts to gauge the crime-preventive (for example, deterrent or incapacitative) effects of sentences.

6. See his proposal for the treatment of the crime of purse snatching, where he would have a range of probation to six months' incarceration.

7. In Minnesota, for example, reliance on the ordinal requirements of desert were critical in helping the commission decide questions of relative severity of punishments.

8. For a fuller discussion of this aspect of punishment, see generally R. Wasserstrom, *Philosophy and Social Issues: Five Studies* (1980), 112–51.

9. See generally J. Rawls, *A Theory of Justice* (1971).

10. See N. Morris, *The Future of Imprisonment* (1974), at 80–84.

11. Card, "On Mercy," 81 *Phil. Rev.* 182 (1972).

12. *Id.*, at 184–87, 201.

4.5
Gauging Criminal Harm: A Living-Standard Analysis

Andrew von Hirsch
Nils Jareborg

1. Introduction: Scope of This Essay

The present topic, of gauging criminal harm, is part of a larger subject that we have been mulling over for some time: the seriousness of crime. The question of how to assess crime seriousness had been gaining importance in recent years, with the increasing influence of desert-oriented or "proportionalist" conceptions of sentencing—conceptions which make the severity of punishment depend principally on the gravity of the offense of conviction.

Seriousness of crime has two dimensions: harm and culpability. Harm refers to the injury done or risked by the act; culpability, to the factors of intent, motive, and circumstance that determine the extent to which the offender should be held accountable for the act. Both dimensions affect crime seriousness; to use familiar examples, murder is more serious than aggravated assault because the injury is greater, and it is more serious than negligent homicide because the actor's culpability is greater. The problem is to develop criteria for harmfulness and culpability that are more illuminating than simple intuition.

With respect to culpability, there is some existing theory that can be drawn upon. It comes from the substantive criminal law: the doctrines of

---

criminal intent and excuse. Those doctrines address whether the defendant is culpable (and hence criminally answerable) at all, but comparable ideas could be carried over to an assessment of degree of culpability at the sentencing stage. Existing substantive-law notions of excuse, for example, could be used to help develop doctrines of partial excuse (e.g., partial duress, partial mental disability, and provocation).[1]

With respect to harm, matters are otherwise. Virtually no legal doctrines have been developed on how the gravity of harms can be compared. The substantive law provides little guidance, because the occurrence of harm is not explicitly made a general condition of criminal liability. The legal definitions of offenses simply describe various kinds of prohibited conduct—which the legislature is assumed to have considered harmful enough to be criminalized.[2] The philosophical literature also has not addressed criminal harm much, with the exception of a recent volume by Joel Feinberg[3] to which we will refer. We devote this essay to the subject of harm because we think it particularly in need of exploration.

We have limited the scope of our analysis of harm in various respects, and should explain at the outset what those limitations are. The present essay addresses only the harmfulness of *criminal* conduct which injures or threatens *identifiable victims*. In thus focusing on victimizing conduct, we are fully aware of the existence of other forms of criminal harm. Some crimes (e.g., certain environmental offenses) have harm that is primarily collective or aggregative: no identifiable person has his or her interest set back by activity of an identifiable actor; but if a sufficiently large number of persons engage in the conduct, the public's interests are adversely affected. In focusing on individual victimizing crimes, we do not wish to suggest these other crimes are necessarily any less important, only that their harmfulness is a more complicated matter to analyze. Having a theory of victimizing harms should be a useful first step.

This essay will be concerned chiefly with the *standard harm* involved in a given category or subcategory of crime. We will thus be assessing the injuriousness of a standard instance of (say) burglary, or of burglary of a certain kind—not the injury done to Mary Smith when her apartment was broken into and her favorite vase stolen on June 24 of this year.

How hurtful a given intrusion is depends on the situation of the victim, and the particular victim's situation varies greatly. The theft of an auto from a rich person may be no more than a temporary inconvenience; that theft from a poor person in a rural area may leave him bereft of any means of transportation. We thus need to assume, in rating the standard case of a given species of crime, that injury occurs to someone who is neither especially vulnerable nor resilient.

Why this emphasis on standard harm? Particular criminal acts are too diverse to be rated on an individualized basis. The analysis is aided when one (1) rates the standard case of an offense, and then (2) addresses unusual cases through principles of aggravation and mitigation. The first of these tasks will keep us amply occupied here. The second, on aggravation and mitigation, is complex enough to call for separate treatment.

2. Harm and the Living Standard

In gauging harms, the hard task is that of comparing the harmfulness of crimes which involve different interests. How is car theft to be compared with burglary, when the former involves a significant property loss and the latter a smaller financial setback but an invasion of privacy as well? Making such comparisons calls for a common criterion, or at least a common guiding idea, for assessing the interests involved.

The guiding idea which we have come to find most natural is one concerned with the quality of a person's life. The most important interests are those central to personal well-being; and, accordingly, the most grievous harms are those which drastically diminish one's standard of well-being. Mayhem is so serious because it makes its victims live in misery; burglary seems less serious because it does not create such misery but still has a significant impact on the quality of life in its intrusion on the person's privacy and comfort.

We required a term for this idea, and came upon Amartya Sen's useful essay, *The Standard of Living.*[4] Economists traditionally have used "living standard" to refer only to the degree of economic affluence or want. Sen, however, suggests a richer use for this term, one that includes not only economic means but other, noneconomic capabilities that affect personal well-being. We decided to adopt the term "living standard," understood in this broader sense,[5] which is used also in quality-of-life studies such as a recent Stockholm survey.[6] It refers to the quality of persons' existence, embracing not only material support and amenity but other noneconomic capabilities that affect the quality of a person's life.

The living standard is one of a family of related notions, including well-being, that refer to the extent of human flourishing. Well-being, however, can be highly personalized. The quality of my life depends upon my particular focal aims. To the person who wants to devote his life to contemplation and prayer, material comfort and social amenities may matter little. Thus, to determine a particular person's well-being, one ordinarily needs to know much about his life goals and his reasons for adopting them.

The living standard, however, does not focus on actual life quality or goal achievement, but on the *means* or *capabilities* for achieving a certain quality of life.[7] It is also standardized, referring to the means and capabilities that would *ordinarily* help one achieve a good life. Consider the person who is in good health, affluent, and with a wide social network from which to draw friends and acquaintances. If his chief goal in life is to write great poetry and he lacks the requisite talent, he may still be frustrated and unhappy. Nevertheless, it would be appropriate to say that he has a good standard of living, not merely because of his wealth but because he has the other means that people ordinarily can use to live well—whether or not he chooses to use those means or actually enjoys their fruits. These features are important for our present purpose because, as noted above, we are primarily concerned with standard harms.

A given capability or resource can support achievement of a variety of ends of a person's choosing. One thus can make living-standard judgments without having either to know a particular person's focal aims or to specify in detail what the standard person's aims are or ought to be. The judgments, in other words, assume a certain degree of pluralism. One may judge, for example, that undisturbed possession of a person's home has a certain degree of importance to his living standard. The judgment can hold, notwithstanding the varying uses of the home in people's lives: that one individual may use his or her home as the locus of family life, another as a place for study, another as a place in which to conduct orgies. One does not need to assume which of these ends are preferable, or even to assume that a person *should* choose personal goals that involve spending much time at home. The judgment is merely that the home plays a significant role in a variety of lives people choose to live in our society. This pluralism is important for our purposes, for it will permit us to make living-standard judgments without an ambitious specification of what people's ultimate focal aims are or ought to be.

Why rely on the living standard in order to gauge harms? A simple answer is that it appears to fit the way one ordinarily judges harms. Why is mayhem more harmful than burglary? It is because the overall quality of the victim's life is more adversely affected.

In adopting a living-standard criterion, we are not claiming that goodness or badness of conduct depends, as a general matter, on the conduct's effect on the quality of people's lives.[8] Our claim is more modest: that the living standard provides, not a generalized ethical norm, but a useful standard which the law can use in gauging the harmfulness of criminal acts. We think this is so for several reasons.

Victimizing harms involve intrusion into various personal resources or interests people have. If one asks why the state should seek to protect such interests through the criminal law, the most plausible answer would be that people require those resources to live decent lives. Robbery, burglary, and theft are prohibited because people need safety, shelter, and certain possessions to live tolerably. It thus makes sense to gauge the gravity of criminal harms by the importance that the relevant interests have for a person's standard of living.

Much of a modern state's protective concern for its citizens is aimed at safeguarding interests of theirs that constitute the generalized means for pursuit of a satisfactory life. Social-welfare programs (where they exist) concern the provision of a minimum of economic support to live decently; health and safety regulations serve to ensure the physical condition people require to have a comfortable existence; and so forth. Our conception sees the criminal law as having a comparable primary role.

The living-standard approach also has the advantage of a certain modesty; no "deep" theory of preferred life aims or appropriate social roles is presupposed. It recognizes, as noted earlier, a certain pluralism in the uses and ends to which people put their various interests.

3. Elements of a Living-Standard Analysis

Having sketched our rationale, we need to explain how criminal harms can be graded through a living-standard analysis. Let us, then, sketch the main elements of that analysis.

Rating the Living Standard: The Four Levels

If harms are to be gauged according to the extent to which they affect someone's living standard, then the living standard needs to be graded. Any grading scheme is bound to be somewhat arbitrary, but one should be able to make rough distinctions: for example, between suffering an intrusion that affects an adequate standard of comfort and one that reduces the person to the mere subsistence level. To accomplish this, we propose a four-level scale. The four living-standard levels may be formulated as follows:

Level	*Category*	*General Description*
1°	Subsistence	Survival, but with maintenance of no more than elementary human capacities to function. No satisfactions presupposed at this level.
2°	Minimal well-being	Maintenance of a minimal level of comfort and dignity.

3°	Adequate well-being	Maintenance of an "adequate" level of comfort and dignity.
4°	Enhanced well-being	Significant enhancement in quality of life above the mere "adequate" level.

This scale is designed to gauge the degree to which a given intrusion affects the person's living standard. If, for example, crime X intrudes into interests required for subsistence (living standard level 1°), it qualifies as gravely harmful. If crime Y intrudes only into interests needed to maintain the quality of the person's life at the "adequate" level (level 3°), this renders the harm less grave but still significant. Intrusions that only marginally (or do not at all) affect the living standard are the least harmful.

Having four grades is by no means inevitable. Since we are dealing with a continuum, a larger or fewer number of notches could have been cut. We propose these four gradations because the differences among them seem reasonably apparent. Having a larger number of living-standard gradations would make it easier to rate harms once the gradation affected by the criminal conduct was determined; but it would make the latter determination more difficult, as the differences among the grades would be less easy to discern.

There will also be variations in well-being *within* the four grades. Subsistence, for example, ranges from bare survival to survival without substantial debilitation: both homicide and mayhem invade subsistence, albeit to different degrees. Again, this should not be surprising, if one keeps in mind that we are dealing with a continuum, not neatly demarcated steps.

The function of these four gradations is to measure the extent to which a criminal act typically intrudes into a person's living standard. The (numerically) lower the level that is involved, the greater the intrusion. To take an obvious example: an aggravated assault threatens subsistence (1°) and thus is substantially more harmful than a theft affecting only level 4°. This explains why we are using a "positive" conception (the living standard) to rate harm (something negative, involving a taking-away). Criminal harm consists in the intrusion into legally protected interests, and its seriousness depends on the importance of the interests involved. We are gauging those interests' importance in terms of their significance for someone's living standard.

Let us consider the four living-standard levels more closely, then, and give a gloss on their meaning.

Subsistence (1°). We have defined subsistence as "survival, but with maintenance of no more than elementary human capacities to function." This means barely getting by. Included would be preservation of one's major physical and cognitive functions and preservation of a minimal capacity for social functioning. Being killed obviously destroys subsistence, but being maimed or made destitute would intrude upon subsistence also.

Critical to our definition of subsistence is that no satisfactions are presupposed at this level. Comfort thus is not part of subsistence—although avoidance of intense pain would be. Neither is privacy or self-respect included: one can survive or get by without privacy and despite repeated humiliations.

Minimal Well-Being (2°). This level we have defined as "a minimal level of comfort and dignity." It means having a bit more than barely getting by. In addition to surviving, certain elementary human satisfactions are assumed: *some* comfort, a modicum of self-respect.

Part of minimal well-being is thus a certain level of material support: shelter from inclement weather, nutritious food, etc. Another part is some degree of privacy and personal autonomy. One can subsist without the slightest privacy, but one hardly can be said to have even a barely satisfactory life. Protection against grossly demeaning or insulting treatment falls in this category also: one can subsist despite such treatment, but it impedes the maintenance of any degree of self-respect. Nevertheless, we are speaking only of a minimum of comfort, privacy, etc.: an existence at this level would still be having a substandard quality of life.

Adequate Well-Being (3°). We have defined this level as "maintenance of an 'adequate' level (but no more) of comfort and dignity." The term "adequate" is used here not in the sense of being satisfactory, but in the more restricted sense of being non-substandard. Included would be a level of material amenity needed for a comfortable, but no more than just comfortable, existence. It also includes that additional degree of privacy and avoidance of demeaning treatment that would be needed to warrant the conclusion that one is not leading a substandard or deprived existence.

Enhanced Well-Being (4°). This we have defined as "significant enhancement in quality of life above the mere 'adequate' level." It addresses those concerns that improve someone's quality of life significantly. A Swedish example of an interest at this level would be the ownership of a "sommarstuga"—the small country cabin that many Swedes own and use for the summer holidays. Having a sommarstuga is not needed for the third level of well-being: one is not plainly deprived (even in prosperous Sweden) if one lacks a summer cabin. Nevertheless, the sommarstuga does substantially enhance the quality of many Swedes' lives, and its destruction would have a significant impact on the quality of the person's existence.

We remain slightly uncomfortable with the term "enhancement," as it applies more naturally to material amenities than nonmaterial interests.

One might readily say that a sommarstuga is not needed for adequate living but improves life significantly. It seems a bit odd to talk about privacy or dignity that way: to say, for example, that freedom from verbal harassment is an "enhancement" of life quality. While one may not be entitled to a sommarstuga, is not everyone entitled to be free of harassment? Remember, however, that when we speak of "enhancements" we are not characterizing the interest itself, but rather its significance for the quality of life. It does make sense to say that freedom from occasional harassment is not necessary for an adequate life, but does enhance one's existence significantly above the mere "adequate" level.

Marginal Impact. Some criminal harms have no impact, or only a marginal one, on the quality of a person's life. Paradigmatic of harms in this category are petty thefts. The conduct may cause brief inconvenience, but typically has no significant lasting impact on the person's well-being.

The Generic Interest Dimensions

A criminal act can intrude upon a variety of different kinds of interests. An assault affects both the person's safety and self-respect; a burglary, a person's material comfort and privacy. The crime can affect these various dimensions in different degrees, and with differential impacts on the living standard: the privacy intrusion in a burglary, for example, may affect the standard of living more than the comfort intrusion does. Our analysis thus needs to distinguish various generic interest dimensions. We suggest four, to wit:

—Physical integrity
—Material support and amenity
—Freedom from humiliation
—Privacy/autonomy

We do not claim this list is complete, and have used no deep theory of interests to derive it. Instead, we rely on our impressions of the main kinds of legally protected interests that seem typically involved in victimizing crimes. Adding supplemental interest dimensions would not alter the mode of analysis.

How are these interest dimensions to be used? One would first identify and separate out the interest dimensions involved in an offense. Next, one would apply the living-standard criteria to each dimension successively. To illustrate, consider simple residential burglary: the offender, during the residents' absence, breaks into an apartment and steals a television set. First, one identifies the interest dimensions. Here, those chiefly involved appear to be (1) material amenity, and (2) privacy. The material loss consists in the loss of a useful home appliance (a TV), the inconvenience of having locks repaired, etc. The privacy intrusion consists of the unauthorized entry into the dwelling place itself. Second, one applies the rating criteria to each dimension, successively. With respect to the comfort dimension, the impact on the living standard is small: a workable replacement TV, for example, can be obtained at modest cost. However, the rating is higher when the privacy/autonomy dimension is taken into account.

Let us examine the four interest dimensions more closely.

Physical Integrity. This embraces health, safety, and avoidance of physical pain. An intrusion into physical integrity can, depending upon its extent, affect any of the living-standard gradations: from a homicide that destroys subsistence (living-standard level 1°) to a jostling causing only momentary discomfort that scarcely disturbs the quality of one's life.

Material Support and Amenity. This embraces someone's material interests. These range from the most basic ones needed for subsistence (e.g., food, drink, and minimum shelter), to the various material amenities needed for a life of tolerable comfort, to various luxuries. An intrusion into a person's material interests may thus range from those that are very serious (affecting living standard level 1°) to those that are quite trivial and do not affect the living standard at all.

Freedom from Humiliation. We considered various terms to describe this dimension: for example, "self-respect" and "dignity." These, however, seemed overbroad—as one's self-respect and dignity depend on one's own self-conceptions as well as on what harm befalls one. The narrower term—"freedom from humiliation or degrading treatment"—therefore seemed more apt, because it refers to those injuries to self-respect that derive from others' mistreatment.[9] That this is a dimension of quality of life should be evident: one is worse off when treated in a degrading fashion. This interest is affected by a variety of criminal acts, from physical assault to verbal harassment.

Privacy/Autonomy. This affects well-being not only because it promotes self-respect but because it helps one pursue preferences of various kinds. It is affected by various offenses, from burglary through wiretapping to kidnapping. It is a dimension which is culture specific: in our culture it affects well-being considerably, but another culture may give privacy or autonomy less weight.

A corollary of this discussion is that some of the interest dimensions do not run through the entire living-standard scale. Physical integrity relates to all four living-standard levels, depending on the degree of the intrusion. Material support and amenity does also, as we have seen. However, the last two dimensions (freedom from humiliation and privacy/autonomy) are concerns that arise only at living-standard level 2° (minimal well-being) or higher. The reason is that level 1° (subsistence) concerns merely "getting by," and no satisfactions are assumed at that level.

Standardizing the Living-Standard Impact

Estimating the impact of a given intrusion on someone's living standard requires assumptions to be made on what other resources he or she possesses. The more slender those resources, the more devastating the intrusion. How, then, should one determine the standard impact?

Our living-standard analysis is designed to gauge harms affecting a variety of interests, from the most to the least important. It is thus helpful to imagine someone who has various interests at the various living-standard levels, and then ask how deprivation or intrusion into *this* particular interest would affect that person's quality of life. The hypothetical victim would thus be assumed to have interests at each of the various living-standard levels: certain interests or resources needed to subsist; others needed to raise his well-being to the minimal and to the adequate level; and certain other, "enhancing" interests. These assumptions provide a perspective for judging the importance of a particular intrusion: it enables one to judge how important the particular interest or resource intruded upon is to a good life, compared to the various other interests and resources a person may have. Not all actual victims will be in the hypothetical victim's situation: some will have a lower living standard to begin with, and thus suffer disproportionately from any given deprivation. Such cases of greater vulnerability to harm—coupled with questions of foreseeability of that vulnerability by the offender—should be addressed by the rules on aggravation and mitigation.

Temporal Perspective

What temporal perspective should one adopt when judging the impact of a crime on someone's well-being? The perspective makes a difference. Consider having one's pocket picked. If the question is, How was your day? it makes perfect sense to answer that it was awful, because one lost one's wallet with a small sum of cash and all one's IDs. However, if the question is how one's year has been, it is silly to say that it has been awful, merely because one's pocket was picked four months ago.

Living-standard judgments are addressed to the overall quality of someone's *life,* and this suggests a considerably longer temporal perspective than the highly variable quality of experience from day to day. The appropriate perspective is a middle-term one—something approximating, How has your year been? or perhaps even a slightly longer duration. An extremely long temporal duration, however, would be too reductive: even awful experiences diminish in importance if the question were, How was your last decade?—and indeed, such questions are seldom asked in ordinary life.

Our suggested temporal perspective is addressed, however, not to the actual duration of the crime and its effects, but to the importance of the experience from the overall viewpoint of a given time frame. A physical assault, and its immediate trauma, may soon be over; yet if the experience was painful or humiliating enough, it may still loom large in evaluation of, say, the quality of a whole year's experience.

Assault and Battery: An Illustration

How might this scheme be applied in rating harms? Consider the case of assault and battery. The assumed standard case is: A beats up B. Suppose the beating is quite painful, and results in substantial bruises and some lacerations—but not enough to require hospitalization.

Consider, first, the interest dimension of *physical integrity.* From this perspective, being beaten up is no worse than accidentally walking into a solid glass door. It hurts badly when it happens, one has a black eye and a headache for a few days, and then it is over. How serious is that?

—Is the living-standard level involved level 1° (subsistence)? Obviously not. There is no loss of functioning. It is merely uncomfortable, and comfort, physical or material, is not presupposed at this level.

—Is it level 2° (minimal well-being), or 3° (adequate well-being)? Again, no. We hardly think that the person who walks into a glass door and gets a black eye has his overall living standard reduced below such levels of adequacy.

—Is it level 4° (enhanced well-being)? For a brief period, yes. One's quality of existence has definitely gone down—while one is still sore and black-eyed. But the period involved may be too brief to qualify from the middle-term perspective of which we are speaking.

Let us, however, consider another interest dimension: that of *freedom from humiliation*. Here, the intrusion into the living standard is potentially more grave: being beaten up is demeaning. How much it is so is a matter of social convention. In the more gladiatorial societies, losing a (fair) fight may not be regarded as particularly degrading—and this holds even in some of our own subcultures, for example, in the venerable American institution of the barroom brawl. (But even there, being victimized in an *unfair* fight—for example, being ambushed by several assailants—may be regarded as humiliating.) The link between being beaten and being humiliated probably holds in most cultures, and may have deeper roots: even a dog cringes if it is beaten and cannot defend itself. In our culture, at any rate, a beating is ordinarily deeply humiliating. What makes it so is not just the physical intrusion and pain, but the being put at someone else's mercy. The person beaten is literally abased—knocked down, abused—and the beater establishes direct physical dominion over him.

So the question becomes, At which level is this deprivation? It is definitely not as high as level 1°, because subsistence does not presuppose self-respect, in our taxonomy.

Is the intrusion at least at 3°? We would say so. An adequate level of self-respect is surely a part of this level. And the humiliation of a beating strikes us as grave enough to compromise self-respect at the "adequate" level.

Is the intrusion still more serious, that is, at 2°? We would say not. There are humiliations that are so grave as to compromise even a minimal level of well-being—for instance, rape. But we remain unconvinced, for the moment, that the humiliation of a beating, substantial though it is, would be so devastating to a normal person's self-respect that it would place the quality of his life at minimal well-being, that is, barely above the subsistence level.

4. Harm Scales, Combinations, and Discounts

Constructing and applying the living-standard ratings helps, but does not suffice, to grade harms. The reasons should be apparent from the preceding illustrations. First, an offense may give rise to multiple living-standard ratings in different dimensions. A beating, as just noted, has not only a given living-standard impact in the physical-integrity dimension, but a (different) impact in the humiliation dimension. We thus need a way of combining these diverse living-standard impacts into a net harmfulness grade. Second, discounts need to be made for risked or threatened harm. An armed robbery, for example, risks subsistence; it can be described as a "discounted" 1°. But it makes little sense to discount directly onto the living-standard scale: if one reduced the robbery rating to 2°, for example, that would not be saying the offense risks subsistence, but rather that it actually affects the living-standard level of minimal well-being—which is not an accurate characterization.

[*The article then contains a discussion of how a harm scale might be constructed so as to take account of combinations of harm and discounts for risked harms. It concludes with suggestions about how the analysis might assist in the task of sentencing reform.*]

Notes

1. See Martin Wasik, "Excuses at the Sentencing Stage," *Criminal Law Review* 450 (1983); Andrew von Hirsch and Nils Jareborg, "Provocation and Culpability," in Ferdinand Schoeman (ed.), *Responsibility, Character, and the Emotions* (Cambridge: Cambridge University Press, 1987) 246.

2. The Model Penal Code, for example, has no general requirement of harm, comparable to its general culpability requirements in § 2.02. Rather, particular kinds of conduct, apparently deemed by the legislature to be harmful, are described: for example, § 223.2 defines theft as the taking or exercise of unlawful control over the movable property of another. There is no express requirement that the taking be injurious to anyone.

3. Joel Feinberg, *Harm to Others* (Oxford: Oxford University Press, 1984); see also John Kleinig, "Crime and the Concept of Harm," 15 *American Philosophical Quarterly* 27 (1978).

4. Amartya Sen, *The Standard of Living* (Cambridge: Cambridge University Press, 1987) 20–38.

5. [In an earlier work, one of the authors espoused a "welfare interest" theory for gauging criminal harms, based on notions of choice. See von Hirsch, *Past or Future Crimes* (New Brunswick: Rutgers University Press, 1985), ch. 6. A portion of the present essay, not excerpted here, argues why a living-standard criterion is preferable to such a "welfare interest" criterion—Eds.]

6. See Robert Erikson and Rune Åberg, *Welfare in Transition: A Survey of Living Conditions in Sweden 1968–1981* (Oxford: Clarendon Press, 1987), ch. 1.

7. See Sen, *supra* note 4, at 30–31, 36–37.

8. Harm consists of being made worse off. One can gauge how much one is harmed, i.e., how much worse off one is, by the impact of the conduct on the quality of one's life. Other evils, however, do not necessarily involve harm as part of their defining characteristics. An example is offense. Being treated offensively does not necessarily involve being made worse off in the sense of having one's personal resources diminished; its evil resides simply in being dealt with without consideration or respect. To gauge the gravity of offensive conduct, one thus may require a standard other than one that refers to reduction in the offended person's living standard. For a useful analysis of offense, and how it differs from harm, see Narayan, *Offensive Conduct* (New Brunswick: Rutgers University, 1990) (unpublished Ph.D. dissertation).

9. This dimension creates a degree of overlap between harm and culpability. Humiliation normally presupposes intent (or at least, apparent intent). I am humiliated by being beaten; but not formally, by being injured through someone's negligent handling of a vehicle.

4.6
Desert and the Role of Previous Convictions

Martin Wasik

[*The author begins by observing that "few people would be likely to argue with the proposition that a defendant's criminal record is an important determinant of his sentence." Given this widely held view, there has been a remarkable "lack of analysis of precisely what information about a defendant's prior record is relevant to sentence selection, and in what ways that influence is manifested." In this respect, maintains the author, "the relation between sentencing and prior record remains obscure." He goes on to suggest that "eight factors of prior record emerge as likely to be perceived by the sentencer as relevant":*
1. *number of previous convictions*
2. *similarity of previous offenses to the current offense*
3. *frequency of reoffending*
4. *seriousness of previous offenses*
5. *previous sentences*
6. *staleness of previous convictions*
7. *age of defendant when he received previous convictions*
8. *previous record as allowing character inference.*]

To what extent are the eight factors identified above capable of being refined and encapsulated in appellate guidance or sentencing guidelines? Traditionally, the Court of Appeal in England has been reluctant, when hearing appeals against sentence, to travel much beyond the instant facts of the case to provide general guidance for sentencers. Recently, however,

---

From Martin Wasik, "Guidance, Guidelines, and Criminal Record," in Martin Wasik and Ken Pease, eds., *Sentencing Reform: Guidance or Guidelines?* (Manchester: Manchester University Press, 1987).

this has begun to change, with an important series of "guideline" judgments providing more generalized assistance for sentencers on important questions of sentencing policy, such as prison overcrowding, or dealing with particular types of cases, such as sentencing in serious drug offenses in *Aramah* (1983) (for a discussion of recent developments see Ashworth, 1984). The Court of Appeal has not so far addressed the general issue of interpretation of prior record in a similar way, but in principle it would seem that some ground rules should be capable of being drawn and indeed must be enunciated if we are to have anything approaching consistent decision making. As the lord chief justice has commented in his seminal speech in *Bibi* (1980): "We are not aiming at uniformity of sentence; that would be impossible. We are aiming at uniformity of approach."

To what extent can there be such uniformity of approach in relation to the interpretation of prior record? In order to achieve uniformity, we have to move away from the still prevalent notion in England that sentencing is a matter of intuition, toward the articulation of general rules and relevant exceptions.

The first substantial difficulty is that prior record may be taken account of for one of two very different reasons. It may be looked at in order to provide a basis for some kind of predictive assessment of the defendant's likely future behavior or response to sentence, or it may be considered as a dimension of the defendant's culpability against which his punishment is to be measured. Some of the eight factors identified above primarily reflect the predictive approach, some primarily reflect the culpability approach, but nearly all are capable of reflecting both.

Criminal Record and Prediction

Some writers have argued that whenever previous convictions are taken into account by the sentencer, a predictive rationale of sentencing must be operating. Take, for example, Fletcher (1978, 466): "The contemporary pressure to consider prior convictions in setting the level of the offense and of punishment reflects a theory of social protection rather than a doctrine of deserved punishment. The rule of thumb is that recidivists are more dangerous and that society will be better served if the recidivists are isolated for longer terms."

While the correctness of this view will be challenged in a moment, it is certainly true to say that previous convictions are more obviously relevant to the sentencer working on a predictive rather than a just deserts basis.

Let us consider the implications of prior record for the predictive approach. To start with, the *number* of previous convictions recorded against a defendant is generally regarded as being the best available predictor of future offending. The research evidence is that the more convictions recorded against a defendant, the greater the likelihood that he will be reconvicted. An English research study (Philpotts and Lancucki, 1979) found that 29 percent of males having no previous convictions who were convicted of standard list offenses in January 1971 were reconvicted within six years. The percentage of offenders who had one previous conviction when convicted in January 1971 who were reconvicted within six years was 54 percent. If they had two to four previous convictions the figure rose to 70 percent, and for those with five or more previous convictions, 87 percent were reconvicted within six years. A sentencer working on a predictive rationale would, therefore, require a full and accurate account of the defendant's previous lawbreaking. A number of American jurisdictions allow the sentencer to have reference to the defendant's "arrest record" as well as previous convictions, on the (surely debatable) basis that this more clearly establishes a criminal "pattern of conduct," and there is some research evidence that the number of the defendant's prior arrests was a very important determinant of sentence in pre-guideline America (Hawkinson, 1975: Johnston et al., 1973).

Criminal Record and "Just Deserts"

There has been a recent resurgence of the notion of "just deserts" in sentencing policy. One of the most difficult matters for the just deserts theorists to resolve has been the relevance of the defendant's previous convictions to the current sentence. Some writers have argued that such a theory cannot support more severe sentences for persistent offenders and that the reasoning employed in taking account of them must be covertly preventive (Fletcher, 1978; Singer, 1979). Most recently, Wilkins (1985) has claimed that it is "because we know that prior convictions are prognostic of future criminality that the strict retributive model is, to most persons, unacceptable." Such criticism has provoked a response from Andrew von Hirsch.

In *Doing Justice* (von Hirsch, 1976), two main arguments were advanced for taking account of prior record in computing culpability. The first was that (at 85): "A repetition of the offense following . . . conviction may be regarded as more culpable since [the actor] persisted in the behavior after having been forcefully censured for it through his prior punishment."

The second was an "evidentiary" one that the more often the defendant is convicted and punished, the more sure we can be that he is actually guilty. In a later article (von Hirsch, 1981) he seems not to pursue the latter claim (wisely, perhaps, for it apparently confuses "evidence of greater culpability" with "greater culpability." He does, however, provide an alternative account of the relevance of previous convictions within just deserts theory.

It is argued by von Hirsch that when a person commits some misdeed in everyday life, he may plead that his misconduct was uncharacteristic of his previous behavior. This plea relates to an inference which is normally drawn from (a) a judgment about the wrongfulness of an act to (b) the disapproval directed at a person. The actor is claiming in mitigation that though this act was wrong he should not suffer full obloquy for it because the act is out of keeping with his customary standards of behavior. Logically, this plea carries greatest weight when the actor has not committed the misdeed before, and it becomes progressively less persuasive with repetition of the wrongdoing. This analysis is then transferred to sentencing. It is clear that the resultant model is very similar, though drawn in more detail, to the "progressive loss of mitigation" theory. It entails that the defendant's criminal record is not appropriate to justify endless successive increases in penalty, but is primarily a means of achieving sentence reduction for those with clean or nearly clean records. Von Hirsch's model provides us with an opportunity to examine the eight factors which were identified above as potentially relevant to prior record in the English sentencing context, to see to what extent they might be compatible with a just deserts sentencing framework.

The first consideration is *number* of previous convictions. It will be recalled that on the basis of predictive sentencing, number provided the best available indicator of future offending. The greater the number of previous convictions, the greater the risk of reoffending and the more pressing the need for appropriate preventive sentencing. In "just deserts" sentencing, however, number is relevant in only a strictly limited way. The defendant is entitled to mitigation for the first few offenses, and then the mitigation is exhausted so that the defendant is visited with the full penalty of the law. The obvious question is how many repetitions can occur before the force of the mitigation is lost? Von Hirsch concedes that he has "no ready answer" to this question, being content to suggest "a certain limited number of repetitions" (1981, 616). We may, for the purposes of argument, select five (as Andrew Ashworth has suggested). The crucial point is that after those five convictions, reconviction would not attract greater severity. Von Hirsch calls this a "closed criminal history score." If we take the Minnesota sentencing guidelines as an example, we see that the defendant is assigned one point for every felony conviction prior to the current conviction. The guidelines have a closed criminal history score in that after six or more previous convictions, the presumptive sentence in the right-hand column of the grid remains unchanged with, for example, twenty-four months representing the "ceiling" for an offense in seriousness category (1).

It must be obvious, however, that in taking account of prior record on a just deserts calculus, number cannot be all there is to it. What of the *similarity* or otherwise between the current offense and offenses appearing in the record? Surely similarity ought to be relevant, for it confirms in the starkest possible manner that such misbehavior is characteristic of the defendant. Von Hirsch is less forthcoming on this point, but in *Doing Justice* (von Hirsch, 1976, 86), he argued that previous convictions might lose some of their significance if they were for crimes "sufficiently dissimilar" to the present one. Of course, the significance of this must depend upon the level of generality at which similarity is identified. Von Hirsch now suggests that the criterion is whether the current act and the prior criminal conduct are "similar in the basic principles they violate" (von Hirsch, 1981, 616). In arguing that "white-collar swindle" is similar to "other frauds," "outright thefts," and "acts of force," since these all "involve willful injury" (617), it is clear that he identifies similarity at a fairly low level. The effect of this is to decrease the relative importance of similarity in the criminal record and increase the relative importance of number. In the Minnesota guidelines no particular importance is attached to repetition of similar offenses. It seems that this may have been for fear of introducing great complexity into the calculation of the criminal history score (von Hirsch, 1982, 201–2).

What about the *staleness* of previous convictions? Again, in *Doing Justice* it was argued that provision should be made "for the decay of offenders' criminal records, with convictions long past being disregarded" (1976, 87). This is because the more distant the conviction the less plausible it is to claim that such acts are characteristic of the defendant's conduct. The commission introduced a "decay factor" into the Minnesota guidelines in this respect. Thus prior felony convictions do not count toward the criminal history score if ten years have elapsed since the date of discharge from or expiration of the sentence, providing that the defendant remained free of conviction during that period. There is also the question of the *seriousness* of the previous convictions. According to von Hirsch (1981, 620):

> . . . the quality of the record should count. Someone convicted of his first serious crime would be entitled to plead that such gravely reprehensible conduct has been uncharacteristic of him, and hence that he deserves to have his penalty scaled down—even where he has a record of lesser infractions. Where the current crime is serious, in other words, the criminal history should take into account the gravity of the prior convictions as well as their number.

If, on the other hand, the current offense is less serious than some offenses which appear on the record, it would seem that the defendant has shown that offending of a nature at least as serious as the current offense is not untypical of him and the argument for mitigation is much less strong. In the Minnesota guidelines relative seriousness is taken into account in computation of criminal history scores, but only to a limited extent. If a previous offense was punished only by way of a fine it will be accorded less weight. If the fine was $100 or less, the conviction does not count at all. Yet the distinction remains crude in that all previous convictions resulting in custodial sentences attract one point, whether the offenses were in fact serious or relatively trivial.

Frequency of repetition does not as such form part of von Hirsch's scheme, though, as we have seen, he advocates giving less weight to older convictions. On the face of it, rapid repetition of offending would seem relevant to desert, as underlining the characteristic nature of the behavior, and it is perhaps odd that specific provision is not made for it. In the guidelines, adoption of the "decay factor" takes account of it to some extent. The Commentary to the guidelines states that "a person who was convicted of three felonies within a five-year period is more culpable than one convicted of three felonies within a twenty-year period." Yet, it is not clear that the ten-year "decay factor" for felonies would operate in either of these cases, assuming the convictions to be evenly spaced.

On a just deserts view, the *age* of the defendant does not qualify as a mitigating factor as such, though it could be relevant indirectly, such as through the issue of degree of participation in the offense (e.g., where a young person was led by experienced offenders into a criminal enterprise). The relevance of the defendant's age to his culpability is a matter which has not so far been adequately dealt with by the just deserts theorists. It is, however, taken account of in the Minnesota guidelines, where for an offender who is under twenty-one when sentenced, only half a point is ascribed to him for each prior felony conviction occurring after his sixteenth birthday. Previous convictions for less serious offenses committed as a juvenile are disregarded. Once the offender attains the age of twenty-one, a nominal one point will be left on his record to indicate to the court the existence of convictions as a juvenile. If he has one such prior conviction, the resultant half-point will be disregarded. It is difficult to discern the rationale upon which the commission proceeded in weighting these factors.

It is apparent from the just deserts model that what is taken to matter is the legal classification of previous convictions, rather than *previous sentences* served by the defendant. The emphasis upon convictions seems also to ensure that in "just deserts" theory, in contrast to predictive sentencing, no attention should be given to "arrest records" or alleged but unproven lawbreaking (see von Hirsch, 1981, 608 et seq.). These limitations are reflected in the Minnesota guidelines. On the other hand, as we have seen, the guidelines refer to sentences served rather than to offense seriousness when drawing the fairly crude distinctions in assigning points to take account of seriousness of previous offenses.

Recently, Walker has criticized von Hirsch's analysis of the relevance of prior convictions by questioning the implications of the "out of character" plea. He says (1985, 44):

> The principal defect of his justification, however, is its failure to distinguish clearly between punishing because punishment is deserved and punishing because punishment expresses disapproval. If his argument is to hold water it must be carried to the length of saying that recidivists should be punished not merely to express disapproval of their character but because the sentencer is entitled to punish them for that character. The Court of Appeal sometimes allows evidence of good moral character—such as bravery—to mitigate sentence . . . but to generalise from this to a policy of sentencing people for their moral character would be a leap into a bog without boundaries.

If Walker is right in this vividly expressed criticism, it seems that factor number eight, above, whereby information about prior record can be used by the court in drawing *character inferences,* must be regarded as being within von Hirsch's theory. Yet this factor must surely be confined to predictive sentencing, having no possible place in just deserts theory. A closer reading of just deserts theory, however, reveals that it does not have the wide implications which Walker claims for it. "Just deserts" relates to punishment for the current offense, though if that offense is the first, there is some room for leniency in the way in which it is sentenced. In no sense, therefore, could this amount to "sentencing people for their moral character." As von Hirsch says, it must be a mistake to assume that using prior lawbreaking in judging someone's actions "must rest on a whole-life notion of good or bad character" (1981, 609). Perhaps, though, von Hirsch's use of the words "typical" and "characteristic" to describe the assessment to be made of the defendant's record in the light of the current offense is unfortunate in tending to suggest an assessment being made of the overall moral standing of the person. It is quite clear from the context of the discussion that this is not what is meant.

References

Ashworth, A. J. (1984), "Techniques of guidance on sentencing," *Criminal Law Review* 519.

Fletcher, G. P. (1978), *Rethinking Criminal Law,* Boston: Little, Brown.

Hawkinson, T. (1975), "The effect of pre-trial release, race, and previous arrest on conviction and sentencing," *Creighton Law Review,* 8, 930.

Johnston, B. L., et al. (1973), "Discretion in felony sentencing—a study of influencing factors," *Washington Law Review,* 48, 857.

Philpotts, G.J.O., and Lancucki, L. B. (1979), *Previous Convictions, Sentence, and Reconviction,* Home Office Research Study no. 53, London: H.M.S.O.

Singer, R. G. (1979), *Just Deserts: Sentencing Based on Equality and Desert,* University of Chicago Press.

von Hirsch, A. (1976), *Doing Justice,* New York: Hill and Wang.

von Hirsch, A. (1981), "Desert and previous convictions in sentencing," *Minnesota Law Review,* 65, 591.

von Hirsch, A. (1982), "Constructing guidelines for sentencing: the critical choices for the Minnesota Sentencing Guidelines Commission," *Hamline Law Review,* 164.

Walker, N. D. (1985), *Sentencing: Theory, Law, and Practice,* London: Butterworths.

Wilkins, L. T. (1985), "The politics of prediction," in Farrington, D. P., and Tarling, R., *Prediction in Criminology,* Albany: State University of New York Press.

4.7
Desert and Prevention: Hybrid Principles

Paul Robinson

Most criminal codes, and most criminal law courses, begin with the "familiar litany" of the purposes of criminal law sanctions—just punishment [desert], deterrence, incapacitation of the dangerous, and rehabilitation. We train and direct our lawyers, judges, and legislators to use these purposes as guiding principles for the distribution of criminal sanctions. The purposes are thus to guide both the drafting and interpretation of criminal statutes and the imposition of criminal sentences in individual cases.

The purposes frequently conflict, however. Conflicts arise because each purpose requires consideration of different criteria; in some cases, a particular fact suggests different sentences or statutory formulations under different purposes. Ultimately a choice must be made to follow one purpose at the expense of another. Yet when faced with conflicting purposes, the judges, legislators, and sentencing-guideline drafters have no principle to guide that decision.

In the absence of a guiding principle, the choices made are, at best, inconsistent. For example, most state criminal codes maintain an insanity defense because it exculpates the blameless (and thus furthers just punishment), even though abolishing the defense might more effectively incapacitate the dangerous. Yet the same codes sacrifice just punishment, in favor of increasing deterrence, by recognizing strict liability. At the same time, rather than increasing the threatened sanction when the temptation or inclination is greater, as a deterrence principle suggests, these codes frequently decrease the deterrent threat—as, for example, in cases of provo-

---

From Paul H. Robinson, "Hybrid Principles for the Distribution of Criminal Sanctions," 82 *Northwestern University Law Review* 19 (1988). Excerpted and reprinted by permission.

cation—because of the offender's reduced blameworthiness. Code drafters are choosing to further different purposes in different contexts.

At worst, the absence of a guiding principle fosters arbitrariness or prejudice. This happens when the inconsistent approach of the code drafters is followed on the level of individual sentencing decisions. For instance, while rehabilitation might be the best means of avoiding future crime by a young addict who is caught selling drugs to support his habit, a judge rationally might decide to impose a long prison term in order to further general deterrence interests. When faced with a young bank teller who embezzled money from her cash drawer, the same judge might decide to sacrifice the general deterrent value of a long prison term and put the offender on probation, under an incapacitative theory—she is no longer dangerous because she will never again be placed in a position of trust. Both of these sentences are justified by one of the purposes of sentencing, but they nonetheless may be the product of arbitrary or biased decision making. Without a principle governing when one sentencing purpose is to be followed at the expense of another, judges and guideline drafters are free to choose whatever purpose justifies the desired sentence.

Why do we not insist that code and sentencing-guideline drafters adopt, and that judges follow, a statement of the interrelation among purposes that will direct the choice among conflicting purposes? A cynic may conclude that the use of "the purposes" to justify a particular code formulation or sentence is a convenient means of rationalizing results for which the decision maker has another, undisclosed reason. This suspicion—that "the purposes" are popular as a method of justification precisely *because* they offer hidden flexibility—is fueled by the almost universal failure to articulate a guiding principle.

Whether the flexibility of rationalization offered by "the purposes" has been used for conscious manipulation or is the result of inadvertent vagueness, a rational and principled system for the distribution of criminal sanctions is needed. Such a system must define the interrelation of the multiple purposes it seeks to further; that is, it must fully articulate a hybrid distributive principle.

Alternative Purposes and Conflict Points

Before discussing alternative approaches to constructing a hybrid distributive principle, two preliminary, related questions must be briefly addressed. First, why do we need a hybrid distributive principle? Why not simply adopt one of the four traditional purposes as the sole distributive principle?

Second, do the traditional purposes really conflict in application? If so, where and why?

Single-Purpose Distributive Principles

One could avoid the inconsistency and abuse of the traditional approach to criminal sanctions by adopting a distributive principle based upon a single purpose. But such a single-purpose distributive principle would produce sentences that are generally seen as unacceptable. Consider, for example, the adoption of a utilitarian purpose, either deterrence, incapacitation of the dangerous, or rehabilitation, as the sole purpose. Each scenario would justify consideration of factors that, in the Anglo-American criminal law tradition, are considered illegitimate bases for distributing criminal liability and punishment.

To the extent that incapacitation determines the distribution of criminal sanctions, statistical data on the probabilities of recidivism is useful. Under a principle designed solely to incapacitate the dangerous, offenders would be sentenced on the basis of backgrounds and characteristics having little or no necessary connection to their crimes. Past employment history, for example, is highly relevant in predicting recidivism. Thus, under such a single-purpose principle, unemployment for the preceding two years should aggravate the grade of an offense or increase the sentence imposed. Age and family situation are also useful predictors of future criminality, and thus also would bear on liability. Indeed, if incapacitation of the dangerous is the only distributive principle, there would be little justification for waiting until an offense is committed; it would be more efficient to screen the general population for dangerous persons and "convict" them of being dangerous and in need of incapacitation.

If pure deterrence were the distributive principle, a potential offender's perception of the probability of apprehension would be highly relevant. To enhance deterrence, offenses with a perceived low probability of apprehension should be graded highly and punished severely. Deterrence theory also suggests that would-be criminals will be powerfully influenced by the perceived likelihood of conviction; therefore punishment should be administered frequently, as well as severely. To that end, it would be appropriate to increase the likelihood of conviction by dispensing with traditional desert-based liability requirements, such as culpability, causation, or complicity requirements, which significantly impede convictions. A pure deterrence principle also logically would base liability upon the extent of the publicity that a sanction receives in a particular case. Just as an advertising executive pays more to place an ad that reaches more people, society may efficiently spend more (that is, impose a greater penalty at a greater cost) if imposition of a sanction will be widely communicated. Thus, news coverage should aggravate the grade of or sentence for an offense. In its most extreme extension, the pure deterrence principle would justify punishment of the innocent; as long as the public perceived the "offender" to be guilty, the deterrence purpose would be served.

To the extent that rehabilitation governs distribution, the actor's amenability to reform or treatment is central. It was in furtherance of the rehabilitative purpose that fully indeterminate sentences were imposed in the recent past. The length of the sentence was to be determined by the length of time necessary for the offender's rehabilitation, which could not be determined at the time of conviction. The offender remained in prison until he or she was rehabilitated. With a pure rehabilitation principle, as with each pure utilitarian principle, there would be little reason to wait for an offense to occur. Incarceration would be justified if the "offender" were shown to have a treatable abnormality.

The utilitarian purposes, if used without desert considerations, not only would permit or compel distribution according to factors that are likely to be judged unacceptable, but also would preclude the consideration of factors that are generally held to be key to the distribution of sanctions under current law. Even the nature of the crime committed may be of little relevance under some utilitarian purposes. As the Model Sentencing Act [see Extract 3.1] proudly points out:

> The [Act] diminishes the major source of [sentencing] disparity—sentencing according to the particular offense. Under [the Act] the dangerous offender may be committed to a lengthy term; the non-dangerous offender may not. It makes available, for the first time, a plan that allows the sentence to be determined by the defendant's make-up, his potential threat in the future, and other similar factors, with a minimum of variation according to the offense.

In contrast to utilitarian single-purpose distributive principles, one might create a generally acceptable system based solely on desert; several writers have proposed just this. But many people will resist such a pure desert system because it may cause unnecessary inefficiency in the use of criminal sanctions to prevent crime. A pure desert principle might impose sanctions that cost more than the crime they prevent and might fail to impose sanctions where the opportunities for efficient crime prevention were great.

Conflict Points among Alternative Purposes

With such differences in criteria, it is no surprise that the purposes frequently conflict in application. If rehabilitation is temporarily excluded from the analysis, because of doubt as to its feasibility and moral objections to its use as a distributive principle, a conflict is likely to reflect one of these three alignments:

1 desert vs. deterrence and incapacitation;
2 deterrence vs. desert and incapacitation;
3 incapacitation vs. desert and deterrence.

1. *Desert vs.*—Desert can conflict with deterrence and incapacitation in two sorts of cases. First, the desert principle gives rise to doctrines like the insanity defense and the voluntary act requirement, which acquit blameless offenders even though they may be dangerous and even though their punishment might serve a general deterrent function. Conversely, in another set of cases, desert is sacrificed to deterrence and incapacitation. For example, the defense for inherently unlikely attempts acquits blameworthy offenders because the inherent harmlessness of the conduct suggests that both incapacitation and deterrence are unnecessary. In both sets of cases, a conflict arises: desert leads to one result while deterrence and incapacitation lead to another.

2. *Deterrence vs.*—Deterrence frequently conflicts with desert and incapacitation where some abnormal condition external to the actor, such as duress, coercion, or nonjustified necessity, contributes to the actor's criminal conduct. Because the conditions rather than the actor are judged responsible for the conduct, the actor is held blameless and nondangerous and thus is acquitted or receives a reduced sentence. On the other hand, the same coercive conditions can create the need for a greater rather than lesser deterrent threat. Greater sanctions would provide a needed additional deterrent in the face of unusual pressure to commit the offense.

If the pressure to commit the offense is so great as to be essentially irresistible, the "special deterrence" rationale (that is, punishment of the offender at hand so that he or she will not commit the same offense in a similar situation in the future) may disappear. In such a situation, any sanction would be futile and thus an inefficient expenditure. There may remain, however, a "general deterrent" purpose in imposing a significant sanction. In *Regina v. Dudley & Stephens,* for example, the sailors who killed the sick cabin boy to stay alive until they could be rescued were hardly shown to be dangerous people (as long as they stayed off boats that would be adrift for weeks) and their blameworthiness was significantly reduced because of the life-threatening conditions. Furthermore, people in their situation, or they again in the same situation, cannot be effectively deterred, because, as is assumed, the pressure they encountered was irresistible. However, there may remain nonetheless some general deterrent value in imposing a significant sanction to reaffirm the strong prohibition against the killing of innocent nonaggressors.

The same conflict arises in applying mitigating principles, like heat of passion, provocation, and mistake as to self-defense by battered wives and abused children. In these cases, an otherwise normal actor reacts less than admirably when confronted with a difficult situation. Such an actor is not as dangerous or blameworthy as an actor who kills absent the mitigating conditions, but, as with instances of duress, coercion, and nonjustified necessity, the need for a deterrent sanction to oppose the tendency and temptation is as great, if not greater.

A similar conflict between purposes arises under many strict liability doctrines when an offender, who is neither blameworthy nor dangerous, is sanctioned as a means of deterring similar violations by other potential offenders. Whenever these sorts of cases arise, a conflict arises in which principles of desert and incapacitation would support a reduction of the degree or scope of liability while deterrence principles would oppose reduction.

3. *Incapacitation vs.*—Incapacitation conflicts with deterrence and desert in setting the grade and sentences for attempted, as compared to completed, offenses, and in the related issue of defining the required causal relationship between an offender's conduct and a prohibited result. Reducing liability for unsuccessful attempts and requiring a strong causal connection between acts and results reflect two judgments: that an offender is less blameworthy when he or she creates no harm, and that efficient deterrence can justify greater sanctions where the offense has occurred than where it has not. The absence of a completed offense does not, however, alter the offender's dangerousness. Thus, whenever cases arise under doctrines giving significance to resulting harm, a conflict arises in which desert and deterrence will take account of resulting harm while incapacitation will not.

Some Alternative Approaches to Constructing a Hybrid Distributive Principle

When alternative purposes conflict, a principled hybrid system must define which of the competing purposes is to be followed. One can identify several rational approaches to establishing such conflict rules.

Establishing Priorities

Under what might be called a "simple priority" approach, whenever purpose *A* (the purpose of highest priority) supports a doctrine or sentence different from that supported by another purpose, purpose *A* shall govern. To the extent that purpose *A* is indifferent as to which of two doctrines or sentences is adopted, but purpose *B* supports one and purpose *C* the other, then purpose *B* (the second highest priority purpose) shall be followed, and so on. Under such an approach, the purpose selected as primary is given greater weight than in any other approach described below. The primary purpose controls whenever it makes a difference.

Somewhat more sophisticated is a "contingent priority" approach. It sets priorities, as in a simple priority approach, but it also sets conditions assuring that a purpose is given priority only in those cases where a defined level of reliability or effectiveness is present. Thus, for example, incapacitation might be given first priority, but that priority can be exercised only if, for example, the empirical data for the given situation shows that the reliability of the prediction of dangerousness exceeds a minimum level. Or, general deterrence might be given first priority, contingent upon, for example, empirical data projecting a deterrence effectiveness of a minimum rate. Under this approach, the decision maker would follow the purpose with the highest priority that satisfies its contingent criteria. The virtue of such an approach is that it permits a purpose to control only to the extent that the assumptions underlying the effectiveness or accuracy of the purpose are true.

Distinguishing Determining Principles from Limiting Principles

The priority approaches generally assume that a particular purpose will call for a particular doctrinal formulation or a particular sentence. Some purposes, however, might be used to limit, rather than determine the distribution of sanctions. That is, their effect may be to exclude a formulation or sentence rather than to recommend one. Where this is true, a purpose may be given first priority, but, if it is treated as a limiting purpose, it is not considered in the initial formulation of the distribution of sanctions; it is consulted only afterwards, to determine whether the contemplated formulation violates the limitations of that higher priority purpose.

To categorize a purpose as a limiting purpose, however, one must conceive of it as simply excluding, rather than requiring, certain formulations or sentences. Some commentators suggest that just deserts is properly treated as such a limiting purpose [see Extract 4.3]. Under this model, desert makes relatively imprecise demands—it conceives of just punishment as simply prohibiting certain "unjust" formulations or sentences—and does not require specific results. Other writers disagree with this conclusion, arguing that desert has, for example, specific ordinal and cardinal ranking requirements [see Extract 4.4].

Even if it is true that desert is not properly characterized as a limiting purpose, however, the determining-limiting distinction might nonetheless be useful in constructing a hybrid distributive principle. One might, for example, treat one of the utilitarian purposes, such as deterrence, as a limiting purpose and thus use it not to formulate doctrines of distribution but to exclude certain formulations generated by a desert principle—such as those that exceed a given net social cost. In other words, deterrence could be employed to set an upper limit on the disutility that society is willing to suffer for the sake of doing justice to individual defendants. Use of deterrence as a limiting purpose might result in a formulation that was less just but significantly more efficient than a pure desert formulation.

The operation of a determining-limiting approach is in many respects similar to a contingent priority approach. The difference is partly formalistic and partly real. Under a contingent priority approach, the first priority purpose is presumed to control as long as the contingencies concerning its effect and reliability are met. Under a determining-limiting approach, the limiting purpose has first priority but is presumed *not* to control *unless* the limitation criteria of the purpose are violated. The difference, then, is partly one of expectations. Assume, for example, that deterrence is the first priority (limiting) purpose and desert the second priority (determining) purpose. Under a contingent priority system, one might describe deterrence as the governing distributive principle except where it is too weak or unproven to be relied upon. Under a determining-limiting system, the same priority puts desert as the dominant principle, except when it undercuts the deterrent effect of the punishment beyond a tolerance level previously set.

The more significant difference between the two approaches is that under a contingent priority approach, a purpose falls from priority only because of its own shortcomings—failing to meet the criteria that assure that it will do what it claims it will do. Under a determining-limiting approach, a determining purpose may be operating as promised, but the punishment or scheme it dictates nonetheless will be rejected if it violates the limiting criteria of another purpose. Thus, a contingent priority approach maximizes reliance upon a single primary purpose so long as the purpose works effectively. Where it is not possible to achieve the goal of the primary purpose—be it deterrence, control of the dangerous, or imposition of just deserts—it is hardly a sacrifice of that purpose to turn to another purpose. Under a determining-limiting approach, by contrast, a determining purpose is indeed sacrificed where it sufficiently conflicts with a limiting purpose.

If a purpose can effectively do what it promises across the full range of cases, as some may think is true in the case of desert, the purpose will have greater effect as the primary purpose under a contingent priority approach than under a determining-limiting approach. If a purpose has proven effectiveness in a more limited range of situations, as is frequently the case with deterrence and incapacitation, the purpose is more likely to influence the formulation of distribution rules as the primary purpose under a determining-limiting approach.

Combining Purposes

Both of the approaches described above are priority systems of a sort, in which one purpose is furthered at the expense of another. One could formulate, however, an approach by which purposes are combined to give a result influenced in part by all purposes, rather than choosing among purposes. Such an approach seems ideal; it seems to further all and sacrifice none.

Unfortunately, while the concept seems perfect, the extent of its realization is limited. The combination of purposes is feasible only if the purposes to be combined share two characteristics. First, all purposes considered must share the same ultimate goal, for example, efficient crime prevention. Second, they must be measurable in a common currency, for example, the "costs" in monetary terms of avoiding or not avoiding certain crimes.

Consider, for example, the combination of deterrence and incapacitation. Assume that from a general deterrence perspective, doctrinal formulation or sentence *A* costs 10 units to gain a benefit of 15 units for a net societal benefit of 5, while formulation *B* costs 15 to save 15 for a net benefit of 0. In this situation, general deterrence as a distributive principle would prefer formulation *A*. Assume that incapacitation finds that formulation *A* costs 20 in order to avoid a harm of 15, for a net loss of 5, while formulation *B* costs 10 to avoid an injury of 15, for a net gain of 5. Thus, incapacitation as the distributive principle prefers formulation *B*. This would be an instance where the two purposes conflict and where any of the previously described priority approaches might be used to decide which of the two conflicting purposes to follow (and thus which of the two formulations to adopt).

But the dilemma can be resolved without giving absolute or conditional priority to one purpose. Because the two purposes have the same goal (efficient crime prevention) and a single currency, the costs and benefits of each formulation for both purposes may be determined and these totals for each formulation may be compared to select the best formulation. Thus, if the incapacitation purpose is significantly increased by a formulation that only minimally hurts the general deterrence purpose in comparison to an alternative formulation, that difference in magnitude of effect might be enough to justify following the incapacitation formulation. The example above generates the following combined analysis:

	Formulation A	*Formulation B*	
Deterrence	−10	−15	
	+15	+15	Deterrence prefers
	+5	0	Formulation *A*
Incapacitation	−20	−10	
	+15	+15	Incapacitation prefers
	−5	+5	Formulation *B*
Combined Assessment	0	+5	Combined purposes prefer Formulation *B*

Thus, by combining the costs and benefits of both purposes one can determine that formulation *B* will best further the common goal of efficient crime prevention.

The difficulty, of course, is that not all purposes of sentencing share a common goal of crime prevention or a common currency of monetary cost and benefit. As the Model Penal Code commentary suggests:

> It is also recognized that not even crime prevention can be said to be the only end involved. The correction and rehabilitation of offenders is a social value in itself, as well as a preventive instrument. Basic considerations of justice demand, moreover, that penal law safeguard offenders against excessive, disproportionate or arbitrary punishment.

Others may disagree. Some suggest that the ultimate purpose of rehabilitation is the same as that of deterrence and incapacitation of the dangerous—that is, crime prevention. On the other hand, some state the difference between the utilitarian goals and desert in even stronger terms than the Model Penal Code commentary does: justice not only bars "excessive, disproportionate or arbitrary punishment," but also requires specific formulations for rules, doctrines, offenses, and sentences. Whatever view one takes, the important point is that the combined approach cannot be used to amalgamize purposes that do not share a common currency and goal.

Relying upon the Purpose with the Greatest Sanction

Some writers have suggested, in the context of sentencing, that one should determine an appropriate sentence under each purpose and then impose the highest of those sentences, under the theory that the highest sentence will assure that all of the purposes are satisfied. Thus, if desert requires seven years, deterrence five years, and incapacitation one year, this approach generates a sentence of seven years. If deterrence requires seven years, incapacitation five, and desert one, seven years is again appropriate. The same process can be used for the selection of criminal law rules and doctrines; after formulating a rule or doctrine using each of the purposes separately, one can simply adopt the formulation that gives the broadest liability to assure that all of the purposes will be satisfied. Rather than choosing among conflicting purposes according to their criteria, this approach selects among them by comparing their results.

But this approach assumes, incorrectly, that to give a sentence higher than a purpose calls for is nonetheless to satisfy that purpose. In the context of doctrinal rules, this approach assumes, equally incorrectly, that a formulation that imposes broader liability than a purpose requires nonetheless satisfies that purpose. "Satisfying" a purpose sometimes requires limiting the sanction or extent of liability. In the first hypothetical above, the seven years required by desert is an inefficient expenditure of sanctions when analyzed according to deterrence and incapacitation principles. In the second hypothetical, the seven years required by deterrence not only violates a principle of efficient incapacitation, but also is grossly undeserved. Such a sentence does not satisfy desert; it violates it. In the context of liability doctrines, desert might support complicity liability of a host for the drunk driving of an intoxicated guest. However, it does not follow that if *more* than such liability is imposed (for example, complicity liability for deaths caused by the drunk driving guest), desert will be satisfied. Such extended liability may further a deterrent purpose yet may violate a just punishment principle.

In the end, then, a hybrid principle that follows the purpose with the highest sentence or broadest liability is not a principled hybrid at all, at least not in relation to the alternative purposes for distributing criminal sanctions. Under such an approach, the selection of the governing purpose among conflicting purposes is not the product of a defined relationship among the purposes that can be articulated beforehand. Instead, the governing purpose is determined ad hoc, depending on the relative results generated in each instance.

Distinguishing the Assignment and Amount of Sanction from the Method of Sanction

The traditional purposes are used to resolve a range of distinguishable issues in the distribution of sanctions: Who should be sanctioned? How much sanction should they receive? How should the sanction be imposed? The first issue is essentially one of liability assignment—who should be held criminally liable. The second issue—how much sanction—goes to both liability rules (that is, what grade or degree of offense is appropriate for certain conduct) and sentencing practice (for example, how long a sentence or how great a fine is appropriate in a particular case). Together, these two issues govern the quantitative distribution of sanction—who will receive how much. The third issue, concerning the method of sanction, is distinguishable from the distribution of amount. Two offenders may merit the same *amount* of sanction yet different *methods* of sanctioning may be suitable for imposing that amount. These two issues—how much for whom and what method—are not only functionally distinguishable but also may properly be subject to different distributive principles.

Each of the distributive purposes may treat the different issues differently. Effective crime control can be furthered through a variety of mechanisms—by setting the amount or the method of sanction, as well as by setting enforcement and prosecution patterns and expenditures. Satisfaction of desert concerns, by contrast, depends almost exclusively on the amount issue—who receives how much; the method issue (as well as the resource allocation issues) is generally not relevant.

The desert requirement of a proper ordinal ranking of offenders by overall blameworthiness, for example, concerns the ranking of *amounts* of sanction. As long as the ordinal ranking is correct, the *method* by which each amount is imposed is not relevant to desert. If one month in the state prison is the punitive equivalent to five months of weekends in the local jail, then desert is satisfied even if the more blameworthy offender gets probation, with a condition of seven months of weekends in jail, while the less blameworthy offender goes to prison for one month. It is critical, of course, that the sanction equivalencies be properly set. Some empirical research has been done on perceptions of relative seriousness of sanctions, but the work is still in its infancy.

With an estimate of equivalencies, one can construct a sentencing system that allows independent determination of the amount and method issues. The principles governing the "amount" issue can generate total "sanction units" for each offender, which can then be allocated to a particular sanctioning method or combination of methods according to a different set of "method" principles. As long as the issues can be effectively segregated in practice, one can develop a hybrid distributive principle for governing the amount of sanction that is different from the principle used to determine the method of sanction. One could, for example, emphasize desert in determining the amount of sanction, but ignore it in determining the method [see Extract 6.6]. The selection of method could be made to maximize pure utilitarian concerns without infringing desert interests—a precious no-loss, all-win opportunity.

The separation of amount and method issues has other important collateral advantages. For example, unwarranted disparity in sentencing primarily concerns disparity in amount, rather than disparity in method. Thus, one might significantly reduce judicial sentencing discretion on the amount issue, in order to reduce disparity among judges, yet maintain broad judicial discretion on the method issue. As long as the total "sanction units" for an offender are satisfied and the sanction equivalencies are properly set, it does not matter what method or methods an individual judge selects; the punitive "bite" will be the same.

The ability to defer to judicial discretion without creating undesirable disparity is particularly useful where method is concerned, because at present the principles for the selection of methods are much less obvious than the principles for the determination of amount. One can do rough ordinal rankings of offense seriousness, for example, but it is more difficult to articulate principles to govern issues such as which conditions of probation are appropriate in what situations.

Suggestions for Further Reading

1. The Theory of Proportionality and Desert

Armstrong, K. G., "The Retributivist Hits Back," 70 *Mind* 471 (1961); McCloskey, H., "A Non-Utilitarian Approach to Punishment," 8 *Inquiry* 249 (1965); Hart, H.L.A., *Punishment and Responsibility* (1968); Feinberg, J., *Doing and Deserving* (1970), ch. 5; Finnis, J., "The Restoration of Retribution," 32 *Analysis* 131 (1972); Murphy, J. G., "Marxism and Retribution," 2 *Philosophy and Public Affairs* 217 (1973); Kleinig, J., *Punishment and Desert* (1973); von Hirsch, A., *Doing Justice: The Choice of Punishment* (1976); Bedau, H., "Retribution and the Theory of Punishment," 75 *Journal of Philosophy* 601 (1978); Murphy, J. G., *Retribution, Justice, and Therapy* (1979); Morris, H., "A Paternalistic Theory of Punishment," 18 *American Philosophical Quarterly* 263 (1981); Mackie, J., "Morality and the Retributive Emotions," 1 *Criminal Justice Ethics* 3 (1982), reprinted in his *Persons and Values* (1985), ch. 15; Davis, M., "How to Make the Punishment Fit the Crime," 93 *Ethics* 726 (1983); Hampton, J., "The Moral Education Theory of Punishment," 13 *Philosophy and Public Affairs* 230 (1984); Murphy, J. G., "Retributivism, Moral Education, and the Liberal State," 4 *Criminal Justice Ethics* 3 (1985); von Hirsch, *Past or Future Crimes* (1985) chs. 3–5; Sadurski, W., *Giving Desert Its Due* (1985); Duff, R. A., *Trials and Punishments* (1986); Sher, G., *Desert* (1987); Duff, R. A., "Punishment and Penance: A Reply to Harrison," 62 *Aristotelian Society—Supplemental Volume* 153 (1988); Primoratz, I., "Punishment as Language," 64 *Philosophy* 187 (1989); Scheid, D. M., "Davis and the Unfair-Advantage Theory of Punishment: A Critique," 18 *Philosophical Topics* 143 (1990); von Hirsch, "Proportionality in the Philosophy of Punishment," 1 *Criminal Law Forum* 259 (1990); Kleinig, J., "Punishment and Moral Seriousness," 25 *Israel Law Review* 401 (1991); von Hirsch, *Censure and Sanctions* (1993, forthcoming), ch. 2.

2. Applying Desert to Sentencing Policy

American Friends Service Committee, *Struggle for Justice: A Report on Crime and Punishment in America* (1971); Gardner, M., "The Renaissance of Retribution: An Examination of Doing Justice," *Wisconsin Law Review* 781 (1976); Clarke, D., "Marxism, Justice, and the Justice Model," 2 *Contemporary Crises* 27 (1978); National Swedish Council for Crime Prevention, *A New Penal System: Ideas and Proposals* (1978); Twentieth Century Fund, Task Force on Sentencing Policy toward Young Offenders, *Confronting Youth Crime* (1978); Singer, R., *Just Deserts: Sentencing Based on Equality and Desert* (1979); von Hirsch, *Past or Future Crimes, supra,* chs. 6–8, 11–12, 14; Galligan, D., "The Return to Retribution in Penal Theory," in C. Tepper (ed.), *Crime, Proof, and Punishment: Essays in Memory of Sir Rupert Cross* (1981); Jareborg, N., "The Coherence of the Penal System," in his *Essays in Criminal Law* (1988); Ashworth, A., "Criminal Justice and Deserved

Sentences," *Criminal Law Review* 340 (1989); von Hirsch, "The Politics of Just Deserts," 32 *Canadian Journal of Criminology* 397 (1990); Braithwaite, J., and Pettit, P., *Not Just Deserts* (1990); von Hirsch and Ashworth, "Not Not Just Deserts: A Response to Braithwaite and Pettit," 12 *Oxford Journal of Legal Studies* 83 (1992); von Hirsch, "Proportionality in Punishment: Some Philosophical Issues," in M. Tonry and N. Morris (eds.), *Crime and Justice: An Annual Review of Research,* vol. 16 (1992); von Hirsch, *Censure and Sanctions, supra,* chs. 3–4.

3. Hybrid Theories

Monahan, J., "The Case for Prediction in a Modified Desert Model of Sentencing," 5 *International Journal of Law and Psychiatry* 103 (1982); Morris, N., and Miller, M., "Predictions of Dangerousness," in M. Tonry and N. Morris (eds.), *Crime and Justice: An Annual Review of Research,* vol. 6 (1986); Tonry, M., "Prediction and Classification: Legal and Ethical Issues," in M. Tonry and D. M. Gottfredson (eds.), *Crime and Justice: An Annual Review of Research,* vol. 7 (1987); Robinson, P. H., "Hybrid Principles for the Distribution of Criminal Sanctions," 82 *Northwestern University Law Review* (1987); Primoratz, I., "The Middle Way in the Philosophy of Punishment," in R. Gavison (ed.), *Issues in Contemporary Legal Philosophy* (1987); von Hirsch, "Proportionality in Punishment: Some Philosophical Issues," *supra;* von Hirsch, *Censure and Sanctions, supra,* ch. 5.

4. Desert and Prior Criminal Record

Von Hirsch, *Doing Justice* (1976), ch. 10; Fletcher, G., *Rethinking Criminal Law* (1978), 460–66; Singer, *Just Deserts, supra,* ch. 5; von Hirsch, "Desert and Prior Convictions in Sentencing," 65 *Minnesota Law Review* 591 (1981); von Hirsch, *Past or Future Crimes, supra,* ch. 7; Stuart, J. D., "Retributive Justice and Prior Offenses," 18 *Philosophical Forum* 40 (1986); von Hirsch, "Criminal Record Rides Again," 10 (2) *Criminal Justice Ethics* 2 (1991).

5. The Politics of Desert

Hudson, B., *Justice Through Punishment* (1987); von Hirsch, "The Politics of 'Just Deserts,'" *supra*; von Hirsch, *Censure and Sanctions, supra,* ch. 9.

Chapter Five

STRUCTURING SENTENCING DISCRETION

Now that four of the leading aims of sentencing have been examined, it is time to turn to the translation of aims and policies into practical sentencing systems. How can sentencing be organized effectively so that it achieves one of the above aims, or a carefully constructed hierarchy of aims?

The question seems to have been little discussed until the last two decades. There was considerable debate about consistency in sentencing one hundred years ago in England, with calls in 1892 for an appellate court to review sentences. In fact, a Court of Criminal Appeal was created in 1907, but six years earlier Lord Chief Justice Alverstone had responded to public debate by overseeing the preparation of a "Memorandum on Normal Punishments," a kind of informal sentencing tariff which the High Court judges agreed to.[1] This debate did not, however, result in any clarification of the general aims or principles to be applied, and for most of the twentieth century sentencing in England and the United States has been characterized by wide judicial discretion. The notion of a sentencing "system" was either not used or, if it was used, it would be applied to an agglomeration of sentencing powers provided by legislatures for courts. The normal approach in most jurisdictions was for the legislature to establish maximum penalties for offenses, to create a range of sentencing options as well as imprisonment, and then to leave the courts to exercise discretion within the wide ranges provided. In a few jurisdictions, most notably England and Wales, the availability of appellate review led to the development of some sentencing principles through case law. In many American jurisdictions, by way of contrast, there was virtually no authoritative guidance beneath the legislative maxima. The result was what Judge Frankel, in Extract 5.1, denounces as "lawlessness in sentencing": decisions on sentence directly concern the basic liberty of citizens—for example, whether those who commit crimes should go to prison and, if so, for how long—and yet the protections of the rule of law seemed to be absent. No standards for sentencing existed, there was no requirement of giving reasons, and therefore no protection was provided from inconsistent or ill-founded decisions.

One justification for the wide discretion enjoyed by sentencers was that it enabled the judge to select a rehabilitative sentence based on a diagnosis of the offender's "needs." This justification began to wear thin as the claims of rehabilitative sentencing were increasingly questioned in the early 1970s (see Chapter 1 above). Interest in sentencing reform was kindled, and the arguments advanced by Judge Frankel and others began to win acceptance. What approach should be taken to the structuring of sentencing discretion? In the last twenty years, many countries have introduced or proposed reforms. It is now possible to identify a number of key factors in the process of structuring. Decisions must be taken on the *content* of guidance, on the *source* of guidance, on the *authority* by which it should be laid down, and the *style* in which it should be formulated; and attention must also be paid to the *mechanics* of putting the guidance into practice. However, before introducing each of these topics, the constitutional dimensions of the subject need to be aired.

In a system which has some attachment, however loose, to the doctrine of separation of powers, which organ of the state should have authority in matters of sentencing? It is widely accepted that the legislature has supreme authority over sentencing policy, at least to the extent that it may lay down maximum penalties for offenses and may decide what forms of sentence are to be available to the courts.[2] It also seems that legislatures may provide for mandatory sentences or mandatory minimum sentences for any offense: mandatory sentences for murder are common to many jurisdictions, without a suggestion that they involve an unconstitutional exercise of power by the legislature, and mandatory minimum sentences have also been held constitutional.[3] However, when legislatures have begun to impinge on what was hitherto a wide sentencing discretion of the judiciary, this has led to claims that the judiciary has some quasi-constitutional right to discretion in matters of sentencing. These claims, heard in many jurisdictions at different times,[4] have sometimes been bolstered by suggesting that sentencing discretion is required by the constitutional principle of the independence of the judiciary. But all such claims are dubious. So long as mandatory and mandatory minimum sentences are accepted as constitutional, the only claim of the judiciary can be to whatever discretion the legislature leaves, which is a somewhat empty claim. The principle of judicial independence is surely designed to protect the impartiality of judges and their freedom from pressure, influence, and bias;[5] it cannot be used to deny the propriety of legislatively authorized restrictions on sentencing, and therefore of legislative supremacy in sentencing matters. The correct position is surely that stated in the recent English White Paper:

"No Government should try to influence the decisions of the courts in individual cases. The independence of the judiciary is rightly regarded as a cornerstone of our liberties. But sentencing principles and sentencing practice are matters of legitimate concern to Government."[6]

Turning to the guidance laid down for sentencers, an initial question concerns its *content*. One of the consequences of the widespread discretion which has characterized sentencing for much of the twentieth century is that a whole variety of principles and policies have influenced sentencing, largely according to the inclinations of the particular sentencer. One of the aims of structuring discretion is to ensure that it is exercised in a principled manner, and one primary point here must be to decide upon a rationale for sentencing. A choice should be made between deterrence, rehabilitation, incapacitation, and desert as the leading aim of the system. Once the leading aim is chosen, then a decision should be taken about whether any other aim or aims should be allowed to influence sentences, to what degree, and in what types of case (see Extract 4.7). Unless decisions of principle are taken on priorities among two or more sentencing aims, the resultant uncertainty would be a recipe for disparity: Extracts 5.3 and 5.4 show how these points have been accepted and acted upon in England and in Sweden, respectively.

There are other decisions of principle to be taken, too. One concerns the promotion of principles such as equality before the law, particularly if there has been evidence of discriminatory sentencing in the past: a declaration that courts may not have regard to such factors as race, color, gender, employment status, and religion might be a step toward this goal. Another issue concerns the use of imprisonment: if there is to be a policy of restraint in the use of imprisonment, this may be implemented, for example, by means of specific legislative declarations or by introducing a prison capacity constraint into the fixing of the sentencing guidance itself (as in Minnesota).

What should be the *source* of any guidance on sentencing? In other words, if guidance is to be given, who should undertake the inquiries necessary to decide upon and formulate the guidance most appropriate to a particular system? The typical English approach, in times of legislative abstention, has been for the senior judiciary in the Court of Appeal to develop guidance through their judgments. The perspective of the senior judiciary is narrow and is unlikely to demonstrate sensitivity to wider criminal justice policies: the British government has now decided to propose new policies itself, as is evident from Extract 5.3 below. However, in other jurisdictions, the government has given the task to a specially appointed drafting committee as a prelude to legislation (as in Sweden); or to a rule-making commission acting with the delegated authority of the legislature (as in Minnesota, for example). The membership of such bodies can be more broadly based, drawing upon the experience of some judges and also including others with wider correctional and criminal justice experience.

Once proposals for the structuring of sentencing have been drawn up, there is the question of the *authority* by which they should be adopted. Should all the standards be contained in legislation, or should use be made of some other form of law or regulation? Some jurisdictions, such as California, have placed all the detailed guidance in primary legislation; this might appear to ensure maximum control by a democratically elected institution, but it brings the danger that a carefully contrived scheme of guidance can be distorted by individual and piecemeal amendments, often proposed for political gain. Another approach, adopted in Minnesota, Oregon, and Washington State, is for the legislature to set out some basic principles in primary legislation, and to establish a rule-making commission to formulate detailed guidance in the form of regulations, which will then take effect unless the legislature resolves otherwise. Much depends here on the competence and sense of commitment of the commission, and its ability to devise a coherent system of guidance which sentencers can be persuaded to adopt. The functions of a sentencing commission are discussed in Extract 5.2. A third approach would be for the primary legislation to set out the basic principles, and leave the judiciary to develop the detailed guidance through appellate judgments. This approach, adopted in the 1988 Swedish sentencing law (see Extract 5.4) and in the 1991 English legislation (see Extract 5.3), depends for its success on the judiciary's willingness to take the principles seriously and to develop them sympathetically.

The next question is what *style* of guidance should be chosen. Mandatory minimum sentences for certain crimes (e.g., gun laws, drug crimes) have been introduced by some legislatures, but this technique seems attractive only to politicians. Mandatory minimums limit discretion only in one direction. They both leave insufficient leeway to deal with mitigating circumstances and fail to impose sufficient restraint on severity—that is, on sentences above the prescribed minimum. The evidence suggests that mandatory minimum sentences have little effect on the crime rate[7] and that sentencers strive to avoid the injustice of having to treat different cases as if they were the same.[8] Determinate or "fixed point" sentencing has normally been the technique used in jurisdictions which place their sentencing guidance in primary legislation, such as California. Once the judge has categorized the crime, there are usually two stages of decision making. The first is whether to impose a prison sentence or a noncustodial penalty, and that decision is (at least, in California) largely discretionary. But if the judge chooses prison, the next stage is narrowly restricted: only three sentences will be available—the standard, the aggravated, and the mitigated. The judge may not go outside that threefold choice, which leaves little scope for taking account of unusual combinations of circumstances. Perhaps the best-known style of guidance in recent times has been numerical guidelines. In Minnesota these take the form of a grid of normal sentence ranges, with scores for the seriousness of the crime and the prior record of the offender. Departure from this range is possible, upon reasons given and subject to appellate review, and a body of jurisprudence on permissible reasons for departure has grown up. In the U.S. federal system the guidelines are approached by means of a stepwise numerical calculation: first the judge categorizes the offense, then takes account of the specific enhancements provided in the guidelines (e.g., possession of a weapon) and certain mitigating factors, and then calculates the criminal history score. This will lead the judge to the applicable range of sentences, from which departure is permissible in certain circumstances. The federal system, which suffers from a lack of any definitive rationale and from complexity in practice, is one of the approaches discussed by Andrew Ashworth in Extract 5.3. A different approach is that of setting out detailed principles, including guidance on how to resolve conflicts of principles, and leaving the courts to translate those into actual sentencing levels: this is the new Swedish law's approach, described in Extract 5.4(a) by Andrew von Hirsch.

These various styles of guidance differ in the extent to which they reduce judicial discretion, but it would be wrong to assume that the pursuit of principled sentencing means that the most constraining approach is necessarily the best. The point is that there will inevitably be questions of detailed application which can be answered differently by different sentencers, so that even if all sentencers were conscientiously pursuing the same aim or set of aims, inconsistencies could result. For example, if the overall aim of the system were incapacitation, it would still be important to have guidance on the types of offense and offender for whom predictive restraint might be justified, on whether limits should be placed on sentences in certain types of cases, and on whether class- or race-related factors such as employment history might be taken into account. If the overall aim is desert, it would be important to have parameters for determining the relative seriousness of different crimes, and for deciding how much weight to give to an offender's prior record. Beyond that, the choices are familiar. "The more detailed the rules and the less room for discretionary choices, the more cumbersome the system becomes, and the more it tends to deal inappropriately and unjustly with unforeseen contingencies. The less the detail and the more interstitial discretion, the greater the risk of inconsistent treatment of similar cases."[9] Much will depend, in practice, on what is deemed appropriate in the context of the legal and political culture of the jurisdiction.

Devising guidance is not, however, enough for the structuring of decisions on sentence. Whatever the content, source, authority, and style of sentencing guidance, it will only be worthwhile if it operates in practice in the way intended. It is abundantly clear that compulsion may not bring this about: the experience of courts circumventing mandatory minimum sentences is sufficient to substantiate this.[10] Where the degree of compulsion is reduced and courts are given the opportunity to depart from guideline sentences upon giving reasons, there may be substantial compliance; but the experience of "adaptive behavior" by both judges and prosecutors in Minnesota demonstrates that the element of flexibility may be exploited to some extent.[11] Appellate review of sentences may be expected to contribute to the practical enforcement of sentencing guidance, but the extent of its contribution will depend on three points. First, the appeal court will need to take a strong line against unwarranted deviations from guidance by lower courts. Second, its decisions should not merely decide the particular case, but serve as precedent for later cases. And third, it must be willing to address issues of principle in its judgments.

In terms of achieving consistency, the ideal position is that sentencers be persuaded of the desirability of the policies and principles underlying the sentencing system, and also that they be fully trained in the approach which it adopts. These training functions can be performed by an academy or center for judges—such as England's Judicial Studies Board. However, judicial training cannot contribute to principled sentencing unless there are clear principles in existence. Another possibility is the introduction of technical aids for sentencers, such as computerized systems with databases which help the judge to discover the relevant laws, policies, and current practice relating to a particular type of case. Information systems of this kind may be particularly useful in collating and presenting relevant guidance from different sources, for example, legislation, judicial decisions, and common practice.[12]

The final extract in this chapter is designed to bring back into view the proposition that sentencing is one part of the wider criminal justice system. It is obvious that the exercise of discretion at other points in the system may reduce the impact of sentencing reform unless it too is subjected to structuring. The effects of prosecutorial discretion and defense tactics are explored by Michael Tonry and John C. Coffee, Jr., in Extract 5.5. Although they suggest that systems of sentencing guidelines like that in Minnesota tend to shift some discretion from court to prosecutor, they argue that the overall effect of such guidelines may still be to constrain the combined discretion previously allowed to courts and prosecutors. Tonry and Coffee do, however, raise several questions about the effects of plea bargaining, "real offense" sentencing, and the sentence discount for pleading guilty, effects which will depend on the response of different kinds of defendant, defense counsel, and prosecutor. At present there is insufficient empirical evidence to assess which of their speculations lies closest to the truth. But if principled decision making and consistency of approach are aims of sentencing reform, the factors to which they draw attention must be carefully considered and monitored.

Reference must also be made to the intimate relationship between sentencing and parole. Indeed, a discretionary parole system could undermine the carefully contrived sentencing differentials established by reformed sentencing structures. One solution, adopted in several U.S. jurisdictions, is to establish parole guidelines which structure decision making on release.[13] Another approach, taken or proposed in some other American jurisdictions, is to abolish discretionary parole release when introducing sentencing reforms. Both these approaches are capable of ensuring that the aims of sentencing are not undermined by discretionary decisions taken later on principles incompatible with the primary aims. Yet parole might serve other goals of criminal justice, and might be retained if those other goals are considered important. For example, in a system which wished to give some limited recognition to rehabilitative or to incapacitative aims, some elements of a discretionary parole system might be retained.[14] The new English system, introduced by the Criminal Justice Act of 1991, is an example of a parole system which seems to incorporate limited elements of rehabilitative and incapacitative thinking into a sentencing system which proclaims desert as its primary aim. The previous system was criticized by the Carlisle Committee in 1988 because, *inter alia,* the increasingly wide gap between the sentence announced in court and the time actually served created "increased unreality in the criminal justice system and handed to the executive too much control over the length of custodial sentences served."[15] But the Committee did not recommend the abolition of parole, since it believed that release under parole supervision could have a beneficial effect. The main proposal was that each part of a custodial sentence should have some meaning for the offender, and the provisions of the 1991 Act follow this by introducing automatic conditional release (after one-half of the sentence) for prisoners serving under four years, subject to some supervision and to recall if they reoffend, and by retaining an element of discretionary release and an element of compulsory supervision for those serving four years or longer. Such compromises are to be found in several present-day systems: many bear the marks of conflicting policies and pressures in criminal justice, but only some attempt to place a clear structure on the decisions and on their relation to other decisions in the criminal justice system.

A.A.

Notes

1. See L. Radzinowicz and R. Hood, *History of the English Criminal Law: The Emergence of Penal Policy* (1986), 755–58, and D. A. Thomas, *Constraints on Judgment* (1978).

2. For further discussion of the constitutional aspects, see A. Ashworth, "Sentencing Reform Structures," in *Crime and Justice: An Annual Review* (1991, forthcoming).

3. *Palling v. Corfield* (1970) 123 *C.L.R.* 52, a decision of the High Court of Australia.

4. For example, the English lord chancellor, Lord Halsbury, made a firm statement to this effect in 1890; see Radzinowicz and Hood, *History of the English Criminal Law,* 754. A century later a similarly vigorous assertion may be found in a memorandum of the judges of Victoria (Australia) on sentencing: see *Victorian Sentencing Committee: Sentencing* (1988), vol. 3, appendix 1.

5. See the declarations of the United Nations, *Basic Principles on the Independence of the Judiciary,* adopted at the Seventh U.N. Crime Congress, 1985, paragraphs 1 and 2:

—The independence of the judiciary shall be guaranteed by the State and enshrined in the constitution or law of the country.
—The judiciary shall decide matters before them with impartiality on the basis of facts, in accordance with the law, without any improper influences or pressures.

6. Home Office, *Crime, Justice, and Protecting the Public* (1990), paragraph 2.1. For the United States, see the dictum of Justice Blackmun in *Mistretta v. U.S.* (1989) 109 S.Ct. 647, at 654, that "the scope of judicial discretion with respect to a sentence is subject to congressional control"; also *Rummel v. Estelle* (1980) 445 U.S. 263.

7. For further discussion and references, see Michael Tonry, *Sentencing Reform Impacts* (1987), chapter 3.

8. In Minnesota the judges succeeded in ensuring that about 25 percent of offenders subject technically to mandatory minimum sentences avoided prison altogether: Dale Parent, *Structuring Criminal Sentencing* (1989), 184; see also the mounting opposition by federal judges, exemplified by the statement of Judge Schwarzer reported in (1989) 2 *Fed. Sent. R.* 186.

9. Andrew von Hirsch, "Commensurability and Crime Prevention: Evaluating Formal Sentencing Structures and Their Rationale," 74 *J. Crim. Law & Criminology* 209 (1983), at 245.

10. See note 8 above, and references.

11. For discussion, see Kay A. Knapp, "Implementation of the Minnesota Guidelines: Can the Innovative Spirit Be Preserved?" in Andrew von Hirsch, Kay Knapp, and Michael Tonry, *The Sentencing Commission and Its Guidelines* (1987), chapter 8, and Michael Tonry, *Sentencing Reform Impacts* (1987), chapter 5.

12. For discussion, see Ashworth (above, note 2).

13. For a summary of the systems and research on them, see Tonry, *Sentencing Reform Impacts* (1987), chapter 7.

14. See Hann, Harman, and Pease, "Does Parole Reduce the Risk of Reconviction?" 30 *Howard J.C.J.* 66 (1991).

15. Report of the Review Committee, *The Parole System in England* (chairman, Lord Carlisle) (London, 1988), Par. 194.

5.1
Lawlessness in Sentencing

Marvin Frankel

The common form of criminal penalty provision confers upon the sentencing judge an enormous range of choice. The scope of what we call "discretion" permits imprisonment for anything from a day to one, five, ten, twenty, or more years. All would presumably join in denouncing a statute that said "the judge may impose any sentence he pleases." Given the mortality of men, the power to set a man free or to confine him for up to thirty years is not sharply distinguishable.

The statutes granting such powers characteristically say nothing about the factors to be weighed in moving to either end of the spectrum or to some place between. It might be supposed by some stranger arrived in our midst that the criteria for measuring a particular sentence would be discoverable outside the narrow limits of the statutes and would be known to the judicial experts rendering the judgments. But the supposition would lack substantial foundation. Even the most basic sentencing principles are not prescribed or stated with persuasive authority. There is, to be sure, a familiar litany in the literature of sentencing "purposes": retribution, deterrence ("special" and "general"), "denunciation," incapacitation, rehabilitation. Nothing tells us, however, when or whether any of these several goals are to be sought, or how to resolve such evident conflicts as that likely to arise in the effort to punish and rehabilitate all at once. It has for some time been part of our proclaimed virtue that vengeance or retribution is a disfavored motive for punishment. But there is reason to doubt that either judges or the public are effectively abreast of this advanced position. And there is no law—certainly none that anybody pretends to have en-

From Marvin E. Frankel, "Lawlessness in Sentencing," 41 *Cincinnati Law Review* 1 (1972). Excerpted and reprinted by permission.

forced—telling the judge he must refrain, expressly or otherwise, from trespassing against higher claims to wreak vengeance.

Moving upward from what should be the philosophical axioms of a rational scheme of sentencing law, we have no structure of rules, or even guidelines, affecting other elements arguably pertinent to the nature or severity of the sentence. Should it be a mitigating factor that the defendant is being sentenced upon a plea of guilty rather than a verdict against him? Should it count in his favor that he spared the public "trouble" and expense by waiving a jury? Should the sentence be more severe because the judge is convinced that the defendant perjured himself on the witness stand? Should churchgoing be considered to reflect favorably? Consistent with the first amendment, should it be considered at all? What factors should be assessed—and where, if anywhere, are comparisons to be sought—in gauging the relative seriousness of the specific offense and offender as against the spectrum of offenses by others in the same legal category? The list of such questions could be lengthened. Each is capable of being answered, and is answered by sentencing judges, in contradictory or conflicting, or at least differing, ways. There is no controlling requirement that any particular view be followed on any such subject by the sentencing judge.

With the delegation of power so unchanneled, it is surely no overstatement to say that "the new penology has resulted in vesting in judges and parole and probation agencies the greatest degree of uncontrolled power over the liberty of human beings that one can find in the legal system." The process would be totally unruly even if judges were superbly and uniformly trained for the solemn work of sentencing.

The kadi, unfettered by rules, makes his decrees swiftly and simply. But we learned long ago that the giving of reasons helps the decision maker himself in the effort to be fair and rational, and makes it possible for others to judge whether he has succeeded. And so we require our federal district judges and many others to explain themselves when they rule whether a postal truck driver was at fault in crumpling a fender and, if so, how much must be paid to right the wrong.

There is no such requirement in the announcement of a prison sentence. Sometimes judges give reasons anyway, or reveal in colloquy the springs of their action. The explanations or revelations sometimes disclose reasoning so perverse or mistaken that the sentence, normally unreviewable, must be invalidated on appeal. Most trial judges (to my impressionistic and conversational knowledge, at least) say little or nothing, certainly far less than a connected "explanation" or rationale of the sentence. Many, sharing a common aversion to being reversed, are perhaps motivated by the view (not unknown on trial benches) that there is safety in silence. It is likely that the judge, not expected to explain, has never organized a full and coherent explanation even for himself. Some judges use the occasion of sentencing to flaunt or justify themselves by moral pronunciamentos and excoriations of the defendant. This has no relation to the serious and substantial idea that the community's "denunciation" is a—possibly the—chief aim of sentencing. It is, in any event, not kin to the reasoned decisions for which judges are commissioned.

The state I have described as lawlessness calls for some immediate, if not immutable, remedies by lawmaking. At least some principles of sentencing should by now be attainable. Both by substantive controls and through procedural revisions the unchecked powers of the untutored judge should be subject to a measure of regulation. The vague, indefinite, and uncritical use of indeterminate sentences calls for restriction through meaningful definitions and discriminating judgments. Matters like the "apportionment of punishment" and its "severity" are peculiarly questions of legislative policy. Believing it has been time long since to start abhorring the vacuum that exists in this area, I propose here to suggest only some beginnings, leaving for wiser heads and fuller time the continuous task of completion and betterment.

Despite all the philosophizing on this most fundamental of subjects in scholarly works and random judicial opinions, we have virtually no meaningful or specific legislative declarations of the principles justifying criminal sanctions.

Beyond dealing with the bedrock subject of sentencing purposes, a new code on sentencing should begin to weigh and decide numerous issues of mitigation or aggravation on which judges are now free to go their disparate ways. It is not acceptable to leave for the normally unspoken and diverse judgments of sentencing courts such questions as: whether a plea of guilty should be considered in mitigation; whether (what is not the converse) standing trial should be considered aggravating; whether waiving a jury or seemingly lying on the stand should be taken into account; whether disruptive behavior and tactics at trial should be considered aggravating; or whether "cooperation" with the prosecutor (furnishing evidence for other investigations, testifying against codefendants, etc.) should be considered mitigating. In addition to such matters of in-court behavior, there are, of course, more fundamental questions touching the criminal acts and the general character and history of the defendant. Students of the subject recall, and generally scorn these days, the efforts of scholars in times past to catalogue such factors—the relative gravity of the specific offense, the cruelty or stealth or deliberateness of the behavior, defendant's age, prior record, character traits, etc.—and evolve a kind of calculus for computing sentences. The short answer to such proposals for detailed sentencing codes has been the familiar, and weighty, aversion to illusory certainty bought at the cost of inflexible laws that torture disparate people and events into identical molds. But, like other short answers, this one is too short. There has not yet been a sufficient investment of energy and imagination in the attempt to codify precise, detailed factors governing sentences. Until the attempt has been made, with at least a measure of the resources and attention befitting a moon-voyaging society, the vague, futile, helpless wailing about disparity remains hypocrisy. Believing this, and risking the misunderstanding likely to greet a proposition conceded to be rudimentary and tentative, I mean to outline (a) the reasons for a detailed sentencing code and (b) the general nature of the contents and uses of such a code.

(a) The argument for codifying sentencing criteria is, very simply, that they now exist and operate, whether we like this or not, in an arbitrary, random, inconsistent, and unspoken fashion. Factors I have repeatedly mentioned—guilty pleas, prior record, defendant's age and family circumstances—are considered every day by sentencing judges, but in accordance with uncontrolled and divergent individual views of what is, after all, the "law" each time it applies. Every factor of this kind calls for a judgment of policy, suited exactly for legislative action and surely not suited for random variation from case to case. It is not a question, then, of seeking out and attempting to apply artificial criteria. It is a question of making explicit and uniform what is now tacit, capricious, and often decisive.

Making such determinations, a detailed sentencing code would eliminate some of the obscurity and the futility now attending the subject. Counsel would have some basis for knowing what to do and how to argue. The sentencers—the single judge or a group, as well as probation officers—would face a task similarly defined and capable of similarly focused appraisal. The defining of concrete issues would lead in turn to the possibility of meaningful appellate review.

(b) To posit at least a theoretical ideal, subject to revision of all kinds in the pursuit, I suggest the goal of codification might be conceived as a fairly detailed calculus of sentencing factors, including such use of arithmetical weightings as experimental study might reveal to be feasible. Again, I disclaim anything beyond the crude diagraming of a preliminary hypothesis. The hypothesis begins with the thought that every sentence under the code, as heretofore urged, would be classified in accordance with its basic purpose or purposes—as deterrent, rehabilitative, etc. For each such category, the code might contain some initial or tentative sentencing guides—

for example, that a purely deterrent sentence should presumptively fall (subject to aggravating factors) in the lowest quartile of the sentencing range for the particular crime, or that a rehabilitative sentence must be categorized initially in terms of the defined need and proposed form of treatment.

Thereafter, within each broad sentencing category or group of categories, particular factors of mitigation or aggravation would be enumerated in the proposed code. Where possible, as I have suggested, numerical weights or ranges would be assigned—as, for example, for the relative gravity of the offense, the defendant's past criminal record, the favorable or unfavorable character of the defendant's work history and abilities. However unromantic numbers sound, or however misleading they may be in foolish hands, their proper uses may guide and regulate judgment. The physician who speaks of a grade 3 heart murmur may not be reporting a measurement as precise as the number of feet in a yard. But he says a meaningful thing that gives information and guidance to others professionally trained. Similarly, at least over time, a score of 5 on a scale of 1 to 5 for "gravity of particular offense" would help to tell what the sentencing judge thought and to test whether his thoughts made sense for the particular case.

For lack of time and competence, I have not attempted to think through how far a scheme of quantification might be carried. Depending upon the resolution of this basic problem, the aim of the sentencing code would be a sentencing form or chart giving possibly an overall "score" or, more likely, a profile of factors and their weights. The end product thus recorded by the sentencing tribunal could be preceded by proposed forms on charts submitted by counsel, probation officers, and others seeking to affect or determine the sentence. All, as I have urged, would have concrete things to aim at and talk about. All would have bases for comparison in assessing differences of ultimate judgment.

If this sounds crass and mechanical, I press it nonetheless as a goal preferable to the void in which we now operate. Outside the somber field of sentencing, it has not been our way to make a fetish of vagueness. Whether numbers and scores are useless is a judgment that ought to follow, not precede, earnest study.

The aspects of sentencing that strike me as most flawed and most urgently in need of law revision have led to the few, somewhat scattered suggestions for legislative reform outlined above. There are needs, however, for action of a more thorough and continuous nature. Ignorance being one of the greatest problems, there is a need to marshal resources and talent for research and experimentation. Because the subject of sentencing is not steadily exhilarating or profitable to political officials, there is a need to fill the gaps in attention between sporadic moments of concern in times of crisis. Another aspect of the same essential point is the lack of political power suffered not only by convicted persons but by their keepers as well. Finally, the need for revision of the law is not a one-time thing: the gross inadequacies of the existing situation require continuing study and reform.

Thoughts along these lines lead to the very possibly impractical but earnest final recommendation of this paper. I propose that there be established a national commission charged with permanent responsibility for (1) the study of sentencing, corrections, and parole; (2) the formulation of laws and rules to which the results of such study may lead; and (3) the actual enactment of rules subject to congressional veto. When I suggest details of the commission's proposed composition and functions, it will be to invite thought rather than to claim anything like certainty or finality. With these caveats I sketch the proposal and its rationale.

Starting with the latter, I have mentioned the need for continuous and prestigious attention to problems of sentencing. The commission, properly launched and populated, could serve in a sense as a lobby within the government for those sentenced and for those charged with their custody and treatment. Other interests, politically significant, have such representation. Agriculture, labor, business, investors, and others have their spokesmen in various departments and agencies. Lately, reflecting a variety of things we seem to care about as a nation, the consumer is elbowing his way into the power structure. Prisoners and jailers, like the poor and others who seemed so distant a while ago, are headed for participation unless we mean to deflect sharply the lines of our recent development. But whether or not that is so, the stakes of everyone in a system of rational sentencing are too great for contentment with the disheveled status quo. The improvements needed will not be achieved through fitful bursts of activity. The task requires the continuous attention of a respected agency.

Membership on the commission would be a matter for discussion. Obvious possibilities suggest themselves—lawyers, judges, criminologists, penologists, more generally based sociologists, psychologists, and, not least but least traditional, former or present prison inmates. This is not to stump for government of prisoners by consent. It is to say we have gone too long without paying much attention to the actual impact upon the recipients of our well-intentioned but ineffectual "treatment" programs.

The commission would not pretend to supersede existing scholarly efforts in universities and elsewhere. Like other agencies of government, the commission would draw upon such enterprises, generate additional ones, and engage in its own study programs. Early in its career, the commission would chart a program of inquiry and action and would set priorities. From this would follow decisions on the commissioning of outside studies and the organization of the agency's own projects.

I envision a highly prestigious commission or none at all. The caliber of those to be sought as commissioners would be a crucial concern. Their roles would be as philosopher-statesmen, charged with both basic scholarship and the formulation of rules, but leaving administrative and operating responsibilities to others. It is conceived, however, that the commission would have significant impact upon the shape and functioning of the affected administrative institutions. It may well be, for example, that the commission would want to consider whether there is any sound reason why the attorney general, the chief prosecutor, should have the Bureau of Prisons and Board of Parole under his jurisdiction. The phrasing here, if it implies a view as to the answer, is accurately revealing, but the commission might discover two sides to the question. The list of provocative possibilities could be extended, but the result might not be to enhance the palatability of my basic suggestion.

Sentencing is today a wasteland in the law. It calls, above all, for regulation by law. There is an excess of discretion given to officials whose entitlement to such power is established by neither professional credentials nor performance. Some measures already in existence—such as sentencing councils and appellate review—seem desirable because they operate to channel the exercise of discretion. On the other hand, the evil of unbounded discretion is enhanced by the uncritical belief that a beneficent "individualization" is achieved through indeterminate sentencing. Indeterminacy in its most enthusiastic forms takes on its literal dictionary quality of vagueness; it means the conferring of power to extend or terminate confinement where the grounds of the power have been misconceived and the occasions for its exercise are not ascertainable. Some aspects of sentencing and the treatment of convicted persons call for prompt legislative attention—in the choice of basic substantive principles, the prescription of basic procedures, and provisions for appellate review. The entire subject, however, is one for study and a steady process of law revision led by an eminent and permanent federal commission.

5.2
The Functions of a Sentencing Commission

Andrew von Hirsch

[*Having described the growing disenchantment in the early 1970s with discretionary sentencing systems, the author continues:*]

The Unsuitability of Legislatively Prescribed Sanctions

As interest in regulating sentencing grew, the method of regulation initially most used was legislative: the legislature would prescribe a detailed schedule of prescribed or recommended sanctions for various crimes. California started the trend in 1976, with its Uniform Determinate Sentencing Law. This law prescribed the terms that were to be served for different felonies when judges committed offenders to state prison. The parole board's releasing power was abolished for most cases, and the offender was to serve the sentence in full, less a one-third "good-time" deduction if he or she behaved peaceably in prison.

The California sentencing code, when first enacted in 1976, had an explicit guiding principle: terms of imprisonment should be proportionate to the seriousness of the criminal conduct. An effort was made by the drafters of the code to grade penalties to reflect the gravity of offenses. The prescribed durations of confinement were based on previous averages for time served, and the legislature resisted proposals for wholesale escalation of penalties when drafting the original statute.

Since its original writing in 1976, however, California's legislation has deteriorated. A number of bills have been enacted to lengthen the prescribed

From Andrew von Hirsch, Kay A. Knapp, and Michael H. Tonry, *The Sentencing Commission and Its Guidelines* (Boston: Northeastern University Press, 1987), ch. 1. Excerpted and reprinted by permission, with changes approved by the author.

terms for various crimes and to restore discretion by widening the range between the presumptive term and the aggravated term. These piecemeal changes were made with little apparent concern for preserving proportionality or consistency among penalties.

In the other states where the legislature attempted to fix definite penalties, the situation was worse than in California from the outset. An example is Indiana. That state's sentencing code bears marks of haste in drafting; it prescribes draconian penalties for many felonies; and, despite its alleged discretion-limiting aim, it reserves vast powers for judges to choose aggravated or mitigated terms and for correctional administrators to confer or withdraw the very large (50 percent) good-time allowance.

Perhaps these jurisdictions' choice of rule maker—the legislature—contributed to the disappointments. When called upon to write specific punishments for crimes, a legislative body has two vulnerabilities. First, it has little time available: given the press of other legislative business, it cannot devote much effort and thought to developing a coherent rationale; comparing proposed penalties with one another; projecting the standards' impact on sentencing practice and on the limited resources of the correctional system; and, once the penalties have gone into effect, reviewing the manner in which they have actually been administered. Second, legislatures face particularly troublesome pressures in the sentencing field. Many voters fear crime and criminals, and few convicted offenders do (or even may) vote. Once a legislative body begins debating specific penalties, legislators have considerable incentives to adopt posturing stances of "toughness" and few incentives for giving thought to the *justice* of proposed penalties—for considering seriously whether the proposed sanctions would treat convicted criminals (that unpopular minority) fairly and deservedly. With such difficulties apparent, observers began to ask whether the legislature might better delegate the task of setting sentencing standards to a specialized body—one more insulated from political pressures and with more time and expertise to devote.

One such alternative rule maker might, surprisingly enough, be the parole board. Traditionally, parole boards were hostile to writing explicit rules for their decisions regarding release. In part because of that hostility, parole authorities in several jurisdictions have lost their authority to decide when to release prisoners. But where authority to grant parole release has been retained, the parole board could become the vehicle of more definite penalties. By writing explicit standards for its release decisions, the board could begin to regulate duration of confinement. The board's standards could reduce prisoners' sense of uncertainty about the lengths of their confinement by requiring that they be informed, soon after entry into prison, of their expected dates of release.[1] The United States Parole Commission developed guidelines of this nature.

Parole guidelines, however, cannot be the ideal solution. Those guidelines cannot regulate judges' critical "in-out" decisions of whether to imprison offenders or not. Parole guidelines, in many states, also only partially control the duration of imprisonment: judges may appreciably influence the length of stay in prison through the decisions they make affecting the date of first parole eligibility and the maximum sentence. Explicit standards for *judges'* sentencing decisions therefore are a necessity. To write such standards, a standard-setting body is needed: not the legislature, but a specialized rule maker.

The Sentencing Commission

The idea for such a rule-making body can be credited to a former law professor and federal judge, Marvin E. Frankel. In a 1972 book he proposed creation of a sentencing commission.[2] The commission would be authorized by statute to write detailed guidelines for sentencing. Its members would be appointed by the jurisdiction's chief executive, with senatorial advice and consent; they would consist of judges, prosecutors, defense attorneys, scholars, and citizens, backed by a full-time professional staff. Judges would be required to follow the guidelines in their sentencing decisions, except where they could give satisfactory reasons for deviation. Under the enabling statute, the guidelines would become law either automatically after the commission approved them (in the absence of a legislative resolution of disapproval), or else upon submission to and approval by the legislature. In either case, the commission would be responsible for writing the guidelines, and was supposed to have enough leisure, expertise, and insulation from outside pressures to draft them with care. After the guidelines went into effect, the commission would collect information on their implementation and amend and refine them accordingly.

The sentencing commission's mission was to be prescriptive: to decide the future direction of sentencing policy. The study of past sentencing practice would be a useful first step, indicating what factors had been given primary emphasis in judges' everyday sentencing decisions. The next and critical step, however, would be a *normative* evaluation of that past practice. Is it rational? Is it fair? Ought the practice continue to be followed? If not, how should it be changed? The sentencing commission, in Frankel's proposal, was supposed to address those issues of policy explicitly. The commission would have its rule-making powers granted by law, in order to give it clear authority to formulate policy.

The commission's guidelines were supposed to structure the judge's discretion, not eliminate it. Judges still would interpret and apply the guidelines and could deviate from them in special circumstances. They would be called upon to do what their legal background has trained them to do: to apply generalized norms to particular cases, with whatever complexities of interpretation that involves, and to decide when there are sufficient grounds for departing from those norms in unusual situations. They would no longer be called upon to act in a legal void—to make decisions about people's liberty without explicit standards to guide their actions.

Frankel's proposal generated a great deal of interest, and by the end of the 1970s, several states began taking action. Of these various efforts, the first—and in some respects the most sophisticated to date—has been Minnesota's guidelines. These guidelines will therefore be the focus of the present discussion.

The Format of the Guidelines

Let me begin a sketch of sentencing commission guidelines with a description of their usual format. The guidelines are numerical and definite. Usually, their principal feature is a sentencing grid: a two-dimensional table of prescribed sanctions. The vertical axis of the grid, or offense score, grades the seriousness of various species of criminal conduct. The horizontal axis, or offender score, rates characteristics of the offender—such as the extent of his prior criminal record. Across the grid is drawn a so-called dispositional (or in-out) line. Above the line are prescribed prison sanctions of varying duration, and below it are lesser sanctions. In each grid cell above the line, a numerical range of imprisonment is prescribed: the grid cell applicable to convicted armed robbers having two prior felony convictions might contain a range of, say, thirty-eight to forty-four months in prison.

The grid is, however, only one of a variety of possible formats for numerical guidelines. It is the one used in the state guidelines that have been adopted to date and thus is the one we shall examine here. Another possible format, however, would be a step-by-step formula: first, crimes are rated by their seriousness; then, adjustments are made for other relevant factors (such as prior criminal history); the result is a "sanction score" that can be converted into periods of imprisonment and appropriate lesser sanctions. Different formats may reflect differences in style more than substance. It may take only elementary mathematics to convert a sentencing grid into a step-by-step formula or vice versa.

In a grid, the range in any particular cell prescribes only the *normally* appropriate sentences. A sentencing court is authorized to deviate from the cell range on account of aggravating and mitigating circumstances. Such deviations are to be invoked, however, only in unusual situations—and the guidelines themselves may contain a suggested list of factors that qualify as mitigating or aggravating.

Once established, the guidelines system is policed through appellate review. The higher courts are authorized to hear sentence appeals and to determine compliance with the guidelines. In so doing, those courts are supposed to develop a supplementary jurisprudence—on, for example, how to interpret the commission's list of aggravating and mitigating factors.

The sentencing commission remains in existence to study patterns of implementation of the guidelines and to note areas of difficulty. Frequent departures from the cell ranges for a particular type of case, for example, may suggest that the ranges themselves need amendment. Through such "feedback," the commission can alter and try to improve the guidelines over time.

The Guidelines and "Disparity"

One of the major charges against discretionary sentencing was its apparent tendency to produce disparate outcomes. It has thus been tempting to define the sentencing commission's mission purely as that of promoting consistency or reducing disparity. Such a formulation of the guidelines' aim, however, is insufficient.

Disparity cannot be determined in a vacuum. It consists of differences in sentence that cannot be accounted for on the basis of the purpose or purposes sought to be achieved. Does it constitute disparity when unemployed offenders receive more severe sentences than employed ones? That depends upon the rationale. If the aim is to punish offenders as they deserve, it *is* disparity—because an offender's employment status ordinarily is not germane to the reprehensibleness of his criminal conduct. If, on the other hand, the aim is to sentence offenders according to their risk of recidivism, it is not necessarily disparity, because available studies suggest a link between joblessness and recidivism. In order to combat or even to identify disparity, the first step needed is the specification of a rationale. Yet that is precisely what is missing in a discretionary sentencing system.

Consistency is, also, no guarantee of the rationality or fairness of a system. Sentencing offenders invariably according to their height or weight would be consistent but nevertheless irrational. What is needed is a *considered* judgment of what the basis of the sentence should be. Only then has a standard been created against which "disparity" can be measured and judged.

What, then, is the mission of a sentencing commission? It is threefold: selecting a rationale, considering prison population constraints, and developing a tariff. Let me examine each of these functions.

Choosing the Rationale

The sentencing commission, in fashioning its guidelines, must choose a rationale. Should the system emphasize punishing offenders proportionately to the gravity of their crimes? Or should it rely, instead, more heavily on the degree of risk offenders pose? Or should there be some other purpose? The choice of rationale is critical because it will determine what features of the offense or of the offender should be relied upon in determining the punishment. On a rationale emphasizing proportionality and desert, the factor primarily to be relied upon is the seriousness of the current crime. On a predictive rationale, however, the primacy would shift to factors that are indicative of risk—chiefly, the offender's previous criminal record and his social and employment history. The commission does not have to choose one rationale to the exclusion of all others, but, where a hybrid rationale is used, it is still necessary to decide which aim should have preeminence [see also Extract 4.7].

A sentencing commission is well suited to this task: it can consider the rationale for the system as a whole and make its choice in an *informed* fashion. When considering treatment or deterrence, the commission can inform itself of the extent and limits of present knowledge of treatment and deterrent effects. When considering incapacitation, it can examine prediction research to see how well we can forecast recidivism, and where the empirical and ethical problems lie. When considering desert, it can—by examining the literature on that subject—acquaint itself with the criteria for proportionality.

With the rationale formulated, the commission is in a position to identify the factors chiefly to be relied upon and the comparative weight they should be given. Choosing between desert and incapacitation, for example, enables the commission to decide the weight to be given the current offense relative to the prior record and other information about the offender.

A striking illustration of this policy-making process has been provided by Minnesota's sentencing commission. The Minnesota commission studied judges' decisions about whether or not to impose a prison sentence. It found that, under previous judicial practice, the main determinant of an offender's going to prison was the length of his criminal record. An offender with a string of lesser felonies would be imprisoned; a first offender with a considerably more serious conviction would not. In other words, the dispositional line on the grid—the line separating prison from nonprison dispositions—would be steep (emphasizing the criminal record) were past practice made the basis of the guidelines. The commission then proceeded to consider whether this practice was desirable and should be continued.

To make that decision the commission developed models comparing the slope of the dispositional line on two rationales: a desert rationale, and an incapacitative one relying on prediction of risk. After consulting the literature on desert and prediction, the commission determined that a desert rationale would have a relatively flat line, giving primary weight to the seriousness of the current offense—whereas a predictive rationale would (because of the link between previous record and recidivism) have a much steeper line, emphasizing the prior record, as the state's previous practice did. With this in mind the commission was able to debate the rationale, and eventually it decided that a more desert-oriented rationale was preferable. The commission thereupon chose as its dispositional line one which, it asserted, reflected a "modified" desert conception; the line was flat for most cases, albeit steep for offenders with lengthy criminal histories. The result of this decision was a substantial change from prior policy. The seriousness of the offense is given considerably more importance in the guidelines than it had under the state's past practice, and the extent of the criminal history is given much less.

Controlling the Growth of Prison Populations

Many jurisdictions, both in the United States and elsewhere, have been experiencing sharp rises in prison populations. The result has been prison overcrowding, with its attendant evils of deteriorating living conditions. If crowding is endemic and serious, the conventional palliatives offer little hope. Emergency release, accelerated parole, and similar stopgap measures are only short-term solutions—and soon generate opposition, as involving the "premature" release of undeserving or dangerous felons. New prison construction is costly, time-consuming, and (if prison commitments continue unabated) creates space that itself soon will be filled. Crowding can be effectively prevented only by controlling the inflow into the prisons and the length of stay there.

Inflow and length of stay can be influenced through sentencing guidelines. Minnesota, again, provides the model. The Minnesota Sentencing Commission devised its guidelines so that, given anticipated conviction rates, the aggregate prison population would not exceed the capacity of the state's prisons. The commission accomplished this by projecting the impact of its tentatively proposed guidelines on prison populations, comparing those projections with the rated capacity of the state's prison system, and then making the appropriate adjustments to yield the final guidelines.

Minnesota's approach involves "freezing" prison populations at existing levels. A variant of the technique might involve setting a population target that is either somewhat higher or lower than existing institutional capacity. Then—as long as any increased commitments were not to take effect until necessary space had been built—the guidelines still would perform the function of restraining prison populations within available space.

The effectiveness of the Minnesota projection technique depends upon grid ranges that are fairly narrow and departure rules that are fairly stringent. With wide ranges, it would be difficult or impossible to project actual sentence levels and hence the impact. Eventually, the Minnesota commission's projections proved reasonably accurate—prison commitments remained roughly within capacity, after a transition period in which some adjustments had to be made.

Why should a sentencing commission adopt such population targets? The plainest reason is ethical. Overcrowding makes the daily discomforts of prison life much worse, and it exacerbates frictions that can lead to violence. A civilized society should not commit offenders to institutions that lack room for them.

A population constraint has another use: it forces those who write sentencing guidelines to treat them as a choice of priorities. When a population constraint is imposed and population projections are systematically used in writing the guidelines, the commissioners are made aware that they are dealing with a system of scarce resources—which cannot possibly imprison all those whom various constituencies might prefer to see confined. With explicit population targets it becomes clear that a choice must be made of whom it is *most important* to imprison: those whose crimes are serious or those who have substantial criminal records can be chosen, but not all of both groups. The need to make such a choice can promote consensus within the commission and can also help the commission explain its work by pointing out the trade-offs: how getting tougher with one group of offenders would necessitate more leniency with another group. In Minnesota, such a strategy of argument proved helpful for obtaining agreement within the commission and for generating outside support for the guidelines.

It is sometimes said to be unjust or inappropriate to let prison space influence punishment levels. This claim seems plausible on a retributive theory of punishment: why should offenders' deserts depend on how much room there is in penal institutions? On closer analysis, however, the claim does not stand. Granted, it would not be appropriate to use space constraints to impose unequal punishments on offenders convicted of equally reprehensible conduct. But if parity among equally blameworthy offenders is maintained, and if punishments are graded according to the gravity of the criminal conduct, then—for reasons elaborated elsewhere [see Extract 4.4]—desert principles allow some leeway in determining the anchoring points and overall severity levels of the penalty scale. To the extent such leeway exists, resource availability may be a legitimate factor in deciding overall severity levels.

Beyond such philosophical arguments stands another, simpler reason for considering prison space: namely, to ensure that the guidelines are implemented as written. To the extent that their full application would overtax available penal resources, the guidelines will have to be disregarded in everyday sentencing decisions. If dissatisfied with existing punishment levels, the commission might decide that increased or reduced aggregate use of imprisonment is appropriate. If it wishes an increase, then it would have to take into account whether the legislature is willing to fund such an increase and how long it would take before the added space becomes available. But to write a sentencing "policy" for which the necessary resources are lacking is posturing, not policy-making.

Developing the Tariff

The third task for the commission is to develop a tariff: to provide specific guidance on the amount of punishment ordinarily called for by various types of cases. Such a baseline for everyday sentencing decisions is what has been lacking from discretionary systems.

If the guidelines use a grid format, the commission develops the tariff by filling in the cells in the grid. By supplying ranges in the grid's cells, the commission indicates when imprisonment is called for, and what periods of imprisonment ordinarily are appropriate. The judges' role then becomes that of applying and interpreting the tariff in their everyday sentencing decisions and deciding when to deviate from the tariff in suitable special circumstances.

This tariff-construction work is the commission's most laborious task. Different species of criminal conduct must be graded in seriousness—which involves assessing the harm and culpability of a wide variety of criminal acts. Offenders' criminal histories, and any other appropriate offender factors, need also to be graded. Finally, the ranges of normally prescribed punishments need to be decided upon—work involving complex comparative judgments, in which the commission needs to bear in mind its chosen rationale and its prison-population targets. The guidelines are only as good as the tariff. Little is accomplished if the chosen rationale is ignored when the numbers are written in the grid cells, or if the prescribed punishment ranges are too broad to provide significant guidance to judges.

Once the tariff is thus developed, the question of departures needs also to be addressed. What burden of persuasion must be met before departures from the grid's ranges are permitted? What are the permitted grounds for departure? If departures are too readily permitted, the guidelines become merely precatory; if they are stringently restricted, then the guidelines become too rigid. The guidelines thus need to address, at least in general terms, what types of aggravating and mitigating circumstances may be taken into account in sentencing decisions.[3]

Notes

1. See Andrew von Hirsch and Kathleen J. Hanrahan, *The Question of Parole: Retention, Reform, or Abolition?* (Cambridge, Mass.: Ballinger, 1979), ch. 9.

2. Marvin E. Frankel, *Criminal Sentences: Law without Order* (New York: Hill and Wang, 1972); and see Extract 5.1, above.

3. For fuller discussion of this issue, see Andrew von Hirsch, Kay A. Knapp, and Michael Tonry, *The Sentencing Commission and Its Guidelines* (Boston: Northeastern University Press, 1987), 102–5.

5.3
Three Techniques for Reducing Sentence Disparity

Andrew Ashworth

During the twentieth century the English Court of Appeal gradually built up, through its precedence, a considerable body of guidance on sentencing. In 1991, however, Britain's Parliament adopted new statutory sentencing principles, but the arguments for reform stopped considerably short of adopting the kinds of numerical guidelines which have been introduced in several American jurisdictions. Of the three different approaches—judicial self-regulation, statutory sentencing principles, and numerical guidelines—what are the principal advantages and disadvantages in terms of structuring sentencing discretion?

Judicial Self-Regulation

Of course, the self-regulation is not total. In England and Wales, as in most jurisdictions, there are and have been maximum penalties set by the legislature for different offenses. Beneath those maxima, however, sentencing has been characterized by a wide judicial discretion with very few other legislative restrictions on what the courts may and may not do. Such an expanse of judicial discretion leaves the way open for disparities in approaches to sentencing, and public and political concern about disparities was rife at the end of the nineteenth century.[1] This was one reason for the creation in 1907 of the Court of Criminal Appeal, now the Court of Appeal. In hearing appeals against sentence the Court, occasionally in the early years and frequently in recent years, has given its authority to various

This essay is published here for the first time.

general principles of sentencing. For example, the Court has held that judges should pass concurrent, not consecutive, sentences where two or more crimes can be said to arise from the same transaction; and it has held that it is wrong for a court to impose a financial penalty (e.g., fine, compensation order) on a wealthy offender where a poor offender would receive a more severe measure. It has also been claimed that the Court's decisions establish the "normal range" of sentences for most crimes.[2] In fact, the Court's jurisprudence on sentence ranges has been rather variable and was, until 1988, limited by its power only to hear defense appeals.

The judicial self-regulation which resulted from this kind of system had the effect of imposing some structure and some limitations on judicial sentencing, but most of these restrictions stemmed from particular appellate decisions and there was rarely any attempt to consider sentencing principles as a whole. The system regards appellate review of sentences as its central pillar, and as such it is the approach adopted in Scotland, in Canada, in Australia, and in many other common-law systems where the appeal court's decision may constitute a binding precedent for other judges. By this means a collection of principles accumulates over time, enabling the judiciary to claim that it has considerable discretion in sentencing but that it regulates the exercise of that discretion itself according to stated principles.

That position, which many judges might regard as close to their ideal, does have the disadvantage that it is purely reactive. The Court of Appeal makes its statements of principle when the cases it is hearing raise the issues. To remedy this, the policy-making role of the English Court of Appeal was developed in the 1960s under Lord Chief Justice Lane. From time to time he delivered so-called guideline judgments, which set out the parameters of sentencing for various manifestations of a particular crime. To take one example, the guideline judgment on rape indicates two main starting points for sentencing this offense—eight years' imprisonment where one of four aggravating features is present, five years in other cases—and then sets out eight aggravating factors and three mitigating factors which courts should take into account when deciding whether the sentence should be higher or lower than the starting point. It also identifies three factors which should not be regarded as mitigating.[3] The strengths of this kind of guideline judgment are that it provides judges with a framework within which they can locate the individual case, without depriving them of the discretion to depart if a particular case has unusual features, and it does so in a narrative form—not by a stark table of numbers, but in the traditional and familiar form of an appellate judgment. One internal weakness is that the judgment may give little indication as to the weighting and effect of the various aggravating and mitigating factors, and this is the very problem likely to arise most in practice. As a policy instrument, however, the guideline judgment as used by the English Court of Appeal has two distinct disadvantages. First, the tendency has been for these judgments to be delivered occasionally and without any sense of an overall strategy or striving for coherence, let alone a settled view of the primary aim or aims of sentencing. They may therefore improve consistency of sentencing within a given offense category, such as rape, without considering the proper relationship of rape sentences to those for burglary, robbery, etc. Second, these judgments have been delivered relatively rarely, and cover only a small proportion of the crimes for which English courts have to pass sentence. Thus, important as the guideline judgment may be as a technique for structuring sentencing, it is fairly marginal in its impact on English practice.

The Court of Appeal's resort to guideline judgments has significant implications. One of those is that the traditional appellate process is not, of itself, a sufficient machinery for providing the degree and style of guidance necessary for consistent sentencing. At the very least, it has to be adapted. A further and deeper implication is that guideline judgments dispose of one much-trumpeted judicial objection to sentencing guidance: "each case is unique, and has its own individual combination of factors, and so guidance will invariably be crude and unhelpful." This is the last line of defense for those who favor unfettered judicial discretion in sentencing. What it seems to assume is that judges share a common evaluation of all the factors which may enter into sentencing decisions, that judges do not differ significantly on the aims of sentencing or in their views on the relative seriousness of offenses, and that it is merely the different combinations of facts in each case which result in the passing of different sentences. Not only does this defy belief at a general level, but it is also controverted by the guideline judgments—which have been welcomed by most English judges as providing a common framework while preserving flexibility for each case.

Guideline judgments have been accounted successful in England because they are constructed *by* judges *for* judges. But the decade which brought guideline judgments into prominence also brought the realization that more could and should be done to foster consistency in sentencing than to rely on occasional judicial utterance. The 1980s ended with proposals to reduce the amount of judicial self-regulation in English sentencing, paying more attention to identifying in legislation the aims of sentencing and the policies which should be pursued, and yet preserving a role for the Court of Appeal and for further guideline judgments in giving detailed guidance in accordance with the leading aims and principles. These developments are discussed next.

Statutory Sentencing Principles

Since 1976, article 6 of the Finnish Penal Code has contained a provision which declares that "[p]unishment shall be measured so that it is in just proportion to the damage and danger caused by the offense and to the guilt of the offender manifested in the offense." Many other jurisdictions have a legislative declaration of sentencing aims, but those aims are sometimes conflicting (as in the German Penal Code). The Finnish code not only articulates a primary rationale but also contains a list of aggravating and mitigating factors which relate to that aim. Beyond that, the application of the guidance in individual cases is left to the courts.

A somewhat more sophisticated version of the same approach is now to be found in the Swedish Penal Code, following its revision in 1988. The code identifies proportionality (desert) as the primary basis of sentencing, and requires the judge to assess the "penal value" (i.e., seriousness) of the offense. Some aggravating and mitigating factors are specified, as are other factors which the court may take into account. There is also guidance on the choice among forms of sentence. The new Swedish law is discussed in detail by Andrew von Hirsch and Nils Jareborg in Extract 5.4 below.

The Finnish and Swedish approaches are notable in that they declare the leading principles of sentencing in legislation, and then leave the judges to apply and to individuate those general norms. In one sense the judges have a great degree of discretion, because they are subject to few legislative restrictions. In another sense their discretion is given guidance, because they should evaluate the factors in individual cases by reference to the principles of sentencing declared in the legislation—they are not free to impose exemplary deterrent sentences if they conceive a desire to do so, because that would be inconsistent with the legislation. The structuring of their discretion is thus achieved through an approach which ties their patterns of reasoning to particular aims and principles, rather than through an approach which sets out numerical guidelines, etc.

The new English approach embodied in the provisions of the Criminal Justice Act of 1991 also sets out statutory sentencing principles, albeit in a somewhat less clear way than the Finnish and Swedish legislation. The origins of the new law were in the government's White Paper of 1990, which stated that desert should be the primary aim of sentencing, that rehabilitation should not be an aim of sentencing but should be striven for within proportionate sentences, and that deterrence is rarely a proper or profitable aim for a sentencer.[4]

Section 1 of the Criminal Justice Act states that courts may (with certain stated exceptions) impose custodial sentences only on the grounds of desert ("the seriousness of the offense"). The Act then provides two further sets of legislative restrictions. If the offense is thought serious enough for custody, section 2 requires courts to ensure that the length of the sentence is "commensurate with the seriousness of the offense." If the offense is not serious enough for custody, section 5 provides that a court may only impose a "community sentence" if the offense is too serious for a fine or a discharge. Once this criterion is satisfied, the court must ensure that the restrictions on liberty entailed by the community sentence are "commensurate with the seriousness of the offense." In these respects the legislation provides repeated affirmation of desert (proportionality) as the primary basis for sentencing, although its provisions on aggravation, mitigation, and previous convictions (section 3) are less clear and less satisfactory.

The White Paper envisaged that the Court of Appeal would, through its judgments, translate the general provisions of the Act into detailed guidance on the sentencing of particular types of offense. In the past the court has shown little enthusiasm for giving general guidance on sentences for the kind of middle-range offenses (burglary, theft, deception, handling stolen goods) which occupy most courts for most of the time, but if the new legislation is to be successful, this is what the Court of Appeal will have to do. Moreover, within the statutory framework it will be expected to adopt desert-based reasoning when giving guidance. It will not be free to draw on deterrent, protective, and desert arguments as promiscuously as it has done in the past. Except for a relatively narrow range of cases which qualify for an incapacitative sentence ("necessary for the protection of the public from serious harm"), the concept of "seriousness" should govern the court's reasoning. The English statute articulates the policy of using community sentences for many offenders who have hitherto received custodial sentences, and that is also a step forward.[5]

Numerical Guideline Systems

Among the most powerful techniques for reducing disparity in sentencing are numerical guidelines. American jurisdictions provide illustrations of several systems of this kind, varying in the form in which they are promulgated, in the presence of absence of overall aims and policies, and in the degree of latitude left to the court in each case. The best-known system is that of Minnesota, which will be discussed first. It will then be contrasted with the distinctly less successful federal guidelines, emanating from the United States Sentencing Commission.

The sentencing commission in Minnesota began work in the late 1970s.[6] One of its earliest decisions was to decide upon a primary rationale for sentencing: desert. It then went on to make some crucial policy decisions. Sentences for property offenders were to be made less severe, and those for violent offenders proportionately more severe. Prior criminal record was to be less influential than the seriousness of the offense. And overall sentencing levels were to be calculated so as to ensure that the numbers sentenced to imprisonment remained within the capacity of the prisons.[7] The commission then divided all serious offenses into ten categories of relative gravity, and developed a seven-point scale for calculating the seriousness of a person's criminal history. The result was Minnesota's "Sentencing Guidelines Grid," in operation since 1981, which enables a judge to find the presumptive sentence in each case by placing the offense within the appropriate category, calculating the criminal history score, and then locating the cell where the two intersect. The judge is obliged to impose a sentence within the range of the presumptive sentence unless there are substantial and compelling circumstances in the individual case for departing from that range. In such circumstances, departure is permitted upon giving reasons, and the guidelines include a list of factors which may and factors which may not be used as reasons for departure.

The Minnesota guidelines have proved reasonably successful in attaining their objectives.[8] A relatively high degree of consistency has been achieved, property offenders go to prison less frequently, and the prison population in Minnesota has been kept somewhat in check. The state's supreme court has developed a jurisprudence of permissible and impermissible departures which places a gloss on the basic guidelines. There are, on the other hand, various respects in which the Minnesota model could be improved. Dividing all serious offenses into only ten categories is somewhat crude; the elements of discretion remaining in the Minnesota system have enabled judges and prosecutors to circumvent the guidelines and restore some of their former practices (e.g., prosecutors have modified their charging practices so as to build up the previous history scores of offenders more quickly); and the guidelines leave a wide discretion in respect of noncustodial sentences, with neither guidance nor articulation of principle.

The success of the Minnesota system has been attributed as much to the personality and style of the chairman and members of the sentencing commission in its early days as to the intrinsic merits of the scheme adopted.[9]

It has been followed in some other states—notably, Oregon and Washington State—with modest success.[10]

The approach of the United States Sentencing Commission has been different, as have been the consequences of the guidelines they drafted. The Commission was established by the federal Sentencing Reform Act of 1984 and was directed to draft sentencing guidelines within certain legislative constraints. The guidelines became law in 1987 but in practice have reflected the structural defects apparent from the outset.[11] Four areas of concern may be identified.

First, the Commission declined to declare a primary rationale for sentencing, and instead opted for a scheme with an indiscriminate mixture of rationales. This is not a mere question of academic elegance: it is a matter of fundamental practical importance when it comes to deciding what factors would mitigate or aggravate and on what basis judges should exercise the discretion left to them within the system. Without a guiding aim, consistency will be difficult to achieve.

Second, the Commission declined to adopt a principle of restraint in the use of imprisonment, despite a reference to resource constraints in the Sentencing Reform Act. The position has been worsened by the mandatory and mandatory minimum sentences enacted by Congress, particularly for drug offenders and career criminals. Federal imprisonment rates are soaring, and judicial opposition to mandatory minimum sentences is widespread.

Third, the federal guidelines themselves are high on complexity and low on clarity. The Commission's "Sentencing Table" has some forty-three "offense levels" on one axis and six "criminal history categories" on the other. For each type of offense a "base level" is indicated by the guidelines; there are then various "enhancements" which the judge must use to raise the offense level, and there are also some factors such as "acceptance of responsibility" (an ambiguous and practically troublesome reference to a plea of guilty) which should reduce the offense level. To take a practical example, robbery carries a "base level" of 18 on the scale. The amount stolen increases this, so that if $100,000 were taken, this would add three points to the offense level. There are further enhancements if a weapon was involved: if a gun was brandished but not used, for example, this would add three further points. Then if the judge thought that the offender's plea of guilty showed acceptance of responsibility, the level would be reduced by two. Next the judge would turn to the offender's prior record: the calculation takes account not only of the number of previous convictions but also of their seriousness. There are also the augmentations for career criminals. The result of this should lead the judge to a cell in the

"Sentencing Table" indicating the appropriate range of sentences. Courts may depart from this range whenever it seems "reasonable" to do so. The guidelines specify some factors which may not and others which may justify departures, and there are also certain "policy statements" whose authority seems to have caused judicial confusion. Since one such statement is that personal characteristics of the offender are "not ordinarily relevant," this has inhibited some judges from mitigating sentence where they might otherwise have done so.

Fourth, the apparent rigidity of the guidelines in practice (with a compliance rate of over four out of five sentences) has resulted, as the Federal Courts Study Committee found,[12] in a transfer of considerable power to federal prosecutors. Although this is a natural consequence of tightly drafted guidelines, the situation is more complex here because there is some uncertainty and confusion about the sentencing discount for a guilty plea. Nevertheless, research has found a significant degree of guideline evasion through plea bargaining.[13]

It is fair to say that the political climate in which the federal guidelines have grown up has been much more conducive to severity than that in Minnesota in the early 1980s. But that does not excuse the structural defects in the guidelines themselves.

Conclusions

References to these and other approaches to sentencing guidance demonstrate that there is no single formula which is likely to work for all, or most, jurisdictions. Much will depend both on the political climate and on the legal tradition of the country or state. Judicial self-regulation provides an excellent basis for the development of principles which are closely sensitive to the practical problems of sentencers, but it is not a good means for deciding the overall aims of sentencing or the policies to be pursued with respect to imprisonment, victims, etc. It must be supplemented by some statutory sentencing principles, formulated after wide consultation and presented as a framework for judicial decision making. The Finnish and Swedish approaches propound general principles and leave the courts to apply them sensibly, which seems to be appropriate according to their legal traditions. The English approach foresees a partnership in which the legislature establishes the framework and the courts develop the more detailed numerical guidance; however, as was suggested above, the framework established by the Criminal Justice Act of 1991 is less clear than one would have hoped for. The Minnesota system accords with the Finnish and Swedish in adopting a primary rationale for sentencing, but goes on to present its guidance largely by means of numbers (although there are also some principles for the exercise of discretion). While its numerical scheme may seem very (perhaps unduly) simplified, the federal sentencing guidelines go to the opposite extreme of detailed prescriptions—combined, however, with some unclear and ambiguous provisions on crucial issues such as the discount for pleading guilty and the permissibility of personal mitigation.

In addition to legal tradition and political climate, another important element is the quality of leadership given to sentencing reform. Personalities assume particular importance when it is a question of persuading people to abandon an approach taken unquestioningly for many years—an approach which, for example, is suspicious of the idea of "guidelines" or which resents as interference any legislative provision on sentencing. Even beyond this, however, lie the penological and philosophical arguments which are needed to convince people of the value of consistency in sentencing; of the need to scrutinize the claims of deterrence, rehabilitation, incapacitation, and desert as sentencing aims; and of the reasons for reducing reliance on imprisonment as a sanction.

Notes

1. Sir Leon Radzinowicz and Roger Hood, *The Emergence of Penal Policy* (1985).

2. Notably by D. A. Thomas, *Principles of Sentencing* (2d ed., 1979), whose pioneering work in rationalizing and reconstructing the Court of Appeal's decisions has had considerable effect on the development of its jurisprudence.

3. The decision is *Billam* (1986) 82 *Cr. App. R.* 347.

4. Home Office, *Crime, Justice, and Protecting the Public* (London, 1990), ch. 2.

5. In this respect the Act builds upon statutory restrictions on the use of custodial sentences for offenders under twenty-one, which have existed in roughly this form since 1982. The Act refines these criteria and applies them generally to offenders of all ages.

6. For the history and the experience of the early years, see Dale G. Parent, *Structuring Criminal Sentences* (Butterworth, 1989).

7. For detailed analysis and discussion, see Andrew von Hirsch, "Structure and Rationale: Minnesota's Critical Choices," in A. von Hirsch, K. Knapp, and M. Tonry, *The Sentencing Commission and Its Guidelines* (1987), ch. 5.

8. See Parent, op. cit.; and Kay A. Knapp, "Implementation of the Minnesota Guidelines: Can the Innovative Spirit Be Preserved?" in von Hirsch, Knapp, and Tonry, op. cit., ch. 8.

9. See Parent, op. cit., and M. Tonry, "The Politics and Processes of Sentencing Commissions," 37 *Crime and Delinquency* 307 (1991).

10. See von Hirsch, Knapp, and Tonry, op. cit., ch. 2 and appendix, for discussion of Washington guidelines.

11. See the critique by Andrew von Hirsch, "Federal Sentencing Guidelines: Do They Provide Principled Guidance?" 27 *Am. Crim. L. Rev.* 367 (1989).

12. *Report,* Federal Courts Study Committee (Washington, D.C., 1990).

13. S. Schulhofer and I. Nagel, "Negotiated Pleas under the Federal Sentencing Guidelines: The First Fifteen Months," 27 *Am. Crim. L. Rev.* 231 (1990).

5.4 The Swedish Sentencing Law

5.4(a) The Principles Underlying the New Law

Andrew von Hirsch

[*This first extract describes the principles underlying the Swedish reforms, and was written at the time when they were proposed. The actual law, which differs little from the proposals, is set out and explained in Extract 5.4(b).*]

The Rise of Swedish "Neoclassicism"

In the decades after the Second World War, Sweden became internationally noted for its interest in penal rehabilitation. Actually, it did not go so far as foreigners imagined: the idea of a graded tariff of penalties retained considerable influence. Indeterminate sentences were used only for special offender categories, such as youthful offenders and habitual criminals. The Swedish Penal Code did not have much to say on choice of sentence for offenders outside these narrow categories. It mentioned rehabilitation and general prevention in broad terms, but provided scant advice on how those aims should be implemented by the courts.

During the 1970s and 1980s, Sweden witnessed growing disenchantment with its law and conceptions of sentencing. The Penal Code, it was felt, gave insufficient guidance for choosing the sanction. It began to be recognized that only limited capacity exists to fashion sentences for rehabilitative

From Andrew von Hirsch, "Guiding Principles for Sentencing: The Proposed Swedish Law," *Criminal Law Review* 746 (1987). Excerpted and reprinted by permission.

effect. Questions were raised about the fairness of basing sanctions on supposed responsiveness to treatment or on likelihood of future offending. There was a strong revival of interest in the idea of proportionality—of punishments that fairly comport with the seriousness of the defendant's criminal conduct.

The new thinking received considerable stimulus with the publication in 1977 of *A New Penal System: Ideas and Proposals.*[1] This report, written for the Swedish National Council on Crime Prevention by a working group of judges and penologists, attracted widespread debate and comment. The report emphasized ideas of structuring sentencing discretion and proportionate sanctions. Similar ideas—sometimes referred to as "neoclassical"—were echoed in an influential essay collection that appeared three years later. Such ideas continued to surface in the Swedish literature, affected in part by Finnish writings and by American writings on "just deserts."

Writing the Proposed Law

The Swedish neoclassicists' first success was in their campaign against the indeterminate sentence. We have, they asserted, neither the capacity to identify persons who are long-term risks nor the ability to treat such persons, as these measures assumed. Above all, they argued, indeterminacy was unfair, in its potential disregard of the seriousness of the offender's conduct in deciding whether and how long to confine. Indeterminate confinement for youths was abolished in 1979, and "internment" for adults eliminated in 1981.

The next step was to address the Penal Code's general provisions on sentencing. In 1979, the Swedish minister of justice appointed a study commission, the Committee on Imprisonment (*Fängelsestraffkommittén*) to examine the matter. The Committee issued its report, *Sanctions for Crimes,* six years later, in the spring of 1986. The report, among other things, recommended a lowering of the statutory maxima and minima for many crimes, an expansion of the system of day fines, and changes in the rules on parole release. Its most notable proposal, however, concerned the principles governing the choice of sentence. The Committee put forward two wholly new draft chapters of the Penal Code, dealing with the subject. The chapters emphasize notions of proportionality in sentencing.

As is customary with study commissions in Sweden, the Committee circulated its proposals to a wide group of scholars, judges, prosecutors, lawyers, correctional administrators, union officials, and other interested parties. The provisions on choice of sentence received generally favorable comment—and early in 1987 the Ministry of Justice, after reviewing the responses, tentatively decided to support those proposals. Ministry support means that the proposed new chapters—after some technical amendments to reflect comments received—will become a government bill, with reasonably good chances for passage. [In fact they were enacted in 1988 and came into force in 1990: the key provisions are set out in Extract 5.4(b), which follows.]

How Much Guidance?

The existing Swedish Penal Code, as I mentioned, provides little guidance to sentencing judges. The so-called penalty scales (that is, the ranges between the statutory maximums and minimums) are fairly wide, especially for the more serious crimes—albeit not as wide as they have been in the United States. The Penal Code provides that sentences should (1) promote general obedience to law and (2) foster the defendant's rehabilitation. It is far from clear, however, how the courts are to accomplish these potentially conflicting aims—especially given the paucity of effective treatments and the tenuous connection between general law-abidingness and the sentence in any particular case. The code fails to suggest what features of the offender or his offense should ordinarily be given emphasis. And it leaves important issues unaddressed—especially, the issue of proportionality between the gravity of crimes and the severity of punishments. Guidance was thought necessary, therefore, to supply a coherent policy for sentencing: to help choose which penal aim should predominate, and thereby to help decide what features of the offender or his offense should be given most weight.

How much guidance should there be, and who should supply it? The Imprisonment Committee considered various solutions. At one extreme was the English approach—of leaving the task of guidance to the appellate courts, without substantial assistance provided by statute or regulation. At the other was Minnesota's approach of a numerical sentencing grid that prescribes specific terms or narrow ranges as the normally recommended sentences. The Committee adopted an intermediate solution: the legislation should provide general principles but no numbers. The courts are then to apply those principles in deciding the *quantum* of sentence.

Leaving guidance to the appellate courts—the English solution—has been defended by D. A. Thomas. The decisions of England's Court of Appeal (Criminal Division), he asserts, have coalesced into a case-law jurisprudence of sentencing: no general legislation on choice of sentence is needed because the Court of Appeal has matters well in hand. Other British observers have been less sanguine—and the Swedish Committee, in any event, was unpersuaded. Appellate courts, acting alone, might be able to establish *some* kind of tariff: imprisonment recommended for this kind of case, probation for that kind. But without external policy guidance, the appellate courts tend to have difficulty fashioning a *principled* resolution of sentencing issues. That difficulty has manifested itself in the English sentencing cases: guideline judgments issued without a clear statement of supporting rationale; claims about deterrence or treatment made with little regard for the availability of supporting evidence; proportionality among dispositions not carefully considered or maintained. Such deficiencies may be understandable, given the pressure of other court business and judges' limited time to peruse and consider sentencing research and theory, but they do not bode well for a well-thought-through sentencing jurisprudence developed by courts alone.

At the other pole lay Minnesota's solution: a table of numerical sentencing ranges. The commonly expressed objection to such a scheme is that it is merely mechanical—"sentencing by computer." That is not accurate. Courts may deviate from the grid ranges for aggravating and mitigating circumstances. The decision whether to remain within the grid range or to deviate is a matter of judgment—around which a considerable body of case law has been accumulating in Minnesota.

The grid has, however, another potential disadvantage: the numbers tend to overshadow the underlying principles. Minnesota's guideline-writing agency purportedly chose a rationale emphasizing proportionality similar to that adopted by Sweden's Imprisonment Committee. Under that rationale, the seriousness of the current offense would be the primary determinant of the sentence—and the criminal record would have only a secondary role. When the drafters of Minnesota's guidelines started filling in the numbers on the grid, however, they decided to impose prison sentences on lesser felons having long criminal records. This was done to enhance the political acceptability of the guidelines, but it was inconsistent with the guidelines' rationale and eventually generated a host of practical problems as well. Deciding on the numbers took on a life of its own that made principled choices more difficult to implement.

The Swedish Imprisonment Committee's proposals on choice of sentence consist, instead, of *principles*. The primary factors to be considered in deciding the sentence are set forth, not the actual sentencing outcomes. The proposed statute thus provides that the seriousness of the crime should be given principal emphasis, directs how seriousness ("penal value") should be judged, and gives general directives on the use of imprisonment and of lesser sanctions. The numbers—the actual *quanta* of sentences—are to be evolved later by the courts. This is designed to permit the statute to focus on what is most important: the *policy*. Consider Minnesota's problem of what should be done with offenders who are convicted of crimes of lesser penal value but who have substantial criminal records. The Imprisonment Committee's proposals offer a general policy: since the seriousness of the crime should count most, such offenders ordinarily should not receive the severe sanction of imprisonment. Such a general statute need not specifically address the extraordinary cases: what should happen if the offender's criminal record is extremely long—for instance, the case of the person convicted of a routine theft for the twentieth time. The courts would deal with such extraordinary cases, bearing the statute's general principles in mind. The drafters did not need to distort the general principles to supply a politically "acceptable" solution for the special cases.

Rationale

The proposed statute—as the Imprisonment Committee's report makes clear—rests on the idea of proportionality: that the offender's punishment should be fairly proportionate in its severity with the seriousness of the criminal conduct for which he stands convicted.

Why should punishments comport with the gravity of crimes? As I have addressed the question elsewhere [see Extracts 4.2 and 4.4], let me just summarize. The idea of proportionate punishments presupposes no deep "metaphysical" notions of requital for evil or of guilt and atonement. There is, instead, a simpler explanation. Punishment is a *condemnatory* institution. The difference between a criminal and a civil sanction lies, generally, in the fact that the former levies censure on the actor. Penalties should, in fairness, be allocated consistently with their blaming implications. The more one downgrades the role of the gravity of the criminal conduct in deciding the sentence, the more the censure imputed through punishment will fail to reflect the blameworthiness of the offender's choices.

Swedish neoclassicists tended also to feel that proportionality in punishment might serve general preventive aims. American and some English general preventionists have focused on deterrence, that is, the intimidating effect of punishment—a notion which may offer little support for principles of commensurability and desert. Scandinavian neoclassicists have taken a different tack: their discussion of general prevention has focused on punishment's "moral" and "educational" effects in reinforcing people's inhibitions against criminal behavior. People's sense of moral self-restraint, the authors of *A New Penal System* argued, might well be enhanced if they are treated as responsible for their conduct, and are sanctioned in a proportionate manner that reflects ordinary offenders' own sense of justice.

Penal Value

How, then, should proportionate sentences be determined? The proposal's central concept is that of a crime's penal value, and the draft begins with a general definition: "The penal value (*straffvärde*) of a crime is determined by its seriousness." To determine a crime's seriousness, the statute goes on to state, special regard should be given to (1) the harmfulness of the conduct and (2) the personal culpability of the actor. This definition—of seriousness in terms of the conduct's harm and culpability—is standard in the recent literature on desert.

Harm

That harm is an important element in a crime's seriousness should be obvious. Murder is more serious than assault because the harm characteristic of such conduct is greater: death instead of injury or attempted injury. Harm has always been important in determining the statutory penalty scales—which is why the legal maximum and minimum for murder are so much higher than those for assault. What the proposed law would do is to direct the judge to give more careful consideration to the conduct's harmfulness *within* the applicable scale: that is, to try to distinguish among types of assaults in terms of the degree of actual or potential injuriousness.

Giving harm this central role should stimulate the development of more sophisticated doctrines on how to assess harm. A simple criterion would be that of violence: crimes are to be deemed more injurious, as the extent of physical injury they visit or threaten increases. But this would not suffice: a variety of seemingly quite serious offenses, such as major economic crimes, are not crimes of violence. [An attempt to develop a fuller theory for grading harm is to be found in Extract 4.5 above.]

Culpability

It is a peculiarity of the Swedish language that the word "culpability" does not exist. Hence the drafters had to resort to the more old-fashioned term "guilt." While the word "guilt" may for some readers evoke theological connotations, those are *not* intended. When the draft speaks of "the offender's guilt manifested in the conduct," it is *not* referring to an elusive evil state in the criminal's soul which the conduct reflects. The draft is referring, instead, to what in English would be denoted by the more neutral word culpability: the degree of intent, recklessness, or negligence involved, the presence of partial excuses, and so forth.

Existing substantive law can thus provide some guidance in interpreting the culpability concept. Consider the role of intent. The law relies already upon the degree of intentionality, recklessness, or negligence of the conduct in fixing the statutory *maxima* and *minima*. The difficulty has been that, within these statutory ranges, the courts have not had the incentive to accord such distinctions much weight. By explicitly emphasizing culpability, the law would call upon the courts to gauge the individual sentence more carefully according to the degree of personal fault involved.

Swedish substantive law has also had elaborate doctrines of excuse—but the sentencing analogue, of partial excuse, has been given less attention. The draft's provisions on culpability would require this attention to be given. Here, the courts will also be given assistance by the draft's special provisions on mitigating circumstances. Cases where the actor's mental condition makes him less than normally culpable are explicitly addressed. Provocation is extended beyond the law of homicide, to become a possible mitigating circumstance for any charge.

Criteria for Choice of Sanctions

The proposal sets forth, for the first time in Swedish law, criteria for imprisonment. These criteria indicate when imprisonment ordinarily is to be imposed, in preference to the lesser sanctions of probation or conditional sentence. The criteria—when read together with the draft's other provisions—prescribe imprisonment in two main kinds of cases. The first is where the crime of conviction is serious: in the words of the draft, where it has "considerable penal value." The courts will have to assess which crimes thus qualify as serious, but crimes of violence such as armed robbery presumably would be included, as would major economic offenses. Those convicted of such crimes could expect to be imprisoned, unless they were able to establish mitigating circumstances indicating reduced culpability for the crime. The fact that the defendant was a first offender would *not* justify withholding imprisonment. The rationale is plain enough. If punishment is to reflect the gravity of the conduct, then the system's most severe type of sanction, imprisonment, becomes appropriate for the worst conduct.

The second type of case where imprisonment would be invoked concerns the criminal record. The Committee's proposals generally attempt to restrict the role of the prior record: serious offenders would be confined even if not previously convicted, and lesser offenders would be given noncustodial sanctions even if recidivists. However, the prior record would continue to play a role with respect to offenses in the middle range of seriousness, such as, perhaps, burglary. Offenders convicted of such crimes would be imprisoned only after having accumulated a significant criminal record.

The draft contains parallel provisions on the use of noncustodial penalties. The fine would continue to be the sanction most extensively utilized. It would be the sanction of choice for crimes of low penal value. It would also be so for crimes of intermediate penal value except where the defendant's prior criminal record was extensive. The more substantial fines would be day fines, scaled according to the offender's income [see also Extracts 6.3 and 6.4].

Between the fine, below, and actual imprisonment, above, would be the two other alternatives—conditional sentence and probation. To ensure that these sanctions are more onerous than a fine alone, they could be supplemented by monetary penalties.

Supplementary Principles

A few other provisions of the proposed statute are worth noting:

1. The draft contains a list of aggravating and mitigating circumstances, as noted already. These are generally desert-related—concerning increased or decreased harm or culpability of the conduct.
2. The draft calls also for reduced sanctions when special circumstances make the penalty uncharacteristically onerous. Ill health or advanced age are included. So, more controversially, are situations where specially adverse employment consequences are involved. The rationale still is one of proportionality—these questions bear (albeit indirectly) on the severity of the sanction. The employment provision may present problems of implementation, however, since punishment can so readily have employment consequences.
3. The draft authorizes deterrent penalties (in excess of what the conduct's penal value would indicate) for certain crimes, such as drinking and driving. This authorization, however, is restricted to conduct which the Swedish Parliament has found (1) to have unusually harmful consequences and (2) to be more than usually amenable to deterrence. The imposition of such sanctions is treated as a departure from the normal standards, for which a special burden of justification must be met.[2]

These supplemental principles would permit the court to address, in sophisticated fashion, a variety of issues that have long been of concern to courts in other countries. Only now, the applicable principles would be spelled out, and would reflect a consistent set of purposes. Mitigation of sentence, for example, would no longer have to be treated ad hoc. Instead, the courts would have statutory guidance in developing coherent doctrines of extenuation.

Notes

1. Brottsförebyggande Rådet, *Nytt Straffsystem: Ideer och Förslag* (1977). For English summary, National Swedish Council for Crime Prevention: *A New Penal System: Ideas and Proposals* (1978).
2. For discussion of such hybrid systems, see Extract 4.7 by Paul Robinson.

5.4(b) The Details of the New Law

Andrew von Hirsch
Nils Jareborg

The proposed Swedish law, with certain charges, was enacted in June 1988. The statute consists of two main parts. Chapter 29 addresses "punishments." In Swedish legal tradition, only two sanctions are termed "punishments": fines and imprisonment. Where an offender qualifies for a fine, only the provisions of this chapter apply. If the case is somewhat more serious and a fine alone is not appropriate, then the reader must turn also to the next chapter, chapter 30. This chapter addresses the choice between (1) actual imprisonment and (2) substitutes for imprisonment—viz., conditional sentence or probation.

The statute thus creates three graded levels of sanction. The lower level is the fine—which includes day fines levied as a proportion of income [see also Extract 6.3]. The next level is conditional sentence or probation—which may be supplemented by monetary penalties. The highest level is incarceration in a penal institution.

The distinctions are significant, because the statute becomes confusing when they are overlooked. There are, for example, *two* provisions governing prior criminal record. Chapter 29, § 4, addresses how prior record affects the choice between fines and imprisonment and how it affects the

From Andrew von Hirsch and Nils Jareborg, "Sweden's Sentencing Statute Enacted," *Criminal Law Review* 275 (1989). Excerpted and reprinted by permission.

amount of fines or imprisonment. Chapter 30, § 4, governs how prior record affects the choice between probation or conditional sentence and actual imprisonment.

Swedish legal tradition permits (indeed, requires) the courts to consult legislative history in interpreting a statute. The statute, therefore, needs to be read in the light of the report of the Committee on Imprisonment, and of the Ministry of Justice's report accompanying submission of the bill. Those texts clarify certain language that may appear ambiguous on the statute's face:

1. *Reasons for Imprisonment* (chap. 30, § 4). This section addresses the choice between imprisonment and its substitute sanctions, probation and conditional sanction. It has applicability, therefore, only to the higher-ranking offenses—for which fines would not be the sanction of choice. For these crimes, according to the section's second paragraph, imprisonment may be invoked in three kinds of situations. The first is where the crime has a high penal value—that is, is quite serious—irrespective of whether the offender has a record. The second is where the penal value (seriousness) is of the upper-middle range (that is, high enough to preclude a fine alone) and the person has a significant criminal record. The third (referred to by the "nature of the criminality" clause) is a *restricted* authorization for deterrent penalties for certain crimes—provided there has been a special parliamentary finding of the appropriateness of such sanctions—the main instance being drinking and driving.

2. *Predicted Risk* (chap. 30, § 7). The statute generally rules out predictive sentencing: proportionality is sacrificed when those defendants who seem good risks are given substantially less punishment than equally culpable offenders who seem bad risks. The objection diminishes, however, when prediction is used to change the character of the penalty but not its severity by much. This provision thus allows the sentencing judge, when choosing between a conditional sentence and probation, to opt for conditional sentence—if the offender appears unlikely to offend again. Probation, with its supervision of the offender, may be unnecessary for low-risk offenders—and is not much more severe than a conditional sentence. However, this provision is *not* intended to permit the court to substitute conditional sentence for imprisonment on predictive grounds, as those sanctions differ so greatly in their severity.

Changes in the Final Version of the Law

The law, as proposed by the Ministry of Justice and enacted by the Swedish Parliament, contains certain changes from the recommendations of the

Committee on Imprisonment [described in Extract 5.4(a)]. However, those changes are of limited scope.

1. *Definition of "Penal Value"* (chap. 29, § 1). The seriousness of a crime depends on the harmfulness (or risk of harm) of the conduct and the culpability of the actor. The Swedish language lacks the term "culpability," so the Committee on Imprisonment used the old-fashioned term "guilt." That term's connotations evoked objections, so the law has substituted, "What the accused realized or should have realized . . . and the intentions and motives of the accused." However, no substantive change is intended, and the idea remains what is denoted in English by "culpability."

2. *Prior Record* (chap. 29, § 4). The Committee on Imprisonment proposed narrow restrictions on considering the criminal record. For upper-middle level crimes, as noted, a criminal record would be grounds for invoking actual imprisonment, instead of conditional sentence or probation. It would also affect the severity of fines. However, the record could not be used to affect the duration of imprisonment. The Ministry's proposals, and the statute as enacted, have relaxed this latter restriction.

3. *Rehabilitation* (chap. 30, § 9). The Committee on Imprisonment's draft authorized reduction of sentence in situations where "through the offender's own efforts, a considerable improvement has occurred in his personal and social situation that bears on his criminality." The intention, apparently, was to qualify the statute's general emphasis on proportionality, in order to permit treatment-based sentences in the most plausible and sympathetic-seeming kind of case, viz., where the change was wrought by the efforts of the offender himself or herself. The enacted version eliminates the reference to the offender's own efforts. The legislative history, however, makes clear that any departures from the statute's proportionality requirements on rehabilitative grounds should be quite sparingly invoked.

The Statute

The text of the statute is as follows:

Chapter 1 *On Crimes and Sanctions*

. . .

§ 3

In this code, sanctions for crime are the punishments of fine and imprisonment, as well as conditional sentence, probation, and commitment to special care.

. . .

§ 5
Imprisonment is to be regarded as a more severe punishment than a fine.
The relation between imprisonment and conditional sentence and probation is regulated in chapter 30, § 1.

§ 6
No one may be sentenced to a sanction for a crime he committed before he reached fifteen years of age.
. . .

Chapter 29 *On the Measurement of Punishment and Remission of Sanctions*

§ 1
The punishment shall be imposed within the statutory limits according to the penal value of the crime or crimes, and the interest of uniformity in sentencing shall be taken into consideration.
The penal value is determined with special regard to the harm, offense, or risk which the conduct involved, what the accused realized or should have realized about it, and the intentions and motives of the accused.

§ 2
Apart from circumstances specific to particular types of crime, the following circumstances, especially, shall be deemed to enhance the penal value:
1. whether the accused intended that the criminal conduct should have considerably worse consequences than it in fact had,
2. whether the accused has shown a special degree of indifference to the conduct's adverse consequences,
3. whether the accused made use of the victim's vulnerable position, or his other special difficulties in protecting himself,
4. whether the accused grossly abused his rank or position or grossly abused a special trust,
5. whether the accused induced another person to participate in the deed through force, deceit, or abuse of the latter's youthfulness, lack of understanding, or dependent position, or
6. whether the criminal conduct was part of a criminal activity that was especially carefully planned, or that was executed on an especially large scale and in which the accused played an important role.

§ 3
Apart from what is elsewhere specifically prescribed, the following circumstances, especially, shall be deemed to diminish the penal value:

1. whether the crime was elicited by another's grossly offensive behavior,
2. whether the accused, because of mental abnormality or strong emotional inducement or other cause, had a reduced capacity to control his behavior,
3. whether the accused's conduct was connected with his manifest lack of development, experience, or capacity for judgment, or
4. whether strong human compassion led to the crime.

The court may sentence below the statutory minimum when the penal value obviously calls for it.

§ 4

Apart from the penal value, the court shall, in measuring the punishment, to a reasonable extent take the accused's previous criminality into account, but only if this has not been appropriately done in the choice of sanction [see chap. 30, § 4] or revocation of parole [see chap. 34, § 4]. In such cases, the extent of the previous criminality and the time that has passed between the crimes shall be especially considered, as well as whether the previous and the new criminality is similar, or whether the criminality in both cases is especially serious.

§ 5

In determining the punishment, the court shall to a reasonable extent, apart from the penal value, consider

1. whether the accused as a consequence of the crime has suffered serious bodily harm,
2. whether the accused according to his ability has tried to prevent, or repair, or mitigate the harmful consequences of the crime,
3. whether the accused voluntarily gave himself up,
4. whether the accused is, to his detriment, expelled from the country in consequence of the crime,
5. whether the accused as a consequence of the crime has experienced or is likely to experience discharge from employment or other disability or extraordinary difficulty in the performance of his work or trade,
6. whether a punishment imposed according to the crime's penal value would affect the accused unreasonably severely, due to advanced age or bad health,
7. whether, considering the nature of the crime, an unusually long time has elapsed since the commission of the crime, or
8. whether there are other circumstances that call for a lesser punishment than the penal value indicates.

If, in such cases, special reasons so indicate, the punishment may be reduced below the statutory minimum.

§ 6
The punishment is to be remitted entirely when, with regard to circumstances of the kind mentioned in § 5, imposition of a sanction is manifestly unreasonable.

§ 7
If someone has committed a crime before the age of twenty-one, his youth shall be considered separately in the determination of the punishment, and the statutory minimum may be disregarded.

Life imprisonment is never to be imposed in such cases.

Chapter 30 *On the Choice of Sanctions*

§ 1
In choosing sanctions, imprisonment is considered as more severe than conditional sentence and probation.

Provisions on the use of commitment to special care are set forth in another chapter.

§ 2
Unless otherwise provided, no one is to receive more than one sanction for the same crime.

§ 3
Unless otherwise provided, someone convicted of more than one crime is to be given one sanction.

If there are special reasons, however, the court may combine a fine for some criminal conduct with another sanction for other conduct, or combine imprisonment for some conduct with conditional sentence or probation for other conduct.

§ 4
In choosing the sanction, the court shall especially pay heed to circumstances that suggest a less severe sanction than imprisonment. In so doing, the court shall consider circumstances referred to in chapter 29, § 5.

As a reason for imprisonment the court may consider, besides the penal value and the nature of the criminality, the accused's previous criminality.

§ 5
For a crime committed by someone before the age of eighteen, imprisonment may be imposed only if there are extraordinary reasons.

For a crime committed by someone between the age of eighteen and the age of twenty-one, imprisonment may be imposed only if there are, with respect to the penal value of the crime or other grounds, special reasons.

§ 6
For a crime committed by someone under the influence of mental disease, mental deficiency, or other mental abnormality of such a substantial nature as to be comparable to mental disease, the court may only impose commitment to special care, a fine, or probation.

If no such commitment or sanction should be imposed, the accused shall be free from sanction.

§ 7
In choosing sanction, the court shall consider, as a reason for conditional sentence, whether there is no special reason to fear that the accused will relapse in criminal conduct.

§ 8
Conditional sentence shall be combined with day fines, unless a fine would be unduly harsh, considering the other consequences of the crime, or there are other special reasons that militate against imposition of a fine.

§ 9
In choosing sanction, the court shall consider, as a reason for probation, whether there is reason to suppose that such sanction can contribute to the accused's not committing crimes in the future.

As special reasons for probation the court may consider

1. whether a considerable improvement has occurred in the accused's personal or social situation that bears upon his criminality,
2. whether the accused is being treated for abuse or other condition that bears upon his criminality, or
3. whether abuse of addictive substances, or other special condition that calls for care or other treatment, to a considerable degree explains the criminal conduct and the accused has declared himself willing to undergo adequate treatment, in accordance with an individual plan that can be arranged in connection with the execution of the sentence.

§ 10
In judging whether probation should be combined with day fines, the court shall consider whether this is called for with regard to the penal value or nature of the criminal conduct or the accused's previous criminality.

§ 11
Probation may be combined with imprisonment only if it is unavoidably called for, with regard to the penal value of the criminal conduct or the accused's previous criminality.

. . .

Chapter 34 *Certain Provisions concerning Concurrence of Crimes and Change of Sanction*

. . .

§ 4

. . .

In judging whether parole should be revoked and in deciding on duration of reconfinement on revocation, it shall be considered whether the previous criminality and the new criminality are similar, whether the criminality in both cases is serious, and whether the new criminality is more or less serious than the previous criminality. In addition, the time that has passed between the crimes shall be considered.

. . .

5.5
Plea Bargaining and Enforcement of Sentencing Guidelines

Michael Tonry
John C. Coffee, Jr.

The recent debate over sentencing reform has led to a broad range of proposals and innovations, including plea-bargaining bans and rules, parole abolition and guidelines, mandatory sentence laws, and various forms of sentencing guidelines and presumptive sentencing statutes. Our aim here is to consider the problem of eliciting compliance with major changes in substantive sentencing policies, using presumptive sentencing guidelines for illustrative purposes. By presumptive guidelines we mean sentencing guidelines that were developed by a specialized rule-making agency and that have some degree of formal legal authority.

Presumptive sentencing guidelines can take a variety of forms. In this chapter we assume the existence of relatively detailed guidelines like Minnesota's, although the issues considered are general and—in attenuated form—will bedevil any presumptive guideline system.

A variety of interrelated questions arise concerning the impact of presumptive guidelines on sentencing outcomes and official behavior. Can such guidelines be enforced? How will guidelines affect plea bargaining? To

---

From Michael Tonry and John C. Coffee, Jr., "Hard Choices: Critical Tradeoffs in the Implementation of Sentencing Reform through Guidelines," in Michael Tonry and Franklin E. Zimring, eds., *Reform and Punishment: Essays on Criminal Sentencing* (Chicago: University of Chicago Press, 1983). This essay was republished, with some alterations, in Andrew von Hirsch, Kay A. Knapp, and Michael Tonry, *The Sentencing Commission and Its Guidelines* (Boston: Northeastern University Press, 1987), ch. 9, and that is the version from which the present selection is drawn. Reprinted by permission.

what extent will they shift discretion from the sentencing judge to the prosecutor, and will this mean increased pressure on the defendant to plead guilty?

Once the issues of enforcement and compliance are candidly faced, complexity quickly arises. The design of any structure for dispositional decision making after conviction is necessarily confronted by a variety of ethically troubling trade-offs between civil libertarian values and pursuit of various sentencing-reform goals. In particular, three distinct clusters of problems confound any proposal for reform.

Substance and Illusion in Plea Bargaining

The goal of sentencing equity—provisionally defined as the treatment of "like cases alike"—is in direct conflict with every criminal defendant's desire to secure favorable treatment. Under the most prevalent form of plea bargaining—namely, "charge bargaining"—the defendant agrees to plead guilty to a lesser included charge, or to fewer than all of the charges against him. The effect of this plea concession is uncertain. Sometimes it is small because the court continues to sentence the defendant on the basis of the original or "real" offense. At other times the court may reward the defendant with leniency over and above that conferred by the prosecutor in his plea concession. Because of this inherent uncertainty, a problem arises: it seems unfair that the defendant should surrender constitutional rights (and, in some cases, the real possibility of acquittal) for illusory consideration. Yet if the benefits of the plea were made concrete and overt by means of a "discount" or "charge reduction guidelines," this would create a sentencing penalty for not pleading guilty and arguably chill the willingness of future defendants to go to trial. A hard choice is thus inevitable, and any proposal for enforcing sentencing guidelines must be evaluated in light of this trade-off between possible unfairness and possible coercion.

Adaptive Responses and Enforcement

Sentencing reforms by definition are attempts to change sentencing outcomes from what they otherwise would have been. External interventions (whether by the legislature or by a sentencing commission) are likely to encounter serious organizational resistance. A major difference in perspective exists between those operating at the abstract level of sentencing-policy formulation and those participating at the adversarial level of individual sentencing hearings. Draftsmen, whatever their philosophical premises, are likely to give primary attention to the grading of offense severity and the achievement of reasonable proportionality between sentences for offenses of differing gravity. Yet this concern with proportionality and the overall coherence of sentencing outcomes is substantially lost once one shifts to the viewpoint of the individual participants. The attention of those in the courtroom is always focused on the individual case before them—the general goal of sentencing equity has no organizational champion to take up arms on its behalf. Aggressive counsel are likely to view sentencing standards as simply the going tariff off which they expect to receive a substantial discount. Prosecutors do not have comparably strong interests in resisting discounts. Conventional wisdom suggests that prosecutors often define their professional success in terms of conviction rates, not sentence severity. Moreover, they often share the defense counsel's interest in the expeditious disposition of the cases and can sympathize with such counsel's need to win something for his client and thereby his fee.

A possibility more subversive for externally imposed reforms is that the participants may tacitly share a common set of sentencing criteria that guides their negotiations. Some social scientists view the sentencing decision as the product of a "work group' of regularly interacting professionals who accept common criteria for the determination of sentences. In this view, the judge is neither the lone decision maker nor the powerless ratifier of plea agreements but an influential member of the group. Much in the work-group perspective can be questioned, but it again suggests that sentencing reforms—however well designed in principle—could produce little net change without some means of enforcement that can, when necessary, restrict the powers of the work group.

Early experience with legislative reform of sentencing in California and elsewhere, while uneven, suggests that reform has produced fewer changes than its proponents had expected. Even clearer is the experience with "voluntary" guidelines adopted by sentencing judges in Denver, Philadelphia, and Chicago and in Maryland and Florida; the reductions in sentencing variance appear to have been negligible.[1] This evidence need not be read to confirm the pessimistic hypothesis that nothing works and that reform is always futile.

Minnesota's and Washington's experiences with presumptive sentencing guidelines have been different; judges and lawyers appear in general to have cooperated with guidelines that significantly altered prior sentencing practices.[2] Still, the experience outside these states underscores the likelihood of adaptive responses by those participants who do not desire to have their behavior changed. Sentencing guidelines are particularly vulnerable to this problem because they necessarily use information which is manipulable. Manipulation can be most easily accomplished by plea bargaining for a charge reduction that reduces the likely sentence to one that the defendant will accept. Or, if this is formally prohibited, the parties can agree (tacitly or otherwise) to ignore factors that the guidelines deem significant (for example, whether the defendant was armed). To the extent that such practices can be attributed to the work group's willingness to reward the defendant for pleading guilty, the prosecutor has little incentive to contest sentencing decisions in which he has participated willingly. In short, the problem of enforcement dovetails with the problem of incentive, and for those whose objective is the reduction of unwarranted disparity, the critical issue becomes how to find or create a participant in the process who has as strong an interest in achieving sentencing equity as do the existing players in encouraging expeditious resolutions through pleas of guilty.

Judicial and Prosecutorial Discretion: The Trade-off

Most recent efforts at sentencing reform have been frankly designed to confine judicial discretion. In so doing, they risk reallocating discretion in ways that are unintended and possibly perversely counterproductive. If, as some have argued, the movement toward determinate sentencing shifts power from the judge and the parole board to the prosecutor, then sophisticated policy planning must predict the likely impact of the shift and, perhaps, find some means for offsetting the prosecutor's increased powers.

To this point, we have sketched distinct scenarios for the frustration of sentencing reform. These are competing scenarios, because they involve inconsistent premises. The sentencing process cannot be simultaneously bureaucratic and adversarial. The judge cannot be both the neutral referee and the busy broker of mutually acceptable plea bargains. Similarly, if sentencing decisions result from collegial processes within work groups, then the danger that the prosecutor will use the enhanced discretion available in established sentencing standards to coerce guilty pleas seems less serious than if the prosecutor had a substantially different view of the appropriate sentence from that of the other participants. We need not resolve which of these scenarios most accurately characterizes sentencing. A diversity of legal cultures exists within the United States and within most states and must be anticipated by the intelligent policy planner.

We now turn to the possible options by which the guidelines' policy can be enforced. We focus on how presumptive guidelines affect the defendant's decision whether to plead guilty; consider proposals that are designed to regulate plea bargaining; and, finally, examine appellate review and internal administrative procedures for securing greater compliance. In each case, our intent is not to present an optimal policy, prepackaged and ready for implementation, but to outline choices. The stance we have adopted—that of impartial policy analysts—is somewhat contrived. The present writers differ—in some cases vigorously—about the desirability and practicability of various of the policy choices discussed in this chapter. Many of these choices, however, are entrenched in the current reform agendas, and it is precisely because of their difficulty and controversy that we attempt to open them to view here.

The Effect of Sentencing Guidelines on Plea Bargaining: Who Wins? Who Loses? What Happens Next?

Other things being equal, sentencing guidelines can be expected to change the prevalent form of plea bargaining from charge bargaining to, in effect, sentence bargaining. Today, considerable uncertainty confronts the defendant offered a charge concession. Will the judge still sentence him on the basis of the real offense (say, armed robbery) instead of the offense of conviction (robbery)? Or, will the judge assign a sentence below even the median sentence for robbery to reward the plea of guilty? Presumptive guidelines, however, inherently reduce this uncertainty by specifying the range of sentences applicable to persons convicted of robbery and enhance the value of the charge concession offered by the prosecutor.

This analysis is, however, overly simple. Another possibility is that sentencing guidelines will reduce prosecutorial leverage by mitigating the potential penalty that he can threaten if the defendant goes to trial. In terms of the allocation of sentencing authority, the discretion gained by the prosecutor under a system of presumptive sentencing guidelines may be substantially less than that lost by the court. Thus, although discretion has been shifted from the judge to the prosecutor, it need not mean that the overall attempt to constrain sentencing behavior has not had substantial success. In principle, the maximum penalty that the court and the prosecutor together can bring to bear on the recalcitrant defendant who refuses to plead guilty may well be materially reduced under a guideline system, even though the prosecutor has gained increased control over the sentencing process. For example, before the Minnesota guidelines took effect, a robbery defendant who went to trial risked a sentence as long as twenty-five years. Under the present guidelines, however, these high statutory ceilings no longer have much relevance because the guidelines radically compress the defendant's real exposure to incarceration. But, as a necessary corollary, the effect of any charge reduction that the prosecutor can typically offer is thereby greatly reduced. Indeed, a charge reduction downward of one seriousness level will seldom reduce the applicable guideline range by more than a year, and often the reduction will be even less. Consequently, we face again an unsettling trade-off: although the prosecutor is a more biased decision maker than the judge, and sentencing guidelines do shift some power to him, the more important variable may be not the relative bias of the decision maker but rather the aggregate pressure on the defendant to plead guilty.

Better insight into this trade-off is gained by focusing on the psychology of the criminal defendant. Concern that plea bargaining under presumptive sentencing guidelines may unduly pressure defendants to plead guilty is implicitly based on the belief that the defendant compares the expected punishment cost of pleading guilty with that of going to trial and opts for the lesser expected cost. But this is not necessarily what the defendant does. At least two other possibilities exist: the defendant may be risk-averse and instead focus on the worst possible outcome (that is, the maximum sentence); or he may be a risk preferrer and focus on the best possible outcome (that is, the minimum sentence or acquittal). There are no compelling reasons to believe that defendants are risk-neutral and simply compare the two expected outcomes.

In fact, under conditions of uncertainty, few of us appear to be risk-neutral. Some of us are risk-averse: when faced with a risk of a substantial loss, we will avoid it even if this means accepting an alternative having a lower expected value. For example, although in theory the certainty of a one-year sentence and the 10 percent prospect of a ten-year sentence are equal (since they have the same discounted value of one year), the risk-averse defendant will opt for the certain one-year sentence (and possibly accept a two- or three-year sentence) before risking the ten-year sentence. For most of us, some risks—such as that of a death sentence or of losing at Russian roulette—are simply unacceptable even if the risk involved is remote; our minds have little capacity to discount them by their limited possibility of occurrence, and so their expected value becomes disproportionately large. Conversely, others may be risk preferrers; rather than focus on the worst possible outcome, such an individual gives disproportionate attention to the best possible outcome (here, acquittal). If so, this possibility may lead a defendant to go to trial, even though a purely neutral evaluation of the relative risks suggests that pleading guilty is the rational course. Either way, the discounting process is skewed by the defendant's subjective evaluation of the penalties.

Most economists who have studied deterrence have tended to assume that the defendant will behave in a risk-averse manner; that is, he will be more deterred by a high potential penalty coupled with a low probability of imposition than by a low penalty coupled with a high probability of imposition.[3] While criminologists have disagreed strongly, arguing that few individuals give much weight to severe sanctions that are only remotely possible and that therefore the probability of apprehension is the more critical variable,[4] the context of plea bargaining is very different from that of deterrence research in general; here, the criminal is already apprehended and the approaching trial date tends, in Dr. Johnson's phrase, "to concentrate the mind wonderfully." The risk of a severe sentence cannot be ignored or disdained in the same manner that the frequently remote possibility of apprehension can be disdained by the competent burglar. Nor does the defendant have the same control over his fate as does the resourceful criminal. His choices are limited: to bargain or not to bargain. Thus, the premise of risk aversion rests on a stronger foundation within this special context of plea bargaining, which leads to the conclusion that the prosecutor can obtain greater coercive pressure over the defendant by threatening the possibility of a severe sentence than by offering a virtually certain but more modest discount off the normal sentence for the crime.

Accordingly, because presumptive guidelines tend to prevent extreme sentences, they should logically be expected to reduce the pressure on the risk-averse defendant to surrender a substantial possibility of acquittal. The trade-off has two elements: presumptive sentencing guidelines may lead a defendant who has little prospect of acquittal to plead guilty (because they make a discount off the mean sentence more certain), but by the same token they protect the risk-averse defendant with a reasonable chance of acquittal from his inability to resist prosecutorial pressure in the form of a threatened lengthy sentence for failing to plead guilty. So viewed, the charge concession arguably becomes only a small bribe that society pays the clearly convictable defendant to surrender the nuisance value that his attorney can create on his behalf, but it is inadequate to compensate the defendant who has a serious chance of acquittal. Thus, it might be argued, guidelines only expedite results; they do not reverse outcomes from the state of affairs that would exist in a world without plea bargaining.

Attractive and benign as such a policy conclusion may seem, we are hesitant to endorse it without considerable qualification. Basically, our reservations stem from the ambiguity inherent in the concept of risk aversion. Much used as the concept is, it is simply not clear what it means. Does it mean only that some severe risks are disproportionately weighted by the defendant? Or, does it mean there is a boundary line beyond which any risk is wholly unacceptable, so that all the prosecutor has to do is credibly threaten a penalty in excess of this level in order to secure a guilty plea to a lesser charge? If the latter, much depends on where this boundary line is located. This idea comes into clearer focus if we suppose that for a hypothetical defendant the boundary line is at the in-out threshold between incarceration and probation; here, introduction of presumptive guidelines may mean that the defendant can escape what is for him the unacceptable risk of incarceration only by pleading guilty to a lesser charge for which probation is the presumptive disposition. Even if our hypothetical defendant had a probability of acquittal, it would be of little importance if we postulate that the defendant will do anything to avoid incarceration. In short, to the extent that the presumptive guideline ranges for the higher and lower offenses straddle the in-out watershed and this line looms disproportionately large to the defendant, concern for prosecutorial overreaching under presumptive guidelines seems to be on much stronger ground. Now the prosecutor has gained an ability to escalate the penalty so as to cross the critical threshold at which the defendant's resistance crumbles.

One other possible type of defendant must be considered: the risk preferrer. The risk preferrer is, in theory, the mirror image of the risk averter; he would prefer a 10 percent probability of $100 to the certainty of $10. Although the tendency in the economic literature is to see such a person as a rare phenomenon, a recurrent observation about plea bargaining is that some defendants who have virtually no chance of acquittal still steadfastly resist their own attorney's advice to plead guilty and insist that they will be acquitted. The impact of sentencing guidelines may often encourage such a defendant to go to trial. Why? Put simply, the introduction of sentencing guidelines is likely to reduce the court's ability (or willingness) to impose a nonincarcerative sentence. Although guidelines need not preclude such a possibility, they do reduce the variance in sentencing outcomes for any offense, at least marginally, and thus move the sentencing court in the direction of the mean sentence. Thus, by reducing the possibility of probation following a conviction for a number of offense categories, they lead the gambler to go to trial as the only means of obtaining the best possible outcome. This conclusion, however, is again subject to the rebuttal that if the guideline for the lesser-included charge is probation, the pure risk preferrer may see this as the best possible outcome and will not seek acquittal.

Who, then, loses under presumptive sentencing guidelines? One loser would seem to be the defendant with a substantial possibility of acquittal who, in the absence of such guidelines, could have negotiated a very substantial reduction in sentence because of the weakness of the prosecutor's case. The only hope for defendants who are so risk-averse that they will not go to trial (or cannot accept the public embarrassment incident thereto or cannot afford the costs of private counsel for a trial) is to negotiate the best possible bargain, and sentencing guidelines tend to reduce the maximum bargain obtainable. Where once prosecutors could have quietly indicated to the court their willingness to encourage a low sentence, the impact of such a signal is at least marginally diminished by the existence of presumptive guidelines that compress the sentencing scale. In short, guidelines encourage the defendant to go to trial where there is a real prospect of acquittal by denying the prosecution the ability to pay the price that the plea is worth in such a case; denied the fair value of the plea, the defendant is forced to make an all-or-nothing choice between trial or an "unfairly" low discount for a plea.

For the especially timid defendant for whom any prospect of imprisonment is unacceptable, guidelines may force a plea of guilty if the charge discount straddles the in-out watershed, even though the defendant would probably have been acquitted at trial. Whether such a defendant should, however, be classified as a loser is more questionable. Although a real prospect of acquittal has been sacrificed, the defendant has achieved his primary end. He has avoided the risk of imprisonment to which he would clearly be exposed in a legal system that did not tolerate plea bargaining. The clearest loser in such a case is once again the goal of sentencing equity, since like cases are not being treated alike.

The reduction in sentencing variance, which presumptive guidelines logically entail, thus poses an unavoidable trade-off: at the same time as it reduces pressure on risk-averse defendants who wish to go to trial but fear a sentence near the maximum, it deprives other defendants of the opportunity to plead guilty in return for a substantial discount.

Given the different impact of guidelines on these different classes of defendants, the next question is obvious: whose interests should the law seek to protect? On a normative level, these two classes *deserve* very different constitutional and jurisprudential protection. From a constitutional perspective, protection of the innocent defendant from the extortionate leverage that plea bargaining can produce deserves primacy among the multiple goals and values that have constitutional recognition. The defendant has a right to be convicted based only upon the level of certainty expressed by the constitutional standard of "proof beyond a reasonable doubt." The defendant has no similar right to trade doubt or nuisance value for a specific sentencing discount. To the extent that a conflict exists, the Constitution must be read to protect the risk-averse defendant, not the bargain hunter. Even if the introduction of presumptive guidelines did harm risk-neutral and risk-preferring defendants more than it aided risk-averse ones, we would argue that only the latter class has a constitutionally or jurisprudentially cognizable entitlement.

The skeptical reader may well have asked by now if there is any empirical corroboration for the hypotheses generated by the preceding analyses. At present, all we can say is that the relevant data are not inconsistent with our analyses.

Findings of the Minnesota self-evaluation seem corroborative of our earlier analyses.[5] Although the percentage of defendants going to trial declined somewhat after the introduction of guidelines, from 5 percent of cases in 1978 to 4 percent among the first 5,500 cases sentenced under the guidelines, these figures camouflage an interesting shift: trial rates fell by half for the five lowest offense-severity levels and nearly doubled for the five highest. These changes might suggest that persons charged with low-severity offenses that are presumptive "outs" became more likely under guidelines to plead guilty in order to receive a nearly certain nonincarcerative sentence rather than risk conviction for a more serious charge and be subject to greater judicial unpredictability. Persons charged with more serious crimes may have felt that the guidelines decreased the risk of an aberrantly long sentence; subject to a prison sentence under the guidelines in any event, they may have been prepared to risk a somewhat longer sentence than a charge bargain might have yielded.

A final lesson from Minnesota concerns the use that prosecutors may make of guidelines. Implicit in critiques of enhanced prosecutorial influence under guidelines is the thesis that the prosecutor will use the guidelines to maximize the pressure on each individual defendant to plead guilty. This may be an oversimplification, however. Other ends—including saving time and achieving better allocation of prosecutorial resources—are also pursued by the prosecutor and facilitated by the introduction of guidelines. Presumptive guidelines serve these goals by simplifying the negotiation process. In so doing, they enable the prosecutor to conserve his investment of resources in minor cases and thereby enable him to focus more intensively on major cases involving more serious crimes.

The Minnesota findings are interesting but preliminary and are based on aggregate data that can tell us little about the experience of defendants who are innocent or who have substantial possibilities of acquittal for other reasons. Much more needs to be learned about the effects of presumptive sentencing guidelines on plea negotiations. For now, it remains an open question exactly how presumptive guidelines will affect plea negotiation practices and whether and when increased leverage afforded prosecutors will increase pressure on defendants who have a significant chance of acquittal.

To this point, we have assumed that sentencing reform is likely to elicit adaptive responses by the parties. Planners are not impotent, however, and measures are possible by which to curtail the more likely forms of evasion. Two possibilities stand out for dealing with circumvention of guidelines through plea bargaining. One is "real-offense" sentencing—under which the court makes use of the guideline applicable to the "actual-offense behavior" determined by it to have occurred, rather than the guideline applicable to the offense of conviction. The other is express discounts for a guilty plea.

Real-Offense Sentencing

The topic of real-offense sentencing tends to produce immediate, intense, and sweeping reactions. One side sees it as a blatant attempt to outflank the fundamental constitutional protections accorded to persons accused of crimes; the other sees it as the only realistic and feasible means to offset plea bargaining, reduce the differential between sentences following pleas and sentences following trial (and the pressure to plead guilty), and achieve equity based on real rather than artificial differences among offenders.

The term "real-offense sentencing" is new, but the practice is not. American judges have probably long given considerable weight to the offense behavior described by the prosecutor or by the presentence report, notwithstanding that such behavior was more serious than the charge to which the defendant pled guilty. What is new are proposals for the formalization of this practice. To date, real-offense sentencing has been adopted in some form by the U.S. Parole Commission's guidelines, several states' parole guidelines, the Model Sentencing and Corrections Act, and several local sentencing guideline systems. Although rationales for real-offense sentencing differ in parole guidelines, voluntary sentencing guidelines, and presumptive sentencing guidelines, it is the last application with which we are concerned.

Three criticisms of real-offense sentencing in a prescriptive sentencing system stand out. First, it downgrades the significance of the trial stage, where various constitutional safeguards protect the defendant, and instead postpones critical determinations to the informal and less reliable dispositional stages. Second, it produces illusory plea bargaining, under which the prosecutor implicitly promises the defendant a concession whose value is then diminished at a later stage by the court or parole agency. Third, it is unrealistic in that it permits no concession for a plea of guilty and hence attempts to erase plea bargaining in a single stroke. Each of these contentions has some undeniable force, but each is also misleading unless examined against the backdrop of existing and alternative practices.

[There follows an extended discussion of these issues.]

Guilty-Plea Concessions

Sentencing guidelines highlight the impact of the guilty plea and thus expose one of the secrets of our criminal justice system. A study by Hans Zeisel compares sentence bargains offered to New York City defendants who turned them down with the sentences imposed on those same defendants after trial. The average penalty imposed was 136 percent of the sentence initially offered. The evaluation of Alaska's ban on plea bargaining concluded that conviction at trial rather than by guilty plea increased sentences for violent offenses substantially both before and after the plea-bargaining ban took effect.

Accordingly, there would seem to be two possible immediate reactions if Minnesota-type sentencing guidelines are introduced in a jurisdiction. First, the incentive to plead guilty will be lessened substantially, with resulting dislocation to the criminal justice system (but also with arguably more than compensating gain to the constitutional values underlying the system); or, second, guidelines in the long run will be subverted, as courts and prosecutors find covert methods to reward guilty pleas. The reaction in most jurisdictions would probably fall somewhere between these two poles, but nonetheless it is understandable that various commentators have recommended that an explicit guilty-plea discount be recognized. One proposal specifies that every cell in the guideline grid contain two different guideline sentences or ranges; the first for defendants convicted at trial, the second for those who plead guilty.[6] A second proposal would make the discount somewhat less stark. Schulhofer has recommended that discounts be awarded by shifting the applicable guideline cell by one row so that, for example, a defendant charged with an offense of severity-level six would be given the opportunity to plead guilty and be sentenced under the guidelines applicable to an offense of severity-level five.[7] A third proposal for guilty-plea discounts, one that predates sentencing guidelines, suggests that guilty pleas be rewarded with a standard percentage discount—say 10 percent—from the other applicable sentence.

We do not devote substantial attention here to the mechanics of any guilty-plea discount system. It suffices to say that any such proposal presents significant policy and operational problems. To be palatable even to those not much troubled by the constitutional implications, any such proposal must strike a difficult balance that encourages pleas from the genuinely guilty but does not coerce them from the innocent. For example, an across-the-board two-year discount for guilty pleas might represent too small a concession to induce a guilty plea from a defendant otherwise subject to a ten-year sentence, while it might exert too much influence over a defendant who otherwise would receive a two- to three-year sentence. Whether such a balance can be struck is open to serious question, once one looks closely at existing systems. The critical problem is that the architecture of existing guideline systems seems to place many defendants in a guideline cell that immediately adjoins the in-out line on either side. This means simply that plea bargains that straddle the in-out line are frequently possible, and as noted earlier such bargains are difficult to resist. Minnesota's experience was that roughly three-quarters of the "imprisonable" cases in their construction sample (on which Minnesota's guidelines were based) fell in cells abutting this in-out line. To offer such defendants a discount that means the difference between the probability of imprisonment and the near certainty of freedom may or may not constitute excessive pressure, but it is highly unlikely that the goal of sentencing equity can be realized under such a structure.

A sentencing guideline system that awards an explicit guilty-plea discount can be seen in three very different lights. First, it is an incentive to plead guilty and so disfavors those defendants who go to trial. Second, it is a limitation on the amount of credit that can be given for such a plea; that is, it is as much a ceiling on the permissible reward as a disincentive to profess innocence. Third, it is a form of consumer protection for offenders. Offenders sometimes plead guilty in return for a valueless consideration: as discussed earlier, the difference between the statutory ceilings for most offenses and for their lesser included offenses may be irrelevant, because the likely sentence for either crime is below the lower ceiling; similarly, when collateral counts are dropped, they may not have much impact on the sentence (as when ninety-nine counts of mail fraud, each based on a different use of the mails, are reduced to fifteen). Underlying such one-sided negotiations may be either a conflict of interest between defense counsel and the client (so that the attorney does not explain to the client the limited value of the benefit) or simply self-deception on the part of a clearly guilty defendant, which requires that he be able to tell himself that he got something in return for his admission of guilt.

In contrast to such illusory consideration, a specific sentence discount off the guideline range (whether stated in terms of months, percentages, or a shift in applicable cells) would ensure that the defendant gets something in return. From the common perspective that sees the private criminal-law practitioner as forced to engage in a high-volume operation which prevents him from representing his clients' interests adequately, such a "reform" arguably represents not pressure on the defendant but a truth-in-plea-bargaining act.

Nonetheless, the civil libertarian will see matters differently, and any attempt to grant explicit concessions for a plea of guilty will provoke a constitutional challenge. At present, all that can be said with respect to such a challenge is that such an explicit credit may be constitutional, at least if done with appropriate artfulness. The key case is a 1978 decision, *Corbitt v. New Jersey,* 439 U.S. 212 (1978), in which the Supreme Court upheld a statutory structure that permitted substantially more lenient sentences for defendants who pled guilty than for those who went to trial. Under New Jersey law, a defendant found guilty of first-degree homicide received a life sentence. But, a defendant who pled *non vult* (no contest) was eligible for a substantially lesser sentence. Stephen Schulhofer has argued that the decision means that the Court "would uphold a guideline system providing separate sentencing ranges for contested and uncontested cases, at least if the two ranges overlapped."[8]

The greatest practical difficulty with discounts involves the predictable attempt by defense counsel to win something extra for his client. In an adversarial system of justice, defendants can be expected to bargain off the lower guideline range. If every defendant is entitled to a guilty-plea discount, a determined defense lawyer will insist also on a charge reduction. The result is double counting. Instead of reducing the pressure to plead guilty by limiting the concession to a modest amount, the original evil is compounded. Various techniques must therefore be considered to prevent such a distortion of the intent of the guideline discount system.

One obvious technique for preventing such double discounts takes us back full circle to our earlier focus on real-offense sentencing. Real-offense sentencing systems could potentially cancel the prosecutor's charge concession and thereby prevent double discounts (unless, of course, the prosecutorial concession interposed a statutory ceiling between the offense of conviction and the guideline range for the real offense). At bottom the proper intent of a real-offense system is to transfer discretion over the sentence back to the court from the prosecutor. This problem of double discounts suggests that guilty-plea discounts are highly unsafe at the sentencing stage unless combined with real-offense sentencing. Yet, as noted in the preceding section, the feasibility of real-offense sentencing remains open to very serious question at the sentencing stage.

We have considered methods of structuring guideline systems to anticipate and counter adaptive responses. It is difficult to place much confidence in either real-offense sentencing or guilty-plea discounts as a means for achieving greater sentencing equity at the sentencing stage. Perhaps workable variations of each can be imagined, but a combination of public opposition and legislative indifference seems likely to interfere with their effective implementation. To work, real-offense sentencing requires some enforcement mechanism that must be independent of the sentencing work group if it is to overcome the natural impulse of the parties to use guidelines as only the opening position for further bargaining. Guilty-plea discounts are on even less firm constitutional ground and predictably face even stronger civil libertarian opposition.

Notes

1. See Blumstein, A., et al., *Research on Sentencing: The Search for Reform* (1983) [and now Tonry, M., *Sentencing Reform Impacts* (1987)—Eds.].
2. See von Hirsch, A., Knapp, K., and Tonry, M., *The Sentencing Commission and Its Guidelines* (1987), chs. 2 and 8.
3. For example, see Polinsky, A. M., and Shavell, S., "Contribution and Claim Reduction among Anti-Trust Defendants: an Economic Analysis," 33 *Stanford Law Review* 447 (1981).
4. Blumstein, A., et al., *Deterrence and Incapacitation: Estimating the Effects of Criminal Sanctions on Crime Rates* (1978).
5. Knapp, K., "The Impact of the Minnesota Sentencing Guidelines on Sentencing Practices," 5 *Hamline Law Review* 237 (1982).
6. Gottfredson, D. M., et al., *Guidelines for Parole and Sentencing* (1978).
7. Schulhofer, S., "Due Process of Sentencing," 128 *University of Pennsylvania Law Review* 733 (1980).
8. Ibid.

Suggestions for Further Reading

1. The Development of Structured Sentencing

Frankel, M., *Criminal Sentences: Law without Order* (1972); A. von Hirsch, *Doing Justice* (1976), ch. 12; Twentieth Century Fund, Task Force on Criminal Sentencing, *Fair and Certain Punishment* (1976); Gottfredson, D. M., Wilkins, L. T., and Hoffman, P. B., *Guidelines for Parole and Sentencing* (1978); Forst, M. L. (ed.), *Sentencing Reform: Experiments in Reducing Disparity* (1982); Blumstein, A., et al., *Research on Sentencing: The Search for Reform* (1983); Ashworth, A., "Techniques of Guidance on Sentencing," *Criminal Law Review* 519 (1984); Martin, S. E., "Interests and Politics in Sentencing Reform: The Development of Sentencing Guidelines in Minnesota and Pennsylvania," 29 *Villanova Law Review* 21 (1984); Shane-Dubow, S., Brown, A. P., and Olsen, E., *Sentencing Reform in the United States: History, Content, and Effects* (1985); von Hirsch, A., "Principles for Choosing Sanctions: Sweden's Proposed Sentencing Statute," 13 *New England Journal of Civil and Criminal Confinement* 171 (1987); Pease, K. G., and Wasik, M. (eds.), *Sentencing Reform: Guidance or Guidelines?* (1987); Tonry, M., *Sentencing Reform Impacts* (1987); von Hirsch, A., Knapp, K., and Tonry, M., *The Sentencing Commission and Its Guidelines* (1987); Robinson, P., "A Sentencing System for the 21st Century?" 66 *Texas Law Review* 1 (1987); Parent, D., *Structuring Criminal Sentences: The Evolution of Minnesota's Sentencing Guidelines* (1988); Council of Europe, *Disparities in Sentencing: Causes and Solutions* (1989); Lovegrove, A., *Judicial Decision-Making, Sentencing Policy, and Numerical Guidance* (1989); von Hirsch, "Federal Sentencing Guidelines: Do They Provide Principled Guidance?" 27 *American Criminal Law Review* 367 (1989); Nagel, I., "Structuring Sentencing Discretion: The New Federal Sentencing Guidelines," 80 *Journal of Criminal Law and Criminology* 883 (1990); Bogan, K., "Constructing Felony Sentencing Guidelines in an Already Crowded State," 36 *Crime and Delinquency* 467 (1990); von Hirsch, "The Politics of Just Deserts," 32 *Canadian Journal of Criminology* 397 (1990); Wasik, M., and von Hirsch, A., "Statutory Sentencing Principles: The 1990 White Paper," 54 *Modern Law Review* 508 (1990); Tonry, "The Politics and Processes of Sentencing Commissions," 37 *Crime and Delinquency* 307 (1991); Wasik, M., and Taylor, R. D., *Blackstone's Guide to the Criminal Justice Act of 1991* (1991); Alschuler, A., "The Failure of Sentencing Guidelines: A Plea for Less Aggregation," 58 *University of Chicago Law Review* 901 (1991); Frase, R. S., "Sentencing Reform in Minnesota: Ten Years After," 75 *Minnesota Law Review* 727 (1991); Ashworth, A., *Sentencing and Penal Policy,* rev. ed. (1992); Lappi-Seppälä, T., "Penal Policy and Sentencing Theory in Finland," 5 *Canadian Journal of Law and Jurisprudence* 95 (1992); Thomas, D. A., Ashworth, A., et al., Special Issue on Criminal Justice Act 1991, *Criminal Law Review* 229 et seq. (1992).

2. *Official Reports*

United States Sentencing Commission, *Sentencing Guidelines and Policy Statements* (1987); Canadian Sentencing Commission, *Sentencing Reform: A Canadian Approach* (1987); Report of the Standing Committee on Justice and Solicitor General on Its Review of Sentencing, Conditional Release, and Related Aspects of Corrections, *Taking Responsibility* (Canada, 1988); Victoria Sentencing Committee, *Report* (1988); Law Reform Commission of Australia, *Sentencing* (1988); Home Office, *Crime, Justice, and Protecting the Public* (England and Wales, 1990); Government of Canada, *Directions for Reform* (1990).

3. *Presentencing and Postsentencing Decisions*

Zimring, F. E., "Making the Punishment Fit the Crime: A Consumer's Guide to Sentencing Reform," 6(6) *Hastings Center Report* 13 (1976); Alschuler, A., "Sentencing Reform and Prosecutorial Power," 126 *University of Pennsylvania Law Review* 550 (1978); von Hirsch, A., and Hanrahan, K., *The Question of Parole: Retention, Reform, or Abolition?* (1979); Schulhofer, S., "Is Plea-Bargaining Inevitable?" 97 *Harvard Law Review* 1037 (1984); Bottomley, A. K., "Sentencing Reform and the Structuring of Pre-Trial Discretion," in K. Pease and M. Wasik (eds.), *Sentencing Reform: Guidance or Guidelines?* (1987); Report of the Review Committee, *The Parole System in England and Wales* (1988); Bottomley, A. K., "Parole in Transition: A Comparative Study of the Origins, Development, and Prospects for the 1990s," in N. Morris and M. Tonry (eds.), *Crime and Justice: An Annual Review,* vol. 10 (1990); McCoy, C., *The Politics of Plea Bargaining: Victims' Rights* (1992).

Chapter Six

COMMUNITY PUNISHMENTS

Sentencing options, in English-speaking Western countries, traditionally were few. This was particularly true in the U.S., where the offender either was sent to prison or jail, or else was placed on probation—usually as part of a large caseload, with perfunctory supervision. Such extremes are ill suited for crimes of the middle range of gravity: incarceration seems unduly harsh, probation scarcely punitive enough.

Dissatisfaction with this state of affairs (and with rising rates of imprisonment and their associated costs) has fueled interest in intermediate sanctions—that is, noncustodial penalties having more punitive bite than simple probation. Monetary penalties (particularly, "day fines" measured by income), community service, intensive probation supervision, required attendance at day-reporting centers, and home detention, all are being tried, especially in the period since the mid-1980s.[1] The present chapter examines such sanctions.

Initially, it was believed that the new options needed merely to be made available to the courts. The judge who invoked imprisonment because he or she was dissatisfied with the alternative of probation would gladly resort to a more substantial noncustodial sanction if authorized to do so. This strategy proved illusory—for reasons examined by James Austin and Barry Krisberg in Extract 6.1. It is not only the absence of other options that creates the tendency to prefer imprisonment, they point out, but also political and ideological pressures within the criminal justice system. Reducing the use of imprisonment will necessitate a variety of legal and administrative measures that restrict the permitted use of the prison sanction and that require intermediate noncustodial sanctions to be employed instead. Such measures may encounter considerable resistance.

Noncustodial sanctions have often been spoken of as "alternatives" to incarceration. This perspective is questioned in the second selection, Extract 6.2, from the 1986 report of the Canadian Sentencing Commission—an advisory body that proposed nationwide sentencing guidelines for Canada. The report begins with an illuminating exposition of the disturbing "net-widening" phenomenon—whereby intermediate penalties intended as replacements for imprisonment become replacements for or supplements to probation instead.

The commission suggests ways in which this net-widening problem may be addressed. First, intermediate noncustodial sanctions should not be thought of as "alternatives" to incarceration—or indeed, as alternatives at all. They should, instead, be treated as penalties in their own right, suited to offenses of the middle range of gravity. The offender convicted of, say, auto theft should receive a significant financial penalty as the sanction of *first* resort. Imprisonment should be invoked only in exceptional circumstances.

Second, the commission proposes that community sanctions' use be structured through sentencing guidelines. (Guidelines generally were discussed in Chapter 5, above.) Existing sentencing guideline schemes, such as Minnesota's, purport to regulate only the use and duration of imprisonment.[2] This does help restrict use of incarceration to the more serious crimes. It is not enough, however, because it leaves the choice among noncustodial penalties for other offenses unregulated. The Canadian Sentencing Commission recommends extending such guidelines to cover noncustodial penalties. Consider monetary penalties. The report proposes much more extensive use of such penalties and suggests the sentencing guidelines should prescribe how such penalties should be graded and used.

The fine—in the form of the day fine (or, as it is called in Britain, the "unit fine")—is the subject of the next selection, Extract 6.3, by Judith Greene. The most obvious drawback of the ordinary fine of a specified monetary amount is that its punitive bite varies with the resources of the offender. A $1000 (or £1000) fine is a devastating penalty to a poor defendant, but trivial to the millionaire. The day fine addresses this difficulty by assessing the fine in income units: the offender is assessed the equivalent of so many days' work (or so many days' worth of disposable income), instead of so many dollars or pounds. The actual monetary amount is then calculated on the basis of the offender's income.

Ms. Greene, in this extract, describes an experimental day fine program developed for misdemeanor courts in Staten Island, a borough of New York City. The experiment is based on European models, but in important respects goes further. Assessing day fines involves two steps: (1) deciding how many day fine units (that is, how many days' worth of income) should be assessed against a defendant; and (2) deciding the actual monetary amount involved per unit, given that defendant's earning power. European day fine systems have guidelines for the second step: a day fine unit consists of the estimated daily income, minus certain specified deductions (e.g., for child support). However, there generally have been no guidelines for step one: it is largely up to the judge to decide, within broad statutory limits, how many day fine units are to be imposed on a particular defendant.[3]

The Staten Island project makes good the latter deficiency, by supplying benchmarks concerning the number of day fine units appropriate for various types of offenses. Misdemeanors, under these benchmarks, are classified in seriousness into six "bands." The recommended number of day fine units is graded according to the "band" involved—that is, according to the gravity of the offense. (The extract's description of the ranking principles is interesting, and should be compared with the more theoretical discussion of crime seriousness in Extract 4.5 above.) A modest downward adjustment in the number of day fine units is then authorized for defendants who lack a significant criminal record; and further adjustments are also permitted for aggravating and mitigating circumstances relating to the offense. The result is a scheme with a coherent (mainly desert-oriented) rationale, and with meaningful guidance provided regarding the number of day fine units to assess. The scheme is not a full sentencing guideline scheme, however, in that it does not apply to felonies, and also in that the judge retains discretion on whether to invoke day fines at all. Under a full-fledged sentencing guideline scheme, the guidelines would prescribe when the day fine is the recommended penalty, as well as how many day fine units are owed (see Extracts 5.2 and 6.6).

A system of day fines results, of course, in offenders convicted of the same crime paying different amounts: the rich defendant pays more per unit than the defendant with only modest means. Is that a disparity? The theory of the day fine is that it is not, but rather a way of *avoiding* disparity: the proportion of income taken from the two defendants is the same, making the punitive bite comparable.[4] Yet the measure of punitiveness used—namely, units of income—is an objective and readily measurable one. Purely subjective differences in sensitivity to punishment would not be considered: the miserly defendant would pay as many units for a given offense as the prodigal one, though payment might subjectively "hurt" more.

The day fine is best suited for defendants with regular, measurable (and legal) income flow. Staten Island, where this experimental project is being tried, generally has lower-middle- and working-class neighborhoods, where most defendants are employed. The judge in Staten Island also retains discretion to choose a penalty other than a day fine, if the particular defendant is indigent. With a full system of guidelines, however, the solution is not so simple: where day fines are normally prescribed but the defendant is indigent, a sanction of comparable onerousness may need to be imposed (see Extract 6.6). The day fine system also requires an efficient system of collection. In Sweden, fines are collected by the agency that collects overdue taxes and other debts owed to the state—and that agency has wide powers of attachment, garnishment, etc. Other jurisdictions, where day fines are new, will have to develop alternate collection mechanisms.

The next selection by Todd Clear and Patricia Hardyman, Extract 6.4, addresses another kind of noncustodial penalty—intensive supervision probation (ISP). It points out some of the hazards encountered when developing intermediate sanctions—and thus supplements Austin and Krisberg's warnings in Extract 6.1. To overcome judicial and public resistance, the sponsors of ISP in various U.S. states try to make this measure as attractive and uncontroversial as possible. This search for "acceptability" has taken several forms: (1) Eligibility criteria are restrictively drawn, to ensure the recruitment of tractable participants who would prompt little public anxiety. Those criteria require ISP participants to have modest crimes of conviction and modest criminal records. (2) To dispel potential judicial objections, broad discretion is retained for judges to decide whether actually to sentence even eligible defendants to ISP. (3) To provide reassurance that ISP participants are not "getting off too easily," the routines of supervision are fairly stringent—including substantial punitive conditions (e.g., numerous hours of community service) and extensive risk controls (e.g., numerous urine tests for drug use). (4) For similar reasons, offenders who defaulted on these requirements can be promptly removed from the program and imprisoned.

The trouble with these four features, Clear and Hardyman point out, is that they tend to defeat the aims of the program. Thus, (1) the narrow eligibility criteria means that offenders convicted of middle-level offenses—that is, those who *should* participate—are largely excluded. The criteria mainly permit inclusion of lesser offenders, who now chiefly receive probation. (2) Leaving judges wide discretion aggravates this problem: only the "easy" (i.e., least serious) cases will tend to receive ISP. (3) Tough supervision routines, when applied to the lesser offenders recruited in the program, merely escalate the overall severity of the system. (4) Easy resort to imprisonment, for breach of program conditions, is particularly problematic. Programs such as ISP monitor supervised offenders' activity much more closely than traditional probation did. Closer monitoring means that program violations are more frequently uncovered. If incarceration is frequently invoked as the sanction, the upshot may be that *more* defendants end in prison than would have, had the program not existed at all.

How does one avoid the pitfalls which Clear and Hardyman describe? What is needed is clearer program objectives that target intermediate sanctions to middle-level offenders, not lesser ones—and guidelines or other guidance methods that help insure that this targeting is implemented. This, however, makes the political and institutional obstacles more formidable. It is easy to promote the new programs for the most tractable offenders whose crimes cause only minimal public anger or anxiety. It is harder to secure implementation of noncustodial sanctions aimed at the more substantial cases in the middle range: for example, at defendants whose crimes are not violent but are still disturbing, such as burglary. It is also harder to insist that such participants should not be imprisoned for routine breaches of program rules but only for quite substantial new infractions. The warning of Austin and Krisberg in Extract 6.1 still holds: securing a meaningful system of intermediate punishments may well evoke considerable resistance.

Suppose, however, that such resistance can be overcome in a jurisdiction—that it is feasible to establish guidelines or other criteria for the use of noncustodial sanctions. Then, the critical question becomes: what should those standards' *content* be? To what extent should the seriousness of the crime determine which penalties should be used, and to what extent should other factors count also? How much "interchangeability" among punishments should be permitted for similar cases? Such questions are addressed in the final two selections of this chapter.

The first of these two selections, Extract 6.5, is a summary by Norval Morris and Michael Tonry of their recent book on noncustodial sanctions.[5] The authors begin with a useful thumbnail sketch of various types of intermediate sanctions being experimented with in the United States. (Comparable developments are occurring in Great Britain.)[6] To structure the use of these sanctions, the authors recommend extending sentencing guideline systems, such as Minnesota's, to address the choice among noncustodial penalties.

What choice should be permissible, under the guidelines? Morris and Tonry propose permitting considerable "interchangeability" among penalties. An offender convicted of a crime in the upper-middle range of seriousness, for example, might receive either a short prison term or else a noncustodial sanction such as a substantial day fine or a stint of community service.

There must, however, be limits on interchangeability—else we are back in the situation of unfettered discretion. How comparable must the penalties be in severity, in order for them to be interchanged in a given type of case? That depends, in large part, on the role given to desert. Norval Morris (as we saw earlier in Extract 4.3) has advocated a "mixed" rationale, in which desert sets only the boundaries on permissible punishments. On this view, offenders convicted of criminal conduct of a given degree of seriousness need not be punished with equal severity: inequality in punishment is permissible, so long as it remains within the supposed desert bounds. In the present selection, Morris and Tonry rely upon this view for their criteria for "interchangeability." Punishments of *different* severity may be interchanged, they state, so long as that difference is not unduly great. It would be unduly great only if the desert limits are breached—that is, if any of the interchangeable punishments are disproportionately harsh or lenient relative to the gravity of the conduct involved.[7]

How defensible Morris and Tonry's stance on interchangeability is depends, of course, on the underlying assumption—that desert supplies only outer limits on permissible punishments. This assumption—versus a more thoroughgoing desert rationale—has been debated already in Extracts 4.3 and 4.4. The workability of their scheme depends also on their ability to delineate what the applicable desert limits are. There are at least two possibilities:

1. The desert limits—while more permissive than under a full desert model—might still be significantly confining. That is, they would substantially shape (albeit not fully determine) the gradation of penalties. The guidelines might, for example, classify intermediate penalties into several bands according to their degree of punitiveness: say, into "mild," "lower-intermediate," "upper-intermediate," and "onerous." Substitutions might be permitted *within* a given band (even if the penalties differ somewhat in punitive bite) but would be restricted among different bands. Thus a short stint in jail and home detention might be interchangeable as both are fairly tough, albeit not equally severe; but a prison term could *not* be interchanged with moderate financial penalties because the disparity in punitiveness is too great. Such a view would set some meaningful limits on what interchanges are permissible and what are not.

2. Alternatively, the desert limits under a "mixed" model could be much more permissive—and bar only *manifest* disproportion. Limits of this kind would serve mainly as a supplement to the statutory maxima and minima. Under such a view, almost any interchange would be permissible—as it largely is today.

Which view of desert limits, (1) or (2), do Morris and Tonry endorse? They do not say in this excerpted summary or in their book (although there are some hints they might prefer the former view).[8] Moreover (as Andrew von Hirsch argues in Excerpt 4.4), Morris does not provide any suggestions in his general theory of punishment about how the width of the desert limits might be ascertainable. One is thus left uncertain about the scope of permitted interchangeability—and indeed about the architecture of their proposed structure.[9]

The final selection, by Andrew von Hirsch, Martin Wasik, and Judith Greene, Extract 6.6, addresses the scaling of noncustodial sanctions under a desert model. The article deals in systematic fashion with a number of key issues that need to be considered in developing a principled system—and thus may be of use even to those who do not subscribe to a purely desert-oriented rationale. Some of the issues are:

1. *The role of rationale.* A desert rationale, the article points out, permits extensive use of noncustodial penalties—namely, for all offenses but those of a rather high degree of seriousness. It would call for noncustodial sanctions to be graded in severity according to the gravity of the criminal conduct—as the illustrative grids in the selection show. Intermediate sanctions would specifically be targeted to crimes of middling and upper-middling gravity. Changing the rationale, as the article points out at the end, could alter the architecture of the scheme considerably.

2. *Interchanges—desert constraints.* The authors' scheme does permit interchange among penalties—but only where those penalties are of roughly equivalent onerousness. This follows the desert-based requirement that criminal conduct of equal seriousness should be punished roughly equally. To the extent this constraint is relaxed, interchanges among sanctions of different punitive bite would become more permissible.

3. *Interchanges—other policy limits.* Should desert requirements constitute the *only* constraint on substitution among penalties? Then—as the "full substitution" model in Figure 2 of the extract shows—there could be very extensive interchangeability, even under a desert rationale. Indeed, a whole smorgasbord of penalties, with extensive mixing, could be employed, so long as the net severity visited on the defendant achieved the prescribed level. The authors point out various problems with such extensive substitutability—for example, that it makes comparisons among penalties difficult. They propose, instead, *limited* substitutability—wherein one type of penalty is the normally recommended penalty for a given band in the grid, and other sanctions (of comparable onerousness) are permitted only where there are special reasons. Mixing and matching—that is, imposing several diverse sanctions in a particular case—would also generally be ruled out.

4. *Breach sanctions.* As pointed out already, the greater intensity of intermediate penalties—as compared with probation—will cause technical violations by offenders to be uncovered more frequently. Unless limits are placed on the severity of the sanctions for such violations—and particularly, on the use of imprisonment as the breach sanction—the net result can be

an *escalation* of severity and larger numbers of persons going to prison. The authors discuss breach sanctions under a desert rationale—and suggest why imprisonment should be the sanction only in exceptional cases.

A.v.H.

Notes

1. See Joan Petersilia, *Expanding Options for Criminal Sentencing* (Santa Monica, Cal.: Rand Corp., 1987).

2. See Andrew von Hirsch, Kay Knapp, and Michael Tonry, *The Sentencing Commission and Its Guidelines* (Boston: Northeastern University Press, 1987), ch. 5.

3. Since 1988, however, Sweden has had statutory principles that address this issue, at least in general terms. See *id.*, ch. 3, and Andrew von Hirsch and Nils Jareborg, "Sweden's Sentencing Statute Enacted," [1989] *Criminal Law Review* 275.

4. Relying on proportions of income in this fashion does not take into account economists' notion of marginal utility. The rich defendant can better afford to lose a given fraction of his income than a poor defendant, because he can live more comfortably with what he has left.

5. Norval Morris and Michael Tonry, *Between Prison and Probation: Intermediate Punishments in a Rational Sentencing System* (New York: Oxford University Press, 1990).

6. These are summarized in Antony K. Vass, *Alternatives to Prison* (London: Sage Publications, 1990).

7. Morris and Tonry, op. cit., ch. 4.

8. *Id.*, ch. 3, where the authors say they envision their system would be an extension of a guideline system such as Minnesota's.

9. For fuller discussion, see Andrew von Hirsch, "Scaling Intermediate Punishments: A Comparison of Two Models," in J. Byrne, A. Lurigio, and J. Petersilia, eds., *Smart Sentencing: Expanding Options for Intermediate Sanctions* (Newbury Park, Cal.: Sage Publications, 1992).

6.1
"Alternatives" to Incarceration: Substitutes or Supplements?

James Austin
Barry Krisberg

The research literature on alternatives to incarceration suggests that their promise remains largely unmet. In each instance, the nonincarcerative options were transformed, serving criminal justice system values and goals other than reducing imprisonment. Sentencing alternatives, such as restitution and community service, are employed to enhance the increasingly criticized sanctions of probation and fines. There is little evidence that sentencing alternatives have substantially displaced incarceration. Similarly, postincarceration release programs often escalate the level of control over clients and have served primarily to control populations within prison systems. Increasing the availability of community facilities has not reduced populations in secure confinement. Community correction legislation appears less likely to reduce incarceration than to change the location of imprisonment from the state institutions to county jails. Moreover, initial declines in state prison commitments can be neutralized by other sentencing or release policies that increase prison populations. Although community correction legislation may have redistributed correctional costs and shifted decision making from state to local levels, it is questionable whether it has made a long-term contribution to reduced imprisonment.

An analysis of why these nonincarceration schemes have failed must confront the question of goals. In each attempted reform, significant crim-

From James Austin and Barry Krisberg, "The Unmet Promise of Alternatives to Incarceration," 28 *Crime and Delinquency* 374 (1982).

inal justice actors added other objectives to, displaced, or replaced the original goals. An even more troubling problem facing reform efforts is the inherent ambiguity in what constitutes successful alternatives to incarceration. Reviews of enabling legislation as well as program descriptions illustrate how multiple and often conflicting objectives characterized these reforms.[1] Harland notes that advocates of restitution often fail to anticipate conflicts with traditional criminal justice goals and procedures.[2] Sentencing occurs within a system dominated by the values of law enforcement, community protection, and punishment. Other values enter the sentencing process during stages of plea negotiation and presentence investigation. Most criminal justice personnel do not endorse the value of reducing incarceration. Quite the contrary, imprisonment itself is valued, and milder forms of punishment such as probation or diversion rest on the threat that incarceration may be applied if the offender fails to conform. Alternatives are employed to the extent that they fit the structure of power and values within specific criminal justice systems and the variety of goals pursued by actors within the system.

Generally, the values of police, judges, and prosecutors are predominant. In correction, the strongest influence is exercised by administrators of prison and jail systems, who control large budgets and often share law enforcement values. Probation and parole agencies exert less influence than do police, court, and correctional organizations; often they are subordinate parts of judicial or prison bureaucracies. Thus, alternatives as a means to reduce imprisonment are advocated by the less powerful divisions of the criminal justice system—or by private reform organizations with minimal political and economic influence, which must rely on the media and the presentation of "new knowledge" to promote decarceration policies and legislation. Within this milieu, alternatives are attractive to law enforcement, court, and prison officials as tools to supplement nonincarcerative sanctions (e.g., probation, fines, and parole). Public opinion opposing the use of socially defined "lenient" alternatives for serious offenders intensifies the system's reluctance to expand the use of alternatives except in crisis situations (e.g., following riots or federal court orders).

In the typical hierarchy of agency values and power within the criminal justice system, it is predictable that sentencing alternatives will be employed for minor offenders whose dispositions rarely produce strong conflict between agencies, or reflect a compromise between competing values. Alternatives tend to become integrated into plea bargaining rituals as part of the local scale of punishments assigned to various constellations of offenses and offenders. The supplementing of probation and jail sentences by "alternatives" reflects a process of compromise between the values of punishment and rehabilitation. Since the rehabilitative ideology has little support from within the criminal justice system or among members of the public, the compromise position embodied by alternatives is likely to consist of the application of more restrictive conditions to minor offenders. Should the rehabilitative ideal gather greater strength in the future, alternatives might be applied to "tougher" cases. Exceptions to this pattern may occur when strong financial incentives such as federal grants or agency budget crises induce shifts in philosophy and practice. The dilemma of criminal justice reform involves restructuring policy at many complex decision points and persuading key decision makers to choose more enlightened sanctioning strategies that sustain desired values.

Changing values and translating these new orientations into practice are difficult enterprises. Traditionally, proponents of nonincarcerative sanctions have made rational and moral arguments to various publics, including criminal justice personnel. Nonincarcerative sanctions are presented as a means of expanding the social control tools of the criminal justice system. Many observers now openly question the strategy of providing a broader range of social control mechanisms, instead proposing to shrink or regulate discretion exercised within the criminal justice system. Harland, for example, argues that community service should be given statutory authorization that specifies the kinds of offenses and offenders appropriate.[3] Furthermore, he argues for legislation equating hours of community service with specific terms of incarceration. Legislation must make it clear that a key aim of community service is to reduce imprisonment. This view is echoed by Galaway, a ten-year veteran of restitution research, who argues that restitution will reduce incarceration only when it is recognized as the fair penalty for certain classes of offenses.[4]

Yet, the promise of such alternatives will not be enhanced merely by legislative enactments. The history of mandatory, presumptive, and determinate sentencing schemes is replete with examples of how new forms of discretionary behavior emerge to frustrate the lawmaker's intent. This can be well understood from observing the role of prosecutors and law enforcement in creating sentencing policies. New efforts to implement nonincarcerative sanctions must examine and respond to the interests and ideology of the most powerful segments of the criminal justice system.

This is not simply a matter of waiting for prevailing values to change. Values influence and are influenced by alterations in the ideology, power, and economic forces within the criminal justice system and society at large. Structural changes may precipitate the reordering of values to enable change in social conditions. For example, the pressures of bulging prisons and scarce public funds may force government officials to reexamine the value of imprisonment versus other forms of social control. Judicial orders mandating reduced prison and jail populations may provide incentives for the system to employ nonincarcerative sanctions for certain classes of offenders. Likewise, legislation forbidding prison administrators from incarcerating more than a specified number could help in expanding alternatives to incarceration by constricting the ability of criminal justice actors to employ imprisonment as punishment.[5] The significance of capping correctional capacity is in its redistribution of resources from the construction and maintenance of correction facilities to nonincarcerative sanctions. It may, moreover, be necessary to create independent public agencies charged with planning, implementing, and monitoring diverse sentencing alternatives that reduce the use of imprisonment.[6]

Explicit legislative delineation of alternatives, substantially greater resources, and more powerful organizational bases might go far in realizing the promise of alternatives to incarceration. To achieve any success in the political arena, the proponents of alternatives must have much better evidence to support their claims that (1) alternatives do not significantly increase risks to public safety, and (2) nonincarcerative sanctions are acceptable to the public, criminal justice practitioners, and victims. Furthermore, we must learn more about how the dynamic criminal justice nets support or impede rational reform efforts.

A radical shift in correctional policy toward the presumptive use of nonprison sanctions, together with fixing (or reducing) custodial capacity, deserves serious debate. One can anticipate intense resistance from actors with opposing ideologies, who stand to forfeit considerable power from such rearrangements. The prospects that change will emanate from within the criminal justice system seem dismal. We might more productively concentrate on forging a new political consensus in which the values of punishment and public safety are rationally balanced with fiscal limits and competing claims for public revenue. Although most elected officials are sympathetic to traditional criminal justice values, their concerns about the costs of punishment provide an opening for discussion.

Notes

1. James Austin, "Instead of Justice: Diversion" (Ph.D. diss., University of California at Davis, 1980); A. T. Harland, "Court-Ordered Community Service in Criminal Law," *Buffalo Law Review,* Summer 1980, 426–86.

2. Alan T. Harland, "Goal Conflicts and Criminal Justice Innovation: A Case Study," *Justice System Journal,* Spring 1980, 291–98.

3. Harland, "Court-Ordered Community Service in Criminal Law."

4. Burt Galaway, "Restitution as an Integrative Punishment," in *Assessing the Criminal: Restitution, Retribution, and the Legal Process*, Randy Barnett and John Hagel, eds. (Cambridge, Mass.: Ballinger, 1977), 331–47.

5. *A New Correctional Policy for California: Developing Alternatives to Prison* (San Francisco: Research Center West, National Council on Crime and Delinquency, 1980).

6. Id.

6.2 Community Punishments as Sanctions in Their Own Right

Canadian Sentencing Commission

The greater use of community sanctions, particularly for property offenses, has been supported by various reform bodies and by public opinion as expressed in public opinion surveys. The use of community sanctions as true alternatives to incarceration in appropriate circumstances was embodied in the sentencing package in the Criminal Law Reform Act, 1984 (Bill C-19). The sentencing provisions of that bill proposed that current community sanctions should be expanded and imposed as sanctions in their own right.

The Commission fully endorses the direction initiated in Bill C-19 toward the development of community sanctions as independent sanctions. In the course of its research, the Commission became aware of other proposals which may warrant further study.

The Commission's recommendation for the greater use of community sanctions and for their further development by a future body should not be construed as an attempt to increase the number of offenders subject to sentencing dispositions.

The Commission makes the following recommendation:

The Commission endorses the general policy in the Criminal Law Reform Act, 1984, that community sanctions be developed as independent sanctions.

Reference has already been made to the necessity of defining the nature of community sanctions. This issue involves a question of whether com-

---

From Canadian Sentencing Commission, *Sentencing Reform: A Canadian Approach* (Ottawa: Canadian Government Publishing Centre, 1987).

munity sanctions are to be viewed as independent sanctions (sanctions in their own right) or whether they are to be viewed as alternatives to incarceration. The difference in these two perspectives relates to the criteria used to measure the success of these dispositions and a determination of their appropriate use. For example, the traditional view has been that community sanctions are substitutes for incarceration and thus are to be used in situations where incarceration would otherwise be imposed. As such, the criteria used to measure their success have often been standards relevant to imprisonment, for example, the degree to which they reduce prison costs or offender populations. The Commission is opposed to the indiscriminate application of principles relevant to custody to assess the merits of community sanctions.

The Commission recommends that community sanctions be defined and applied as sanctions in their own right.

If the Commission were simply to recommend that community dispositions should be viewed as sanctions in their own right, it would not address the important issue of the use of community sanctions to broaden the scope of penal control over Canadian citizens. This phenomenon is often referred to in the literature as the "widening of the net effect."

A widening of the net of penal control is liable to occur when a new sanction is introduced with the intention that it should be used in lieu of another sanction, which is *more severe*. Let us imagine, for purposes of illustration, that 40 percent of dispositions result in incarceration and that the remaining 60 percent result in probation. If a new sanction such as house arrest is introduced as an alternative to the more severe and more costly sanction of incarceration, the expectation is that its introduction will reduce recourse to incarceration. This intended result is illustrated by the following diagrams which depict an anticipated 10 percent decrease in the use of incarceration.

1. Starting point

Incarceration: 40%	Probation: 60%

2. Intended result: a reduction of incarceration

Incarceration: 30%	House arrest: 10%	Probation: 60%

The arrow in diagram 2 demonstrates the reduction in the use of imprisonment which is anticipated by the introduction of house arrest. However, general research about the introduction of alternative community sanctions has shown that the expected reduction in the use of the more severe sanctions does not usually follow from the introduction of a new, less severe substitute sanction (Cohen, 1985; 44–49). Considered in the context of our illustration, this means that the percentage of offenders receiving terms of imprisonment would remain constant. However, 10 percent of offenders who currently received probation would now be subject to house arrest, which is a more severe disposition than probation. As illustrated:

3. Actual result: a compression in probation

Incarceration: 40%	House arrest: 10%	Probation: 50%

The net result of the introduction of house arrest would not be a decrease in sanction severity but an increase due to the percentage of probationers who would receive house arrest in lieu of probation. It is also possible that an offender may be subject to both of these restrictions on his or her freedom: the offender cannot leave his or her home and is supervised occasionally by a probation officer. The direction of the arrow in diagram 3 is intended to indicate that, contrary to the original intention, it is the less severe sanction of probation which is diminished by the introduction of the more severe sanction of house arrest.

Unfortunately, the process does not stop at this point. Although 10 percent of the offenders who normally would receive probation will now be placed under house arrest, there is no real decrease in the overall use of probation. Hence, the "missing" 10 percent of probationers will be recruited from among those offenders who used to receive the less severe sanction of a community service order. This process is similar to tumbling dominos which fall in the direction of the most severe to the less severe sanctions. The last domino falls into the arena of those offenders who previously were diverted from the courts entirely and thus received no penal sanction at all for their criminal transgressions. This progressive intrusion of penal sanctions into civil life is what is properly called the widening of the net effect. It may be illustrated as follows:

4. The widening of the net effect

		Expanded use of probation 50% + 10%	
Incarceration: 40% (unchanged)	House arrest: 10%	Compressed probation: 50%	Community service orders: reduced by 10%
	Former use of probation: 60%		

The widening of the net effect is evident from a comparison of the relative use of probation and incarceration in Ontario and Quebec. One study found that although courts in Ontario impose terms of probation four times more frequently than those in Quebec, this has not resulted in a concomitant reduction in the use of imprisonment in Ontario.

The Commission is of the view that the widening of the net effect can only be contained by adoption of a policy which represents a fundamental shift in the perception of community sanctions. The traditional emphasis in sentencing has been on incarceration as the pivotal sanction, as illustrated by use of the term "noncustodial" to describe community sanctions. However, the Commission's scheme of presumptive dispositions reflects the policy that imprisonment has been excessively and inappropriately used. To reverse the disproportionate use of incarceration, the Commission has presumptively assigned "out" and "qualified out" designations for a number of offenses, many of which currently result in custodial sentences. In this context, community sentences are being used as "alternatives" to incarceration in the sense that they are more appropriate dispositions than custodial sentences for these offenses.

The policy reorientation inherent in the Commission's approach to community sanctions is appropriate for a number of reasons: it accords with the Commission's emphasis on the principle of proportionality. As indicated earlier, public concern in sentencing focuses primarily on violent offenses. The use of community sanctions for property offenses is supported in both the public opinion polls and in the briefs submitted to the Commission. Second, an emphasis on the use of community sanctions for a greater number of offenses also accords with the Commission's commitment to the principle of restraint. Finally, this approach complements the Commission's sentencing principle that the sentence should be the least onerous sanction appropriate in the circumstances. To the greatest extent possible, the offender's social and economic ties with the community should be maintained. There would appear to be no social benefit to imposing sanctions for lesser offenses which disrupted those ties and thereby hindered rather than enhanced the offender's opportunity to resume a normal life in future.

The Commission proposes that one concrete way to reduce the likelihood of the criminal justice system intruding further into civil life is to develop guidelines based upon the above-noted policy that community sanctions must be considered as sanctions in their own right which, for a greater number of offenses, are to be used in lieu of incarceration.

The Commission has invested its time and resources in addressing the pressing issues raised by incarceration and could not attend to the more detailed aspects of the development of guidelines for community sanctions. However, the Commission sees the development and implementation of such guidelines as the ongoing task of a future sentencing body (e.g., a permanent sentencing commission). These guidelines particularly relate to two issues: a further refinement of the imposition of custodial as opposed to community sanctions (the "in/out" decision) and additional guidance respecting the appropriate circumstances for the use of a particular community sanction relative to other sanctions. The Commission anticipates that the latter type of direction would discourage the substitution of one type of community sanction for an inappropriate alternative.

The Commission is of the view that there is no inconsistency in maintaining that community sanctions should be considered as sanctions in their own right and at the same time arguing that for many offenses, they should also represent alternatives to incarceration. If community sanctions are considered to be sanctions in their own right, then the criteria used to measure their use and success will no longer be imprisonment-oriented. This approach is complemented by the Commission's recommendation respecting the greater use of community sanctions which is premised on the policy that for many offenses, they are the most appropriate dispositions available. In this sense, they truly represent alternatives to incarceration.

However they are defined, community sanctions should not attempt to resemble incarceration by attracting conditions which are so arduous that they approximate the degree of constraint implied by custody. They must be viewed as sanctions which, in many cases, are more appropriate than incarceration because they are proportionate both to the gravity of the offense and the degree of responsibility of the offender.

Reference

Cohen, S. (1985). *Visions of Social Control: Punishment and Classification*. Polity Press.

6.3
Day Fines: Monetary Sanctions Apportioned to Income

Judith Greene

As public officials and criminal justice policy experts around the country struggle with the surging costs of our prison and jail population explosion, interest in credible and enforceable, but nonincarcerative, punishments has been renewed. During the past decade, while the use of imprisonment has doubled, alternative penalties once considered experimental—intensive probation, community service orders, house arrest (with and without electronic surveillance)—have become commonplace. However, the track record of the alternatives movement in reducing levels of incarceration is not encouraging. The popularity of the more established alternative sentencing options seems related primarily to their use as a way of augmenting probation supervision, rather than as sanctions in their own right.

Widespread, systematic use of noncustodial penalties can be encouraged by emphasizing sanctions, such as fines and community service, that can be calibrated in direct proportion to the seriousness of the crimes, and that are relatively simple and inexpensive to administer and enforce. When measured against the long-standing requirements in American jurisprudence—that sentences be proportionate, clear of purpose, broadly applicable, widely available, and enforceable—the initial attractions of alternatives that are highly individualized (i.e., crafted case by case) appear fleeting.

From Judith A. Greene, "Structuring Criminal Fines: Making an 'Intermediate' Penalty More Useful and Equitable," 13 *Justice System Journal* 37 (1988). Excerpted and reprinted by permission, with changes approved by the author.

The Criminal Fine: An Underutilized Resource

After seven years of work to develop a model for the effective imposition and enforcement of community service orders as a sentencing alternative to short jail terms for recidivist property offenders (McDonald, 1986), planners at the Vera Institute of Justice in New York City have turned to restructuring the use of a more traditional sanction—the criminal fine. A decade of work by Vera researchers, in collaboration with colleagues at the Institute for Court Management of the National Center for State Courts, informs this planning effort. The research has documented a sharp contrast between the manner in which fines are used in American sentencing practice and their use in some Western European criminal justice systems. In the latter, fines are systematically imposed across a broad spectrum of criminal offenses as the primary noncustodial penalty, and are effectively administered after imposition.

Broad interest in the United States in this research on fines stems from American policymakers' growing attention to credible, enforceable alternatives to incarceration. The criminal fine has many characteristics which are well suited to its sytematic application as an intermediate penalty. Its basic punitive aim is compatible with a desert-based rationale for sentencing. The fine is also viewed as having value as a deterrent. It is also a compensatory sentence—the offender literally pays his or her debt to society—thereby falling within penalty systems which stress offender accountability. Fines are a flexible sentencing device and, as will be demonstrated below, they can be scaled to cover a broad range of offense severity, while at the same time adjusted to account for differences in income levels among individuals convicted of comparable offenses. The fine is an available sanction, currently authorized in all American jurisdictions, large and small, urban and rural. Moreover, its expansion is practical: the fine is inexpensive to administer, requires relatively few supervisory personnel, and generates revenue, often over and above the costs of administration.

Examination of European courts provides further evidence of the untapped potential of the criminal fine (Casale, 1981; Greene, 1987). The court systems of Sweden, England, and West Germany impose fines as the sole penalty in 80 to 85 percent of all convictions. Fine-alone sentences are not restricted, as is common in American courts, to traffic offenders, first-time criminal offenders, or those charged with the least serious crimes. In West Germany, for example, the fine is now used as the sole penalty for three-quarters of all offenders convicted of property crimes, and two-thirds of those convicted of assault (Gillespie, 1980).

Survey research indicates that, although patterns of fine use are highly variable from court to court, American judges generally impose fines well below statutory limits—despite increased legislative action to raise these limits as a means of expanding the fine's punitive range (Hillsman, Sichel, and Mahoney, 1984). The difficulty seems to center on the basic organizing principle American judges commonly use to assess the amount of a fine: the fixed-sum fining system in which approximately the same fine amount is imposed as a flat sum for all offenders convicted of the same or similar offense. This approach to setting fines has led courts to adopt informal tariff systems, or "going rates," for specific offenses. Given the modest economic circumstances of most offenders in state courts, these flat dollar rates tend to cluster at the bottom of the legislatively set ranges, further restricting fine use to the lesser categories of offenses. Thus, low dollar fine amounts restricted to the least serious crimes have become the norm in most courts (Hillsman, Sichel, and Mahoney, 1984; Hillsman and Greene, 1988).

The American tendency to use a fixed-sum fining system presents another difficulty for sentencing judges. Because such tariff systems are tacitly grounded in the notion that consistency in sentencing requires that all offenders convicted of a given crime will pay the same fine amount, they give an obvious advantage to offenders with higher incomes. When fines are set in equal sums for similar crimes, the disparate punitive impact of the fine across differing income classes distorts both the principles of proportionality and equity.

At the same time, however, research suggests that some judges do attempt to make the rigid tariff system more flexible by tailoring fine amounts within tariff ranges more clearly to the means of individual offenders. This suggests, therefore, that if judges are provided with streamlined methods to set equitable fines more systematically, the impediments created by fixed tariff systems can be overcome, freeing the criminal fine to become a more central punishment option (Mahoney and Thornton, 1988).

The European Day Fine System

Contrasts between American and Western European courts suggest that if the basic approach to fining embodied in European sentencing practices—the day fine—can be translated for use in the American legal context, and tested in a typical court setting, the results could enhance the credibility of the criminal fine and broaden its usefulness in the United States (Hillsman and Greene, 1988).

First developed in Scandinavia in the 1920s and 1930s, and introduced into West Germany during the late 1960s and early 1970s, the day fine system of setting variable rather than fixed fine amounts rests upon a simple two-step process that embraces both proportionality and equity. First, the court sentences the offender to a certain number of fine units according to the gravity of the offense, but without regard to his or her means. The value of each unit is then established as a share of the offender's daily income (hence the name "day fine"), and the total fine amount is determined by simple multiplication. The share of income used to value the day fine units varies across the different countries that use this system, as do methods for accounting for capital wealth or family responsibilities, but the basic idea assures routine imposition of variable, but equitable, fine sentences, the punitive impact of which are in proportion to the crime. The day fine approach has also ensured that courts can administer these monetary penalties without overburdening collection and enforcement efforts, and without resorting to high levels of imprisonment for default (Albrecht and Johnson, 1980).

Adaptation for American Practice

To explore the viability of using the day fine approach in an American court, a collaborative planning process was undertaken by planners of the Vera Institute of Justice, in conjunction with the Richmond County Criminal Court (Staten Island, New York) and the county district attorney's office. The goal was to adapt Western European day fine models to this American court to test how sentencers will use fines when freed from the constraints of a tariff system, and whether courts can administer them effectively and efficiently (Hillsman and Greene, 1987).

The selection of a trial court of limited jurisdiction reflected several considerations. Planners wanted a type of American court in which improvements in fining would be immediately relevant and thus of substantial practitioner interest. Traditionally, lower courts in the United States have been the primary users of fine sentences, used both alone and in combination with other penalties. These courts are followed by general jurisdiction trial courts which handle a wide variety of misdemeanor as well as felony cases; general jurisdiction courts handling only felonies are the one type of American criminal court that tends to use fines sparingly as sole sanctions (Hillsman, Sichel, and Mahoney, 1984).

Another consideration was an interest in exploring the impact of restructuring fines on the displacement of short sentences of incarceration. It seemed practical to test this innovation in a court which routinely handles the lower range of cases now receiving custodial sentences. Because short terms of imprisonment are used increasingly in lower courts, judges who deal primarily with felony cases may be reluctant to experiment with noncustodial sentences when cases of lower severity are being jailed by judges on the misdemeanor bench. Until sentencing practices in our lower courts effectively incorporate a credible schedule of criminal penalties which do not rely upon incarceration, it is unlikely that alternatives to incarceration will gain wide acceptance in the higher courts.

The Staten Island Criminal Court is a desirable site for such a pilot test. It already uses fines as a sole sanction in almost half its cases. It also disposes of cases displaying a broad range of offense seriousness. As a court of original jurisdiction, the criminal court arraigns and processes all cases, whether charged by the district attorney as felonies or misdemeanors, before they are either indicted and transferred to the court of general jurisdiction (the New York City Supreme Court), or disposed as misdemeanors in the criminal court. Because case screening is vigorous at the lower level, only cases with a high probability of felony conviction are indicted; therefore, Staten Island's criminal court disposes of many felony complaints. Of all cases charged as felonies in 1986, for example, almost three-quarters remained in the criminal court for final disposition (Hillsman and Greene, 1987).

Finally, the Staten Island court is relatively rich in sentencing options as compared with many lower courts. These include probation sentences, supervised restitution and community service orders, imprisonment, conditional and unconditional discharges, as well as fines. Thus, day fines compete with a well-developed range of traditional options, and do so in a context characterized by serious jail overcrowding.[1]

The Staten Island community served by the court also makes it a desirable site for experimenting with day fines. Although part of New York City, this county is similar to many middle-sized, suburban communities in the United States. It is distinguished by a sound economic base and a high degree of social stability; but it also has a significant crime problem and a sizable, if not dominant, resident population characterized by poverty and unemployment.

The goal of the initial planning process was to develop a workable design for introducing day fines into the Staten Island court and for studying its implementation. The planning involved close collaboration between Vera Institute of Justice planners and researchers and a court planning group composed of the bench, the bar, court administrators, and policy experts from across the United States and Western Europe.

The central components of the plan developed by the planning group involved (1) a system of sentencing benchmarks to guide the number of day fine units set for specific offenses; (2) a method for collecting the necessary means information and for valuing the day fine units imposed on a particular offender; (3) strategic improvements in the court's collection and enforcement system so that it can respond to the potentially higher fine amounts and broader range of fined offenders under a day fine system; and (4) a microcomputer-based information system to record collection and enforcement activities and to provide statistical reports to the court (see Cummings, 1988). In the design and development of each component, court administrators were essential to the process of planning new systems within existing court procedures for administering fine sentences and for managing case records.

Sentencing Standards: The Benchmark Scales

To guide the transition from a fixed-sum to a day fine system, a set of scales or benchmarks was devised by the court work group to provide informal sentencing standards to judges for determining the number of day fine units to be imposed. The basic architecture for the scales was a rank ordering of seventy-one penal law misdemeanors and violations frequently found as conviction as well as arraignment charges in the court. The range of charges encompassed lesser victimizing crimes (including those charged by prosecutors as felonies but disposed as misdemeanors); a broad spectrum of property offenses; minor street-level drug and contraband offenses; and a variety of offenses involving the obstruction of legal process and the breach of public decorum and community standards of behavior. These offenses were rank ordered by the work group by classifying the relative degree of seriousness represented by the specific criminal behaviors typically coming before this court under each penal law category, as deduced from discussions among the court officials and from analysis of actual sentencing patterns.

Assessment of the relative seriousness of these offenses was guided by the general analytic principles, rather than solely by their formal classification in the New York State Penal Law. These principles suggest a three-fold hierarchy of victimizing crimes (see von Hirsch, 1985, ch. 6). At the highest level are crimes which damage or destroy the welfare interests of individuals, that is, those harming a person's life, health, or economic livelihood at the level of basic subsistence. Next are crimes which threaten a person's security interests by threatening or damaging physical well-being, or the enjoyment of a tolerable living environment. Crimes affecting accumulative interests are ranked next; these involve property beyond that necessary for preservation of basic subsistence or a tolerable living environment.

This conceptual framework was broadened to allow the court work group to develop standards for ranking the wide array of petty, nonvictimizing offenses that also come before the Staten Island court. Classification of these offenses began with those which, while not violating the interests of an identifiable "victim," nonetheless present a risk of resultant harm. Some common vice crimes (for example, trafficking in drugs and gambling activities) may result in quite serious harm even though, it may be argued, consumers of these goods and services have willingly assumed the risks involved. There are also vice crimes which involve no direct harm, but constitute conduct offensive to community sensibilities (for example, prostitution). The third category of nonvictimizing crime are those involving a breach of citizenship duties. The most serious is the corruption of public officials. Less serious are those which interfere with or undermine the proper administration of justice or other governmental operations including, at the lowest end, such minor crimes as the false report of an incident.

To anchor these offenses in relation to each other, the planning group followed some general ranking principles:

—among victimizing crimes, property and theft offenses generally should be weighed as less serious than those involving physical harm;

—nonvictimizing crimes which present a clear potential for tangible harm should be considered only slightly less serious than property crimes, while those presenting no risk of harm should be ranked in the lowest ranges of severity; and

—"breach of duty" crimes should range from medium to low severity, according to the degree of their interference with proper governmental operations.

These principles were then applied by distributing the seventy-one penal law offenses across and within a framework containing six severity levels. Offenses involving substantial physical harm were ranked in the highest levels. The lowest levels were devoted primarily to harmless nonvictimizing and public decorum offenses. Property offenses and the more serious drug and gambling offenses were distributed primarily in the middle bands. In some instances where the scope of a particular offense, as defined in the penal law, spanned widely dissimilar conduct or a broad range of harms in terms of actual criminal behavior, the offense was broken down into subcategories.

To illustrate, assaults were distinguished by the gravity of the injury—substantial or minor—and then further categorized according to the type of victim involved. The most serious type of assault (e.g., where the victim is especially vulnerable and the injury is substantial) was anchored at severity level one, while the least serious (e.g., a trivial injury resulting from an altercation between acquaintances) was assigned to level five. Similarly, drug possession cases were distinguished as to the type of drug: possession of street drugs was assigned to severity level three, while criminal possession of pharmaceutical drugs was ranked at level four.

This overall ranking provided an agreed-upon framework for calibrating an appropriate number or range of day fine units for each specific offense. Using the West German day fine scale as a model, the work group assumed that a scale of 360 day fine units could offer sufficient flexibility for the full range of finable offense charges appearing in the New York State codes (from infractions through felonies). The work group then agreed to limit the range for violations through misdemeanors to 5 to 120 units. Setting a floor at 5 units was thought to ensure offenses at the lowest end of the scale were not trivialized. Setting the ceiling at 120 day fines was thought to reflect adequately the less serious nature of the cases disposed in the criminal court, and to reserve the upper two-thirds of the scale for use for felony offenses if the system is extended to the Richmond County Supreme Court.

The resulting range of 115 day fine units was then distributed across the six severity levels for misdemeanors and violations. Relatively broad ranges were assigned to the more severe levels; progressively narrower ranges were assigned as severity decreased, because offenses at the low end of the scale reflect minor criminal behavior at a relatively uniform level of severity, while the upper levels contain a wider range of offense severity.

Using this structure, the final set of day fine scales was crafted for all offenses. One further refinement was added to the full scales. Circumstances other than harm (which was the primary consideration in determining the rank order of each offense) may be important to judges in assessing the severity of a specific crime and thus in determining the appropriate number of day fine units to be imposed in an individual case. For example, although an offender's prior criminal record is likely to have been weighed by the judge in determining the *type* of sentence to be imposed (jail, probation, fine, etc.), an absence of prior convictions might warrant a discount from the normal day fine number, while a criminal record of exceptional length might trigger a move to a higher number. To account for such factors, a separate "discount" day fine scale incorporated a reduction of 15 percent from the assigned number of day fine units. A "premium" scale, incorporating an added 15 percent, was also provided to allow sentences to reflect aggravating factors. These discount and premium scales appear to the left and right of the normal day fine number or benchmark.

Setting a Value for Each Day Fine Unit

To set the value of each day fine unit for individual offenders in relation to financial circumstances, the court planning group decided that any offender with a steady income stream could be fined. The valuation method devised was based on a proportionate share of the offender's net daily income. While the process does not reflect differences in assets or debts, it does take into account an offender's family responsibilities, using a method derived from practices commonly used by American courts to set child support payments by noncustodial parents.[2]

The planning group decided that an additional "flat-rate" discount was needed to calibrate the punitive impact of the day fines to the other sentencing options available to the court, and to current fine amounts. The day fine system in Staten Island was intended to serve in an intermediate position; that is, day fine amounts should be substantial enough, relative to an offender's means, to be viewed as more punitive than a conditional discharge or routine probation supervision, though not so stiff on a routine basis as to approach the severity of typical jail sentences. At the same time, the planning group felt that the day fine amounts for the most trivial violations committed by offenders with the lowest incomes should remain, as fixed fines are now, at very modest dollar amounts.

By testing an array of discount rates, one was chosen that seemed to the court work group to achieve both of these goals. A flat reduction rate of one-third results, for example, in a day fine amount of $30 for a woman supporting three children on welfare who is sentenced to a five-unit day fine for disorderly conduct. Further up the severity and income scales, an offender convicted of theft of property worth $400 would, given a modest gross annual income of $13,000, result in a total day fine amount of $450. However, because any flat-rate system falls more harshly on low-income offenders than on those who have more assets or access to credit, the planning group created a two-tiered discount rate to further reduce the hardship of a day fine for the poorest offenders: Offenders above the official federal poverty income guidelines receive a one-third rate of discount on their day fine unit value, whereas the discount for those living in poverty is one-half.

Applying this valuation system to the range of offenses scaled in the Staten Island benchmark system, total day fine amounts range from a low of $25 (for the welfare mother convicted of the lowest five-unit offense) to a typical high-range amount of nearly $4000 (for a single, self-supporting offender in the $35,000 gross annual income range convicted of the most serious offense on the benchmark scale). To streamline the process of actually sentencing offenders to day fines, all the steps were condensed into a value table for use by judges and other court officials.

Notes

1. For some time, the New York City correctional system has been under court order to reduce overcrowding; in 1983, the federal court required the city to release some defendants from custody to ease the problem. Conditions have not improved much in recent years. However, because Staten Island is the smallest jurisdiction within the city of New York, it does not contribute a significant proportion of the cases which crowd the city's facilities. Thus, while overcrowding as well as substantive sentencing concerns encourage the court's focus on alternative sentences, the situation in Staten Island is not as pressing as it is in some other jurisdictions. This is also a favorable context for careful innovation and experimentation.

2. The offender's net daily income (whether from wages, welfare, or other sources such as unemployment insurance) is reduced by a factor of 15 percent for self-support, 15 percent for the support of two dependents, 10 percent each for the support of two more dependents, and 5 percent each for any additional dependents over these four.

References

Albrecht, Hans-Jorg, and Johnson, Elmer H. (1980). "Fines and Justice Administration: The Experience of the Federal Republic of Germany," 4 *International Journal of Comparative and Applied Criminal Justice* 3.

Casale, Silvia S. G. (1981). "Fines in Europe: A Study of the Use of Fines in Selected European Countries with Empirical Research on Problems of Fine Enforcement," Working Paper #10, *Fines in Sentencing*, New York: Vera Institute of Justice.

Cummings, Laird (1988). "Developing a Microcomputer-Based Management Information System for Fines Administration," 13 *Justice System Journal* 80 (1988).

Gillespie, Robert W. (1980). "Fines as an Alternative to Incarceration: The German Experience," 44 *Federal Probation* 20.

Greene, Judith A. (1987). *Report to the German Marshall Fund of the United States on Day Fine Study Tour and Richmond County Day-Fine Planning Conference*. New York: Vera Institute of Justice.

Hillsman, Sally T., and Greene, Judith A. (1987). *Improving the Use and Administration of Criminal Fines: A Report to the Richmond County, New York, Criminal Court Day-Fine Planning Project*. New York: Vera Institute of Justice.

——— (1988). "Tailoring Criminal Fines to the Financial Means of the Offender," 72 *Judicature* 38.

Hillsman, Sally T., Sichel, Joyce L., and Mahoney, Barry (1984). *Fines in Sentencing: A Study of the Use of the Fine as a Criminal Sanction*. Washington, D.C.: National Institute of Justice.

Mahoney, Barry, and Thornton, Marlene (1988). "Means-Based Fining: Views of American Trial Court Judges," 13 *Justice System Journal* 51.

McDonald, Douglas C. (1986). *Punishment Without Walls*. New Brunswick, N.J.: Rutgers University Press.

von Hirsch, Andrew (1985). *Past or Future Crimes*. New Brunswick, N.J.: Rutgers University Press.

6.4
Intensive Supervision Probation: How and for Whom?

Todd R. Clear
Patricia L. Hardyman

There have been two quite distinguishable intensive supervision movements in the last quarter century. The first, which occurred in the 1960s, has been characterized as the "search for the magic number" (Carter and Wilkins, 1984) because it was primarily a series of experimental projects designed to determine the optimal number of clients to be supervised in a single caseload. The second movement, which began in the mid-1980s and continues today full force, might be called a "response to crowded prisons" because most of these new programs have resulted from alarm about crowding in U.S. prisons and jails. The difference in the nature of these two movements is significant because it helps to make understandable the considerable contrast between the traditional meaning of intensive supervision programs (ISPs) common in the 1960s and today's versions of the same general idea.

The impetus for the new ISP movement does not come from careful study of the literature on community corrections. It is instead a product of the serious problem of prison crowding in the 1980s. Without jail and prison crowding, it is hard to imagine that the current support for ISP would have materialized of its own accord. In most jurisdictions in the United States, courts are imposing levels of control or punishment for which the system simply lacks resources, and ISP is presented as an alternative

From Todd R. Clear and Patricia L. Hardyman, "The New Intensive Supervision Movement," 36 *Crime and Delinquency* 42 (1990).

that occupies the crevice between available resources and demands for them. In short, overwhelming institutional crowding created an irresistible demand for alternatives to incarceration. But because of its extremely limited public credibility, probation was poorly equipped to meet the need. The solution to this dilemma was approached in part as a public relations problem: Corrections would bring about a version of "new, improved probation" that would be so richly endowed and tightly run that it could do what regular probation could not.

With a few exceptions, most of the new ISPs are quite brazen in their claims about the clients served. Partly as justification for the intensive methods employed, the client target group is referred to as the "serious," "dangerous," "recidivist," or "high-risk" offender. The image is created of a predatory group of offenders who must receive close supervision so as to keep the community from peril. These labels are often applied as broad generalizations about the persons who will be eligible for ISPs. It is important to clarify the use of these labels.

The term "high-risk" offender refers to a person whose characteristics, including the length and diversity of criminal record, indicate that he or she has a high probability of some future, serious law violation (Gottfredson and Gottfredson, 1986). This is normally established through the use of a statistical assessment instrument, but it can also be the result of a clinical assessment of certain types of offenders (Monahan, 1981). A "dangerous" offender is a subclass of high-risk offenders for whom there is some reason to believe that any future criminality will involve violence. Thus, ISPs that claim to work with "high-risk" or "dangerous" offenders are really saying that they tap the high end of a spectrum of offenders arrayed according to probability of a new, serious offense.

A person is defined as a "serious" offender due to the nature of the current offense. Usually, the label "serious" is restricted to designate only the most heinous, predatory personal crimes. Thus, when an ISP is focused on a serious offender, it selects criminals from among those whose curent offenses are the most repugnant.

In the specification of target group criteria, most ISPs establish certain bases for exclusion. One common reason for exclusion is a violent (i.e., "serious") current offense—and some programs go so far as to exclude a person with any prior history of violence. Another common requirement for exclusion is a long criminal record or an otherwise unusual risk to the community. New Jersey's ISP, for example, is available only to "low risk inmates who are sincerely motivated to change" (New Jersey Administrative Office of the Courts, 1985).

When the new ISP establishes exclusionary criteria based on current offense and prior record, it restricts itself to a target group that is not likely to tap either high-risk or serious offenders, not to mention dangerous ones. ISP administrators may be pleased that they can avoid responsibility for these offenders, but the irony is that regular probation usually cannot. In many cases, offenders who are ineligible for ISP due to their record or risk are nonetheless eligible for regular probation. Remarkably, some of those who would be ineligible for ISP because of their purported risk level or crime seriousness instead are placed on regular probation.

In Georgia, for instance, over 30 percent of the ISP (there called "IPS" clients) score as "minimum risk" on their assessment instrument, while less than 20 percent are "maximum" risk (Erwin, 1986). This profile is not very different from that of regular probationers across the state. In New Jersey's program, 50 percent of the ISP cases score low risk and 20 percent high risk, compared to 45 percent and 17 percent, respectively, for a regular probation group that matched ISP crime criteria (Pearson, 1988). In both of these highly successful and widely touted programs, the ISP client is not a considerably higher risk than the regular probationer in the same jurisdiction. Moreover, in both cases, the ISP client is hand-selected for the program.

In other words, there are almost certainly numerous persons on regular probation who represent a considerably higher public safety problem than the ISP client. Yet markedly greater time and attention—on the order of three to ten times the commitment of resources—is invested in the ISP client. Stated in another way, these two examples of ISP programs have been able to develop a concentrated level of supervision heretofore unheard of, with a degree of community control that exceeds any previously experienced in this country. This supervision is applied to a target group of client volunteers, one-third or one-half of whom represent a minimal level of community risk—this, while the ordinary probationer (who looks much the same in terms of risk) receives the usual degree of (often scant) attention.

Advocates of ISPs respond that while this may be true, the real justification of these programs lies in the prison space they save and, hence, in tax dollars. These offenders are being diverted from prison, and that is the main intent of the ISP. Such claims of program priority are certainly legitimate, but they leave unanswered a troubling question. If these ISP clients are truly bound for incarceration and yet look not remarkably different from regular probation cases in terms of risk and crime seriousness, then why are they bound for incarceration? And how much of the current crisis of prison crowding is a product of irrational allocation of incarcerative resources rather than a scarcity of those resources? More to the point, if ISP clients look like regular probation cases except for being prison-bound, then why do they need such intensive supervision?

This raises a concern about viewing ISPs as contributing to an improvement in public safety. If ISPs for the most part deal with a relatively ordinary set of offenders, then by definition they will have trouble enhancing community protection because their clients represent such low risk, in general, to begin with. This seems incongruous, because the public is so used to viewing prison-bound offenders as being by definition "dangerous." Yet if the data from these early studies of the new ISPs can be taken as an indication, there are many persons bound for prison who are neither serious offenders nor high risk, compared to regular probationers. The fact that they get thoroughly intensive supervision cannot be considered a major contribution to public safety.

The problem of target group criteria has already been described. Especially when a program is new and vulnerable to criticism, there is considerable pressure to apply exclusions to the target group such that those with lengthy criminal records and/or serious current offenses are ineligible. When this is done, the vast majority of incarceration-bound offenders are excluded, and this makes it all the more difficult to obtain cases for supervision.

The success that many ISPs—such as those in New York, Arizona, Georgia, New Mexico, and New Jersey—have had in acquiring clients is impressive. A great deal of this success is a result of selection processes.

The best way to guarantee high numbers of clients is to allow judges to sentence directly to the program. Judges frequently sentence offenders to probation even though they are uncomfortable with the sentence. They are more than happy to have additional alternatives available. For these cases, ISPs can serve more as an alternative to probation than as an alternative to incarceration.

When judges sentence directly to ISPs, it is difficult to know the true diversion rate. Both Arizona and Georgia allow direct sentencing of offenders.[1] Arizona claims a diversion rate of about 90 percent, but this is based on an internal study that reviewed a sample of ISP cases and found that 90 percent *could* have gone to prison under Arizona law. Of course, *could* and *would* are very different. Because there is so much of an overlap between probation and prison case profiles, there is a large probability that the direct-sentence cases would have gone to regular probation without the ISP alternative. Georgia officials privately estimate that only about three-fourths of their cases are true diversions, for example, even though every judge signs a document for each ISP assignment stating that the offender would have gone to prison had the program been unavailable.

In order to avoid the net-widening problem, some ISPs have tried to wait until later in the sentencing process before selecting the case. An Oregon program considered cases only after a presentence report recommended that the person receive an incarcerative sentence. Even so, their own studies show that a portion of those cases would get regular probation anyway (Clear et al., 1988).

ISP offenders in New Jersey must actually be sentenced to incarceration before they can apply to the program. Even this approach may not be problem-free. Early in the program there were rumors that some judges were sentencing offenders to prison in order to make them eligible for ISPs. While New Jersey officials have taken steps to reduce this problem, "hedged" sentences are a common complaint in programs that use resentencing to divert offenders.

The methods of the new ISP movement are unapologetically strict. The typical program calls for at least twice-weekly contact, home visits at night, community service, and restitution; many programs use curfews, urine monitoring, and electronic surveillance. Surveys of ISP requirements have shown them to be quite varied but truly intensive by any reasonable criteria (Byrne, 1986).

One impressive aspect of the new ISP movement is the degree of intensity it appears to have achieved. Regular audits of caseloads in Georgia and New Jersey show that probation officers routinely exceed the very ambitious supervision contact requirements the programs' promotional literature presents.

The use of stringent methods combined with strict enforcement raises three issues: appropriateness of conditions, interaction effect, and costs.

In many of the ISPs, conditions are applied across-the-board without much attention to the individual circumstances of the case. For instance, a punitive condition such as community service may be required, even though similarly situated offenders on regular probation would not face a similar requirement. Conversely, risk-control conditions such as urinalysis are applied even when there is no evidence that the use of drugs has ever been a problem in an offender's life.

The inordinate use of punitive conditions means that the scale of punitive sanctions is further muddied under the ISP. If every ISP offender performs 140 hours of community service regardless of the offense, then the service loses much of its punitive value as a sanction because everyone gets it. One of the reasons it is so hard to justify ISPs for serious offenders is that the scale of punishments is already thrown off by the heavy unnecessary reliance upon prison as a core sanction. Overly punitive ISP conditions exacerbate this problem as it applies to community supervision.

A different, but equally serious, problem is created by the unrestrained use of risk-control conditions. Once information exists that a rules violation is occurring, a response is necessary, even if it is unwise. In Georgia, for example, routine use is made of urine screening, even for offenders for whom there is little reason to be concerned about drug use. A large proportion of urines come back dirty, many of them indicating marijuana use only. When this happens, it puts agents of the law in a bind. The use of marijuana is still against the law in Georgia, and the urine is clear evidence of continuing law violation. Yet for many offenders, the adjustment to supervision has been otherwise acceptable (or even laudable) and to return the person to prison would be ridiculous, given the goals of the program. So the probation officer is forced to play a type of game—warning the offender and noting the violation but trying to avoid action unless something else happens in the case.

The problem here is both conceptual and practical. The imposition of a condition is a "threat": The offender should either abide by the requirement or suffer the consequences. When the threat is hollow because there can be no intent to follow it with action, or when it appears arbitrary because it is out of scale with other threats, the law is mocked. The resources simply do not exist to carry out all the threats made in the ISPs—and nobody in the new ISPs would claim they should all be fully enforced. The primary role of the threats is to show how "tough" the new alternative really is and to thereby generate public support for it. Whether it is appropriate to use conditions in this way, with their enforcement left to discretion and potential abuse, is a troubling question.

There are only two types of savings that can occur as a result of an ISP alternative: Actual dollars are saved because a facility is closed down or substantially reduced in its use, or costs are avoided because the need to build a new prison is reduced due to diversion. Most of the claims of savings will take the latter form, and so they are more symbolic than actual tax savings.

However, even cost avoidance can be reduced by close enforcement strategies.

Assume that an ISP is supervising 1,000 offenders who, as a group, would have served an average of 9 prison months each—a total possible savings of 9,000 cell months. Assume as well that offenders who fail under an ISP serve a premium of an average of 24 months per offender, and assume further that 25 percent fail.[2] That reduces the net savings to merely 3,000 cell months. If the true diversion rate for those original 1,000 offenders is only 70 percent, then the net savings is only 300 cell months. If 33 percent of the nondiversion are low-risk cases who otherwise would have failed at a rate of 15 percent without the close supervision and would have received a lesser premium for a penalty for failure of, for example, 12 months, then there is actually a net *loss* of 120 cell months. Whether these assumptions are completely accurate is open to debate, but as speculations they are certainly not outlandish. In any event, they show how an ISP that is very successful at diversion can, through interaction effect and overenforcement, result in a net loss in prison space at financial cost to the public.

Notes

1. Only a percentage of Georgia's ISP offenders are diverted to the program directly upon sentencing. The remainder are diverted after sentencing, but the use of the postsentencing option is getting less frequent.
2. This is the percentage of failures that the new ISPs commonly produce.

References

Byrne, James (1986). "The Control Controversy: A Preliminary Examination of Intensive Probation Supervision in the United States," 50 *Federal Probation* 2–16.

Carter, Robert, and Leslie T. Wilkins (1984). "Caseloads: Some Conceptual Models," in *Probation, Parole, and Community Corrections* (2d ed.), edited by Robert Carter and Leslie T. Wilkins. New York: Wiley.

Clear, Todd, Carol Shapiro, Suzanne Flynn, and Ellen Chayet (1988). *The Probation Development Project: Successes, Failures, and Question Marks.* Newark, N.J.: School of Criminal Justice. (mimeo)

Erwin, Billie S. (1986). *Final Report of the Georgia Intensive Probation Supervision Project.* Atlanta: Department of Corrections.

Gottfredson, Stephen E., and Don M. Gottfredson (1986). "Accuracy of Prediction Models," in *Criminal Careers and Career Criminals, Vol. II,* edited by Alfred Blumstein, Jacqueline Cohen, Jeffrey Roth, and Christy A. Visher. Washington, D.C.: National Academy Press.

Monahan, John (1981). *Predicting Violent Behavior: An Assessment of Clinical Techniques.* Beverly Hills, Calif.: Sage.

New Jersey Administrative Office of the Courts (1985). *Intensive Supervision Program.* Trenton, N.J.: Author.

Pearson, Frank (1988). *Final Report of the Evaluation of New Jersey's Intensive Supervision Program.* New Brunswick, N.J.: Rutgers University Center for the Study of Crime and Delinquency.

6.5
Between Prison and Probation

Norval Morris
Michael Tonry

Many offenders are jailed or imprisoned because credible community punishments do not exist and judges believe their crimes *too serious* to be sanctioned solely by an ordinary probation sentence. Many offenders are sentenced to probation because credible community punishments do not exist and judges believe their crimes *not serious enough* to be sanctioned by an ordinary jail or prison sentence. In both cases, credible, community-based intermediate punishments are lacking.

By "intermediate punishments" we mean all punishments lying between imprisonment and "ordinary" probation. These include fines, community service orders, house arrest, intermittent imprisonment, split sentences, and intensive supervision probation, buttressed where appropriate by electronic and other monitoring techniques.

By "credible," we mean punishments that judges, offenders, and the general public will regard as intrusive, punitive infringements on the offender's liberty and appropriate as punishments for moderately severe crimes.

The United States has lagged far behind Western Europe in the development of intermediate punishments. Community service orders have been common in England and Wales since the mid-1970s. Criminal fines in sizable, punitive amounts are widely ordered in many European countries. In West Germany and Sweden, particularly, "day fines" that calibrate the amount of a fine to the offender's means and the severity of his crime

From Norval Morris and Michael Tonry, "Between Prison and Probation: Intermediate Punishments in a Rational Sentencing System," *N.I.J. Reports* January/February 1990, 8–10. This article summarizes a book of the same title, by the same authors, published by Oxford University Press, 1990.

substitute for short prison terms. In the United States, by contrast, intermediate punishments are used much less commonly. Where they exist, they are often rationalized as "alternatives," sanctions to be imposed in lieu of incarceration. Whatever their rationales, they are commonly applied to offenders who otherwise would not be jailed or imprisoned. The American failure to use intermediate punishments for moderately serious crimes has three causes.

First, too little money, effort, and imagination have been expended to develop programs that are cost effective and protective of public safety. Judges, prosecutors, and the general public too often simply don't believe intermediate punishments are effective.

Second, there is a record of their being started by enthusiasts supported by "soft money," that is, by other than the ordinary budgets of the judicial or correctional systems that launched them. When that money ceases to flow, enthusiasm wanes, enforcement slackens, and another allegedly successful experiment dies.

Third, and of more importance, intermediate punishments have been bypassed by the sentencing reform movement that has influenced all American judicial systems, federal, state, and local. The imposition of intermediate punishments is everywhere ad hoc and idiosyncratic.

This article and the book on which it is based[1] argue for incorporating intermediate punishments into sentencing guidelines and other systems of structured sentencing discretion.

If fairness, rationality, and improved crime control are to be achieved in our systems of justice, the near vacuum between ordinary probation and incarceration must be filled by a graduated series of intermediate punishments imposed in a principled way. Until sentencing guidelines direct judges to use intermediate punishments in appropriate cases and to select among them and between them and jail or prison terms, these sanctions will continue to be underused, little-respected adjuncts of probation.

As one surveys the complexity of punishment processes in the states, cities, and localities, as well as in the federal system, it becomes clear that there has been considerable experimentation with intermediate punishments. Some programs have received substantial publicity and have been applied to large numbers of offenders. In one form or another, intensive supervision probation (ISP), house arrest, electronic monitoring, and community service are in use in nearly every state.

Intensive Supervision Probation

Many states have established ISP programs. Some, like Georgia's, are "front door" programs aimed at diverting prison-bound offenders to community-based programs. Others, like New Jersey's, are "back door" programs aimed at providing early release from prison for lower risk prisoners. Still others, like Massachusetts', are case management efforts by probation departments to subject higher risk probationers to tighter controls.

House Arrest
Many states have established house arrest programs. Here again there are front door and back door versions. Florida's is the best known front door program and claims to have served many thousands of offenders diverted from imprisonment. Oklahoma's back door program operates as an early release device for selected prison inmates.

Community Service
There are numerous community service programs, but little evidence is available that they are used as other than supplements to probation. An exception is the well-evaluated community service program for repeat property offenders operated by the Vera Institute of Justice in New York City.

Fines
Though fines are often ordered in the United States, they are used erratically, are often haphazardly enforced, and are virtually never ordered as a substitute for imprisonment. Innovative projects in Richmond County (Staten Island), New York, and Phoenix, Arizona, are testing the feasibility of day fines in the United States [see Extract 6.3].

Other Intermediate Punishments
Many other kinds of intermediate punishments are possible. Night detention, day detention, shock probation (including a short prison term), shock incarceration (followed by quick release), and "boot camps" are among others now in use. Use of electronic monitoring and drug testing to monitor adherence to conditions of the sentence is common.

Many, though not all, of these punishment programs have been established as responses to prison crowding, either to reduce crowding or to save money by substituting less expensive community-based punishments for more expensive institutional ones. Usually, the argument goes, the intermediate punishment is an appropriate alternative to incarceration because it is punitive, intrusive, and crime-preventive.

Unfortunately, in many cases. though not all, the research evidence and common experience teach that intermediate punishments free up many fewer prison beds and save much less money than their proponents claim. Judges and other public officials too often hesitate to impose a new intermediate punishment on *prison-bound* offenders because they doubt its ability to deliver appropriate punishment and to prevent crime. Judges and other public officials too often leap to impose new intermediate punishments on *probation-bound* offenders. At worst, from the judges' perspective intermediate punishments will be no less punitive and crime-preventive than ordinary probation. If a new sanction promises to fill the void between probation and prison, it is only natural for judges to impose it.

Principled Punishment System Needed

The major reason why these new punishments fail to save prison beds or money is that they are too often applied to the wrong offender. This is because nowhere have they been built into a comprehensive, graduated, and principled punishment system based on defined sentencing policies. They have been scattered and isolated experiments, mostly sailing under the banner of "alternatives" to imprisonment.

The "alternatives" approach to intermediate punishments is defective both in theory and in practice. In theory, it is an error to see intermediate punishments as any more an alternative to imprisonment than an alternative to ordinary probation. In practice, it has not been shown that intermediate punishments much reduce the pressure on scarce cell space because they draw their subjects at least as much from those who would not have been incarcerated as from those who would. A further defect in the "alternatives" approach is that the often-repeated claim that these programs will save money has not yet been shown, at least in the short run. For intermediate punishments to escape the failings of the alternatives movement, they must be incorporated into comprehensive sentencing policies. The sentencing reform movement shifted sentences in many jurisdictions away from indeterminate prison terms with release based on parole predictions of fitness for release, to a variety of relatively fixed-term sentences. The main purpose of the reforms has been to eliminate or reduce unjustified disparities between punishments.

Unfortunately, the debate and the legislative and judicial remedies pursued to that end have been directed almost exclusively to trying to eliminate two types of disparity—disparity in who goes to prison and who does not, and, for those who are sent to prison, disparity in the duration of their incarceration. The appropriate role of intermediate punishments has been almost completely ignored by most sentencing commissions. The U.S. Sentencing Commission, for example, included intermediate punishments in its guidelines only for the most minor offenses.

In *Between Prison and Probation* we survey current practice with the imposition of intermediate punishments. One aspect of our proposals merits mention, since it cuts against the conventional wisdom of "just deserts" which has so influenced American sentencing policy. The idea that what is seen as a justly deserved punishment should define the specific punishment is in our view a fundamental error that accounts for much that is currently wrong with our punishment systems. We believe the justly deserved punishment does indeed define the upper and lower limits of severity of a punishment, but within those limits there must be room for both utilitarian concerns of crime control and humane considerations [see Extract 4.3]. Those utilitarian and humane values will often find their expression in the imposition of intermediate punishments, provided punishments are rigorously supervised and enforced so as to protect public safety.

Between Prison and Probation suggests a principled sentencing system that differs from the usual in-or-out and, if in, for-how-long system. It substitutes principles that allow for interchangeability between imprisonment and intermediate punishments and for interchangeability between probation and intermediate punishments. We argue that it is inappropriate in the name of justice always to treat alike those who have committed similar harms and who have similar criminal records.

Below a level of severity of crime punishable by, say, two years' imprisonment, crime prevention purposes and a humane economy of punishment require principled interchangeability between punishments to be served in prison and punishments to be served in the community and also between probation and more severe or restrictive community-based punishments. Only in such a system is it possible to give a principled role to intermediate punishments. Such a system could reduce class and race bias in criminal sentencing.

For too long in this country intermediate punishments have been seen as interesting experiments in leniency, in reducing the costs of imprisonment without inflicting increased crime on the community. Other countries, as well as many scattered developments in this country, have shown that this is too narrow a view, that intermediate punishments have a much larger role to play. It is time we regained leadership in fashioning an effective, community-protective, and humane system of criminal punishments.[2]

Notes

1. Morris, Norval, and Tonry, Michael, *Between Prison and Probation: Intermediate Punishments in a Rational Sentencing System* (New York: Oxford University Press, 1990).

2. [The authors' interchangeability principles, elaborated in their book, permit substitution among penalties, provided the penalties involved (1) do not breach the upper or lower desert limits on permissible punishments, referred to in this extract and Extract 4.3, and (2) are "equivalent in function" as explained in the book. For a critique of these proposals, and a comparison with those set forth in Extract 6.6, see Andrew von Hirsch, "Scaling Intermediate Punishments: A Comparison of Two Models," in J. Byrne, A. Lurigio, and J. Petersilia, eds., *Smart Sentencing: Expanding Options for Intermediate Sanctions* (Newbury Park, Calif.: Sage, 1992)—Eds.]

6.6
Scaling Community Punishments

Andrew von Hirsch
Martin Wasik
Judith Greene

Punishments in the community have been dealt with only briefly by writers on desert. In a 1976 work, one of us maintained that imprisonment is appropriate only for serious crimes (such as crimes of actual or threatened violence), and that noncustodial penalties should be employed for offenses of intermediate or lesser gravity.[1] However, only a cursory sketch was offered of what those alternatives should be and how they should be arrayed. Later writings on desert have likewise recommended limiting the use of imprisonment but have not examined noncustodial sentences in much depth.[2]

The sentencing guidelines movement has also paid relatively little heed to community sanctions. The Minnesota guidelines—the first such effort and, perhaps, the most sophisticated to date—address only the use of imprisonment. Imprisonment is restricted, under the guidelines, to offenders convicted of more serious crimes (chiefly, crimes against the person), and to those with lengthy criminal records.[3] Other offenders are to receive nonprison sanctions. However, the guidelines do not specify what those other sanctions should be.

This emphasis on incarceration was understandable at the time the writers of guidelines began their work. Noncustodial sentences were little developed—consisting mainly of conventional probation. The use of im-

---

From Andrew von Hirsch, Martin Wasik, and Judith Greene, "Punishments in the Community and the Principles of Desert," 20 *Rutgers Law Journal* 595 (1988). Excerpted and reprinted by permission.

prisonment was expanding rapidly. It seemed sensible to try to regulate and limit the use of imprisonment, before going on to the more complex task of fashioning new noncustodial penalties and scaling their use.

This strategy of focusing on imprisonment has had its costs, however. Guidelines such as Minnesota's did have modest success in making the use of imprisonment more uniform and predictable, but other penalties have remained as ill-regulated and disparate as before.[4] Moreover, the guideline writers—given their failure to address noncustodial sanctions—have been able to offer little or no advice to those other reformers who were beginning to devise novel alternative penalties.

Recently, this latter effort has been much in evidence. With prisons overfilled and the costs of new prison construction rising, the need has become apparent for credible sanctions that can be administered in the community. Whereas a decade ago probation was virtually the only alternative to imprisonment, today a host of other sanctions are being experimented with, including "intensive" supervision, home detention, community service, and day fines.[5]

The proponents of these new sanctions largely disregarded the parallel efforts being made to regulate and scale the use of imprisonment. After all, they were dealing not with the prison but with community sanctions. Why worry about what penal aim these novel sentences served or how they could be arrayed on a scale? Apparently, it sufficed to make the newer options available. Judges invoked prison in borderline cases, reformers believed, when they felt they had no meaningful alternative (that is, none other than routine supervision by a probation officer administering a large caseload). Once more-credible noncustodial penalties were brought into existence, judges could be expected to prefer those sanctions.

This strategy—of simply creating more options—has proven a disappointment, however. In the absence of principles governing their use, the novel sanctions have not necessarily served as replacements for imprisonment. Instead, judges often sentenced people to prison as before and used the new sanctions as substitutes for probation—a measure which they had come to regard as perfunctory. The new measures proliferated at the expense of probation, and at the expense of each other. To enhance public acceptance, programs tended to be targeted at offenders thought most likely to "cooperate," namely, persons whose modest crimes and short criminal records would have made them unlikely candidates for imprisonment in the first place. It is scarcely surprising that more careful recent assessments have questioned the newer "alternatives'" success in reducing reliance on imprisonment.[6]

Now, at last, it is beginning to be recognized that the two reform efforts cannot afford to disregard each other; scaling penalties is as important for noncustodial sanctions as for custodial.

The time has come to apply a coherent penal rationale to the development of, and choice among, punishments in the community. This article concentrates on one such rationale—desert—and discusses how it might illuminate the use of noncustodial penalties. At the end, we will see how much our conclusions might change if desert constraints are relaxed in favor of more utilitarian models.

In this article, we will be using grids to explicate our position. In this country, sentencing guidelines have usually taken numerical form—recommending specific quanta of sentence, or ranges of sentence, for various crimes. The grid has been the device chiefly used to scale durations of imprisonment.[7] The grid is capable also of being used, as the reader will see, to scale noncustodial penalties. It should be emphasized, however, that our use of the grid is for heuristic purposes only—as it best illustrates the relationships among the various elements in our system. Whether it is advisable actually to adopt numerical guidelines in law depends on the legal and political traditions of the particular jurisdiction.[8]

But even where the adoption of statewide guidelines and a grid would be unwise, those concerned with noncustodial sentences will still have to think about how those sentences should be scaled. That thinking is aided by the hypothetical use of grids.

Our article is theoretical: we wish to offer a conception of how noncustodial penalties can be arrayed. To provide a coherent picture in a short space, we do not attempt to address the more practical specifics—for example, how a particular jurisdiction's statutes might have to be amended in order to put our conception into force. We think it is more important to try to specify the objectives of noncustodial sentencing, and that is the purpose of this article.

To remain concise, we assume the reader is familiar with the basic tenets of desert theory—the theory we propose applying to noncustodial sentences. The central thesis of desert theory is well known enough: that comparative severities of punishment should be determined chiefly by the seriousness of offenders' crimes of conviction. The theory's more detailed tenets have been described at length elsewhere.[9] However, two other features of the theory are worth noting.

The first, mentioned already, is that desert theory permits most offenses to be dealt with by noncustodial sentences. A sentence of incarceration is a severe punishment, and the theory requires severe penalties only for serious crimes. For other crimes, a less severe, noncustodial sanction should be the sanction of choice.[10] Indeed, our suggestions in this article should be judged by their usefulness in reducing reliance on imprisonment.

Second, a desert rationale addresses only the severity of penalties, not their particular form. This permits considerable flexibility to use noncustodial sanctions of various types, as we shall see. It also potentially permits substitution among penalties. If A is a sanction that is appropriate for crimes of a given degree of seriousness, and B is a sanction of another type that is approximately of equal severity, then B can be substituted for A without infringing desert constraints. One may then even choose between the two severity-equivalent sanctions, A and B, on crime-preventive grounds since doing so would not alter the onerousness of the punishment.[11] How much substitution there should be, if any, is a question we will next address.

How Much Substitutability? Three Alternative Models

How might noncustodial sanctions be arrayed on a penalty scale? There are three models we might consider. All three reflect desert principles, but they differ from one another in the amount of substitutability of penalties they permit.

The "No Substitution" Model

The simplest model permits no substitution. It can be illustrated by a grid which sets out graded sanctions in the manner represented in Figure 1A. The two axes relate to seriousness of the offense and the prior record.

The relatively flat lines demarcating the different bands reflect the predominance of offense seriousness in deciding the sanction. The sentence, on a desert rationale, is determined chiefly by the current crime of conviction, qualified only to a limited extent by consideration of the defendant's record of previous convictions.[12] Penalties could be divided into mild, intermediate, and severe. For the purposes of illustration, we might place a judicial caution with unconditional release in the mild band, fines in the intermediate band, and custody in the severe band. To achieve ordinal proportionality, there would have to be ranking within these bands, in respect of the severity of the particular sanction involved—for example, the amount of fines.

This very simple model permits no interchange among different noncustodial sentences or between noncustodial and custodial sentences. It would envisage a sharp diminution in the variety of noncustodial sentences available to the courts, since only one penalty would be found within each band. Even this simple model, however, would permit a considerable reduction in the use of custodial sentences—since the intermediate-level crimes which now often receive custody would receive fines instead.

The model could be elaborated through subdividing some of the bands, without departing from the basic design. Custodial sentences could be

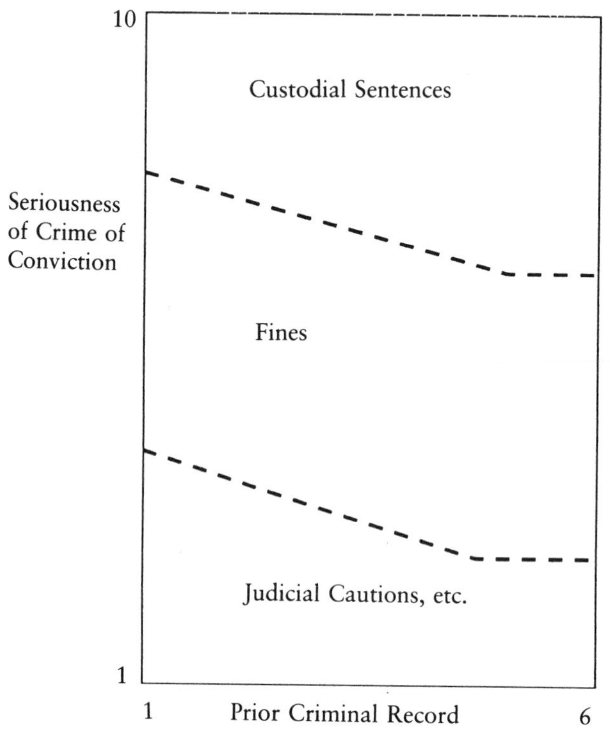

Fig. 1A — Simple "No Substitution" Model

divided into two bands, one more severe requiring residential custody, and one less severe calling for a form of partial confinement. The latter could consist of intermittent custody in a community residence or attendance center for prescribed hours of the day, evening, or weekends. Alternatively, it might consist instead of home detention during nonworking hours (see discussion below).

The band containing fines could likewise be subdivided, with substantial monetary penalties for upper-intermediate crimes, and more modest ones for lower-intermediate offenses. To achieve greater equity of impact, these penalties could be expressed as day fines: that is, as specified numbers of days' earnings, rather than as flat fine amounts [see Extract 6.3]. The lowest band could likewise be subdivided, with small, flat fines in its upper portion and cautions in its lower portion. The model, thus elaborated, is shown in Figure 1B.

By increasing the number of bands in this way, the scheme could further restrict the use of full custody, and would provide more gradual transitions in prescribed severity. However, the model would still permit no substitu-

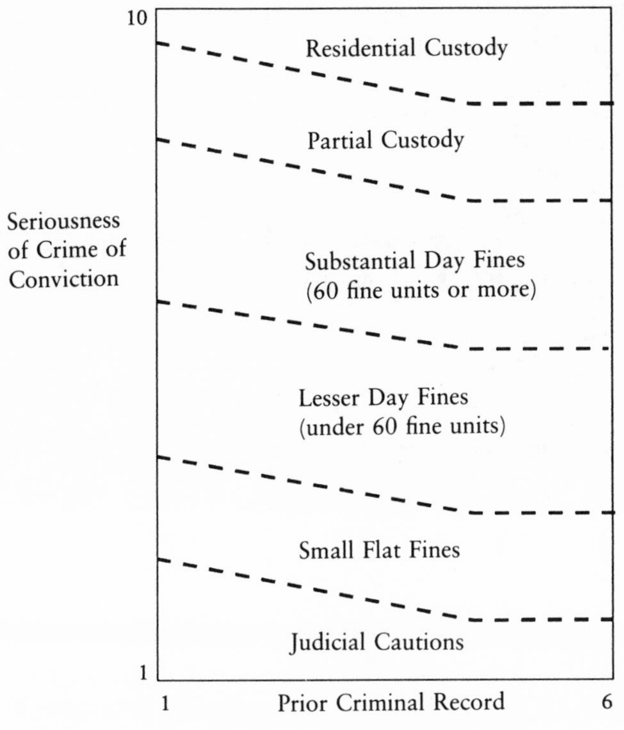

Fig. 1B — A More Elaborate "No Substitution" Model

tions among penalties, and this probably renders it unworkable. The prescribed sanctions may, for example, not be feasible for certain types of offenders. Consider the substantial day fines in the upper-intermediate band. While this sanction is suitable for most offenders to which it would apply, it cannot be used for those who are known to lack any regular earnings on which the fines can be based. A substitute sanction of equivalent severity would be needed in such cases.

The "Full Substitution" Model

Let us, then, consider the opposite: a grid with full substitutability. This model is envisaged in Figure 2.

The grid uses penalty bands computed on the basis of "penalty units," rather than specific types of sentences. Thus the mild penalty band could be indicated by penalty units between 1 and 20, the lower-intermediate by penalty units between 21 and 40, the upper-intermediate between 41 and 80, the moderately severe between 81 and 120, and the severe between 121 and 200. All available custodial and noncustodial sentences would, in

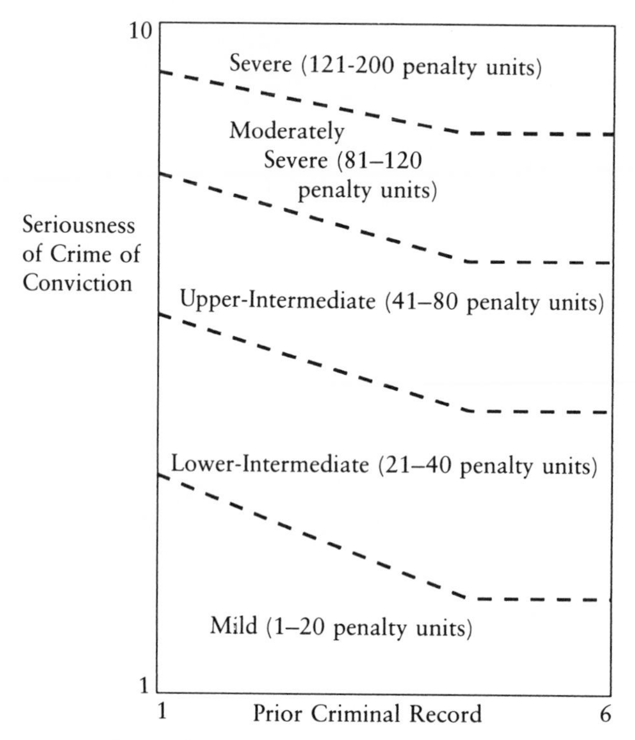

Fig. 2 — "Full Substitution" Model

a separate translation scale, be assigned penalty units, reflecting their comparative severities. This model would operate quite differently from that previously described, since it would allow extensive substitution among penalties. It would be possible, by reference to the translation scale, to equate penalties and to impose the appropriate penalty unit sentence through a variety of sentencing options. Also, the model would allow the combining of different penalties together, so as to achieve the prescribed penalty unit total. Combination of penalties would not be possible under the earlier models.

The full-substitution model would have a number of drawbacks. First, it presupposes a degree of sophistication in our ability to compare and calibrate severities of different species of sanctions that does not now exist and is not likely to exist. In our no-substitution models shown in Figures 1A and 1B, it is not difficult to make the judgment that the sanctions are arrayed in ascending order of severity. It would be vastly more difficult, however, to make comparisons of severity among a large and heterogeneous variety of possible sanctions.

Second, the need for full substitutability is far from obvious. Unless one has a heroic belief in individualization, cafeteria-style sentences can accomplish little more than a restricted substitutability scheme could. We have seen that substitutability is sometimes needed because the normally prescribed penalty cannot feasibly be applied to a particular defendant—as in the case of substantial day fines for defendants who lack regular earnings. But such cases can be accommodated by prescribing a standard substitute—say, a period of community service, instead. A limited substitutability scheme might also be useful for preventive ends—say, in order to supervise offenders convicted of middle-level crimes, who appear to be particularly amenable to such treatment. However, our present capacity to affect offenders' criminal behavior through supervision is fairly limited—and supervision targeted to a few discrete subcategories of offenders would probably be sufficient to accomplish the desired results.[13]

The "Partial Substitution" Model

What remains—and strikes us as most sensible—is *limited* substitutability. A standard type of punishment would be prescribed for each band in the grid, and would be the normally recommended type of disposition. However, there would be substitution rules which would allow that sanction to be replaced in specified types of cases.

A limited-substitution model might have the form of Figure 3. A presumed sentence type would be indicated for each penalty band.

However, limited substitution would be permitted within some of the bands. The substitute penalty would have to be of equivalent severity, and it could be invoked only for certain stated reasons. Those reasons could be crime-preventive (where, for example, the sentencer has special reason for believing that the alternative sanction might encourage the defendant to remain law-abiding) or administrative (where, for example, the standard sentence could not effectively be enforced against this type of defendant). Desert requirements would be satisfied nevertheless, because the substituted penalty is required to be of approximately the same onerousness as the normally prescribed grid sanction.

The standard sanctions in Figure 3 might be the same as those in Figure 1B. However, the substitution rules might permit the following possibilities:

1. The severe band would involve full custody, for periods of six months or more. No substitution of noncustodial penalties would be permitted, as these would be substantially milder.
2. The moderately severe band would normally involve partial custody—served, perhaps, at specified hours of the week or weekend at a community residence. However, short periods of full custody—say, of several

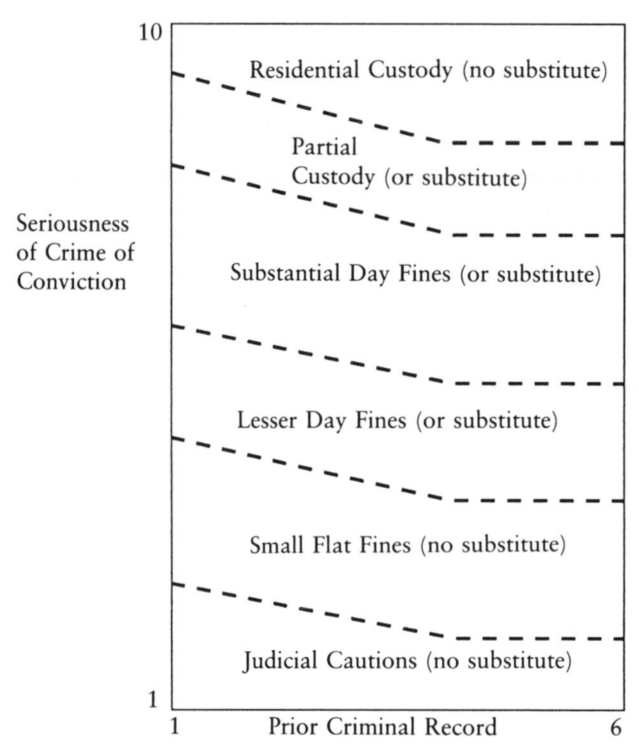

Fig. 3 — "Limited Substitution" Model

days or one or two weeks—would be the permitted substitute. The substitute might be invoked, for example, for offenders whose previous records of absconding suggests they would not comply with the prescribed terms of the normal penalty—for example, for offenders who would not attend a community residence during the prescribed hours. The duration of such full custody, however, would be calibrated so as to be comparable in onerousness to the normally applicable sentence.

3. In the upper-intermediate band, the normally prescribed penalty might be a substantial day fine. (By "substantial" we mean day fines representing a substantial number of days' earnings, perhaps sixty days' earnings or more.) However, other sanctions of comparable severity might be substituted to a limited extent. These might include intensive supervision for amenable individuals, and community service for those lacking the income on which such fines are based.
4. The lower-intermediate band would normally have more modest day fines—say, those involving less than sixty days' earnings. Substitution would still be needed for those lacking the means to pay. This might

take the form of community service—but for shorter periods than that which could be invoked as a substitute in the preceding level (see 3 above).

5. The low bands would consist of small, flat fines; and below them, judicial cautions with unconditional release. Little need for substitution would exist here.

The reader should note that the particular penalties mentioned here are only for the sake of illustration. One could construct a limited-substitution model using other sanctions as the normally recommended ones or their substitutes.

Gauging Sentence Severity

The limited-substitution model still requires the substitute sanction to be of comparable severity with the normally prescribed one. Hence, the model presupposes criteria for gauging the comparative severity of noncustodial sentences. How should this be done?

Desert theorists have largely ignored this subject. They focused primarily on the questions of whether to imprison and the duration of imprisonment, to which common sense suggests some simple answers: imprisonment is more severe, generally, than noncustodial penalties and its severity can be assessed by its duration.

Several criminologists have been trying to measure the comparative severity of sanctions through opinion surveys. A selected group of respondents is shown a list of penalties—some custodial sanctions, others non-custodial sanctions such as probation, fines, and community service—and each respondent is asked to rate their severity on a numerical rating scale. These surveys tend to show a considerable degree of consensus in comparative severity rankings.[14]

These studies, however, do not attempt to elucidate what is meant by severity, or elicit from respondents the reasons for their rankings. It is important that, before adopting the severity rankings indicated in these and similar studies, we clarify, in principle, what *should* be the basis for comparing penalties. In short, we need a theory of sentence severity.

One possible conception of severity relies upon the degree of pain or discomfort felt by those upon whom the punishment may be inflicted. A punishment is thus ranked as more severe when it is characteristically experienced as being more onerous by potential recipients.

On this theory, opinion surveys would be helpful. What these surveys can measure is how averse people feel to various possible intrusions. One of us has criticized relying on opinion surveys to gauge the seriousness of crimes.[15] Seriousness concerns the harmfulness and degree of culpability of the criminal conduct,[16] and people's unsupported opinions are not necessarily a measure of either. Discomfort, however, is a subjective quantum. On a discomfort theory of severity, it becomes appropriate to measure what people feel. If penalty A is generally experienced to be more unpleasant than penalty B, then that makes it so.

One problem with a discomfort index is finding a target audience. If persons are surveyed who think themselves unlikely to be punished, their answers might be influenced by ignorance of how the penalty is actually carried out, or by indifference to the sufferings of others. However, convicts or ex-convicts can be included as one of the populations surveyed to provide a control for this. Sebba and Nathan found the severity rankings of convicts to be comparable to other groups.[17]

Another problem is that of unusual individual sensitivities. Misers might find fines particularly onerous, for example. However, the surveys themselves would indicate the extent of this problem by the degree of variance in responses within a given population of respondents. Individual sensitivity is not a problem unique to noncustodial penalties, but applies to the entire range of sanctions. Desert-based schemes, typically, deal with the problem by relying on the degree of severity *normally* or *typically* characteristic of various sanctions—and then, perhaps, by making some allowance for special sensitivities in restricted categories of cases where the impact of the penalty is most obviously unusual.[18]

How useful, then, might surveys be? That depends on how ambitious we wish to be about substitution of penalties. A full-substitution model would require a capacity to compare the severity of numerous penalties in a more highly discriminating fashion than surveys would probably be capable of providing. However, the limited-substitution model would be less demanding: it should be possible to measure perceptions of the comparative onerousness of the penalties normally recommended and of the limited number of their potential substitutes. Of course, one would need new surveys that consider the particular types of sanctions which the proposed scale is to use—as existing research addresses more traditional penalty structures.

An alternative theory is that relative severity should be measured by way of the normative importance of the personal interests compromised by operation of the penalty. The more basic the interests infringed, and the greater the extent of their infringement, the more severe the penalty. According to the extent to which the penalty affects a person's liberty, autonomy, or comfort, the various penalties could be ranked in order of relative intrusiveness. Regard could be had to recent jurisprudential writings on the relative gravity of harms.[19]

Any such definition and ranking of interests would by no means be precise—and hence could not sustain the elaborate severity comparisons that a full-substitution model would involve. But it might be helpful, again, for the more modest purposes of the limited-substitution model. The comparisons could be made with the aid of common sense. When one asks whether a stint of community service is comparable in severity to, and hence substitutable for, a day fine, an analysis of interests might help. Both day fines and community service are economic sanctions (the latter, because it exacts unpaid labor), but community service also restricts liberty of movement by requiring the work to be done at a particular place. The equivalences should take that difference into account—for example, requiring that each day fine unit should be treated as equivalent to substantially less than an eight-hour working day in community service.[20]

Backup Sanctions

Noncustodial penalties require backup sanctions for willful defaulters—as in the case of the individual who refuses to pay his day fine even though he is capable of paying. How should those backup sanctions be devised?

Traditionally, backup sanctions have relied on imprisonment. The form of the noncustodial penalty often called for such a response: the offender received a conditional sentence whereby, if he failed to perform the prescribed penalty in the community, the condition was violated and the prison sentence held in reserve could be invoked. Such a response is troublesome both for pragmatic reasons and in principle.

The pragmatic difficulty is that—to the extent that noncustodial sentences are meant to diminish reliance on imprisonment—systematic resort to confinement as a backup sanction will be self-defeating. A considerable number of lesser and intermediate-level offenders will be confined as defaulters, for periods that substantially exceed the terms they might have received had imprisonment been the initial response to their crimes. Such a severe sanction, moreover, is likely to be invoked unevenly: some defaulters will go to prison when others, whose default is no less flagrant, are allowed to remain in the community.

The theoretical difficulty is that reliance on imprisonment as a potential backup sanction can infringe desert principles. Suppose an offender commits an offense in the lower-intermediate band of the grid, receives the prescribed noncustodial sanction, and then defaults without good excuse. Since he has not fully undergone his penalty, he still "owes" the not yet completed portion, in some comparable form. Imprisonment will not serve this purpose, however, as it is much more severe than the offender's original penalty and could not have been imposed, under the grid, for his crime.

One might argue that his act of default (although not necessarily a statutory offense) itself is a reprehensible act, for which he "owes" more. But how much more? Unless one is prepared to argue that default *per se* is *very* reprehensible, it would not suffice as grounds for invoking the severe sanction of imprisonment. We need, then, to devise nonincarcerative measures as backup sanctions. How, under a desert model, should their severity be determined?

We might begin by trying to identify a penalty that is equivalent in severity to, but more readily enforceable than, the initially imposed punishment. Where the offender has completed a portion of his noncustodial penalty before defaulting, the substitute would correspond to the severity of the unserved portion. Next, one might treat the act of default (if willful) to be itself a reprehensible act, deserving of some increase in the punishment. How serious that act is considered to be would depend on one's general criteria for gauging seriousness. However, default *per se* does not strike us as extraordinarily reprehensible, and would not warrant more than a modest increase in the severity of the sanction.[21] The increase might involve, perhaps, a step-up to the next band in the grid immediately above the band in which the initial penalty was located.

Were our suggested "limited substitution" model (see Fig. 3) employed, and such a one-band-upward standard used for defaults, it might have the following consequences: A person convicted of a lower-intermediate level offense, for which a modest day fine is the normally recommended penalty, would upon willful default be subjected to a substantial day fine—the penalty prescribed for the upper-intermediate band. To ensure the penalty was paid, measures of distraint (i.e., attachment or garnishment) could be employed. Defaulters convicted of crimes in the upper-intermediate band, for which substantial day fines would be the normal sanction, would similarly face the penalty in the next band up. This would consist of intermittent confinement (or else, for the sufficiently recalcitrant, a short, equivalently severe period of full confinement).

Specific Noncustodial Penalties

Let us turn now, briefly, to consider specific noncustodial sentences and their place within the framework we have envisaged. It is helpful to consider first those measures which have traditionally been regarded as penalties in their own right, as these can fit readily within a just deserts framework. Next, we will consider the measures which might only be accommodated with a considerable shift of emphasis in the way the penalty is thought of and used.

Penalties Which Readily Fit

The most obvious such penalty is the *fine*. The straightforward punitive character of the fine comports well with a desert model. Fines are particularly suited for offenses in the middle range of seriousness—where incarceration is too severe a sanction, but a response of some significant degree of punitiveness is called for. Fines can, moreover, be readily calibrated in their comparative severities. In the penalty scales suggested above, the fine would be the penalty most frequently employed.

Any rational system emphasizing desert would surely require, to a substantial extent, the adoption of a system of fining similar to that of the European day fine, where fine units are computed as a percentage of disposable income. Whether the additional administration involved in such a system is justified for smaller fines is debatable, but for more substantial monetary penalties the case for moving to a day fine system of some sort seems unanswerable.

The Vera Institute's pilot project in Staten Island illustrates the potential for day fines.[22] Like its European counterparts, the Vera project levies fines in fine units; and provides a formula, based on the offenders' income, for translating the units into actual monetary amounts. The project goes beyond the European systems, however, in providing explicit standards on how many day fine units should be levied for various offenses. The number of units is made explicitly to depend on the gravity of the crime, as a desert model would require. Strengthened procedures for collecting unpaid fines are also established.

While some argue that *community service* should be regarded as primarily therapeutic, its actual rehabilitative usefulness is doubtful, as empirical research has demonstrated.[23] A more plausible view of community service is as a punishment: a sanction that deprives the person of leisure, and exacts unpaid labor, in a community setting. The most elaborate community service program, operated by the Vera Institute, treats the sanction in this fashion—as a sanction that is punitive, but less severe than imprisonment.[24] Community service thus can fit comfortably within a desert rationale. The severity of community service varies considerably, however. In Vera's project, the work consists of a specified number of full days of manual labor at a designated, supervised work site.[25] Such a sanction comes close to partial confinement for an equivalent period. Other forms of community service may be much less intensive.[26] Community service is not so much a single sanction, but rather a spectrum of sanctions—the severity of which can be graded according to how onerous the work is, how many hours per day are required, and how many days are involved.

In our suggested "limited substitution" scheme, we utilize community service only as a substitute penalty for the intermediate band of crimes—one to be imposed on those unable to pay day fines. The day fine, we think, is more capable of being routinely administered—as it is in Germany and the Scandinavian countries. Community service, the experience of the Vera Institute project has indicated, calls for intensive staffing—both to supervise offenders at work and to ensure that they attend.[27] Given limitation of resources, it seems preferable to us to use the sanction more sparingly, as a substitute penalty when the day fine is not feasible.

Partial custody is our term for penalties that deprive the offender of his freedom of movement, but to a lesser extent than does the full-time residential restraint which incarceration involves. One form of partial custody is intermittent confinement, served during specified daylight or evening hours at a facility in the community—such as a halfway house, treatment facility, or attendance center.[28] Another possible form is home detention—where the offender must remain at home except during specified working hours.[29] These kinds of sanctions, likewise, represent a spectrum of punishment rather than a single penalty. The onerousness of partial confinement depends upon what portion of the day and week the offender is restrained.

Cautions are the form of penalty appropriate at the bottom of the scale, for the least serious infractions. The sanction consists of a judicial caution or warning, followed by unconditional release. England has a sanction like this—the absolute discharge. In the U.S., its availability varies with state law. Often the discharge is conditional (with imprisonment or some other penalty threatened for violation of the conditions), but the conditions are then routinely ignored. Such conditional discharges raise problems which are discussed below. To our mind, the unconditional discharge would be more appropriate, as the mildest penalty in the system.

Penalties Fitting Only Partially

Some traditional noncustodial penalties do not fit so easily into our scheme. To accommodate them, their structure and criteria would have to be significantly altered.

Probation has been the most common nonincarcerative penalty. The offender is released conditionally, and subjected to specified conditions designed to encourage him to lead a law-abiding life. A probation officer supervises the offender, and is supposed to see to it that the conditions are observed. Violation of any of the conditions, at the court's discretion, can result in imprisonment.[30]

Traditional probation involves large caseloads, and a (supposed) mission of providing support to the offender. The newer "intensive" probation (ISP)—now being tried in several U.S. states—involves smaller caseloads, more stringent release conditions, and a greater emphasis on surveillance and control. Some forms of probation may actually involve partial or full confinement—as where the offender is required to reside in a residential treatment center or group home. Probation (and its supposedly novel variant, ISP) is thus not so much a single sanction but a wide array of sanctions, depending on the character of the release conditions and of the supervision. On a desert model, probation would (to the extent used at all) have to be graded according to its severity. The fact that probation might have positive results in reeducating or maintaining surveillance of offenders should not make us overlook its punitive character.

We have recommended that probation should not be a presumed sanction, and not be forced into a single slot in the tariff. It should be an alternative to the normally recommended sentence within specific (middle-range) penalty bands. There, its severity rating should depend on the conditions imposed, and it should be invoked only when there is a particular reason to believe this type of offender is potentially responsive. The backup sanction for violators would also have to be altered to reflect the principles we have suggested, rather than permitting easy resort to imprisonment.

The more intensive and surveillance-oriented forms of probation supervision may also raise problems of intrusiveness. Frequent unannounced home visits may be involved. Electronic monitoring, where used, now mainly consists of a device which issues a signal when the offender leaves the home or some other specified area,[31] but monitoring the offender's activities *within* the home could eventually become a possibility. Such measures raise troublesome ethical questions—concerning both the right to dignity of the offender, and the privacy rights of unconvicted third persons living with the defendant.[32]

Impact on Use of Imprisonment: The "Net-Widening" Problem

How much could our proposed scheme of noncustodial sanctions reduce reliance upon imprisonment? We suspect the reduction might be considerable. Full custody could be invoked routinely only for the serious offenses in the top band of the grid. Its only additional permitted use would be quite restricted—as a substitute sanction (but for very short periods) for the next most serious band, and as a backup sanction for defaulters in the band below that. Other offenders could not be confined, and incarceration could not be invoked to back up lesser noncustodial penalties as it may be today.

The scheme would also help resolve the "net-widening" problem.[33] This much-discussed problem is that noncustodial sanctions, meant to replace imprisonment, come to be used, instead, as substitutes for more traditional community sanctions such as probation; meanwhile, the use of imprisonment goes on as before. When one looks more closely at this phenomenon, two things are going wrong. First, imprisonment continues to be used *inappropriately* for crimes that are not serious. Intermediate-level crimes, particularly, continue to attract imprisonment rather than one of the new community sanctions. Second, the more substantial community sanctions are being used inappropriately. Instead of being employed for middle-level offenses, they are employed for the least serious—where they are disproportionately onerous. Grading community sanctions, as we have suggested, would help resolve both of these problems. Imprisonment would be restricted chiefly to the serious crimes. Noncustodial penalties that have significant punitive "bite"—for example, substantial fines, community service, or intensive supervision—would be utilized where they belong: for crimes of medium gravity, not for lesser offenses.

Just how much effect would our scheme have in reducing incarceration? That is an empirical question. The amount of reduction depends on how much imprisonment is used in the particular jurisdiction, and for which kinds of offenses. To predict the extent of the reduction, one would need to conduct prison-impact analyses of the kind pioneered in Minnesota in which one simulates the application of the proposed standards to a representative caseload of offenses.[34] Those simulations, in turn, will have to be adjusted as experience begins to indicate how plea-bargaining practice is affected by the standards.[35]

Effects of Shifting Toward a More Utilitarian Rationale

In the foregoing sketch of noncustodial penalties, we have assumed full adherence to desert constraints. Crime prevention, in our model, may be considered only insofar as it does not infringe proportionality requirements.[36]

Not everyone will agree with these assumptions, however. Some will prefer a rationale giving less emphasis to desert constraints and more to utilitarian concerns. What would the effects of such a shift be on the penalty structure? The answer will depend, of course, on which utilitarian concerns are invoked. A deterrence rationale may produce a different array of noncustodial penalties than a rationale emphasizing restraint of potential recidivists. Let us consider the latter for present purposes—as more is known about prediction than about deterrence or treatment.[37] As predictive concerns are given more weight, how would the penalty structure change?

First, the seriousness of the current crime would have less influence, and the prior criminal record more, since previous crimes tend to be the better predictor of future criminality.[38] On a grid, this would be reflected by altered slopes of the bands of the grid. Those bands—particularly the band containing custodial sentences—would tilt more toward the vertical, so as to emphasize the prior record.[39] In addition, the horizontal axis of the grid may come to include additional factors, other than the criminal record, that are found to be useful predictors.[40]

The backup sanctions may also change. When willful default is indicative of increased probability of offending, a stiffer sanction could be invoked where that would be useful to restrain the offender. Relaxing desert requirements would thus allow the system to be more permissive with backup sanctions.[41]

Two features of our suggested scheme should be retained, however. First, a limited-substitution system would remain preferable to one that allows unlimited substitution. Even if one accepts a rationale that gives more emphasis to incapacitation and less to desert, there is no obvious reason why cafeteria-style sentencing would be needed.

Second, when one penalty is substituted for another, it should still be considered whether it is of equal severity. Even on a more predictively oriented rationale, there is an important difference between (1) replacing a sanction with another equally severe one and (2) replacing one sanction with another that is *more* severe. Where one is increasing severities on the basis of a prediction, firmer supporting evidence as to the reliability of the prediction should be required.[42]

Conclusion

We have tried to show that it is indeed feasible to design a sentencing framework based on desert principles which makes extensive use of noncustodial penalties. Such penalties can be scaled and interrelated in a far more consistent manner than is the case at present. Instead of being regarded merely as substitutes for incarceration, they would be penalties in their own right,[43] ranged on a scale below custody, and involving varying degrees of punitiveness.

Extensive reliance upon noncustodial sanctions is to be distinguished from mere proliferation of such sanctions. We have argued for a system involving a relatively small standard group of penalties, with limited substitution. Such a system would be conceptually coherent and would avoid many of the problems which beset the present system.

We have outlined some areas in which further research needs be done—particularly, in measuring the comparative severities of different noncustodial penalties. Work along these lines would facilitate judgments concerning the substitutability of penalties.

Ours is only a brief sketch, and more thinking needs to be done—both about the structure of penalties and the practical problems of their implementation. Penal theory *can* provide a useful framework in scaling noncustodial penalties, but only with more thought than has been given to the subject in the past.

Notes

1. A. von Hirsch, *Doing Justice: The Choice of Punishments* 107–17 (1976).
2. See, e.g., A. von Hirsch, *Past or Future Crimes: Deservedness and Dangerousness in the Sentencing of Criminals* 92–101, 160–66 (1985); R. Singer, *Just Deserts: Sentencing Based on Equality and Desert* 97–110 (1979).
3. For a fuller analysis of the Minnesota guidelines' structure, see A. von Hirsch, K. Knapp, and M. Tonry, *The Sentencing Commission and Its Guidelines* 84–106 (1987).
4. *Id.*, at 105, 130–32.
5. For an overview of recently developed noncustodial penalties, see J. Petersilia, *Expanding Options for Criminal Sentencing* (1987); M. Tonry and R. Will, *Intermediate Sanctions* (1989).
6. See, e.g., *Intermediate Sanctions* [and Extracts 6.1 and 6.4].
7. A. von Hirsch, K. Knapp, and M. Tonry, *supra* note 3, at 8–15.
8. Some European countries, most notably Finland and Sweden, have statutory principles concerning choice of sentence, instead of numerical guidelines and a grid. For the possible advantages of this approach, see *id.*, at 47–61. For further details of the Swedish legislation, see von Hirsch, "Principles for Choosing Sanctions: Sweden's Proposed Sentencing Statute," 13 *New England J. Crim. and Civil Confinement* 171 (1987). Since publication of this latter article, the Swedish proposals have been enacted into law as *Swedish Penal Code*, chs. 29–30 (1989). [See also Extracts 5.3 and 5.4.]
9. A. von Hirsch, *supra* note 2, at 31–101. [See also Extracts 4.2 and 4.4.]
10. A desert rationale's most stringent requirement is that of *ordinal* proportionality, which calls for punishments to be ranked in severity to reflect the comparative seriousness of offenses. *Id.* at 40–43. This requirement can be satisfied by grading the severity of the noncustodial penalties prescribed. The other, less constraining requirement is that of *cardinal* proportionality, which requires—in setting the anchoring points of a penalty scale—that penalties not manifestly devalue or overvalue the gravity of the conduct. *Id.* at 43–46. This requirement can be satisfied by a scheme that limits the severe sanction of imprisonment to fairly serious offenses, and prescribes scaled noncustodial sanctions for other crimes. See *id.* at 160–66.

11. *Id.* at 112; Robinson, "Hybrid Principles for the Distribution of Criminal Sanctions," 82 *Nw. U.L. Rev.* 19, 34–36 (1987).

12. For discussion of the weight of the prior criminal record under a desert model, see A. von Hirsch, *supra* note 2, at 77–91; Wasik, "Guidance, Guidelines, and Criminal Record," in *Sentencing Reform: Guidance or Guidelines?* 105–25 (K. Pease and M. Wasik eds. 1987); von Hirsch, "Desert and Previous Convictions in Sentencing," 65 *Minn. L. Rev.* 591 (1981). [See also Extract 4.7.]

13. Certain subcategories of offenders having identifiable problems linked with criminal behavior—e.g., certain alcoholics and drug users—*might* return to crime less often under supervision. We emphasize the qualifier "might," however, as careful evaluations of such programs remain a rarity. For discussion and bibliography, see M. Tonry and R. Will, *supra* note 5. There is no evidence that supervision could have significant preventive effects on offenders generally. *Id.*

Even though supervision is preventively oriented, its use as a substitute would not violate desert constraints *provided* that the supervision's degree of onerousness—that is, its severity—is approximately the same as that of the deserved, normally prescribed penalty. See von Hirsch, "Hybrid Principles in Allocating Sanctions: A Response to Professor Robinson," 82 *Nw. U.L. Rev.* 64, 65–66 (1987).

14. Sebba and Nathan, "Further Exploration in the Scaling of Penalties," 24 *Brit. J. Criminology* 221 (1984). See also Erickson and Gibbs, "On the Perceived Severity of Legal Penalties," 70 *J. Crim. L. and Criminology* 102 (1979); Sebba, "Some Explorations in the Scaling of Penalties," 15 *J. Research Crime and Delinq.* 247 (1978); Buchner, "Scale of Sentence Severity," 70 *J. Crim. L. and Criminology* 182 (1979); Kapardis and Farrington, "An Experimental Study of Sentencing by Magistrates," 5 *L. and Hum. Behav.* 107 (1981).

15. A. von Hirsch, *supra* note 2, at 65.

16. *Id.* at 64–65.

17. Sebba and Nathan, *supra* note 14.

18. Von Hirsch, *supra* note 8, at 188. Cases of ill health and advanced age are examples of special cases calling for reduced sanctions.

19. See, e.g., von Hirsch and Jareborg, "Gauging Criminal Harm: A Living-Standard Analysis," 11 *Oxford J. Legal Studies* 1 (1991), excerpted in Extract 4.5 of this volume. Here we are speaking not of criminal harm, but of the onerousness of the penalty. However, the penalty's onerousness could be gauged by how much it sets back the punished offender's interests.

20. Possibly these two approaches could be combined. A model scale of penalties could be developed, using normative "interest analysis" for gauging their comparative severities. Then the severity gradations could be tested through survey research.

21. A. von Hirsch and K. Hanrahan, *The Question of Parole: Retention, Reform, or Abolition?* 64–66 (1979).

22. See Extract 6.3, this volume.

23. See D. McDonald, *Punishment Without Walls: Community Service Sentences in New York City* 164–74 (1986).

24. *Id.* at 45–46.

25. *Id.* at 36.

26. M. Tonry and R. Will, *supra* note 5, ch. 5.

27. D. McDonald, *supra* note 23, at 46–49.

28. We are referring here to attendance for only a *portion* of the day or week in such facilities. Full-time residence in a treatment facility should be considered a species of full custody.

29. M. Tonry and R. Will, *supra* note 5, ch. 3.

30. See, e.g., *Model Penal Code* § 301.1 (1962).

31. See M. Tonry and R. Will, *supra* note 5, ch. 4.

32. Von Hirsch, "The Ethics of Community-Based Sanctions," 35 *Crime and Delinq.* 162 (1989).

33. See Austin and Krisberg, "The Unmet Promise of Alternatives to Incarceration," 28 *Crime and Delinq.* 374 (1982). [See Excerpt 6.1 of this volume.]

34. A. von Hirsch, K. Knapp, and M. Tonry, *supra* note 3, at 107–16.

35. *Id.* at 142–76.

36. For fuller discussions of which crime-prevention strategies are consistent, and which inconsistent, with desert requirements, see A. von Hirsch, *supra* note 2, at 160–66. See also von Hirsch, *supra* note 13, at 65–66.

37. A. von Hirsch, *supra* note 2, at 7–9, 12–16.

38. *Id.* at 132–34.

39. *Id.*; see also von Hirsch, "Commensurability and Crime Prevention: Evaluating Formal Sentencing Structures and Their Rationale," 74 *J. Crim. L. and Criminology* 209, 218 (1983).

40. A. von Hirsch, *supra* note 2, at 136–38.

41. See A. von Hirsch and K. Hanrahan, *supra* note 21, at 70–71.

42. Even Norval Morris, who has advocated the use of prediction (within broad desert limits), recommends that increases in sentence severity based on prediction be supported by strong statistical evidence. See Morris and Miller, "Predictions of Dangerousness," 6 *Crime and Justice: An Annual Review of Research* 1, 37–38 (M. Tonry and N. Morris eds. 1985). By contrast, a substitution that involves no increase in severity might be based on more subjective risk judgments.

43. [See also Extract 6.2 in this volume.]

Suggestions for Further Reading

1. Recent Surveys and Analyses of Intermediate Punishments

Petersilia, *Expanding Options for Criminal Sentencing* (1987); Bottoms, A. E., "Limiting Prison Use: The English Experience," 26 *Howard Journal of Criminal Justice* 177 (1987); Tonry, M., and Will, R., *Intermediate Sanctions*, A Report to National Institute of Justice (1988) (unpublished manuscript, available from National Institute of Corrections, Washington, D.C.); NACRO, *The Real Alternative: Strategies to Promote Community Based Penalties* (1989); Vass, A. E., *Alternatives to Prison* (1990); Byrne, J. M., Lurigio, A., and Petersilia, J. (eds.), *Smart Sentencing: Expanding Options for Intermediate Sanctions* (1992).

2. Community Service

Young, H., *Community Service Orders* (1979); Pease and McWilliams, W. (eds.), *Community Service by Order* (1980); Pease, K., "Community Service Orders," in M. Tonry and N. Morris (eds.), *Crime and Justice: An Annual Review of Research*, vol. 6 (1985); McDonald, D., *Prisons without Walls: Community Service Sentences in New York City* (1986); Tonry and Will, *Intermediate Sanctions*, *supra*, ch. 5; Vass, A., and Menzies, K., "The Community Service Order in England and Ontario," 29 *British Journal of Criminology* 225 (1989).

3. Fines and Day Fines

Friedman, M., "The West German Day-Fine System: A Possibility for the United States?" 50 *University of Chicago Law Review* 281 (1983); Hillsman, T., Sichel, L., and Mahoney, B., *Fines in Sentencing: A Study in the Use of the Fine as a Criminal Sanction* (1984); Thornstadt, H. "The Day Fine System in Sweden," [1985] *Criminal Law Review* 307; Hillsman, S., and Greene, J., "Tailoring Criminal Fines to the Financial Means of the Offender," 72 *Judicature* 38 (1988); Hillsman, S., "Fines and Day-Fines," in M. Tonry and N. Morris (eds.), *Crime and Justice: An Annual Review of Research*, vol. 12 (1990); Gibson, B., *Unit Fines* (1990); Moxon, D., Sutton, M., and Hedderman, C., *Unit Fines: Experiments in Four Courts* (1990).

4. Probation

McAnany, P., Thomson, D., and Fogel, D., *Probation and Justice: Reconsideration of a Mission* (1984); Shaw, R., and Haines, K. (eds.), *The Criminal Justice System: A Central Role for the Probation Service* (1989); McWilliams, W., and Pease, K., "Probation Practice and an End to Punishment," 29 *Howard Journal of Criminal Justice* 14 (1990); Petersilia, J., and Turner, J., "An Evaluation of Intensive Supervision in California," 82 *Journal of Criminal Law and Criminology* 610 (1992). Several useful analyses of intensive supervision probation (ISP), along with bibliographical materials, are set forth in a special issue, 36 *Crime and Delinquency* No. 1 (3–191) (1990).

5. Home Detention and Electronic Monitoring

McCarthy (ed.), *Intermediate Punishments: Intensive Supervision, Home Confinement, and Electronic Surveillance* (1987); Tonry and Will, *Intermediate Sanctions, supra*, chs. 3 and 4; Lilly, R., "Tagging Reviewed," 29 *Howard Journal of Criminal Justice* 14 (1990); Mair, G., and Nees, C., *Electronic Monitoring: The Trials and Their Results* (1990); von Hirsch, A., "The Ethics of Community-Based Sanctions," 36 *Crime and Delinquency* 162 (1990); von Hirsch, A., *Censure and Sanctions* (1993, forthcoming), ch. 8.

6. *Scaling Intermediate Punishments*

Bottoms, A. E., "The Concept of Intermediate Sanctions and Its Relevance for the Probation Service," in Shaw, R., and Haines, K. (eds.), *The Criminal Justice System: A Central Role for the Probation Service, supra*; Morris, N., and Tonry, M., *Between Prison and Probation: Intermediate Punishments in a Rational Sentencing System* (1990); von Hirsch, "Scaling Intermediate Punishments: A Comparison of Two Models," in Byrne, J. M., Lurigio, A., and Petersilia, J. (eds.), *Smart Sentencing, supra*; von Hirsch, *Censure and Sanctions, supra*, chs. 6 and 7.

Chapter Seven

LOOKING BEYOND THE SENTENCE

No discussion of sentencing policy can be complete without looking at some broader perspectives. How should a sentencing theory fit into broader social welfare concerns? What relation should sentencing have to the earlier stages in the criminal process? How should sentencing address itself to the concerns of the victim? Space does not permit a selection of readings, so we present a narrative of our own, raising some of the main issues.

1. Sentencing and the Wider Society

We select for brief discussion three recent works which lay emphasis on the social aspects of sentencing. The first is Barbara Hudson's *Justice through Punishment*,[1] which is subtitled "A Critique of the 'Justice' Model of Corrections." The critique offered by Hudson may be reduced to three main arguments. First, she suggests that desert theory can be co-opted by those who wish to "get tough" on crime, and so has been used in various jurisdictions to raise the levels of punishment.[2] This, she argues, is no coincidence: the emphasis of desert theory on the gravity of offenses rather than the motivations of offenders makes it readily available as a legitimating rhetoric for those who wish to increase the amount of control and punitiveness against disaffected, and often disadvantaged, groups in society.

Hudson therefore questions whether desert theory really does promote liberal values, and argues that it has no potential for bringing changes in the approach to offenders and offending. Her second point, then, is that desert ignores the notion that the law has a reformative function, in that it "emphasises abstract classes of behaviour as the targets for action, rather than the problems of whole human beings."[3] Real concern for the rights of individuals can only be demonstrated through rehabilitative approaches which do not "privilege events over people" but which offer understanding and help to offenders on a personal level. This means devoting adequate resources to rehabilitative forms of sentence.[4]

Her third argument is that there is a need to go much further than this, and she commends "radical" approaches which insist on viewing sentencing, and criminal justice policy as a whole, in its social context. Greater attention should be devoted to the reduction of crime, not just through situational crime prevention but also through structural crime prevention—which means the pursuit of economic and social policies aimed, for example, at full employment and wider educational and recreational facilities.[5] The overuse of imprisonment should be tackled head-on by a program of closing prisons and defining the small group of offenders for whom incarceration really is justified.[6]

This third argument is taken up at the end of this section, but a few questions must be raised here in relation to the first two points. She supports her claim that desert theory leads to increased severity by reference to the California experience. There, sentencing has been highly politicized, and the legislature set the actual sentence levels. However, a look at the experience of other jurisdictions leads one to question the existence of any necessary link between desert theory and severe penalty levels. On one hand, several jurisdictions have adopted the principle of proportionate punishments without concomitantly increased sanctions: in Finland, sanction levels have actually fallen considerably since adoption of a desert-based sentencing statute in 1976; in Sweden, a comparable 1988 statute was designed to be neutral in its impact on imprisonment levels; and in three U.S. sentencing-guideline states—Minnesota, Oregon, and Washington State—there have been increases, but less drastic ones than elsewhere in America.[7] On the other hand, U.S. states whose criminal justice politics were comparable to California's—such as New York State—experienced sharp rises in prison populations without having adopted either a desert philosophy or sentencing guidelines. Hudson's arguments also overlook the structural aspects of desert theory: its emphasis on the seriousness of the current offense helps ensure that persistent lesser felons do not receive severe sentences. As for her second argument, this leads in the direction of a rehabilitative theory of sentencing, which is open to the criticisms advanced in Chapter 1 above (especially Extract 1.6).

The second of the recent works is *Not Just Deserts,* by John Braithwaite and Philip Pettit.[8] The authors construct what they term a republican theory of criminal justice. It is a theory which justifies punishment in terms of its consequences for what they call "dominion," which they regard as the supreme value:

A person enjoys full dominion, we say, if and only if:

1. she enjoys no less a prospect of liberty than is available to other citizens;
2. it is common knowledge among citizens that this condition obtains, so that she and nearly everyone else knows that she enjoys the prospect mentioned, she and nearly everyone else knows that the others generally know this too, and so on;
3. she enjoys no less a prospect of liberty than the best that is compatible with the same prospect for all citizens.[9]

Punishments would then be justified if and to the extent that they advance dominion, in terms of increasing the dominion of victims and potential victims with the least loss of dominion to the offenders punished. The sentences this would yield would bear no relation to a proportionality scale: they would be governed by preventive calculations of the results of various strategies, and in some instances by predictions of dangerousness. There would be maximum penalties, and there would be conscientious efforts to lower the overall level of punitiveness, but beyond that the touchstones would be prevention and prediction. Moreover, these form part of a wider theory of criminal justice, since Braithwaite and Pettit pursue the same approach as both Hudson and Nicola Lacey in insisting that sentencing issues should not be abstracted from their criminal justice context.

Braithwaite and Pettit differ from Lacey (below) and from desert theorists in arguing that censure can and should be kept separate from punishment. Their view is that, although the criminal justice system does have a censuring function, this can be fulfilled by measures such as adverse publicity and other ways of producing stigma. Therefore it would be quite possible to impose on a white-collar criminal a more lenient sentence than on a similar blue-collar criminal, and to ensure that the white-collar criminal was subjected to adverse publicity (which would probably be effective in altering his future conduct, but possibly ineffective for the blue-collar offender). The inequality of punishment between the two is unimportant: the crucial point is that by using other forms of stigma the necessary amount of censure has been brought to bear, with a parsimonious use of punishment. Proportionality of sentence is not a significant value for Braithwaite and Pettit, although they do suggest that the maximum penalties for crimes should be set in such a way as to provide "moral education" to citizens.[10] Beneath those maxima, however, it is risk, prediction, and other preventive considerations that hold sway.

What is unclear about the theory is how "dominion" operates to prevent punishment and sentencing policies from trampling on the values of liberty and choice which Braithwaite and Pettit purport to respect. The theory is consequentialist and plainly requires a calculation of risk as a key issue in sentencing. This undoubtedly excludes any individual right not to be punished more than is proportionate to the seriousness of the offense: such a right, which is respected by desert theory and which is implicit in core liberal values,[11] is contradicted by the emphasis on prevention and prediction. It is not just that Braithwaite and Pettit are prepared to go above proportionate levels in the sentencing of "dangerous" offenders,[12] it is that proportionality seems to play little or no part in their sentencing scheme at all. Persons committing serious offenses could receive relatively low sentences if the incidence of those crimes could thereby be kept low, whereas those committing less serious offenses could be punished more severely if that were thought necessary for deterrence or risk prevention. It is not clear how well this would accord with people's moral sense, yet the authors seem to attribute considerable weight to the fears of citizens,[13] if not to their beliefs and values. If they really believe that punishment is justified wherever the net gain in dominion to potential victims exceeds the net loss to offenders, have they advanced significantly beyond Bentham? How, if at all, does the primacy of "dominion" protect individuals against excessive state punishment grounded in deterrence or predicted risk? While one might agree wholeheartedly with their espousal of the principle of parsimony in punishment, is it proper to use it, in conjunction with their attempt to separate censure from punishment, in such a way as to produce lower sentences for affluent and "respectable" offenders when others continue to receive full punishment?

A third theory, which is concerned with the social and political aspects of sentencing, may be found in Nicola Lacey's book *State Punishment*,[14] which is subtitled "Political Principles and Community Values." Lacey argues against all four "traditional" theories of punishment (those discussed in Chapters 1 to 4 above) and moves toward a communitarian approach. The foundations for this are constructed on principles of legal and political obligation. The state must respect the autonomy of individual citizens not merely in the sense of negative freedom (from the depredations of others), but also in the positive sense of providing an adequate range of facilities and options for individual self-development. Moreover, autonomy is regarded as only one of the basic political values relevant to criminal and social justice. Equally important is welfare, which regards individuals primarily as social beings and which points the need to promote social goals. Thus individual commitment to the law and to the criminal justice system would be enhanced if the state took a positive role in fostering a sense of community, providing facilities and enabling participation in decision making. It would then be clearly seen that the chief function of state punishment may be found in "a collective need to underpin, recognise and maintain the internalised commitments of many members of society to the content and standards of the criminal law," and in the need to demonstrate that people cannot break those standards with impunity.[15] Punishment is therefore functional within the community: the limitations stressed by desert theory are largely upheld in the name of autonomy, but desert and other liberal theories of punishment are found deficient in their lack of interest in public goods and collective values. Punishment can have social benefits which advance welfare, and a properly pluralistic theory should take these into account.

It follows from this, Lacey argues, that it is unduly simplistic to think in terms either of a single aim of punishment or of a single principle for the distribution of punishments. Both questions involve the two "core values" of welfare and autonomy, and inevitably there will be some "trade-offs" between them in practice. The trade-offs may be in terms of more or less of one value, but should not lead to the total sacrifice of a value: there should be no punishment without requiring criminal conduct, and no kind of sentence "so severe as to reflect a complete absence of respect for or denial of the offender's autonomy."[16] Within those limits, however,

> proportionality to socially acknowledged gravity could serve a useful function in underlining community values, but the symbolic element in punishment will probably detract from the tendency towards a rigid hierarchy of punishments according to gravity of offences.[17]

Lacey goes on to argue that deterrence research supports a lowering of present levels of penality, but little more is said about the criteria for distributing punishments.

The last point is of some importance, since Lacey had previously subjected desert theory to criticism on the basis that it provides insufficient guidance on how to set the overall level of punishments and on how to make judgments of ordinal proportionality between different kinds of offense.[18] In fact, the communitarian theory appears to supply less, rather than more, guidance on these issues. Its stance on overall levels of penality is similar to that espoused by some desert theorists,[19] whereas on criteria for the comparative grading of punishments it has no clear prescriptions to offer. However, the chief target of Lacey's book is not the detailed working-out of sentencing principles but the foundations for the theories. Is there, then, any reason why the precepts of desert theory, as outlined in Chapter 4 above, should not be accepted by a communitarian?

It will be evident from this brief outline of the theories of Hudson, Lacey, and Braithwaite and Pettit that they raise important questions about sentencing theory. In particular, their emphasis on the wider social and criminal justice context of sentencing is a valuable perspective. However, it is important not to *over*emphasize this broader context. It is one thing to keep in mind the interrelationship between sentencing and other parts of the criminal justice system, and between sentencing and broader social concerns. It is quite another thing to neglect the distinct functions of sentencing and to give no clear prescriptions about the basis on which those functions should be carried out. All three books are either vague on the principles of distribution in sentencing or seem to subscribe to forms of preventive theory containing elements of prediction, rehabilitation, and/or deterrence—theories which were discussed critically in Chapters 1, 2, and 3 above.

Moreover, the potentials of sentencing may be much more limited than these authors sometimes suggest. The preventive functions of sentencing are rather modest, and it is the existence of a penalty system rather than moderate changes in sentencing levels which exerts the preventive effect. Social policies to bring about greater equality, to reduce discrimination, and to ameliorate the position of minorities are of great importance, but is *sentencing policy* the right method by which to pursue these goals? Surely the sentencing process is concerned with offenses and with offenders in relation to those offenses, and should aim to express censure on that basis rather than attempting to become a tool of social engineering—an attempt which is likely to meet with little success, in view of the limited power of sentencing decisions to bring about significant social change. The link between sentencing and social policy does indeed require further exploration, but that link is more subtle than these three books would suggest.

2. Sentencing Theory and Prosecutorial Processes

One close relationship, already discussed in Chapter 5 and particularly in Extract 5.5, is that between sentencing and the many pretrial decisions which filter and shape the cases which courts receive for sentence. In most jurisdictions these decisions are largely discretionary, and yet they constitute an exercise of official power which may be no less significant for defendants than the sentencing decision itself. Some cases may not be prosecuted at all, despite a sufficiency of evidence; some prosecutions may be dropped or otherwise discontinued; some defendants may be charged with higher offenses than others; some cases may be brought in higher courts, some in lower courts; and, as elaborated in Extract 5.5 above, a "bargain" between the prosecutor and the defense may alter the nature of the case which is presented for sentence.

There are several reasons why greater interest has recently been shown in these pretrial decisions. It has been increasingly recognized that the whole process of prosecution may be regarded as punitive, in the sense that it puts the defendant and his or her family under considerable pressure, as well as bringing inconvenience, stigma, and probably expense. Once the criminal process is regarded as, in a sense, punitive, the question of justifying criminal prosecution is raised.

These concerns are not necessarily inconsistent with the aims of sentencing outlined in the earlier chapters. For rehabilitationists there is a question of whether prosecution, conviction, and sentence might not reduce the probability of succeeding with a treatment program for the defendant; those who appear to have good prospects of rehabilitation might therefore be diverted from prosecution. For deterrence theorists there is a question whether the object of prevention cannot be achieved at a lower cost and with no loss in efficiency by diverting certain cases from prosecution: some lesser response, such as reparation, a prosecutor's fine, or merely an official caution, might be just as effective in terms of both individual and general deterrence. And for desert theorists, the fact that the prosecution process can be seen as a kind of punishment in itself raises the question whether a more proportionate response to certain less serious forms of offense with relatively low culpability might be to avoid prosecution and seek a milder form of response.

The variety of diversionary programs available in different jurisdictions in the United States and the United Kingdom is extremely wide. Many of them are local in origin and application, but four broad approaches may be mentioned here. One is diversion involving reparation, which is discussed in section 3 below. A second is nonprosecution conditional on the defendant participating in some community activity, which may vary from mere deprivation of leisure time to supervised or treatment-oriented activities.[20] A third is a prosecutor's fine, used more in continental European systems.[21] A fourth approach, much used in England and Wales, is the formal police caution: the defendant has to attend at a police station and be cautioned by a senior officer, usually in uniform. Police cautioning has been developed so strongly that two-thirds of male juveniles believed to have committed offenses are now cautioned instead of prosecuted, a proportion rising to five-sixths for juvenile females. Recidivism rates appear to be no worse than previously, and the juvenile crime rate is no higher. Once again, fears about the social effects of lowering the level of penal response have not been borne out.

On what criteria are cases diverted from prosecution, and on what criteria should they be diverted? The answers to the first questions are variable. In some jurisdictions there is a wide and unreviewed discretion, the effects of which are felt throughout the subsequent decisions in the criminal process (including sentence). Other jurisdictions have attempted to structure decision making at these crucial early stages. For example, in England and Wales there are criteria or guidelines both for the police and for Crown prosecutors. These seem to be generally consistent with the proportionality principle: prosecution should be avoided where the case is so minor that it would probably receive only a nominal sentence if it were taken to court, or where the defendant's culpability is low (e.g., mental disturbance, extreme stress at the time of the offense, advanced age or extreme youth, etc.).[22] One key factor in the decision not to prosecute a juvenile is whether it is the first offense: almost all juvenile first offenders are cautioned, and a substantial number of second offenders also receive a caution. This can be connected with the reasons for modifying the penal response to first offenders, discussed in Extract 4.6 above. However, there are other criteria, allowing nonprosecution where the offender is suffering from a serious or terminal illness and allowing some account to be taken of the wishes of the victim.

The decision whether or not to prosecute is perhaps the most important of the pretrial decisions, but there are further decisions of significance. Where a case is prosecuted, the court's sentencing powers and the defendant's bargaining position may be affected by the charge which the prosecutor decides to bring. Sentencing powers may also be affected by the level of court in which the prosecution is brought. And then there are the various practices known as charge bargaining, plea bargaining, etc. (discussed in Extract 5.5 above).

On what basis should the guidelines or criteria for the exercise of discretion by prosecutors and other pretrial decision makers be formulated? Rehabilitationism appears to have little to offer, beyond basing the initial decision whether or not to prosecute on considerations of the approach most likely to result in the improvement of the offender. Deterrence theory is concerned with achieving maximum deterrence at minimum cost, and so its approach at each stage would be that the prosecutor should choose the less onerous and less costly option (i.e., nonprosecution, lesser charge, lower court) if the prospects for deterrence are not materially weakened thereby. The approach of desert theory would be that prosecutors should grade their responses proportionately to the seriousness of offenses, choosing nonprosecution for minor offenses with low culpability and being guided by seriousness when deciding on the charge, the level of court, and whether or not to enter into a bargain. In practice, these ideals are unlikely to be maintained, because of the pressures of the system—the need to process cases rapidly, the benefits of choosing certain conviction of a lesser offense rather than the uncertainties of a trial for a higher offense, the need to maintain cooperative relations with other advocates and attorneys, etc.[23] The resilience of these working practices raises questions about the means of attaining a consistent exercise of discretion, whether through guidelines, training, professional discipline, or other methods. These early decisions have a considerable effect on sentencing, and it is desirable that they should be based on principles consistent with those prevailing at the sentencing stage.

3. Confiscation, Compensation, and the Role of the Victim

It is plainly wrong that a person who has profited from crime should retain those profits to enjoy after the completion of the sentence imposed by the court. In recent years many countries have redoubled their efforts to strip offenders of the profits of crime,[24] and there is now legislation of this kind in the United States and in the United Kingdom. The primary target of the legislation is the dealer in narcotics and other controlled drugs, but the principle can be applied to organized crime and, indeed, to many forms of offending.

The rise of the "victim movement" in recent years has also forced some fundamental rethinking in sentencing theory. It has become increasingly recognized that the criminal justice system ought to care more for the needs and rights of the victims of crime, and policies have been developed to provide for personal support for the victims after the crime, for state compensation for the victims of violent crime, and for compensation orders to be made at the sentencing stage. A landmark here was the adoption of a charter of victims' rights by the United Nations in 1985, in its Declaration on the Basic Principles of Justice for Victims and Abuse of Power. In some jurisdictions there have also been the beginnings of alternative schemes of criminal justice based on victim-offender mediation, where victim and offender are invited to come together to discuss the crime and its effects.[25]

There are powerful arguments in favor of the state ensuring that compensation is available for the victims of violent crime and that support is available for all crime victims. The element of support is a proper object of social policy for those suffering misfortune. A policy of compensation may be supported as demonstrating the state's concern for those who fall victim to criminal violence, but it may also be regarded as a victim's right. It can be argued that the state is responsible for maintaining law and order and therefore ought to assure compensation to those who suffer from the failures of the policies pursued. There is the further pragmatic argument that the criminal justice system could not operate without the cooperation of victims (in assisting detection and in giving evidence), and so it is only fair that their suffering is recognized when their help is accepted.[26] The preamble to the European Convention on Compensation for the Victims of Crimes of Violence expresses as possible justification that

> the State is bound to compensate the victim because—it has failed to prevent the crime by means of effective criminal policy; and it introduced criminal policy measures which failed.[27]

The role of the state in these matters should not displace the primary responsibility of the offender to provide compensation. In practice, however, many offenders are impecunious, and others are imprisoned for serious crimes and therefore unable to earn the money with which to pay compensation: this is why state compensation schemes have grown up. But one must not overlook the point that some offenders can afford to pay some compensation to their victims, and therefore should be required to do so.

What should be the relationship between punishment and compensation? The question raises a number of issues of principle, three of which can be considered briefly here.

First, when a criminal court orders the offender to pay compensation to the victim, is it merely acting as a makeshift civil court? In other words, are such orders of compensation supportable chiefly on the pragmatic ground that the criminal court is already seized of the case, and it would be unduly onerous to expect the victim to bring a separate civil action to recover damages from the offender? This is a significant argument in favor of compensation orders: by empowering criminal courts to make these orders, the state is giving practical assistance to victims by obviating the need for them to sue the offender in the civil courts.

Second, if criminal courts are to be able to order offenders to pay compensation, should this have any effect on the sentence passed? One answer to this is that the criminal court is simply ordering the offender to pay what a civil court could have ordered him to pay. On this view, the compensation issue is entirely separate from sentencing. But there may be a distinct lack of realism about this. If one reason why criminal courts are empowered to order the offender to pay compensation is the pragmatic one that most victims would find it too burdensome to sue, does it not follow that in reality the criminal court is ordering the offender to pay money which, in the vast majority of cases, he would otherwise not be required to pay? If this is accepted, the compensation order is a burden imposed by a criminal court. As Bentham recognized:

Exacted at the expense of the evil doer, compensation necessitates suffering; exacted in consideration of, and in proportion to, the evil done by him, that suffering, by the whole amount of it, operates as punishment.[28]

English law now recognizes this, by giving priority to a compensation order over a fine when the offender has insufficient money to pay both, and by empowering a court to make a compensation order as the sole order in a case.[29]

A third and related issue is whether the amount of compensation ordered by a criminal court should be reduced where the offender has little money and few resources. In many legal systems it is a principle that fines should be adjusted to the means of the offender. If one considers whether the same principle should apply to compensation orders, their mixed parentage becomes apparent. On the one hand, the whole purpose of compensation is to repay or restore the victim. On the other hand, fairness to offenders in criminal proceedings indicates that courts should not impose heavy burdens on offenders with only modest resources. The acute conflicts of principle are apparent in English law, which gives priority to a compensation order over a fine, and yet limits the amount of the compensation order according to the offender's means.

This leads to a deeper issue of principle. Thus far it has been assumed that justice for victims is to be sought and achieved mostly through additions to conventional sentencing systems. Two pieces of U.S. federal legislation, the Victim Witness Protection Act of 1982 and the Victims of Crime Act of 1984 are examples of this. This approach can be developed so that the state has obligations to pursue crime prevention policies and to ensure proper services, support, and compensation for victims, while at the same time requiring courts to order offenders to pay compensation to victims wherever possible.[30] A more radical approach, however, would be to aim for a fully restorative theory of criminal justice, putting fairness to the victim first rather than fairness to the offender. Restorative theories vary in their details, but three major principles stand out.[31]

First, the aim of criminal justice should be to ensure that the offender compensates the victim and the wider community for the loss inflicted by the crime. Victim compensation may be onerous in some cases, where the loss is great and the offender's resources meager. Compensation to the community may also be required, especially where the harm inflicted was low but the danger and fear arising from the crime was considerable.

Second, the restorative approach prescribes measures which make a constructive effort toward the reintegration of the offender into the community. The measures imposed may make considerable demands on offenders, but restorative theorists argue that the purpose of the sanction is always and clearly explainable in terms of the damage done.

Third, the restorative approach would move away from the primarily adversarial nature of the criminal process toward a system based primarily on mediation and compensation, with resort to prosecution and to custodial sanctions only in rare cases. The victim would be the key figure rather than the public prosecutor, and victim satisfaction would be given priority over any supposed community interests.

There are many possible criticisms of the restorative approach at a practical level. Despite the apparent success of some schemes of victim-offender mediation, there are questions about whether it can cope with serious crimes—What should happen if the victim wants neither a meeting nor any dealings at all with the offender? What happens if the mediation makes things worse rather than better between victim and offender? What happens if the offender is impecunious?—is it realistic in times of world recession to construct a theory based on offenders working for years to pay off their crimes?[32] There are also doubts about fully restorative theories at the theoretical level. Is it true, as Nils Christie implies,[33] that the state has insufficient interest in lawbreaking to be allowed to control the response to offenses? Christie's view is that crimes are conflicts between the individuals concerned: apart from its exclusion of the many "public" offenses and crimes against the state, this raises the question whether or not there is a distinction between compensation (civil) and punishment (criminal). Measures like compensation orders made by criminal courts tend to blur the distinction for the pragmatic reasons given earlier, but is there not a fundamental distinction here? Compensation repays for damage done, with little regard for culpability. Punishment, on the other hand, is concerned that the public response to the wrongdoing should vary with the culpability of the offender. The theories may give similar results in cases of deliberate damage or intentional injury, but the two awkward types of case are attempts to commit serious crimes and minor assaults which lead to unexpectedly devastating consequences. A case of attempt may require relatively little compensation, but it remains a serious crime with high culpability. The minor assault would require substantial compensation if its consequences were considerable, whereas neither desert theory nor deterrence would rank the offense high on the punishment scale.[34]

The fundamental difference between restorative theories and theories of punishment, such as deterrence and desert, is that restorative theories hold that compensation is a sufficient response to an offense whereas punishment theories generally do not.[35] It is true that some restorative theories go further and refer to reparation to the community in addition to compensation to the victim; but the notion of symbolic social reparation comes close to punishment, in practice if not in theory.[36] Other restorative theories argue for rehabilitative measures in addition to compensation, and they have all the weaknesses of rehabilitative theories (see Chapter 1 above). Punishment theories may place greater emphasis on the state's role in ensuring general prevention through punishment, on the insufficiency of compensation as a response to many offenses, and on the fairness of a system of proportionality based on culpability rather than chance occurrences. Moreover, fairness on these issues is a matter for the state to determine through public and arguable principles, not for individual victims to determine according to their feelings in the particular case. To ensure that victims' rights to compensation and support are properly honored is important in its own right and is perfectly consistent with the theories of punishment. Few restorative theorists would go so far as to suggest that punitive measures can be dispensed with entirely, for recalcitrant or extremely serious offenders.[37] The question is whether restorative approaches are sufficiently sound in theory and feasible in practice to advance beyond a position in which they are merely forms of diversion or adjuncts to punishment systems, and to emerge as a sufficient response to middle-range and moderately serious crimes.

A.A.

Notes

1. London: Macmillan, 1987.
2. See, for example, *id.*, 161 and 163.
3. *Id.*, 166.
4. *Id.*, 173–76; cf. Extract 1.5 above from Cullen and Gilbert, and the further discussion of this approach in the Introduction to Chapter 1.
5. *Id.*, 177–78.
6. *Id.*, 182–84.
7. For fuller discussion, see A. von Hirsch, "The Politics of Just Deserts," 32 *Canadian J. Criminology* 397 (1990); see also A. von Hirsch, *Censure and Sanctions* (forthcoming, 1993), ch. 9.
8. Oxford: Oxford University Press, 1990. For a critique of Braithwaite and Pettit, see A. von Hirsch and A. Ashworth, "Not Not Just Deserts," 12 *Oxford J. Legal Studies* 83 (1992); von Hirsch (1993), ch. 3.
9. Braithwaite and Pettit, 64–65.

10. *Id.* 127–28.

11. See the arguments of A. E. Bottoms and R. Brownsword, in "Dangerousness and Rights," in J. Hinton (ed.), *Dangerousness: Problems of Assessment and Prediction* (1983); and N. Lacey, *State Punishment* (1988), 160–67.

12. Braithwaite and Pettit, 125–26.

13. *Id.*, 153.

14. London: Routledge, 1988.

15. *Id.*, 183.

16. *Id.*, 195.

17. *Id.*, 194.

18. *Id.*, 21.

19. See the arguments for lowering the overall levels of punishment discussed in the Introduction to Chapter 4.

20. For the United Kingdom, see A. Bottoms, et al., *Intermediate Treatment and Juvenile Justice* (1990), although intermediate treatment has now developed chiefly as an alternative sanction at the sentencing stage.

21. For a survey in English, see the report of the Stewart Committee, *Keeping Offenders Out of Court: Further Alternatives to Prosecution* (London, 1983).

22. The guidelines for the police have been revised from time to time, and now appear in Home Office Circular no. 59/1990. They are largely the same as the *Code for Crown Prosecutors* formulated by the Director of Public Prosecutions pursuant to the Prosecution of Offences Act 1985. For comments, see A. Ashworth, "The 'Public Interest' Element in Prosecutions," [1987] *Crim. L.R.* 595.

23. J. Baldwin, *Courts, Prosecution, and Conviction* (1981); S. Gottfredson and the summary by A. Ashworth, "Criminal Process and Criminal Justice," 28 *Brit. J. Criminol.* (1988).

24. See the report of a committee chaired by Sir Denys Hodgson, *The Profits of Crime and Their Recovery* (1984).

25. For the United States, see P. Tomasic and M. Feeley (eds.), *Neighborhood Justice: Assessment of an Emerging Idea* (1982); for the United Kingdom, see T. Marshall, *Alternatives to Criminal Courts: The Potential for Non-Judicial Dispute Resolution* (1985), and T. Marshall and S. Merry, *Crime and Accountability: Victim/Offender Mediation in Practice* (1990).

26. See particularly J. Shapland et al., *Victims in the Criminal Justice System* (1985).

27. Council on Europe, *European Convention on the Compensation of Victims of Violent Crimes* (1984), para. 9.

28. *Id.*, cited by Martin Wasik, "The Place of Compensation in the Penal System," [1978] *Crim. L.R.* 599.

29. Criminal Justice Act of 1982, section 67, strengthened by the Criminal Justice Act of 1988, which imposes a general duty on courts to consider making a compensation order in every case and to give reasons if no order is made.

30. See the discussion by A. Goldstein, "Defining the Role of the Victim in Criminal Prosecution," 52 *Mississippi L. Rev.* 515 (1982).

31. Of the many writings listed in the Suggestions for Further Reading, below, see particularly R. Barnett, "Restitution: A New Paradigm of Criminal Justice," 87

Ethics 279 (1978); G. del Vecchio, "The Struggle against Crime," in H. B. Acton (ed.), *The Philosophy of Punishment* (1969); and H. Zehr, *Retributive Justice, Restorative Justice* (1985).

32. For discussion and purported rebuttal of some of these criticisms, see M. Wright, *Justice for Victims and Offenders* (1991).

33. In his much-quoted lecture "Conflicts as Property," 16 *Brit. J. Criminol.* 1 (1976).

34. See discussion by A. Ashworth, "Punishment and Compensation: Offenders, Victims, and the State," 6 *Oxford J. Legal Studies* 86 (1986).

35. Although, as was argued in section 2 above, the aim of deterrence or desert may be fulfilled by some form of diversion from prosecution, perhaps involving reparation, where the crime is minor.

36. Cf. del Vecchio (1969) and Wright (1991), chs. 2 and 6.

37. For example, Wright (1991, 125–27) contemplates the use of prison in extreme cases.

Suggestions for Further Reading

1. Sentencing and the Wider Society

Hudson, B., *Justice through Punishment: A Critique of the 'Justice' Model of Corrections* (1987); Lacey, N., *State Punishment: Political Principles and Community Values* (1988); von Hirsch, A., "The Politics of Just Deserts," 32 *Canadian Journal of Criminology* 397 (1990); Braithwaite, J., and Pettit, P., *Not Just Deserts* (1990); Garland, D., *Punishment and Society* (1990); von Hirsch, A., and Ashworth, A., "Not Not Just Deserts: A Response to Braithwaite and Pettit," 12 *Oxford Journal of Legal Studies* 83 (1992); von Hirsch, A., *Censure and Sanctions* (1993, forthcoming), ch. 9.

2. Sentencing Theory and Prosecutorial Processes

Newman, D. J., *Conviction: The Determination of Guilt or Innocence without Trial* (1966); Alschuler, A., "Sentencing Reform and Prosecutorial Power," 126 *University of Pennsylvania Law Review* 550 (1978); Sanders, A., "Class Bias in Prosecutions," 24 *Howard Journal of Criminal Justice* 176 (1985); Mansfield, G., and Peay, J., *The Director of Public Prosecutions* (1985); Bottomley, A. K., "Sentencing Reform and the Structuring of Pre-Trial Discretion," in K. Pease and M. Wasik (eds.), *Sentencing Reform: Guidance or Guidelines?* (1987); Galligan, D., "Discretion and Pre-Trial Justice," in I. Dennis (ed.), *Criminal Law and Justice* (1987); Ashworth, A., "Criminal Justice and Criminal Process," in P. Rock (ed.), *A History of British Criminology* (1988); Gottfredson, M., and Gottfredson, D. M., *Decision-Making in Criminal Justice* (2d ed., 1988); McConville, M., Sanders, A., and Leng, R., *The Case for the Prosecution* (1991).

3. Sentencing and the Role of the Victim

Schafer, S., *Compensation and Restitution to Victims of Crime* (1970); Christie, N., "Conflicts as Property," 16 *British Journal of Criminology* 1 (1976); Hudson, J., and Galaway, B. (eds.), *Victims, Offenders, and Alternative Sanctions* (1980); Galaway, B., and Hudson, J. (eds.), *Perspectives on Crime Victims* (1981); Abel, C. F., and Marsh, F. H., *Punishment and Restitution* (1984); Shapland, J., Willmore, J., and Duff, P., *Victims in the Criminal Justice System* (1985); Zehr, H., *Retributive Justice, Restorative Justice* (1985); Marshall, T., *Alternatives to Criminal Courts: The Potential for Non-Judicial Dispute Resolution* (1985); Waller, I., *The Role of the Victim in Sentencing and Related Processes* (1986); Ashworth, A., "Punishment and Compensation: Offenders, Victims, and the State," 6 *Oxford Journal of Legal Studies* 86 (1986); Maguire, M., and Corbett, C., *The Effects of Crime and the Work of Victim Support Schemes* (1987); Maguire, M., and Pointing, J. (eds.), *Victims of Crime—A New Deal?* (1988); Walklate, S., *Victimology: The Victim and the Criminal Justice Process* (1989); Matthews, R. (ed.), *Informal Justice* (1989); de Haan, W., *The Politics of Redress* (1990); Zehr, H., *Changing Lenses:*

A New Focus for Criminal Justice (1990); Murphy, J. G., "Getting Even: The Role of the Victim," in E. F. Paul, F. D. Miller, and J. Paul (eds.), *Crime, Culpability, and Remedy* (1990); Wright, M., and Galaway, B. (eds.), *Mediation and Criminal Justice: Victims, Offenders, and the Community* (1990); Rock, P., *Helping the Victim* (1990); Wright, M., *Justice for Victims and Offenders* (1991).

Index